MARKETING MANAGEMENT CASES

MARKETING MANAGEMENT CASES

Planning and Executing Marketing Strategy

SECOND EDITION

William M. Weilbacher

Vice-Chairman of the Board of Directors, Dancer-Fitzgerald-Sample, Inc.
Formerly Adjunct Professor of Marketing, Graduate School of Business
New York University

Macmillan Publishing Co., Inc.
NEW YORK
Collier Macmillan Publishers
LONDON

MACMILLAN PUBLISHING CO., INC.
866 Third Avenue, New York, New York 10022

COLLIER MACMILLAN CANADA, LTD.

Library of Congress Cataloguing in Publication Data

Weilbacher, William M
  Marketing management cases.

  1. Marketing management—Case studies. I. Title.
HF5415.13.W38 1975   658. 8   73–22625
ISBN 0–02–425080–5

Printing: 4 5 6 7 8   Year: 7 8 9 0

This book is for Barbara Taylor Weilbacher

PREFACE

THIS is the second edition of a book of marketing cases. It deals, as did its predecessor, with formulating and executing marketing strategy.

The second edition is very much like the first edition in concept and style. And yet this second edition represents a very substantial revision in case content. Of the sixteen cases included, nine are totally new, two more have been extensively changed, and five are similar to those that appeared in the first edition. Several of the new cases reflect topic areas that seem now to have particular urgency for marketers and thus for students of marketing. These new subject areas include corporate social responsibility, government regulation, industrial marketing, package design, and psychological market segmentation.

Beyond this, a major effort has been made to strengthen the questions that accompany the cases. In every instance these questions are now designed to relate specifically to the major issues of the case. In addition the questions are posed in such a way as to relate more generally to the central issues in marketing.

As those who have used the first edition know, I have tried to develop these cases with a strong sense of marketing reality. The cases are long rather than short because reality is dense and ambiguous; short cases miss these central characteristics.

In my own teaching experience with available marketing case material, I have found it hard to impart the sense of fascination and involvement that the world of marketing offers. The need, it seems to me, is for case material that is neither abstract nor unreal. Marketing is many things. It is not merely facts and figures. It is not cut-and-dried decision situations, nor does it involve only decisions that are rationally made. And marketing is a business in which people interact with one another—real people with real prejudices and aspirations and enthusiasms and blind spots.

I have tried to inject some of the personal side of marketing and marketing decision making into the facts and assumptions and techniques and logical structures. In addition, I have tried to make the formal content (which, of course, still constitutes the core and the bulk of the cases) sufficiently extensive and normal to project a sense of what the issues faced by the marketer are really like.

The student is served in two ways. First, he is better prepared to relate his inside marketing training to the outside marketing world. Second, the business context is not discrete and single-topic-oriented and neither are these cases. The student knows this instinctively and this case material thus confirms his instincts.

The book is designed to supplement standard marketing texts; it is particularly relevant to texts in marketing management. It can be used with both undergraduate and graduate students. It is neither elementary nor advanced: it simply reflects reality. The more mature the student, the more of this reality will be absorbed and resolved, but the situations and issues remain the same regardless of the sophistication of the student or, one might add, the marketer. No compromises are made with reality because such compromises do not make the life that the case reflects easier for the student—only more frustrating.

The book is divided into three main parts. These seem logical to me, and I hope that they will to others. A variety of issues tend to come up in every case, and the division of the material tends to reflect each case's dominant characteristics rather than all of its specific content.

There are no real situations in this book, with one exception. Case 12 is based on the experience of Master Jazz Recordings, Inc., a jazz record company of which I am president.

All of the other cases are imaginary. One characteristic of a career in the advertising agency business is its diversity of exposure to business situations and personalities. This exposure is even more extensive when one has been concerned with marketing planning and marketing research. So I have worked with drug companies and food manufacturers and distillers and household product manufacturers and television set manufacturers and so on. But no one of my clients, past or present, serves as a model for Allgood Drug, or Wonder Foods, or Bourbon Brothers, or Home Products Universal, or Cacaphony Sound. My students often seem to want to make these purely imaginary companies into real companies. This is harmless enough, I suppose, but I must emphasize that, with the exception noted, the firms and people are not real. The important point is that they *could* be real, and this possibility breeds involvement of the student with the material.

There are no real data in the book. All the exhibits are labeled "specimen data" because they are only specimens of the real thing.

In assigning material of this kind to my students, I always make several suggestions to them about how it should be handled.

1. I urge them to immerse themselves in the case itself—to read it through carefully and with thorough concentration. Almost all of the material in the case is relevant in one way or another to an understanding of the situation portrayed and to the questions that are raised at the end of the case. An understanding of the arguments and the issues of the case is an imperative first step toward solution.

2. After they believe that they *understand* the case, I propose that they try to identify the significant issues and the relevant marketing decisions related to these issues. Paper and pencil help here. I suggest that the students jot down what might have to be decided as a result of the material in the case and what the most appropriate marketing moves

might be in each instance. A development of this sense of context makes it easier to answer whatever actual questions are to be answered because the student has begun to feel—if he has done the job—all of the conflicting pressures and issues that the actual decision-maker becomes aware of in reaching a marketing decision.

3. Finally, I suggest that the student begin to develop his answers to the assigned questions. I implore him to be succinct, that is, to have thought through the implications of the case and his specific answers so that they may be stated with simple directness and clarity rather than in muddled verbosity. And I encourage the student to make explicit the assumptions that he has made in answering the questions. I tend to accept almost any reasonable explanation, as long as its underpinnings are explicit, and I tend to mark down unwarranted or unexplained leaps of fancy.

Much of the material in the book has been used, in one form or another, in my marketing courses at the Graduate School of Business Administration of New York University. To a great extent the form of the cases has resulted from the reactions of my students to more traditional case material, which suggested the need for a text like this. Indeed, their forbearance and constructive criticism have helped mold the book into its final form.

Marlene Gavagan typed and retyped the manuscript with an industriousness and cheerfulness that belied the frustrations and drudgery involved. She made the whole enterprise notably easier for me and I am very grateful to her for it.

W. M. W.

New York City

CONTENTS

xi

THREE
Choosing Alternative Marketing Tactics

PART ONE

Central Issues in Marketing

The Marketing Concept

Home Products Universal Develops DB–14

HOME PRODUCTS UNIVERSAL is a medium-sized Midwestern manufacturer of household cleaning and maintenance products. The Company has managed to build market shares ranging from 5 to 25 per cent for each of the seventeen products that it manufactures. It has successfully competed with the giants in the field through aggressive marketing, an insistence on quality products, and an imaginative program of cost cutting in warehousing, transportation, and production. Its president, Alfred Herbert Knutson, is the first grandson of founder, Eleazer Hudson, born to the founder's favorite child and only daughter, Sarah, in 1934. Knutson assumed the presidency on the retirement of the founder in 1971, after fifteen years' apprenticeship in all facets of the business.

Established in 1911 by Hudson, HPU is something of a phenomenon in the home cleaning and maintenance products industry: it is a successful regional operation. It has maintained its market position fundamentally because of its historic ability to produce products equal or superior to those marketed by the giants in the field. "Equal or superior to" means, according to HPU, product parity or superiority on critical laboratory characteristics and, in addition, a consumer preference of at least 55 per cent in direct, blind paired comparison tests with consumers.

To this end, HPU has maintained an excellent product research and development program through its technical laboratory and has consistently recruited into this program superior graduate-degree holders in the physical and biological sciences. A very basic part of the product research and development program has been to establish critical performance factors for every product category manufactured by HPU and to evaluate each of its products on these performance factors and relative to the market leader or leaders. These competitive evaluations are made once every six months. This program keeps the company in constant touch with the technical characteristics of leading products in the market. As the key characteristics of the market leaders are changed, HPU knows it and can decide whether or not to change its own product to or beyond the level of performance achieved by the market leader. This program of testing has beneficial effects in keeping the HPU management in touch with its developed market and in ensuring that the necessary information to maintain the "equal or superior to" product quality policy of the company is continuously available. But it is fundamentally a defensive laboratory program and policy.

When Allen R. Scala was promoted to the job of director of product research and development in June of 1973, he also inherited this product evaluation program. He recognized the importance of the program in the overall scheme of HPU product research and development activities and appreciated the key role that it had played in the successful and profitable history of Home Products Universal. Nevertheless, he was certain that this program should not be the end of research and development activities. He noted that, in its history, HPU had been a follower in the development of new products rather than a leader. HPU had never, in its entire history, introduced a totally new product into the market place. It was not a matter of having tried and failed. To the contrary, it was a matter of never having tried at all. The HPU style had been to wait for others to innovate and then to follow, after basic consumer receptivity had been assured, with an equivalent or superior product developed in the HPU laboratories.

Scala recognized that this achievement was a very significant one. It was no mean trick to consistently duplicate or outperform the laboratory work of the leading "soapers" of the nation, and the success of HPU reflected an unusual level of competence among its laboratory people.

But the past success of this policy and its research and development program could not be depended upon to provide HPU with the base for successful and profitable operations in the second half of the 1970's, thought Allen Scala. There were three things wrong with it from his viewpoint.

First, the policy eliminated the possibility of developing totally new products. Of course, the odds against were relatively high in new-product development work, but the opportunity for very significant new sales volume and profits was very high too, if one knew what he was about and if his laboratory and technical support were of the first order.

Second, the existing policy was tied to the regional operation of the company. Scala believed that the company should be a national operator and he believed that totally new products offered the easiest way to extend the operations of the company from regional to national. A hot new product could be handled through the HPU sales organization in that fraction of the country where the company was established and could be offered to brokers in the outside area. This would bring in extra sales and profits, with only marginal extra effort.

But the third effect of the traditional policy upset Scala the most. He was finding it increasingly difficult to attract talented people to his laboratories as employees. The fact that Home Products Universal's home office was situated in an Indiana town of modest size and crushing inelegance was problem enough. But the fun in product development work, the opportunity for fame, and the chance for fortune all came from working on totally new products. And if one could not offer this prospect to the potential employee, he had two strikes against him from the start. The clincher was that HPU was not a national company and had neither prospects nor intention of going national. Alfred Knutson was quite firm about this; he intended, apparently, to follow his grandfather's policies to the letter, at least until the old fellow passed on and was no longer looking over young Al's shoulder. Who, mused Scala, would want to come to central Indiana to work on old products that could be marketed only regionally? And how could he, Scala, do his job without a steady influx of new talent?

But Allen R. Scala was, after all, only the director of product research and development and it was apparent even to him that some of his thoughts were on a somewhat grander scale than he was entitled to by position alone. In theory, he reported directly to the president, Knutson himself. (See Exhibit 1–1.) For practical purposes he reported to two other men.

First of these was Arthur V. Pensa, vice-president and director of product marketing. Pensa was an old hand at HPU. He had been hired by Eleazer Hudson in 1955 and had been appointed to the directorship of product marketing in 1969, shortly before founder Hudson retired from active participation in the affairs of the company.

The second was Alphonso Caravelle, vice-president and director of manufacturing operations. Caravelle was a newcomer, having joined the company in 1970. But he was outspoken and important since everyone knew that Knutson himself knew nothing about the manufacturing side of the business.

As Scala was not a vice-president and as his slot on the organization chart was at a level below that of Pensa and Caravelle, he found it prudent, in practice, to make sure that both of these men supported any project or proposal that he intended to pursue or forward to President Knutson. So, before making any of his views about new products marketing public, Scala decided first to discuss them informally with Art Pensa. This was easier said than done because Scala had a lot of ground to cover and because Pensa seemed to have a congenitally short attention span. The appropriate moment arrived when the two men set out on an air journey to the West Coast to attend a Chemical Specialities Manufacturers Association seminar. The airplane trip from Chicago to San Francisco provided Scala with just the opportunity he needed: there was,

EXHIBIT 1–1
Excerpt of Home Products Universal Master Organization Chart
As of October 1, 1974

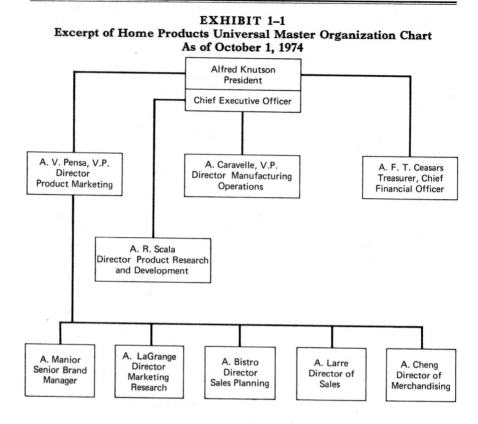

providentially, no in-flight movie, and dinner was served almost immediately after they boarded the aircraft.

So Scala introduced the topic of new product development and then proceeded to a discussion of national marketing and the problem of recruiting talented young people into the organization. Pensa listened to all of this with considerable patience at first, but as the presentation went on and on, he seemed to lose interest and toward the end appeared quite bored. Most of this was Scala's own fault: he had not mastered the art of organizing his ideas crisply and presenting them succinctly. But, anyway, he had delivered the viewpoint in its entirety to Pensa.

Pensa's response astonished Scala. He simply said, "Why do you tell me all of this?"

"Because I thought it was of interest and because you own a lot of our stock and want to see the company grow and prosper."

Pensa seemed to warm up a bit at this and smiled very slightly as he said, "All I want to do is cash in in six years and enjoy my retirement. So long-term plans and projects really don't interest me all that much.

But I'll tell you this. I think you're dead right about new products. I don't know about national distribution. The only one that knows about that is Mr. Knutson and I wouldn't try to talk to him about it, if I were you, because it's not your job, it's my job, and if he asks me I'll tell him I advised you not to bother him about it. Maybe some other time, but not now. As far as your not being able to hire good guys, I don't think you sell hard enough. All it needs is a little determination and belief in our company—you've got to get that across, Scala. If you can't find good guys to work for Home Products Universal, there must be something wrong with your approach because the company's OK, solid as a rock." With this Pensa excused himself and wandered off in the general direction of the washroom.

Scala's next move, on returning home, was to solicit the support of Al Caravelle. In his approach to Caravelle, he decided to dispense with any talk of national expansion or his personnel recruitment problem and concentrate on the need for new products. Caravelle, as director of manufacturing operations, was the only man who could make new products become a physical fact, and without his ungrudging support, Scala's ambitions were doomed.

He talked to Caravelle over a hasty luncheon in the company cafeteria. "Al, I've been talking with Art Pensa about new products—I mean really new products, not just copies of other guys'—and he thinks we really ought to get into that kind of thing."

"Do you have people of that caliber in your R and D operation, Al?" asked Caravelle with a manner that made it difficult to judge whether he was inquiring innocently or putting Scala on a bit.

Scala assumed the best and responded, "My gang is OK—not P and G, but OK—and they won't come up with anything that's too tough to make, that's a sure thing."

Caravelle finished the conversation with a blunt response. "If you come up with anything we can make and Pensa thinks he can sell, we're with you. But I'm not going to waste any of my people's time with crackpot ideas that old Mrs. Consumer won't buy."

Scala chose to interpret this as an endorsement of his proposal. He was now left with the problem of coming up with products that could be made and would be bought by the consumer. The first issue that Scala faced was developing ideas for new products.

Where do such ideas come from? They come out of people's heads, and in one sense, one person's head is as good as another for generating new product ideas. Some people are more efficient at it than others because they are inherently smarter or have had more experience in juxtaposing different thought and experience fields to produce "creative" responses. Some people have greater technical knowledge of one field or another and can see solutions to obvious problems in terms of the technology that they have mastered. And some people have a greater innate sense of market opportunity because they are intuitively aware of both sales volume potential and the possibility of positive consumer response. But any consumer is a potential new product source.

Scala may have dimly perceived all of this, but he was in no position to seek out smart creative people, or a broad range of technologists, or consumer-market–oriented people. He had to make do with what was available to him, and this consisted, basically, of his staff of six and his wife. He described the problem to his staff in a special meeting called for this purpose. He rambled on about the need for new products, and the support of Pensa and Caravelle, and how they should be mindful that established company distribution systems would restrict the area of exploration to products sold in grocery stores, and that this work should not and could not impinge upon their regularly assigned tasks, and on and on.

After an hour and forty minutes Scala had exhausted both the subject and his listeners. But the staff had the point and it excited them and they went to work with enthusiasm, at least for the break in the routine of laboratory analyses that the quest for new products afforded them. And Scala's wife was duly briefed too, in even greater detail on the strength of a predinner cocktail, and she agreed enthusiastically to think and think hard, if for no other reason than to end Allen's lengthy exposition.

* *
*

In three weeks' time Scala had accumulated a list of six new product possibilities. Three of these had come from his wife, one from the departmental secretary, and two from the newest professional employee in his group. Scala was embarrassed that he himself had drawn a complete blank.

The six products were these:
1. A liquid enzyme to break down and convert garbage to a harmless liquid.
2. An electrically powered hand-held vegetable slicer.
3. A powdered laundry bleach.
4. A soft drink for dogs.
5. A liquid detergent for dishwashing machines.
6. A floor-sweeping compound for domestic use.

Scala rejected all but two of these ideas. He believed that there was not adequate technology or understanding of enzyme activity available either in the literature or among his own staff to make the enzyme-garbage-product idea a good candidate for laboratory development. He suspected that a lot of time would be wasted on the project with relatively little hope of success. The vegetable chopper did not seem like a food store product to Scala, and again, none of his staff had any idea of how to put motors on chopping blades; they were chemists, not physicists. Scala thought that the idea of a soft drink for dogs might be promising but considered it off the HPU beaten track and one for which perhaps Pensa, and certainly Caravelle, would have little but ridicule. Finally, Scala rejected the liquid dishwashing product because it would, presumably, require an alteration in all those dishwashing machines that had been designed for and could only accommodate dishwashing powders.

This left the powdered bleach and the floor-sweeping compound for domestic use. Scala's next move was to go to Pensa and unveil these two ideas as potential new products. He asserted in this meeting that he believed that either could be formulated with relative ease by the research and development staff. Pensa seemed enthusiastic about both ideas but counseled that only one be forwarded to Knutson, because, after all, the very idea of the development of a totally new product was alien to HPU, and it seemed to him to make good sense to put a single best exploratory foot forward.

The two men talked at length about the two ideas. Scala was especially intrigued with the floor cleaner because he had swept out his basement only the preceding weekend and had had a severe allergic reaction to the dust that was raised in the sweeping process. But he believed that he could make a significantly safer and gentler powdered bleach with no sacrifice in product performance if he were to pursue the powdered bleach idea.

At length, Pensa interrupted Scala in the midst of a rather pointless soliloquy about dry bleach ingredients and said, "Work on the bleach product, Al. Our liquid bleach is just like the competition's and we don't get more than 5 or 6 per cent of the business. But there's a big market sitting waiting for an innovation and we'll generate a lot of sales if you come up with something. The garage floor thing could be socko but I don't think Alfred[1] is allergic to anything and I know he's never swept out a cellar or a garage in his life—best to talk to him about something that he might vaguely understand."

The two gentlemen then went to Caravelle and outlined their thoughts to him. "We've got a carport and it doesn't ever need sweeping and our basement is hooked into the built-in suction vacuuming system so we wouldn't use that floor product, and I bet there are a lot of people like us," said Caravelle, and that was that. It was not clear that Caravelle endorsed the powdered bleach. It was only clear that he did not endorse the floor cleaner. This, Scala subsequently observed, was a characteristic of Caravelle.

---

[1] It was understood within HPU that the first name Alfred, in conversation, referred to Mr. Knutson and that all other names that could be shortened to Al were shortened to Al. This created considerable confusion because either a malevolent god or a perverse personnel department had stocked the company richly in names that could become Al. See Exhibit 1–1.

Caravelle often spoke out against a proposal, but he rarely endorsed anything. In this way he was rarely responsible for failure and could often point out that he had personally opposed a course of action in the event that it did not pan out. Scala was, in due course, to learn how this tactic worked out in practice, to his annoyance and chagrin, but for the moment all was blue skies and clear sailing.

* * *

At this point the professionals took over. The job of actually exploring the ways in which a superior powdered bleach might be formulated was turned over to Robert J. Johnson, one of the senior lab technicians employed under Scala. In previous assignments Johnson had shown a sophisticated knowledge of chemical brighteners and phosphorus derivatives that might be expected to produce the effect of bright whiteners in clothing. In addition, he had a very impressive general background in inorganic chemistry and had specialized in developing methods and concepts to ensure that HPU products were both safe to humans and non-destructive of natural and man-made materials and fibers.

Johnson immersed himself in the relevant literature for a period of six weeks. Toward the end of this period he began to experiment with various combinations of dry ingredients that, although they technically were not bleaches at all, did accomplish what liquid bleaches are supposed to accomplish, only better and with total fabric and color safety.

Another four weeks passed, and finally, Johnson had assured himself that one of his formulae passed all of his tests and satisfied each of his developmental criteria. This formula—the laboratory designation of the product was DB–14—had the following characteristics:

1. It was concentrated. A packet weighing three tenths of an ounce was sufficient to bleach a fully loaded automatic washer.
2. It outperformed regular bleach: tests show that it produced 20 per cent greater brightness (reflected light) on white sheets than did the leading liquid bleach when used as directed on full washing machine loads.
3. It would not bleach out colors under any circumstances: it was totally color safe.
4. It had a pleasant perfume—a pine-scent odor rather than the harsh acrid scent of typical liquid bleaches.
5. It was mild to fabrics and hands. Fabric deterioration due to bleaching was reduced by a full 38 per cent on extended-use tests of white sheets using identical washing machines with all other factors held constant.
6. Although this product was somewhat more expensive to produce than liquid bleach, some of this extra cost could be recaptured through lower transportation costs, and it was anticipated that it

could be marketed at a price about one third higher than liquid bleach on a completed-washload basis.

Johnson was immensely pleased with his accomplishment. He had produced a superior product on all counts, and he had done it in a relatively short period of time. But even more important was the opinion of Home Products Universal's legal counsel that the particular combination of ingredients and the method of combining them was, in fact, protectable by patent.

Scala was ecstatic. He seemed to have struck oil on his very first new product enterprise. His first step was to deliver the wonderful news to his president, Alfred Knutson.

Scala, Pensa, and Caravelle agreed that the proper way for this communication to take place was in the form of a formal stand-up/chart presentation by Scala to Knutson. They settled on this device as a succinct way to summarize all of the steps leading to the final product development. Knutson had not been informed that the project was afoot and thus a heavy dose of background was in order for him. A chart presentation seemed a feasible way to discipline Scala's descriptions and conserve Knutson's valuable time. And so the presentation was made. Scala got through it all in about forty minutes and at the conclusion he waited with bated breath for Knutson's reaction.

It was short and to the point. "Have any housewives used the stuff in their homes?" asked Knutson. Scala said, "No." Knutson said, "Let's get the consumers' reaction before we go any further."

"Well, Allen," said Pensa "maybe the old man makes a point. You know this product is better than anything else on the market, and I know it's better, too. But maybe the consumer won't feel the same way. I can't imagine any consumer not preferring this new bleach, but we don't know that she will, and now we've got to prove it, whether we want to or not."

* *
*

At this point, Scala called upon Aloysius LaGrange, director of marketing research for Home Products Universal. LaGrange specialized in two kinds of marketing research: sales analyses to determine where and under what conditions HPU sales were favorable or not; and blind product-testing to establish consumer reactions to products.

Scala took LaGrange through the same presentation that he had just given to Knutson and said at its conclusion, "Alfred wants the product tested by consumers. Can you do it?" LaGrange said that he would be delighted to take a crack at it, but he emphasized that research work on a new product might involve considerably different and more sophisticated procedures than those used in the standard Home Products Universal blind comparison test of established and known products.

First of all, LaGrange proposed that samples of the product be distributed to two hundred housewives who were regular users of liquid bleach. Each of these housewives would receive, in addition to the bleach samples, a brief *factual* description of exactly what the product was and its unique characteristics. Then these consumers would be asked to use the new powdered bleach in their next regular wash. In a callback interview they would then be questioned concerning their overall reaction to the product; their views of its strengths and weaknesses; their evaluation of its performance relative to the liquid bleach they usually used; an appraisal of the likelihood they would purchase it; and a projection of what price they would expect to pay for the product.

At the same time, LaGrange suggested that a basic study of consumer attitude and usage of bleach products should be undertaken to determine demographic patterns of bleach usage and basic knowledge about the kinds of wash items that were regularly bleached; the frequency with which they were bleached; consumer attitudes about what bleach actually accomplished; the major shortcomings of available liquid bleaches; and the major advantages of available bleach products.

LaGrange pointed out that the second study might well have been undertaken before the laboratory had started development so that the development of the new product, once initiated, would respond insofar as possible to expressed consumer needs and to the shortcomings perceived by consumers in the existing products in the marketplace. But LaGrange still believed that the results of such research work would be helpful in appraising the market potential of the new bleach product. LaGrange prepared formal research proposals for these two projects. These proposals described in some detail just how the research work would be carried out, how much time it would take, and how much money would be involved in the recommended studies.

The estimated cost of the first, the home placement study, was $6,500. It was anticipated that the work would require approximately ten weeks to complete, although a preliminary or top-line report could be expected in approximately seven weeks from the date of authorization. The attitude and usage study would also take approximately ten weeks to complete, with top-line results again in about seven weeks, and the estimated cost was $26,300.

Scala was disturbed by two factors about these proposals: their cost and the amount of time that they were expected to take. He asked LaGrange to prepare a brief memorandum justifying the time and cost requirements. LaGrange relished this request, because he knew that his time and cost estimates were reasonable and because he knew that Scala had no choice but to accept them.

Here is his memorandum:

HPU Internal Communication

September 18, 1974

FROM: A. LaGrange
TO: A. Scala

You have asked me to explain in some detail our estimates of time and cost supplied to you in connection with two research proposals for product DB–14.

As you know, it is the policy of the Marketing Research Department to farm out all field work and tabulation for such studies, reserving to ourselves only the functions of study planning, data analysis, and interpretation of results. Thus, the major elements in our cost and time estimates are developed for us by the outside suppliers who are always subjected to the discipline of competitive bidding. Our internal time estimates are relatively modest, and our costs are computed on the basis of standard-work-grade hourly rates supplied to us by the central accounting office.

The attached exhibits detail these factors for the studies in question.

EXHIBIT 1–2
Cost Estimates for Market Research Job 27–347
(In-Home Placement DB–14)

	BID I*	BID 2*	BID 3*	FINAL ESTIMATE
Internal time	—	—	—	$1,700
Field work	$4,000	$4,250	$3,650†	4,000
Tabulation	800	1,000	1,275	800
				$6,500

* Supporting documents in MR File 27–347–001.
† Required fourteen weeks for completion at this cost.

EXHIBIT 1–3
Cost Estimates for Market Research Job 27–349
(Consumer Bleach Attitude DB–14)

	BID I*	BID 2*	BID 3*	ESTIMATE
Internal time	—	—	—	$4,900
Field work	$20,000	$18,500	$21,500	18,500
Tabulation	2,000	2,900	4,000	2,900
				$26,300

* Supporting documents in MR File 27–349–003
(All bids were solicited for field work and tabulation together, as a "package," because of the size and complexity of the job.)

You have also asked for a draft of the factual description of product DB-14 that would be given to consumers in the home placement test. Here it is.

Dry Bleach

This product is to be used in the same way as liquid bleach: one packet to each automatic washer load. The product is an extremely effective bleach as you will see, and it is very mild to hands, and to fabric fibers. It is guaranteed safe for colored fabrics: it will absolutely not cause color fading or bleeding. The product delivers full power performance with total mildness and safety.

Your approval of the research plans and of this description of the product is awaited.

Scala immediately authorized the research work to proceed but entreated LaGrange to do everything in his power to speed it up while minimizing the cost. The inconsistency of these wishes amused LaGrange. He delivered the research reports exactly when he said that he would and within 7 per cent of the estimated costs.

LaGrange presented the results of the two studies when they became available. These presentations were made to all of those who had been either interested or involved in the development of DB-14, but Mr. Knutson was not invited. When Scala had first proposed that Knutson be included in the group receiving first exposure to the research reports, Pensa exploded.

"You really don't get it, do you, Al? We are hired to provide solutions for Alfred, not to give him an opportunity to share our problems. Let's take a look at these studies and then we'll figure out what to do. Maybe we'll even let him see them, but let's keep control, huh, Al? Let's not give him, or the old man, a shot at providing an afternoon's entertainment at our expense."

But it was not to be. Knutson had been in the organization for fifteen years. He knew it like the back of his hand and he had developed excellent informal sources of information about what went on within its walls. More often than not, he "knew" what went on because he had a superb memory for detail as well as an excellent intuitive understanding of how his key people worked and how they were likely to respond in a particular situation. Knutson either sensed, or overheard, or was told that the new product research on the bleach was available, and he advised LaGrange, upon finding this out, that he would be pleased to review it in his office the next morning at 8:45 A.M.

LaGrange informed his superior, Pensa, of this development, Pensa informed Scala and Caravelle, and these latter three appeared uninvited and without joint consultation in Knutson's office for his "review" of the consumer research work.

The material seen by Knutson is summarized in Exhibits 1–4 through 1–9 (the product placement study) and in Exhibits 1–10 through 1–16 (the usage and attitude study).

EXHIBIT 1–4
DB–14 Placement Study
Specimen Data:
Overall Reaction to Product
(5-point scale supplied to testers)

Base: All testers	
Number	206
Per cent	*100*
DB–14 is	
Excellent	12%
Good—above average	4
Average	38
Not so good—below average	30
Poor	16

EXHIBIT 1–5
DB–14 Placement Study
Specimen Data:
Reported Advantages of Product DB–14

Base: All testers		
Number	206	
Per cent	*100*	
Product has an advantage*	37%	
Mild to hands		21
Pleasant odor		7
Safe for colors		7
Safe for fabrics		6
Convenient		4
All other responses		1
Product has no advantage	63	

* Some testers gave more than one advantage.

EXHIBIT 1–6
DB–14 Placement Study
Specimen Data:
Reported Disadvantages of Product DB–14

Base: All testers		
Number	206	
Per cent	*100*	
Product has a disadvantage*	74%	
Doesn't get clothes whiter		51
Not strong enough, too mild		47
I don't bleach colors		8
Packet is too small		2
Doesn't smell strong enough		1
All other responses		6
Product has no disadvantages	26	

* Some testers gave more than one disadvantage.

EXHIBIT 1–7
DB–14 Placement Study
Specimen Data:
DB Performance Relative to Liquid Bleach Regularly Used

Base: All testers	
Number	206
Per cent	*100*
Liquid bleach better	72%
DB–14	18
No choice	10
Reasons liquid bleach better	
Base: Liquid bleach preferrers*	
Number	148
Per cent	*100*
Gets clothes whiter	72%
Is stronger	64
Best for me	31
The powder is too mild	10
All other responses	6
Reasons DB–14 better	
Base: DB preferrers*	
Number	37
Per cent	†
Good odor	(12)
Mild to hands	(11)
Mild to fabrics	(10)
All other responses	(8)

* Some respondents gave more than one reason.
† Small base: only absolute numbers are reported.

EXHIBIT 1–8
DB–14 Placement Study
Specimen Data:
Purchase Intention for Product DB–14
(5-point scale supplied to testers)

Base: All testers	
Number	206
Per cent	*100*
Definitely will purchase	6%
May purchase	7
Not sure	21
Probably won't purchase	12
Definitely will not purchase	54

EXHIBIT 1–9
DB–14 Placement Study
Specimen Data:
Price Testers Expect to Pay for DB–14

Base: All testers		
Number	206	
Per cent	*100*	
Expect to pay more than liquid bleach	13%	
1–5¢ more		10
6–10¢ more		3
11¢– or more		—
Expect to pay the same as liquid bleach	12	
Expect to pay less than liquid bleach	75	
1–5¢ less		21
6–10¢ less		42
11¢– or less		12

EXHIBIT 1–10
DB–14 Usage and Attitude Study
Specimen Data:
Bleach Usage and Intensity of Bleach Usage

Base: All households		
Number	1,479	
Per cent	*100*	
Use bleach	78%	
Heavy bleach users		
(more than 1 quart a month)		20
Light bleach users		
(less than 1 quart a month)		58
Do not use bleach	22	

EXHIBIT 1–11
DB–14 Usage and Attitude Study
Specimen Data:
Bleach Usage and Intensity of Bleach Usage
by Standard Demographic Characteristics*

	USE BLEACH	HEAVY BLEACH USAGE†	LIGHT BLEACH USAGE‡
All Households	78%	20%	58%
Income			
Under $5,000	88%	34%	54%
$ 5,000–$ 7,999	84	21	58
$ 8,000–$ 9,999	78	16	62
$10,000–$14,999	64	6	58
$15,000–$24,999	58	4	54
$25,000 and over	50	4	46
Education of household head			
Grade school or less	85%	33%	52%
Some high school	82	24	58
Graduated, high school	78	16	62
Some college	60	4	56
Graduated, college	49	2	47
Age of household head			
24 and younger	56%	4%	52%
25–34	68	10	58
35–49	78	18	60
50–64	98	42	56
65 and older	96	42	54
Geographic area			
Northeast	72%	18%	54%
Central	76	20	56
South	88	24	64
West	78	20	58

* The percentages are based on the number of households falling in each demographic category.
† A heavy-bleach-using household consumes more than 1 quart of bleach a month.
‡ A light-bleach-using household consumes less than 1 quart of bleach a month.

EXHIBIT 1–12
DB–14 Usage and Attitude Study
Specimen Data:
Items Most Frequently Bleached and Estimated Bleaching Frequency*

Base: All households using bleach

Number	1,154	
Per cent	*100*	

ITEMS BLEACHED†		ESTIMATED BLEACHING FREQUENCY‡
White fabrics	100%	1.00
Sheets, pillowcases	97	1.00
Towels, bathroom linen	94	1.00
Undergarments	42	.25
Outer garments	77	.62
Shirts	82	.76
Others	36	.31
Colored fabrics	12	.10
Delicate fabrics	6	.05
Synthetic fabrics	2	.05

* Respondents were asked to mention the three or four kinds of fabrics they bleached "most often."
† There is duplication in this classification. A white nylon undergarment would show up as a white undergarment, a delicate fabric, and a synthetic fabric, for example. If a garment could be classified in more than one catagory, it was so classified.
‡ The proportion of washes out of total washings in which bleach is used, as estimated by respondents. White undergarments are bleached, for example, in .25 washings, or one in four.

EXHIBIT 1–13
DB–14 Usage and Attitude Study
Specimen Data:
What Consumers Think Bleach Accomplishes for Them*

Base: All bleach-using households

Number	1,154
Percent	*100*

Gets clothes whiter, brighter	98%
Gets clothes cleaner	96
Gets colored clothes brighter	14
Saves work in getting out dirt	10
All other mentions	6

* Some respondents gave more than one answer.

EXHIBIT 1–14
DB–14 Usage and Attitude Study
Specimen Data:
Major Advantages of Liquid Bleaches*

Base: All bleach-using households	
Number	1,154
Per cent	*100*
Does the job, gets clothes whiter, cleaner, brighter	100%
Strong	85
Economical	76
Chlorine ingredient does the job	40
Odor denotes cleanliness	26
Flexible—easy to measure and works better	21

* Some respondents gave more than one answer.

EXHIBIT 1–15
DB–14 Usage and Attitude Study
Specimen Data:
Major Shortcomings of Liquid Bleaches*

Base: All bleach-using households		
Number	1,154	
Per cent	*100*	
Harsh, too harsh	52%	
Too harsh on fabrics		32
Too harsh on hands		26
Ruins colors	26	
Can't use on synthetic fabrics	24	
Clumsy and heavy to carry around	22	
No shortcomings	41	

* Some respondents gave more than one answer.

EXHIBIT 1–16
DB–14 Usage and Attitude Study
Specimen Data:
Characteristics of an Ideal Bleach*

Base: All bleach-using households	
Number	1,154
Per cent	*100*
Gets clothes totally white and bright	98%
Gets clothes totally clean	94
Same price as liquids	82
Safe for colored clothes	22
Safe for synthetic fabrics	16
Safe for skin	8
Light and easy to carry	6

* Some respondents gave more than one answer.

When the material had been presented by LaGrange and discussed by the group, Knutson said, "Al, have you reached any conclusions about where we should go from here?" When Knutson could be referring to more than one Al, the company custom was for the senior man to respond.

And so Pensa said, with a rather indicative quietness, "No, Alfred, these studies have only just become available, and we haven't had a real opportunity to explore all the ramifications of them. We'll be back with our joint recommendation early next week if that's OK."

But it was not OK with Knutson: "I'll tell you what, Al; this is kind of a new venture for us, right? And none of us has had much experience with this kind of information [his left had jerked spasmodically in the direction of LaGrange's reports], and if we are going to do more of it, I'd like the chance to see how each of you goes at it as an individual. Why doesn't each of you write me a private note telling me where you come out on DB-14 and why, if that's OK."

And this second proposal was OK, whether anyone except Knutson liked it or not. Here are the three memoranda received by Knutson:

HPU Internal Communication

December 5, 1974

FROM: A. Caravelle
TO: Alfred Knutson

We can make DB-14 and we can make if profitably, under the proposed pricing structure. As far as the product itself is concerned, it's a beauty. It really does all of the things that Johnson in R&D says that it will. I have to conclude that we have an important breakthrough in technology. To achieve a result of this importance on our very first try in new product development strikes me as extraordinarily lucky and all I can say is I'm glad we're the ones that have this product to put on the store shelves under the HPU name.

But, my question has always been whether we should be developing any new products at all. This way, we have to shoot dice with consumers, and we all know how fickle they are—LaGrange's research proves that, if nothing more. Before we got into new product development, we let our competitors spend their money trying to please the consumer, and while they blithely threw money away, we profited by their errors.

I say let the other guys make the mistakes for us. I say let's not throw any more good money after bad with this bleach product, good as it may be, that consumers won't buy.

I recommend we forget the whole thing.

HPU Internal Communication

December 5, 1974

FROM: A. Pensa
TO: Alfred Knutson

The DB–14 research poses a real dilemma for us.

The research indicates that the consumer does not want a bleach product that has the characteristics of DB–14. DB–14 apparently doesn't do the job as far as consumers are concerned. We know, from our own laboratory tests, that it *will* do the job for them. Somehow we have gotten the consumers off on the wrong track. Maybe it's because we emphasize the safety of the product rather than its performance. But we know the product is a good one.

If a competitor came along with this product, and it was patented, we would have a devil of a time equaling or surpassing the formulation. And yet the consumers say they don't like it. I know all about the science of sampling and all, but I really wonder if we should take the word of a few hundred women and run off the end of the dock with it. I believe the best bet is to introduce the product as it stands into a test market and try to develop advertising that will overcome the consumer negatives that have been uncovered by the research. It could be that the research is wrong, but maybe by developing a new positioning for the product, we can convince the consumer.

I recommend that we introduce the product into two medium-sized test markets as soon as we see advertising copy that we like.

HPU Internal Communication

December 5, 1974

FROM: A. Scala
TO: Alfred Knutson

It is clear from the consumer research that DB–14 should not be introduced into the marketplace. Good as it is, it is not what the consumer wants. The research results are simply too negative and too conclusive.

The research results suggest that the product should be reformulated:

a. Liquids are the preferred form and seem to suggest strength.
b. DB–14 smells too mild.
c. DB–14 should have all of its current performance attributes but should not appear in any way to be mild, or lacking in effectiveness.

The research results suggest even more strongly that we should change our description of the product:

a. The reformulated DB–14 should only be described in terms denoting strength, cleaning power, whitening power.
b. All mention of gentleness and safety should be omitted.

In order to get some idea about the importance of the words in describing the product, I would like to recommend that a second home placement test be run with DB–14, unchanged, but with a new description along these lines:

Powerful Dry Bleach

This powerful dry bleach should be used in the same way as liquid bleaches—one packet will clean and whiten a normal automatic-washer load.

For loads containing deep soil or stains, use a second packet.

This powerful product is extremely effective in whitening and cleaning clothes —its bleaching agents surround individual fabric fibers and wrench dirt and grime away. You'll be amazed at the difference.

My second recommendation is that I immediately be authorized to develop a new form of bleach that is totally consistent with consumers' expectations in this product category. This new product may be a liquid—if we can find ways of stabilizing our active ingredients in solution. But it may be a powder if the recommended new consumer research indicates that the proper product positioning will strip away consumer resistance to dry bleaches.

Questions for Case 1

1. Define the "marketing concept." How does the marketing concept relate to the facts presented in this case?
2. Summarize the consumer placement research findings given in Exhibits 1–4 through 1–9.
3. Summarize the usage and attitude research findings given in Exhibits 1–10 through 1–16. What are the implications of these findings for a new product in the bleach market?
4. Home Products Universal's laboratory evaluation of the product DB–14 appears to be contradicted by the consumer research findings. Is it possible that consumers may prefer a product that does not meet the highest performance specifications?
5. Evaluate the memoranda written by Caravelle, Pensa, and Scala in response to Knutson's request. Do you agree with any of these men? If so, tell which one and why. If not, prepare a memorandum to Mr. Knutson that is properly responsive to his request.
6. When Mr. Knutson receives the three memoranda, how should he proceed?

Case 2

Market Segmentation

Wonder Foods Company, Inc.
Reviews Its Franchise in the
Hot Cereal Market

THE WONDER FOODS COMPANY, INC. is the third largest food manufacturer and the forty-ninth largest company in the United States. It produces and distributes a wide line of food products. In addition, in recent years the company has diversified widely, operating as separate units nineteen distinct nonfood companies ranging from a greeting card manufacturer to a producer of bicycles and diving boards.

Among the food products are 80 distinct branded items. Of these, 17 are supported with advertising and/or sales promotional expenditures. These 17 advertised promoted brands contributed the bulk of Wonder Foods' sales and profits. These brands include, among others, Picture Pretty DeLuxe Cake Mixes, Fluffy Quick Brand preprocessed rice, Pucker Brand Pickles, the Tremendous W Dry Cereal line, Happy Red Brand Tomato Condiments, Plenty Good Brand Gelatin Desserts, and the Perfect Puritan Brand Hot Cereal line.

In addition to the advertised brands, there are some sixty-odd Wonder Foods products not actively advertised or promoted by the Wonder Foods Company, Inc. These non-advertised/promoted brands (which include wet and dry cooking ingredients and spices and jams and jellies) are less important to Wonder Foods in sales and profit terms, but in aggregate they make an important contribution to the good health of the corporation. Cost-accounting analyses confirm that each of the nonpromoted brands is profitable in its own right and that they all absorb their proportionate share of corporate overhead.

In a company like Wonder Foods, the major marketing effort tends to be given to the brands with the largest sales volume. There are three of these: the cake mixes, the preprocessed rice, and the gelatin desserts. Considerably less attention is paid the remaining advertised brands. One index of this relative neglect was the total amount, in 1973, of advertising and promotional funds devoted to them as a group ($6,000,000) as contrasted to the three leading brands in aggregate ($27,000,000). Each of these leading brands has its own product manager; the fourteen remaining advertised/promoted brands are shared by two men.

In this situation, it was possible, but relatively improbable, that one of the less important brands would suddenly receive an unusual amount of product-manager attention or that a major program would be initiated to investigate the true potential of the particular product category in which one of these lesser brands was an entrant.

Wonder Foods is truly a forest of brands; a triumph of manufacturing and distribution skills; a company that knows how to generate sales of myriad products without undue emphasis on any save the three major breadwinners. In this approach, Wonder Foods is quite different from its leading competitors, who depend upon a relatively short line of heavily advertised and promoted items. These competitive companies simply do not bother with long lines of relatively small sellers with little or no marketing or advertising support. When one of these competitors looks for expanded sales volume it is usually necessary for it to consider launching a new brand in a new product category heretofore unexplored by that company. The opposite is more likely to be true for Wonder Foods. When Wonder Foods seeks new horizons it is forced to examine its existing product lines, because within these is likely to be found almost every kind of product that could provide significant new volume to the company.

Early in 1974, Theodore W. MacMahoner faced a decision. MacMahoner is the general marketing manager of Wonder Foods. The decision that he faced concerned the succession to one of the two product managerships for the minor advertised brands. These two jobs held an identical title; Product Manager–Advertised Lines. Albert W. Kinselver was about to retire after forty-two years of service with Wonder Foods, mostly in sales, but for the past three and one half years as one of these product managers for advertised lines.

Over the past twenty or so years these Product Managers–Advertised Lines positions had been held by a succession of mediocrities. Two primary sources dominated the background of these men: either they had failed as product managers of one of the three major advertised lines or they had come out of the field selling organization, generally from the district manager level. There was a quiet understanding throughout the organization that men did not move upward from an assignment as product manager for advertised lines. This was as high as an appointee would ever go. He might receive other comparable assignments within the organization, or more likely retire from the post, but his upward progress halted when he was appointed a product manager for advertised lines. And so the incumbents in the post at any given point in time tended to receive neither respect nor excessive cooperation from the rest of the corporation. When they wanted something done, it always seemed to take a day or two longer. If an obscure secretary or assistant librarian was more interested in arranging a bridal shower than responding to a request from one of the advertised-lines men, the request was put off with the smug assurance that such insolence merely reflected the understanding of the entire organization as well as the PM–AL's, themselves.

The status of these men within the organization ensured, therefore, that very few marketing innovations occurred within their brands. The brands involved were not managed as much as they were perpetuated. Cost-to-sales ratios stayed the same year after year and promotional programs were also repeated almost endlessly with only minor change.

At some previous time it had apparently been decided that the sole objective of the advertised lines would be to generate consistent yearly profits. This decision may not have been a decision at all, rather the unconscious consensus of a management unwilling to make or approve any overt moves for the advertised lines over a long enough period of time to become a de facto decision—overt enough, even though unspoken —and, thus, an agreed-upon policy for the company. Once the organization assimilated this, the status of the PM–AL's merely reinforced it, and, in fact, it is hard to say who really caused the final state of affairs: the management, the rest of the employees in the organization, or the PM–AL's themselves.

However all of this had come to pass, it was real enough, and Mac-Mahoner was a good enough executive to understand it thoroughly, even if perhaps he could not articulate it. The decision that he faced coldly in 1974 was a relatively simple one. Should he find another Kinselver, a man whose career would effectively stop with the appointment, or should he undo the decision of the past and make an attempt to upgrade the PM–AL job, and by implication attempt to vitalize the advertised lines themselves?

On its surface, this seemed to be no decision at all. MacMahoner had been general marketing manager for Wonder Foods since 1960 and had appointed five product managers for advertised lines during the fourteen years. Every one of them had been a mediocrity, and MacMahoner himself had done as much as any man to ensure the status of the PM–AL's within the organization and to reinforce the perpetuation of the status quo for the advertised lines themselves. There was no reason at all for anyone to expect that MacMahoner should do anything except what he had done on five previous occasions.

And yet MacMahoner found himself under very heavy pressure from corporate management to increase sales and profits. If someone had asked the question at any time during his fourteen years of stewardship, MacMahoner would always have responded vehemently that he was "under very heavy pressure from corporate management to increase sales and profits." It is, after all, the only responsibility of the senior marketing executive in a corporation to sell as much as he can with the maximum achievable profit. So the senior marketing executive should always feel a compelling pressure to exceed previous sales accomplishments and profits. Sales can never be high enough, and profits are always lower than the shareholders would wish them to be. But there was something tangibly different in the 1974 atmosphere, and if MacMahoner always felt the pressure of his management, he could say with conviction that they expected more from him now than they had in the recent past.

Wonder Foods' corporate sales had fallen for two consecutive years. It was, in fact, fair to say that 1972 and 1973 were two of the most disappointing sales years in the history of the corporation. True enough, the Wonder Foods Company as a distinct entity, and the third largest producer of food products in the United States, had relatively good sales and profits in 1972–73. It was the acquisitions that were lagging. One—a computer software company purchased in 1967 through stock exchange at a wildly exaggerated price-earnings multiple for the software company against a moderately depressed market valuation for Wonder Foods—failed completely in November of 1972. The bicycle company, producing in 1971 at the upper limit of its production capacity against surging consumer demand, installed faulty brake cables in over 278,000 bicycles. A district court in Selma, Alabama, ruled, on a consumer complaint, that the recall regulations that protect consumers against automobile failure also applied to bicycles. The court ordered that all 278,000 defective bikes be recalled and that the defective cables be replaced at company expense. Before the dust settled, it was clear that the loss of this unit came to over $2,978,000 in 1972 and about $4,500,000 in 1973. No one of the nineteen acquired companies showed a significant profit in either 1972 or 1973 and most operated at a flat loss in both years.

Even if MacMahoner's operations had performed well in both years, and they certainly had, the profit problems of the corporation were his to share. Corporate management was, after all, responsible for overall corporate performance, and although they knew well enough where the problem lay, they exerted pressure throughout the corporation for improved performance. Maybe, reasoned the corporate managers, the proven products could deliver even more and thus save everyone a lot of trouble. Corporate life is, after all, corporate life, thought MacMahoner, biting the mental bullet and placing his figurative shoulder to the wheel.

It was in this context that MacMahoner approached the selection of a new Product Manager–Advertised Lines. Would it be possible, he wondered, to turn up increased sales and profits from the advertised lines if a talented young marketing man was put in place and given an injunction to proceed in any way he wished as long as it was aggressive? After all, there was a variety of accepted products, with achieved distribution, established advertising and promotion budgets, and a decade of perpetuative marketing management from marketing managers that had been chosen because they had demonstrated only the abilities of thinking slowly and unimaginatively and standing pat. Did this not represent an opportunity for significantly improved sales and profits?

As he reviewed all of this it seemed clear to MacMahoner that his best move would be to break sharply and unequivocably with the past. He would find the most aggressive and the most promising product manager available and then give him his head. But where to find this man? Should he be moved from within or would it be best to recruit him from outside? MacMahoner considered these options for a week or more and then decided to move from within. He knew that the only way that he could convey to the whole organization that the ball game had radically changed was to move a man that was the opposite of all the things that the PM–AL's had historically been and a man who was widely recognized within the organization to be just this.

Such a man was readily at hand. He was Huntington James Johnson— "Hunty" to everyone at Wonder. Hunty Johnson had been with Wonder Foods throughout his entire fourteen-year business career. He had started with the sales force, worked for a year in marketing research, gone back to sales, and then entered the product manager ranks, first as an assistant to John O'Neale on cake mixes. He had then been promoted to Product Manager–Gelatin Desserts in early 1971 and had been as effective in this role as in all others he had held within the company. Bright, alert, aggressive, subtle in his assessments of people, and, with all, a totally dedicated Wonder Foods man, Hunty Johnson was MacMahoner's bright star. He would, in fact, replace MacMahoner himself if no shadow crossed his record in the six or eight years ahead. With all this thinking done, it only remained for MacMahoner to convince young Hunty that a move to PM–AL was, in fact, a great opportunity and a way station on the trail to future heights rather than an early warning that corporate oblivion was to be his final reward for dedication.

MacMahoner broached the subject just before Hunty was scheduled to leave on a two-week vacation. "I want you to think something over while you're away, Hunty. It'll sound damned funny when you first hear it, but I want you to really think it over, and two weeks ought to fill the bill." Ted MacMahoner held rather primitive views on the need for and virtue of vacations for his employees. MacMahoner prided himself that he had not taken a day off for any reason, including vacation and sickness, for almost fifteen years—ever since his promotion to the position of general marketing manager in 1960.

Hunty Johnson had all-American-boy trappings, but he wasn't a fool. When MacMahoner asked someone to think something over, it was known throughout the organization that the something inevitably was unpleasant and usually involved either a move to a remote corporate outpost or a switch to some unappetizing home-office assignment.

"I can't think of anything that you would suggest to me that could require two weeks of thought, Mac—even two weeks of vacation thought," countered Hunty. "What's up?" MacMahoner knew the response for what it was: a quiet challenge to MacMahoner and the entire organization to recognize Johnson's demonstrated competence and loyalty. Maybe what was coming wasn't too good, but Johnson was carefully implying that it had better not be too bad, because they both knew that his performance warranted a promotion or an increase in salary, or both. But MacMahoner was not to be deflected from his purpose. Hunty Johnson was his man, and he was going to make Hunty do what was best for MacMahoner and the corporation.

"Hunty, I'm going to bump your salary $5,000 on the first of October. And I'm going to ask you to accept a new assignment—a really tough one. I want you to take over from Al Kinselver as a PM–AL when he retires." Hunty didn't have anything to say. He was quiet for almost two minutes and then, out of the total stillness, he said, "I guess I'd like to know exactly what's in your mind, Mac. You know and I know that the PM–AL spot is a graveyard and that the people you put there are put there to do nothing. The less they do the better the choice. That's not for me, Mac, and we both know it. What's this all about?"

This gave MacMahoner just the right opening: "You got it right away, Hunty. I can't kid you, and I won't try to, you know that. We've got to breathe some life into the advertised lines. You know that upstairs[1] is having a rough year between the failure of Motivational Software Dynamics for Management Involvement and the recalls on Regal Wings bikes and all the other acquisitions lying down. You know and I know that profits have to come from somewhere, and in this company that means the food company, and that means us—you and me, Hunty. If I keep putting Yo-yos into the advertised lines I won't get any results. But maybe we can really do something in there and you're the man to do it. And you know that if I pick you, everybody will know it's a new ball game, and that's why we're going to do it that way. Makes sense, doesn't it?"

From the look on Johnson's face it was pretty clear that it made very little sense at all at the moment, and MacMahoner decided not to press it when Johnson looked at him and quietly said, "I don't know whether it does or not, Mac, but I'll think it over for the next few days and give you a ring."

In the end Johnson said "Yes." As of October 1, 1974 he was a product manager for advertised lines and MacMahoner did everything in his power to support him in his new role. Years later, Johnson looked back upon his appointment to PM–AL as a sharp upward turning point in his career, but he did not think of it as such at the time and came near to turning it down. But once committed, he put all of his considerable

---

[1] *Upstairs* meant the management floor, and more specifically, the corporate management of Wonder Foods, Inc.

talents to work against the problem of squeezing more sales and profits out of the advertised lines that fell under his immediate jurisdiction. There were seven of these: Pucker Brand Pickles; Happy Red Tomato Condiments; Golden Delicious Pancake, Waffle, and French Toast Syrups; Shady Cellar Mushrooms; Perfect Puritan Brand Hot Cereals; Breath of Genoa Fancy Garlic; and Silver Shavings Iodized Salt.

Johnson's first move was to assemble relevant sales and profit statistics for these brands. These are summarized in Exhibit 2–1. He studied this exhibit with great care. (The gross profit figures should be reduced to one fourth to get an idea of the actual after-tax corporate profit contribution of the brands.) He was looking for a brand, or brands, with relatively large sales and with high and steady profits. If he could find such a brand, he reasoned that its existing sales position would reflect good consumer acceptance and that its high, steady profitability would reflect favorable market pricing and stable and controlled cost factors within the corporation.

The brand that most nearly met these criteria was Perfect Puritan Brand Hot Cereals. Its sales were significant and growing and its profit high and stable. Johnson was also pleasantly surprised by some of the other brands under his jurisdiction, notably Shady Cellar Mushrooms and Pucker Brand Pickles. There seemed to be a great deal of potential in their figures, as shown in the exhibit, but he intended to take one step at a time and concluded that the greatest present opportunity existed

EXHIBIT 2–1
Specimen Data: Sales and Gross Profits for Selected Advertised Lines
1971, 1972, 1973

	Sales (000 omitted)			Gross Profits (Before Corporate Overhead and Taxes) (000 omitted)			Gross Profits/Sales (Per Cent)		
	1971	1972	1973	1971	1972	1973	1971	1972	1973
Happy Red Tomato Condiments	34,320	36,177	40,127	12,124	12,321	12,916	35.3	34.1	32.2
Perfect Puritan Brand Hot Cereals	21,426	27,321	29,440	10,724	13,421	14,560	50.1	49.1	49.5
Shady Cellar Mushrooms	10,723	12,639	14,822	3,214	4,289	6,433	30.0	33.9	43.4
Pucker Brand Pickles	8,542	10,978	16,247	2,453	3,601	5,721	28.7	32.8	35.2
Golden Delicious Pancake, Waffle, and French Toast Syrups	3,211*	8,724	9,821	13*	411	3,241	0.4	4.7	33.0
Breath of Genoa Fancy Garlic	2,944	3,279	3,998	1,211	1,312	1,526	41.1	40.0	38.2
Silver Shavings Iodized Salt	1,243*	6,729	8,544	−324*	47	2,411	−	0.1	28.2

* First national advertising year.

with hot cereals. "Let's increase sales significantly on Perfect Puritan and hold the profit percentage just as it is," thought Hunty Johnson to himself, "and we'll be heroes soon enough."

The Perfect Puritan line of hot cereals consisted of four basic items: Oatmeal, Bacon Flavored Oatmeal, Snowflake Wheat Puree, and Snowflake Rice Puree. Each of the four basic items was available in both regular (or long-cooking) and "instant" forms. The average preparation time of the regular items was twenty-eight minutes, and the average preparation time for the "instant" forms was eleven minutes. Each product was available in two package sizes (sixteen ounces and thirteen ounces.) Prices varied with the item: the regular products were sold, at retail, for about 25 per cent less than the "instant" products, and the purees were about 20 per cent more expensive than the oatmeal products.

Johnson requested from the Wonder Foods marketing research department a summary of all the information held by them that they considered pertinent to the current marketing of the Perfect Puritan line of hot cereals. About ten days later, he received the following memorandum from J. Q. Martindale of the Wonder Foods marketing research department:

WONDER FOODS MEMORANDUM

October 15, 1974

TO: H. J. Johnson
FROM: J. Q. Martindale
SUBJECT: Review of Hot Cereal Information

Mr. Bartley H. Bogardus, Manager of the Marketing Research Department, has asked that we respond to your recent request for a "complete review and interpretation of all Hot Cereal Marketing data, that might be pertinent to a vitalized new marketing posture for Perfect Puritan Brand."

We are delighted to comply with this request and summarize in the following paragraphs our evaluation of all the Hot Cereal data in our files.*

1. The hot cereal market consists of three major types of products:

   a. The rolled oat products.
   b. The preprocessed full-husk wheat products.
   c. The creamed or pureed products.

The oat products have held more than half of the total market since 1960; the preprocessed full-husk wheat products and the creamed or pureed products each hold about half of the remainder, but the pureed products have slowly but steadily gained market shares in the last decade or so. (See Exhibit 2–2.)

* (These data are quite sparse compared to those in hand for the company's major advertised brands. There are, all told, eight custom-market research studies for the Perfect Puritan Brand as well as the usual spate of syndicated studies covering competitive distribution and sales information, etc. But the material that is available appears to indicate clearly the major marketing issues that face you as you set out to vitalize the Perfect Puritan Brand. A recapitulation of each of the major studies is presented in the appendix, following the interpretative summary of highlights.)

EXHIBIT 2–2
Specimen Data: The Hot Cereal Market—Major Product Types, 1960–73

	TOTAL	ROLLED OAT (Per Cent)	PREPROCESSED FULL-HUSK WHEAT (Per Cent)	CREAMED OR PUREED (Per Cent)
1960	$120,086,050	52	34	14
1965	117,824,931	48	33	19
1966	117,806,321	51	30	19
1967	116,421,067	50	27	23
1968	116,438,072	53	28	19
1969	115,997,831	51	25	24
1970	115,821,342	49	27	24
1971	114,682,421	50	26	24
1972	113,841,321	51	22	27
1973	112,421,320	52	23	25

S O U R C E : Modeled on the reports of the A. C. Nielsen Company and Market Research Department projections.

2. The market is gradually declining. Total retail sales have fallen from $120,086,050 in 1960 to $112,421,320 in 1973. The actual decline in servings per capita has, of course, been considerably greater because the population has increased about 19 per cent in this period and we estimate that the price of hot cereal at retail has increased about 50 per cent in the period. (This price increase is a function of these two basic factors: inflation, about 30 per cent; and upgrading of product from the "regular" to the more expensive "instant" forms, about 20 per cent. A third, minor factor is the increasing popularity of the somewhat more expensive pureed products and the decline in popularity of the somewhat less expensive preprocessed full-husk wheat products. No effort has been made to estimate the net effect of this last factor.) Thus, we estimate that the 1973 retail dollar sales level reflects about 48 per cent as many actual servings as the 1960 total of $120,086,050.

3. There has been no significant product innovation in the hot cereal category in the past twenty-five years. I would not believe my ears when our librarian told me this the first time. We have *never*, in the history of the Department, investigated a product category that had no new product entry over a period of twenty-five years. But it is true! I spent a day and a half personally reviewing the new-product-introduction files, which go back to 1948. There has not been a single new product introduction in the hot cereal category in this whole time.

You will understand that this finding excludes the development of the "instant" and "quick-cooking" versions of the three basic types. We viewed these as line extensions rather than new products, even though they are generally sold at a higher price and do absorb additional retail shelf space for the product category.

4. The major competitors are the Smiling Ben line (it held about 30 per cent of the total retail volume in 1973) and the Golden Morn line (with about 18 per cent of the total retail volume). Wonder Foods Perfect Puritan line holds, as you know, about 41 per cent—at retail. The remainder of the business is divided between a host of small-volume regional marketers—no one of which is a significant factor in

the market. Interestingly, private-label merchandise has never been important, or even a factor, in this market.

The breakdown of the leading brands by product type is shown in Exhibit 2–3A and 2–3B for the year 1973. Perfect Puritan is a dominant factor (58 per cent) in the single most important segment of the market—the rolled oat category. It holds somewhat less than half of the smaller but growing segment of the creamed or pureed group. It has no market entrant in the preprocessed full-husk wheat category.

Smiling Ben Brand has a modest position in the rolled oat and preprocessed full-husk wheat category and is the leader in the creamed or pureed category.

Golden Morn is the least important national brand in the Rolled oat category and is the most important brand in the preprocessed full-husk wheat category. It has no pureed or creamed entry.

It seems clear to us that Perfect Puritan must think in terms of new product types or in terms of stronger competitive efforts in the creamed or pureed category if competitive gains are to be made; certainly we cannot look for competitive gains in the rolled oats category and would not want to enter the preprocessed full-husk wheat segment.

5. Distribution is excellent for Perfect Puritan and Smiling Ben. It is spotty for Golden Morn. As the data in Exhibit 2–4 indicate, each of the leading brands has achieved distribution in excess of 80 per cent for each of its leading varieties. (You

EXHIBIT 2–3A
Specimen Data: The Hot Cereal Market—Brand Share of Major Product Types, Total Market Base, 1973

	TOTAL	ROLLED OATS 52%	PREPROCESSED FULL-HUSK WHEAT 23%	CREAMED OR PUREED 25%
Perfect Puritan	41%	30%	—	11%
Smiling Ben	30	10	6%	14
Golden Morn	18	9	9	—
All others	11	3	8	—

SOURCE: Modeled on the reports of the A. C. Nielsen Company.

EXHIBIT 2–3B
Specimen Data: The Hot Cereal Market—Brand Share of Major Products, Market Segment Base, 1973

	TOTAL	ROLLED OATS 100%	PREPROCESSED FULL-HUSK WHEAT 100%	CREAMED OR PUREED 100%
Perfect Puritan		58%	—	44%
Smiling Ben		19	26%	56
Golden Morn		17	39	—
All others		6	35	—

SOURCE: Modeled on the reports of the A. C. Nielsen Company.

EXHIBIT 2–4
**Specimen Data: The Hot Cereal Market—Achieved Distribution for
Leading Brand Varieties, 1973**

BRAND	VARIETY	DISTRIBUTION (Per Cent)	OUT OF STOCK (Per Cent)
Perfect Puritan	Oatmeal	92	2
Perfect Puritan	Bacon Flavored Oatmeal	89	4
Perfect Puritan	Snowflake Wheat Puree	93	3
Perfect Puritan	Snowflake Rice Puree	91	8
Smiling Ben	Oatmeal	84	2
Smiling Ben	Wheat Yummy	91	6
Smiling Ben	Creamed Rice	86	8
Golden Morn	Oatmeal 'n' Grits Mix	49	12
Golden Morn	Smoothee Wheato	57	9

S O U R C E :   Modeled on the reports of the A. C. Nielsen Company.

will recall that distribution percentages are based on the total grocery-commodity sales volume handled by the stores in which distribution for a single item has been achieved. Thus, a distribution of 92 per cent for Perfect Puritan Oatmeal means that it is available to consumers in stores that account for 92 per cent of all grocery commodity volume to consumers.) Out-of-stock is moderate for Perfect Puritan, modest for Smiling Ben, and more serious for Golden Morn.

The general pattern is that the instant products have achieved better distribution than the regular products, at least for Perfect Puritan. The 1973 Perfect Puritan picture is shown in Exhibit 2–5. Taken together, the instant and regular products are widely available (Exhibit 2–4), and distribution is lower for the individual types. This is a relatively normal pattern and is to be expected based on the relative factory sales of the two product types. (The instant products, in aggregate, had factory sales of $17,243,071 in 1973 and the regular products aggregated $12,196,929 in 1973. Comparable data for Smiling Ben and Golden Morn Brands are not available.)

6. The hot cereal user is older, less well educated, down scale in income, and more likely to live in the south and central geographic areas rather than the northeast and Pacific geographic areas. (See Exhibit 2–6).

7. Comparable demographic data for the three varieties of hot cereals (rolled oats, preprocessed full-husk wheat, and creamed or pureed) and for the two types of hot cereals (regular and instant) are not available. It is the belief of the Market Research Department that the demographic distribution for rolled oats and for regular varieties would be somewhat more skewed toward lower income and education and older households in the south and central areas than for preprocessed full-husk wheat and pureed varieties and for the instant type. But we have no hard data to back up this belief.

8. Hot cereals are now in the pantry inventory of 40 per cent of U.S. families. One out of ten U.S. families serves hot cereal every day; 12 per cent serve it

EXHIBIT 2–5
Specimen Data: The Hot Cereal Market—Achieved Distribution for Perfect Puritan Regular and Instant Varieties, 1973

BRAND	VARIETY	DISTRIBUTION (Per Cent)	OUT OF STOCK (Per Cent)
Perfect Puritan	Instant Oatmeal	72	8
Perfect Puritan	Regular Oatmeal	61	6
Perfect Puritan	Instant Bacon Flavored Oatmeal	69	7
Perfect Puritan	Regular Bacon Flavored Oatmeal	43	2
Perfect Puritan	Instant Snowflake Wheat Puree	81	2
Perfect Puritan	Regular Snowflake Wheat Puree	42	4
Perfect Puritan	Instant Snowflake Rice Puree	88	1
Perfect Puritan	Regular Snowflake Rice Puree	52	7

S O U R C E :   Modeled on the reports of the A. C. Nielsen Company.

occasionally; 18 per cent say they have served it sometime in the past four years. (See Exhibit 2–7.)

Multiple variety/brand stocking is the rule. More than three quarters (34 per cent out of 40 per cent) of the stocking homes have two or more brands or varieties of hot cereals on hand. (See Exhibit 2–8.)

As one might expect, depth of home inventory is positively correlated with intensity of hot cereal usage. That is, the more frequently hot cereal is served, the more likely is a home to have more varieties/brands in inventory. (See Exhibit 2–9.)

9. Package design—both functional and aesthetic—has remained unchanged over the past twenty-five years for the Perfect Puritan Brand and over at least the past nine years for the competition.

Our files on Wonder Foods packaging go back to the beginning of the Marketing Research Department in 1949. Competitive packaging records in this category were started in 1964.

Oatmeal comes in a cylindrical cardboard box: this convention has been accepted by all manufacturers. Preprocessed full-husk wheat and pureed products come in rectangular top-opening boxes: this convention has also been accepted by the entire industry. Every manufacturer uses a metal pour spout in all packages, that is, for all varieties, types, and sizes.

It is interesting, and indicative of the stagnation in package design that has descended upon this product category, to observe that when the instant type was introduced, not one manufacturer designed new package graphics. Instead, they all mortised the word *instant* in block letters over the face of the existing packages. We, uniquely among the manufacturers, made one further change; our instant

EXHIBIT 2-6

Specimen Data: Characteristics of All Hot Cereal Using Families and Characteristics of Heavy* Hot Cereal Using Families, 1964

	ALL FAMILIES	HEAVY* HOT CEREAL USING FAMILIES	ALL† HOT CEREAL USING FAMILIES
Base			
Number	5,247	525	2,103
Per cent	*100*	*100*	*100*
Income			
Under $5,000	28%	45%	42%
$ 5,000–$7,999	32	30	31
$ 8,000–$9,999	24	15	16
$10,000 and over	16	10	11
Education of household head			
Grade school or less	21%	32%	30%
Some high school	18	24	23
Graduated, high school	35	27	30
Some college	16	15	12
Graduated, college	10	2	5
Age of household head			
24 and younger	26%	6%	7%
25–34	28	10	14
35–49	18	11	16
50–64	12	31	26
65 and older	16	42	37
Geographic area			
Northeast	28%	20%	22%
South	20	32	30
Central	27	36	34
Pacific	25	12	14

* A "heavy using family" is one in which hot cereals are served every day.
† A "using family" is one in which hot cereals have been served sometime within the past two years and that currently has a hot cereal on hand.
S O U R C E : Market Research Department Study, 1964.

product packages are in pastel shades of the dominant colors of the regular packages for the respective varieties. But the basic design is the same for both types.

10. We maintain, as you know, a file of trade information. The file is simply a repository for any report—published or verbal—about any of our competitors. Its purpose is to codify rumor, fact, and fancy, as we at Wonder Foods hear it. The TI file for most product categories, including hot cereals, go back to 1964. The typical file bulges with undigested information, largely fantasy but always interesting because it suggests the degree and character of the sound and fury that surround a particular product category. It came as no surprise to us to discover that the TI file for hot cereals was totally empty. Its contents had not been lost or stolen—there have never been any entries in the file! Granted, the instant products had been

EXHIBIT 2–7
Specimen Data: The Hot Cereal Market—Hot Cereal Serving Frequency, 1964

Base: Total households		
Number	5,247	
Per cent	*100*	
Have a hot cereal on hand, in pantry	40%	
Serve hot cereal every day*		10%
Serve hot cereal occasionally*		12
Serve hot cereal some time in past two years*		18

* A "heavy using family" is one in which hot cereals are served every day. A "using family" is one in which hot cereals have been served some time within the past two years and that currently has a hot cereal on hand.

s o u r c e : Market Research Department Study, 1964.

EXHIBIT 2–8
Specimen Data: The Hot Cereal Market—Hot Cereal Varieties in Pantry Inventory, 1964

Base: Total households		
Number	5,247	
Per cent	*100*	
Have a hot cereal on hand, in pantry	40%	
Have one variety of hot cereal on hand*		6%
Have two or three varieties/brands of hot cereal on hand*		31
Have four or more varieties/brands of hot cereal on hand*		3

* A "variety" would be rolled oats, preprocessed full-husk wheat, or creamed and pureed. A "brand" is a brand of a variety.

s o u r c e : Market Research Department, 1964.

EXHIBIT 2–9
Specimen Data: The Hot Cereal Market—Hot Cereal Serving Frequency by Number of Varieties/Brands in Pantry Inventory,* 1964

	NUMBER OF VARIETIES/BRANDS IN PANTRY INVENTORY			
SERVING FREQUENCY†	ONLY I	2–3	4 OR MORE	TOTAL (Base)
Every day	22%	25%	31%	525
Occasionally	27	29	36	630
Sometime in past two years	51	46	33	945
TOTAL (Base)	315	1,627	157	2,100

* Cross-tabulation of data presented in Exhibits 2–7 and 2–8.
† Serving frequency of families who have served a hot cereal at least once in the past two years and who now have a hot cereal in pantry inventory.

s o u r c e : Marketing Research Department Study, 1964.

introduced prior to the establishment of these files. But what kind of a product category is it that generates no trade rumors at all in almost ten years?

One additional point. You will note that most of the foregoing information is largely up to date. There are two important topics for which this is not so. These are the demographic characteristics of consumers and the inventory and serving characteristics of hot cereal families: all of the information underlying paragraphs 6, 7, and 8 above. Because the market for hot cereal is skewed toward older people it is probable that the customers for this product category are dying off faster than they are being replaced. If this is so, then the market for hot cereal probably consists of fewer families today than in 1964 and these few families probably eat hot cereals less often and hold fewer brands/varieties in inventory. This estimate is reflected in our conjectures about the decline in servings of 52 per cent since 1960 presented in paragraph 2. The important point is that the 1964 data are way out of date and should be updated, if you are really serious in your intention to attempt to vitalize this part of our business.

* *
*

Hunty Johnson studied this memorandum for several days. On the basis of his analysis of the information that it contained, he determined to explore possibilities for sales development in four areas: expanded consumer use of existing products; manufacturing innovations on existing products; improved or expanded promotional activity; and exploration of potential for totally new hot cereal products. With these objectives in mind, he wrote the following four memoranda:

WONDER FOODS MEMORANDUM

October 21, 1974

TO: Marshall J. Ellender (General Production Manager)
FROM: H. J. Johnson
SUBJECT: Hot Cereal Products Manufacturing

As you know, I have recently been appointed to the post of Product Manager–Advertised Lines. It is my intention to vitalize the sales and profits of several, if not all, of the products now entrusted to my care.

Our first major effort will be with the Perfect Puritan line of hot cereals. In this connection, I am interested in your thoughts on the following:

1. Can current manufacturing procedures on our hot cereal products be modified in any way that will
   a. Significantly reduce manufacturing costs without changing product character or quality?
   b. Significantly improve product character or quality without significantly increasing manufacturing costs?
   c. Reduce manufacturing costs *and* improve the character and quality of our products?

2. Have there been, or should there be, research and development projects to determine whether any of the objectives in question 1 can be accomplished?

3. Have there been or should there be research and development projects to determine whether totally new kinds of hot cereals are feasible? In this connection, I am thinking not only of the rolled oat, preprocessed full-husk wheat, and pureed cereal types, but also of totally new cereal types heretofore not available to the consumer.

Please have an answer to these questions in my hands within ten days.

WONDER FOODS MEMORANDUM

October 21, 1974

TO: Anita L. O'Weeke (Director of Home Economics)
FROM: H. J. Johnson
SUBJECT: Hot Cereal Product—Expanded Uses

As you know, I have recently been appointed to the post of Product Manager–Advertised Lines. It is my intention to vitalize the sales and profits of several, if not all, of the products now entrusted to my care.

Our first major effort will be with the Perfect Puritan line of hot cereals. In this connection, I am interested in your thoughts on the following:

As far as I can discover, the Home Economics section has never made any serious attempt to discover ways to extend the consumer use of hot cereal products. I suppose that you did develop the oatmeal cookie recipe that we have carried for several years on the regular oatmeal box, but I notice that it is not carried on the instant oatmeal box. Why not? Doesn't the recipe work with the instant product, or what?

You know your business better than I do, but I wonder if it might be worth our while to explore thoroughly all the ways that our oatmeal and pureed products might be used as an ingredient. Can either one or both be used, for example, as an ingredient in breads, cakes, gravies, soups, muffins, or pastries? How many different kinds of cookies can be made from the hot cereal products in our line? If we wanted to do a Christmas baking promotion based on these products, what kinds of Christmas goodies could you and your associates dream up? What are all the other ideas that you have about this product category that have escaped me?

Please have at least a preliminary answer to these questions in my hands within ten days.

WONDER FOODS MEMORANDUM

October 21, 1974

TO: Ambrose M. Follensbee (Director of Sales)
FROM: H. J. Johnson
SUBJECT: Hot Cereals Promotion

As you know, I have recently been appointed to the post of Product Manager–Advertised Lines. It is my intention to vitalize the sales and profits of several, if not all, of the products now entrusted to my care. Our first major effort will be with the Perfect Puritan line of hot cereals. In this connection, I am interested in your thoughts on the following:

My investigations reveal that we have never had a trade promotion on the Perfect

Puritan line of cereal products. I am appalled at this. Do you believe that the trade is so apathetic to sales possibilities for hot cereals that we can in no way encourage them to build displays of our brands in their stores; or price-feature them; or offer them with tie-ins during health food promotions, or whatever? Have we ever experimented with the trade on this line of products? If so, what was the outcome? If not, why not?

I sense an atmosphere of lethargy from your people on all of the advertised-line products. Granted, you've done a bang-up job in achieving distribution, but I don't think that's enough. Remember what we did for gelatin desserts when we promoted them with Bertram Bunny strawberry jam and the mystery ring tie-in! Now is the time for us to find the trade keys to moving these products.

Please let me know what you think within ten days.

WONDER FOODS MEMORANDUM

October 21, 1974

TO: Bartley H. Bogardus
FROM: H. J. Johnson
SUBJECT: Hot Cereal Consumption Patterns and Opportunities

Thanks so much for the nifty job that Jack Martindale did with the summary of available information on the hot cereal business. I've studied all of the material in detail and I would like to raise the following questions:

1. How would you proceed to update the consumer demographic information data that was last studied in 1964? I don't want an elaborate plan: a memorandum outlining costs, timing, and subject areas to be covered will be good enough for me.

2. I suspect, but cannot prove, that the potential market for hot cereals is considerably larger than the actual market that now exists.

   Perhaps there are groups of consumers that are quite anxious to eat a hot cereal, but not any of the hot cereals currently being offered. That is, there may be hot-cereal-prone people who do not now buy hot cereals because they don't like any of those offered.

3. Beyond this, it strikes me as possible that we can make competitive inroads if we know more about the people who now eat hot cereals. Is it possible to find out more about the personality traits that are attracted to hot cereals? If we knew more about these people, could it be that we could improve the effectiveness of our marketing and advertising?

   Perhaps an updating of the demographic/usage pattern study is as far as we can or should go. But somehow I have the feeling that there must be other information that can be obtained that will be of help to us.

Please let me have your thoughts within a week.

WONDER FOODS MEMORANDUM

October 29, 1974

TO: H. J. Johnson
FROM: Marshall J. Ellender
SUBJECT: Hot Cereals—Product Manufacturing

This responds to your memorandum of October 21, 1974, same subject.

We know of no way to modify current hot-cereal manufacturing procedures to

a. Reduce manufacturing costs.
b. Improve product character/quality.
c. Reduce manufacturing costs *and* improve product character/quality.

There have been no research and development projects to produce totally new hot cereals since the development of the instant varieties.

We would recommend, with your concurrence, that research and development activity should be directed toward reducing cooking time of the current instant products from eleven minutes to under three minutes. We believe that this objective is totally feasible, and we believe that if it is achieved no important increase in cost of goods will be involved relative to the currently marketed instant products.

This work would not involve more than 18 per cent of the time budget for professional research and development allocated to Advertised Lines for fiscal 1974–75.

Hunty Johnson scrawled the following note across the top of this memo: "Marsh Ellender: Excellent—I concur totally, approve the use of professional time and entreat you to move fastest—Hunty."

WONDER FOODS MEMORANDUM

October 31, 1974

TO: H. J. Johnson
FROM: Anita L. O'Weeke
SUBJECT: Hot Cereal Products Expanded Uses

We in Home Economics think you are so right about hot cereals! All of my associates have ideas about how to use them in recipes, particularly baking. I've encouraged them to pursue them in their spare time. I really don't know how much we can do in terms of a Christmas goody collection for this year, but I imagine you meant 1975.

One thing that we think should be an active project right now is how to make hot cereals more palatable as cereals. We mean, what can the consumer find easily in his very own pantry to put on hot cereals to make them more yummy?

There are lots of old-fashioned ways—like brown sugar and butter. But we'll try a lot of things in the next week or two and suggest them for a revised box-back.

Incidentally, we can find no record of having developed the cookie recipe that's on the back of the current oat meal box. Just reading it, I know it's not ours. I suspect that a product manager must have gotten it somewhere else—maybe from his wife or mother: but he didn't get it from us. It doesn't work very well and we'd love to get it off the boxes as quickly as we can.

WONDER FOODS MEMORANDUM

November 5, 1974

TO: H. J. Johnson
FROM: Ambrose M. Follensbee
SUBJECT: Hot Cereal Promotions

There ought to be trade promotions on hot cereals!

We've been saying this for years to all your predecessors!

We believe that a couple of juicy price-off deals—say two free with twelve, or 10 percent off on a display unit, would work fine!

As you know, we enjoy very cordial relations with the A&O food chain in Southwest, and they like tests and can run them beautifully because of their computerized buying setup, which is a model for the industry!

We'll be back with a test plan within a week!

WONDER FOODS MEMORANDUM

November 5, 1974

TO: H. J. Johnson
FROM: Bartley H. Bogardus
SUBJECT: Hot Cereal Consumption Patterns and Opportunities

Thank you for your memorandum of October 21.

We can do a demographic/consumption pattern study that exactly parallels the 1964 work. Probably we should investigate the following subject areas too:

1. The specific ways in which the various cereal types are served in the home. (I know Anita is working on this, feels strongly about it, and would welcome complementary information from Marketing Research.)
2. The degree to which hot and cold cereals are served in the same home. When and under what conditions and by whom hot cereals are eaten in preference to cold and vice versa.
3. Demographic information for each of the main hot cereal varieties and for the two hot cereal types.

We estimate that work of this kind based on a total population sample of 10,000 homes to yield about the same number of hot-cereal–using families as in 1964 (the population sample was about 5,247 in 1964, but we believe incidence of use has fallen off dramatically in the interim) would cost about $60,000 and could be completed in about ninety days. If this sounds right to you, we'll prepare a research authorization for your approval.

There is one other thing that should be done. We should attempt to identify population segments that have specific personality orientations toward hot cereals and determine the optimum product/communication mix to exploit these segments. It is possible that the population will not array itself in meaningful personality groupings vis-à-vis hot cereals, but our experience with other product categories has been that such segmentation can often be found and that, once found, it is likely to prove exploitable in market/profit terms. When I say "personality grouping," I mean to suggest that we study all of the aspects of the consumer that influence his decision to buy or not buy hot cereals and for those who do buy, all the aspects of his decision to buy particular varieties, types, and brands. Procedures now exist for analyzing the consumer in this total sense and they frequently yield results that go considerably beyond traditional demographic analyses.

The procedure follows a fairly structured series of steps:

1. First of all, it is important to do qualitative interviewing to determine the way in which consumers perceive hot cereals and specific hot cereal varieties; when and how they serve hot cereals and why; the attitudes that consumers hold about hot cereals and specific hot cereal varieties; the benefits they expect to derive from consuming hot cereals; the relation of their overt personality characteristics and hot cereal consumption; the relation of their overt demographic characteristics and hot cereal consumption; and so on.

At this stage in the qualitative work, we are simply looking for hints of the types of variables that might be crucial in separating consumers into meaningful personality groupings or segments. Every product group generates different kinds of segments, of course. But every product group develops its segments upon the basic structure of human personality that has been fairly well worked out by the psychologists over the years.

2. With the results of this work in hand, we analyze it in psychological terms as well as marketing terms and develop a list of personality "items" that relate to the personality dynamics, as we understand them in total, that underlie product usage and brand choice for the category. A personality "item" is a short statement that a respondent can agree or disagree with. In aggregate, a particular respondent's pattern of agreement with these items will identify him as a member of a group with comparable personality traits that may be characteristically associated with a particular market segment's orientation toward the consumption of hot cereals.

At this point the question is whether or not meaningful personality segments exist, in fact, for the product group in the population as a whole. We may guess that they do, on the basis of both this qualitative work and the general experience we have had with comparable product categories. But the important point is that we do not *know* this for sure, and the problem is really too complicated to permit us to make meaningful predictions at this stage. We can only know for sure if segments exist after data on all aspects of the personality in relation to the product groups have been processed through the computer, using a series of exceptionally powerful new programs that have been developed specifically for these analyses.

We believe it to be prudent to pilot-test the factor list on about two hundred respondents. The results of the pilot test accomplish two distinct purposes: (a) it gives us fodder for a computer run to determine whether meaningful segments do exist, without committing us to the expense of a full-scale study, and (b) it gives us a basis for refining our lists of factors for the final, full-scale undertaking.

3. On the assumption that the pilot work is successful, one then goes on to the final job—usually about 1,500 product users. In this case, it is totally feasible to combine the demographic study, outlined above, with the segmentation inquiry (the third phase), if the third phase appears feasible and desirable on the basis of phases one and two. If we were to follow this approach it would mean delaying the demographic work by the amount of time required to complete phases one and two: about three months. The major reason for proceeding this way is because of the cost savings involved.

The cost of the segmentation study, alone, is approximately $125,000. If it is combined with the demographic study, the cost will not increase by more than $10,000. This seems to us to indicate the desirability of proceeding with the two studies jointly. May we have your comments?

* *
*

Three days later, Hunty Johnson reluctantly authorized the Wonder Foods marketing research department to proceed with the full research program outlined in the Bogardus memorandum. He did this with considerable misgiving—after all, how was one to know whether or not the expenditure of $135,000 would pay off?

Before saying yes, Johnson talked at great length with Bogardus, trying to determine whether he really believed that the segmentation study would return its cost in future profits from hot cereals or whether he was simply doing his best to sell a big research job. Finally, Johnson decided that this risk was a reasonable one. The segmentation study might help him to make really significant breakthroughs in hot cereal marketing simply because there seemed to be a very good chance that it would provide him with significant new knowledge about how these products were consumed. But even if, in the end, its profit contribution did not match its cost, it would at least create the feeling throughout the organization that Hunty Johnson meant business and was willing to put his own reputation and significant amounts of company money on the line in order to achieve success. And that, thought Hunty Johnson to himself, may be worth five times as much to me as the cost of the study.

And so the work itself proceeded. In the end, its results were considered by all concerned to produce a significant breakthrough for Wonder Foods in the marketing of hot cereals. The various reports and analyses generated by these studies came to over 525 pages of text, tables, charts, and whatnot.

Reproduced in the following pages are the key findings and analyses from the studies. Exhibits 2–10 through 2–14 update the demographic data on the hot cereal market. A memorandum dated June 23, 1975 from Bartley Bogardus to Hunty Johnson provides a summary interpretation of the segmentation study findings. Exhibits 2–15 through 2–22 summarize the major findings of the segmentation study.

(A note on research method. The earlier, 1964, study was descriptive of the family consumption patterns of hot cereal. Consumption and demographic data were developed on the basic family unit. This structure was duplicated in the 1975 work for hot cereal consumption and demography. The personality segmentation work was, of course, concerned with individuals. A random sample of individuals was selected from the 9,854 family units within which the basic interviewing was conducted. This random sample of individuals reflects the population as a whole in respect to personality traits. In addition, a complete personality segmentation questionnaire was administered to *every* hot cereal eating individual in the 3,350 family units who used a hot cereal. These 5,477 individuals —there are 1.63 hot cereal eaters in every using family—are presented in the following tables as "hot cereal eaters."

EXHIBIT 2–10
Specimen Data: Characteristics of All Hot Cereal Using Families and Characteristics of Heavy Hot Cereal Using Families, 1975

	ALL FAMILIES	HEAVY HOT CEREAL USING FAMILIES*	ALL HOT CEREAL USING FAMILIES†
Base:			
Number	9,854	493	3,350
Per cent	*100*	*100*	*100*
Income			
Under $5,000	19%	41%	32%
5,000–$7,999	29	29	27
$8,000–$9,999	29	18	21
$10,000 and over	23	12	20
Education of household head			
Grade school or less	12%	39%	29%
Some high school	18	26	20
Graduated, high school	34	20	30
Some college	19	15	14
Graduated, college	17	—	7
Age of household head			
24 and younger	24%	5%	10%
25–34	26	11	16
35–49	17	12	17
50–64	14	32	26
65 and older	19	40	31
Geographic area			
Northeast	26%	22%	26%
South	22	30	26
Central	25	34	32
Pacific	27	14	16

* A "heavy using family" is one in which hot cereals are served every day.
† A "using family" is one in which hot cereals have been served sometime within the past two years and that currently has a hot cereal on hand.
s o u r c e : Market Research Department Study, 1975.

EXHIBIT 2–11
Specimen Data: The Hot Cereal Market—Hot Cereal Serving Frequency, 1975

Base: Total households	
Number	9,854
Per cent	*100*
Have a hot cereal on hand, in pantry	34%
Serve hot cereal everyday*	5%
Serve hot cereal occasionally*	6
Serve hot cereal sometime in past two years*	23

* A "Heavy Using Family" is one in which hot cereals are served every day. A "Using Family" is one in which hot cereals have been served sometime within the past two years, and which currently has a hot cereal on hand.
SOURCE: Market Research Department Study, 1975.

EXHIBIT 2–12
Specimen Data: The Hot Cereal Market—Hot Cereal Varieties in Pantry Inventory, 1975

Base: Total households	
Number	9,854
Per cent	*100*
Have a hot cereal on hand, in pantry	34%
Have one variety of hot cereal on hand*	14%
Have two or three varieties/brands of hot cereal on hand*	18
Have four or more varieties/brands of hot cereal on hand*	2

* A "variety" would be rolled oat, preprocessed full-husk wheat, or creamed and pureed. A "brand" is a brand of a variety.
SOURCE: Market Research Department Study, 1975

WONDER FOODS MEMORANDUM

June 23, 1975

TO: H. J. Johnson
FROM: Bartley H. Bogardus
SUBJECT: Psychological Segmentation of the Hot Cereal Market

I'm delighted to tell you that the psychological segmentation worked. You'll be getting a detailed report from the department on the whole study, but I thought you might like a brief note highlighting the findings.

First of all, we found that hot cereal eaters group themselves quite nicely into four psychological segments called the Self-satisfied Modest Achievers; the Uncertain Self-negators; the Independent Self-asserters; and the Stable Self-appreciators.

And these groups exhibit markedly different behavior and attitude with respect to the hot cereals that they consume. In simplest terms, the first two groups seem

EXHIBIT 2-13
Specimen Data: Usage of Hot and Cold Cereal and Reasons for Preference, 1975

	ALL FAMILIES	COLD CEREALS ONLY	HOT AND COLD CEREALS	HOT CEREALS ONLY
Base:				
Number	9,854	3,939	2,956	394
Per cent	100	100	100	100
Hot cereals only	4%			
Hot and cold cereals	30			
Cold cereals only	40			
No cereals	26			
Use hot cereals because*				
Nutritious			26%	52%
Good for health			14	30
Warm you up on cold days			18	29
Economical			12	16
Always served, habit			6	14
Family member prefers			44	8
Use cold cereals because*				
Nutritious		59%	20%	
Good for health		28	16	
Quick, easy to prepare		48	42	
Good all year round		21	35	
Kids like		35	51	
Always served, habit		6	2	
Good tasting		10	1	

* Some respondents gave more than one reason for liking a kind of cereal.
SOURCE: Market Research Department Study, 1975.

well satisfied with the product assortment available to them.

The Self-satisfied Modest Achievers are heavy consumers, particularly of rolled oats—they have distinct brand preferences—especially Perfect Puritan; they eat hot cereal for health/nutritious reasons; they are more likely to eat the regular than the instant type. The Uncertain Self-negators exhibit a very similar pattern: they, too, are heavy consumers, particularly of rolled oats and also of the creamed, pureed varieties; they have distinct brand preferences and are almost as enamored of our products as are the Self-satisfied Modest Achievers; they eat hot cereals for health/nutritious reasons; and they are somewhat more likely to eat a regular than an instant type.

The remaining two groups are, as you will see, quite another dish of tea, especially in respect to their consumption frequency and stated brand affiliations.

The Independent Self-asserters distribute their variety consumption across the three varieties in about the same proportionate distribution as sales volume would suggest, but almost none of these people are heavy hot cereal eaters—they are rather more likely to be very light or occasional eaters at best; they are very unlikely to state any brand preference at all; they eat hot cereals for nonsubstantive reasons such as warming up on cold days, habit, or because some other family member prefers them; and they are much more likely to prefer the instant to the regular type.

The Stable Self-appreciators are just like the Independent Self-asserters, only

EXHIBIT 2–14
Specimen Data: Characteristics of Hot Cereal-Using* Families and of Those Using Particular Hot Cereal Varieties and Types, 1975

| | VARIETY USAGE | | | | TYPE USAGE | |
	ALL USING FAMILIES	ROLLED OATS	PRE-PROCESSED FULL-HUSK WHEAT	CREAMED OR PUREED	REGULAR	INSTANT
Base						
Number	3,350	2,876	1,542	1,921	1,572	2,421
Per cent	*100*	*100*	*100*	*100*	*100*	*100*
Income						
Under $5,000	32%	38%	33%	29%	40%	27%
$5,000–$7,999	27	29	28	26	28	26
$8,000–$9,999	21	18	20	23	19	25
$10,000 and over	20	15	19	22	13	22
Education of household head						
Grade school or less	29%	36%	28%	27%	36%	28%
Some high school	20	25	21	19	27	24
Graduated, high school	30	21	29	29	22	25
Some college	14	15	15	17	12	14
Graduated, college	7	3	7	8	3	9
Age of household head						
24 and younger	10%	8%	9%	12%	6%	11%
25–34	16	10	17	17	12	18
35–49	17	12	16	16	18	20
50–64	26	33	25	27	28	24
65 and older	31	37	33	28	36	27
Geographic area						
Northeast	26%	38%	27%	24%	39%	21%
South	26	29	29	31	30	24
Central	32	27	30	30	29	27
Pacific	16	6	14	15	2	28

* A "using family" is one in which hot cereals have been served sometime within the past two years and that currently has a hot cereal on hand.
† The average using family has 1.9 varieties of hot cereal in inventory and 1.2 types of hot cereals in inventory.
s o u r c e : Market Research Department Study, 1975.

more so. They are light eaters; fully eight of ten state no brand preference; they eat hot cereals for fortuitous or nonsubstantive reasons; they are instant type eaters.

Incidentally, the demographic characteristics of the four groups do not reveal startling differences—at least the differences that are significant do not suggest anywhere nearly the schism that exists when one looks at the psychological differences of these people.

I know that you like to make your own sense out of the data that we produce for you, but I would certainly like to point out that there seems to be abundant opportunity for products that will truly appeal to the two groups that now eat hot cereals because they are there rather than because they especially like them.

EXHIBIT 2–15
Specimen Data: Summary Verbal Descriptions of Population Personality Segments, 1975

Self-satisfied Modest Achievers—28%

Individuals who are smugly well satisfied with what they are and what their life has been. Typically in the lower middle class, they believe that their accomplishments approach perfection, simplistic as their view of perfection may be. These people are not strongly goal oriented: they tend to aim low and accept what they get. Their daily preoccupation is with maintaining and perpetuating this satisfying resolution of their lives.

Uncertain Self-negators—24%

Individuals who are alien from and threatened by the world about them, typically middle-aged females of limited education. Life is filled for them with doubts, imponderables, and miseries. These people lack confidence in their own ability to cope with the world arrayed against them. They are chronically neurotic and constantly seek ways to alleviate their misery.

Independent Self-asserters—25%

These individuals confidently and willingly control their own destinies. Typically younger men, they are totally self-sufficient. Physical well-being neither concerns nor preoccupies them—they assume it and are ready to take whatever steps seem necessary to overcome their slight indispositions. These individuals sacrifice everyone and everything in their own pursuit of self-realization and pleasure.

Stable Self-appreciators—23%

These typically upper-class men and women believe that they have achieved all the worthwhile goals that exist in life. They accept their consequent emotional and economic comfort as their due. These people are settled, dependable middle-of-the-roaders on the one hand. But their secure achievements mask an ingrained upward strivingness that has driven them to the level in life that they have attained. They revel in their possessions, their modernity, and the achievements of their life, never looking backward, but always around them, comparing their achievements with those of their peers. Placid on the surface, they will do whatever they must to maintain their level of accomplishment and position.

S O U R C E : Market Research Department Study, 1975.

EXHIBIT 2–16

Specimen Data: Hot Cereal Usage by Population Personality Segments, 1975

	TOTAL POPULATION	HOT CEREAL EATERS*
Number	9,854	5,477
Per cent	*100*	*100*
Population personality segments		
Self-satisfied modest achievers	28%	38%
Uncertain self-negators	24	27
Independent self-asserters	25	20
Stable self-appreciators	23	15

* A hot cereal "eater" is an individual who has consumed hot cereal one or more times in the past six months.

s o u r c e :   Market Research Department Study, 1975.

EXHIBIT 2–17

Specimen Data: Usage of Hot Cereal Varieties and Types by Personality Segments, 1975

		PERSONALITY SEGMENTS			
	HOT CEREAL EATERS*	SELF-SATISFIED MODEST ACHIEVERS	UNCERTAIN SELF-NEGATORS	INDE-PENDENT SELF-ASSERTERS	STABLE SELF-APPRE-CIATORS
Number	5,477	2,077	1,476	1,093	831
Per cent	*100*	*100*	*100*	*100*	*100*
Varieties eaten†					
Rolled oats	53%	57%	51%	55%	42%
Pre-processed full-husk wheat	28	28	25	27	35
Creamed/Pureed	35	31	42	35	32
Types eaten*					
Regular	47%	53%	49%	42%	34%
Instant	57	51	52	62	71

* A hot cereal "eater" is an individual who has consumed hot cereal one or more times in the past six months.

† Some "eaters" report eating more than one variety or type.

s o u r c e :   Market Research Department Study, 1975.

EXHIBIT 2–18

Specimen Data: Demographic Characteristics of Personality Segments, 1975

	ALL HOT CEREAL EATERS*	SELF-SATISFIED MODEST ACHIEVERS	UNCERTAIN SELF-NEGATORS	INDE-PENDENT SELF-ASSERTERS	STABLE SELF-APPRE-CIATORS
Base					
Number	5,477	2,077	1,476	1,093	8 31
Per cent	*100*	*100*	*100*	*100*	*100*
Income					
Under $5,000	34%	38%	34%	31%	28%
$5,000–$7,999	28	27	29	26	31
$8,000–$9,999	19	17	19	20	23
$10,000 and over	19	18	18	23	18
Education					
Grade school or less	34%	39%	35%	30%	25%
Some high school	22	24	22	20	20
Graduated, high school	26	25	27	29	23
Some college	12	7	11	14	24
Graduated, college	6	5	5	7	8
Age					
24 and younger	6%	4%	7%	12%	1%
25–34	14	11	15	16	17
35–49	17	16	17	18	18
50–64	28	30	29	24	27
65 and older	35	39	32	30	37
Geographic area					
Northeast	25%	26%	27%	24%	20%
South	23	22	21	25	26 –
Central	24	25	23	24	23
Pacific	28	27	29	27	31
Sex					
Male	48%	46%	44%	58%	47%
Female	52	54	56	42	53

* A hot cereal "eater" is an individual who has consumed hot cereal one or more times in the past six months.
S O U R C E : Market Research Department Study, 1975.

EXHIBIT 2–19
Specimen Data: Reasons for Preference of Hot Cereal Eaters by Personality Segments

	HOT CEREAL EATERS*	PERSONALITY SEGMENTS			
		SELF-SATISFIED MODEST ACHIEVERS	UNCERTAIN SELF-NEGATORS	INDE-PENDENT SELF-ASSERTERS	STABLE SELF-APPRE-CIATORS
Number	5,477	2,077	1,476	1,093	831
Per cent	*100*	*100*	*100*	*100*	*100*
Reasons for preference†					
Nutritious	56%	64%	70%	42%	29%
Good for health	32	34	38	25	25
Warms you up on cold days	31	16	14	54	68
Economical	17	24	16	15	4
Always served, habit	16	2	1	42	43
Other family member prefers	9	—	2	21	28

* A hot cereal "eater" is an individual who has consumed hot cereal one of more times in the past six months.
† Some respondents gave more than one reason for liking a kind of cereal.
SOURCE: Market Research Department Study, 1975.

EXHIBIT 2–20
Specimen Data: Frequency of Hot Cereal Eating by Personality Segments, 1975

	HOT CEREAL EATERS*	PERSONALITY SEGMENTS			
		SELF-SATISFIED MODEST ACHIEVERS	UNCERTAIN SELF-NEGATORS	INDE-PENDENT SELF-ASSERTERS	STABLE SELF-APPRE-CIATORS
Number	5,477	2,077	1,476	1,093	831
Per cent	*100*	*100*	*100*	*100*	*100*
Frequency of eating					
Eat hot cereal everyday	24%	37%	34%	2%	2%
Eat hot cereal occasionally	31	29	27	37	36
Eat hot cereal at least once every six months	45	34	39	61	62

* A hot cereal "eater" is an individual who has consumed hot cereal one or more times in the past six months.
SOURCE: Market Research Department Study, 1975.

EXHIBIT 2–21
Specimen Data: Brand Preference by Personality Segments, 1975

	PERSONALITY SEGMENTS				
	HOT CEREAL EATERS*	SELF-SATISFIED MODEST ACHIEVERS	UNCERTAIN SELF-NEGATORS	INDE-PENDENT SELF-ASSERTERS	STABLE SELF-APPRE-CIATORS
Number	5,477	2,077	1,476	1,093	831
Per cent	*100*	*100*	*100*	*100*	*100*
Brand preference*					
Perfect Puritan	49%	70%	59%	21%	15%
Smiling Ben	30	38	33	26	10
Golden Morn	12	16	18	4	2
Others	6	8	9	2	1
No brand preference	26	5	4	48	88

* Some hot cereal eaters name more than one brand as "preferred."
† A hot cereal "eater" is an individual who has consumed hot cereal one or more times in the past six months.
S O U R C E :   Marketing Research Department Study, 1975.

EXHIBIT 2–22
Specimen Data: Concise Summary of Hot Cereal Predispositions by Personality Segments

I. *Self-satisfied Modest Achievers*

Lower middle class
Female
Older
Heavy users of hot cereals, particularly rolled oats
Frequent users of hot cereals
Users of regular type
Use because of nutrition/health/economy reasons
Strong hot cereal brand preference

II. *Uncertain Self-negators*

Lower class
Female
Neurotic, hypochondriacal
Heavy users of hot cereals, particularly creamed/puree
Frequent users of hot cereals
Users of regular type
Use because of nutrition/health/economy reasons
Strong hot cereal brand preference

EXHIBIT 2–22—continued

III. *Independent Self-asserters*

> Middle class
> Men
> Younger
> Average consumption incidence of hot cereals
> Infrequent users of hot cereals
> Users of instant type
> Use because warms you up/habit/because served to other family members
> No strong hot cereal brand preference

IV. *Stable Self-appreciators*

> Upper middle class
> Men and women
> Low levels of rolled oat consumption
> High levels of preprocessed full-husk wheat consumption
> Infrequent users of hot cereals
> Users of instant type
> Use because warms you up/habit/because served to other family members
> No strong hot cereal brand preference

Questions for Case 2

1. What is a new product? What is a line extension? Can a product be both new and a line extension?

2. The phrase "market segmentation" is used in many ways in marketing. For instance, it is used to describe the loyalties created by particular brands; to describe demographic segments; to describe psychological segments. In what ways do these kinds of "segmentations" differ? Which of these kinds of segmentation is most important in this case? Which is likely to be most important in the general sense?

3. Why did Hunty Johnson not ask the advertising director for his recommendations? Does advertising have only a subsidiary role in the vitalization of a product like hot cereal?

4. In this case, Hunty Johnson decides to undertake the market research program on judgment. What kind of decision criteria might have been set up upon which to evaluate this move? Would the development of such criteria have helped Johnson or would the decision have been a judgment in any case?

5. Demographic data for hot cereal users are presented in Exhibits 2–6, 2–10, 2–14, and 2–18. What conclusions do you draw from each of these exhibits? Which one would be most useful to the marketer?

6. How much responsibility does the market researcher have for interpreting his data? Should J. Q. Martindale suggest the meaning in marketing terms of his work as he does in point 4 on page 33? What is the implication of the Bartley Bogardus statement, "I know you like to make your own sense out of the data, but . . . " on page 49?

7. Do you agree with the Bogardus memorandum on the segmentation study results? For each of his major conclusions, indicate the exhibit or exhibits upon which the Bogardus interpretation depends.
8. What is the significance of Exhibits 2–7, 2–8, 2–9, 2–11, 2–12, and 2–13? Are they necessary or unnecessary to one's understanding of the important marketing issues in the hot cereal market?
9. If you were Hunty Johnson, what moves would you make for the exploitation of the hot cereal products based both on the segmentation study and on the recommendations of Ellender, O'Weeke, and Follensbee?

[Handwritten notes follow:]

def- product line — has 2 elements
1) has the width & breath factor
          very similar

product mix — typewriters, air cooler
Rening ? is wide 15 different
                    lines

2) product line — has breadth (dpth)
6 different models of typewriters
4 G.E different lines.
shoe stores — product width is narrow
all sell is shoes (have depth
          sport shoes, dress, jogging)
          3) product mix narrow
   which but have different models
        establised dpth

ex Sears Roebuck depth of Sears
product mix + product line

product mix—narrow or concentrated
        ↓ or
      wide & with dpth

extend usage of a product thru
modification is a product extension
strategy to increase sale

CASE 3

Consumer Perceptions and Behavior

Bourbon Brothers Distilling Company Introduces Old Carnaby Gin

OURBON BROTHERS DISTILLING COMPANY is a major distiller of various brands of whiskey: bourbon, straight rye, and blended whiskey. Bourbon Brothers also imports several brands of Irish and Scotch whisky and is, through a wholly owned subsidiary, a major importer of French liqueurs, still wines, and sparkling wines. The company also buys gin from a major gin manufacturer and bottles and distributes it under the Old Carnaby label.

Bourbon Brothers was founded in 1907 by the two McPhael brothers of Crystal Springs, Kentucky. Joseph O'Brien Toscano McPhael and Lindbloom Arthur McPhael had learned the time-honored art of distilling Kentucky bourbon whiskey, as lads in their teens, from their father John Brown McPhael. The father had learned the art, in turn, from his father, who had presumably applied his own youthful initiation into the manufacture of Scotch spirits in Blairgowrie, Scotland, to the available raw materials in Crystal Springs, when he arrived there as an immigrant in 1843. With the immigrant McPhael, whiskey production was only a hobby, a pleasant enough one. With John McPhael it was a profitable sideline. He sold a significant fraction of his product to neighbors in the countryside and to one or two emerging taverns in Crystal Springs. Although his reputation for producing fine spirits grew through the years, he never regarded his still as the source of more than incidental income. John McPhael was a farmer first and a distiller second.

The two sons saw things rather differently. They liked to farm middling well but recognized that the potential of their father's farm was small enough as it stood and paltry if split three ways. At the age of forty-four, John McPhael showed no sign at all of giving up the farm. At the same time, he seemed less and less interested in dealing with the whiskey buyers from the hotels and taverns of growing towns like Louisville and Frankfort and Lexington who sought him out because they knew his product and respected him for it. This was enough for the boys. They were alike in many ways and both were adroit in recognizing opportunity. They offered to take the whiskey business off their father's hands, and he was glad enough to see it and their indifferent help on the farm go their way.

So the Bourbon Brothers Distilling Company was founded. Over the years it grew as a producer of bourbon whiskey. Lindbloom McPhael became a wizard at finding ways to expand production without sacrificing quality. Meanwhile, J. O. T. McPhael developed considerable ability in the financial affairs of the companys.

The sales function was handled by L. M. "Turk" Mascagna, a native of Crystal Springs and only son of the single Italian family to settle in the town prior to 1927. Mascagna was small of physical stature and in his youth and adolescence he had found it necessary to develop his personality in order to survive, as he did not enjoy the physical means to defend himself—the acknowledged outlander—against the rest of the boys in town. In his early manhood the skills that had been learned as a defense against assault were easily converted to the ends of salesmanship and Turk Mascagna went to work for the McPhaels in 1908, never to hold another job. He was devoted to both Lindbloom and J. O. T. and always found ways to back them both at the same time, never questioning either or coming between them.

The division of power and authority between the McPhael brothers was convenient enough, and all was happy and harmonious until the opportunities inherent in the acquisition of other companies began to dawn on J. O. T. in the years before World War I. J. O. T. wanted to expand through acquisition, and as his schemes unfolded it became clear that as long as the company made a liquid that was potable and alcoholic, it mattered not a whit to J. O. T. McPhael whether that liquid happened to be bourbon whiskey or not. Expansion was fine with Lindbloom, but he considered any whiskey that was not bourbon an abomination and any alcoholic beverage that was not whiskey a curse upon mankind. The upshot was that J. O. T. bought out Lindbloom's interest in 1916, and Lindbloom started a small bourbon distillery of his own in nearby White Water, Kentucky. Mascagna stayed with J. O. T.

With the onset of prohibition, J. O. T. McPhael switched to the manufacture of medicinal whiskey under government license and survived the dread dryness handsomely. Perhaps there was more to it than that: Turk Mascagna seemed busier than ever in those years, and it appeared possible to some of the townspeople in Crystal Springs that at least some of the Bourbon Brothers production was finding its way into nongovernmental hands. But there was never any trouble about it and over the years J. O. T. McPhael continued to acquire the brand names and technical know-how of other less fortunate firms, as they passed out of existence.

McPhael was shrewd enough and lucky as well. Most of the brands and facilities that he acquired represented a high level of quality. He maintained this and in the years after the repeal of prohibition geared his marketing and selling efforts toward the development of significant consumer franchise.

In 1945 McPhael set up the J. O. T. Company and through a favorable arrangement with Gaston and Gaston, major French liqueur and wine exporters, developed major volume in these specialized fields. In 1946, at the age of sixty-eight, he negotiated an exclusive franchise arrangement for U.S. distribution of the Billowing Sail, Clan MacAdoo, and Jimmie Mackintosh brands of Scotch whisky. These brands were all of excellent quality and McPhael immediately proceeded to build their franchise in the United States through his usual combination of strong retail selling, restrained and rather pompous advertising, and shrewd pricing.

In 1948 J. O. T. McPhael retired, handing the leadership of his company over to his son, J. O. T. McPhael, Jr. The young man was his father's son and had been well trained by him besides, and at thirty-nine he was ready to continue in his father's footsteps and beyond. One of his first steps was to insist quietly that Turk Mascagna, now sixty-six, retire and leave the sales fortunes of the company to several younger men that had been hired and trained by Mascagna with this day in mind.

In 1954 J. O. T. McPhael, Jr. negotiated with a major New Jersey distiller of gin a contract under which the distillers would produce gin for Bourbon Brothers, packaging it under a name to be selected by Bourbon Brothers. An unusual feature of the contract was a sliding-scale price agreement: Bourbon Brothers paid less per gallon of gin the more gin it purchased. This was standard enough, but J. O. T., Jr. insisted that the scale be extended to cover very large gallonages; the end price in the contract was based on a gallonage three times larger than that of the largest gin brand in America. McPhael demanded, and got, a most favorable price for gin in this quantity: it only remained for him to find the marketing means by which a corresponding sales volume might be achieved.

McPhael chose the name Old Carnaby Gin for this product, which he intended to develop into the dominant position in the domestic gin market. No involved decision process was followed in selecting this name. J. O. T., Jr. considered himself rather expert in the choosing of good names. He prided himself on having a good ear and even better intuition, and he believed that when he coined a brand name or chose one from a list of those available, it was likely to be the best name that could be selected. Old Carnaby Gin was one of over seven hundred brand names that Bourbon Brothers had acquired over the prohibition years as they bought the assets of failing companies. There were thirty-two other gin brand names on the list, and J. O. T. McPhael, Jr. thought that "Old

Carnaby" was the best of that lot and could think of none he preferred, and that was that.

McPhael held the standard whiskey-maker's prejudices about non-whiskey potables—perhaps he was not as stubborn about what a decent drink was as had been his Uncle Lindbloom, but he was stubborn enough to know that gin wasn't whiskey and smart enough to suspect that it couldn't be marketed to consumers in the same way either.

J. O. T., Jr. also differed from many of the older hands in the company with respect to his dependence upon experience in the making of marketing decisions. "Experience is OK," he remarked to Johnny Conforte, the new sales vice-president, "but I'm not old enough to have enough, so I've got to have some help along the way." McPhael became, in his quest for help along the way, fascinated by the relatively new art/science of marketing research. He liked his marketing research simple and straightforward with a face trustworthiness, but once he accepted a particular study or finding, he relied upon it very heavily. "When you go for the big buck markets, you have to know who the customers are and what makes them tick," he remarked to Conforte one day shortly after completing the negotiations of the gin supply contract.

Conforte was a rough, bright, hustling salesman who understood the chemistry of the face-to-face sale and had brilliantly exploited this understanding into an outstanding field-selling record. But to Conforte, the customer was the wholesaler or retailer to whom he sold. He had no understanding of, nor interest in, the amorphous masses who subsequently consumed his products by actually drinking them. Abstentious himself, Conforte had little appreciation of the ways in which alcoholic beverages are consumed and even less appreciation of the ways in which the drinkers themselves decided what brands to buy and why. He even felt a little guilty about his own relation to this whole process, because he was a generally honest man and a moral one in his way and he did not like his association, indirect as it was, with the medical, psychological, and social problems associated with alcohol, alcoholics, and alcoholism. He simply dissociated himself from the ultimate consumer and ignored the fact that anything at all happened to the products of his company after they disappeared into the warehouse of his trade customers.

McPhael was much more pragmatic than Conforte. Perhaps it was the fact that the making and selling of whiskey was in his blood, or perhaps it was only that he was more honest with himself than Conforte. McPhael thought of himself simply as a supplier of a particular product demanded by the public. As he remarked to himself one evening as he drove from the company office in Crystal Springs, "If they wouldn't buy it, I couldn't sell it. They do and so I do and if it wasn't me it would be some other son of a gun and it might as well be me—the pay's good." And that was that. Bourbon Brothers ran ads suggesting hot coffee for the road in the daily papers on the thirty-first of December each year, and J. O. T., Jr. made significant anonymous contributions each year to Alcoholics Anonymous and to the alcoholic studies unit of a leading northeastern university. The rest of the year he spent most of his working hours trying to figure out how to sell more and more of his brands of booze.

And so, just as Conforte was rather ill at ease and even apprehensive in conversations having to do with consumer research, McPhael was totally involved, anxious to know everything there was to know. For McPhael, the first step to take in learning how to sell more of anything was to catalogue his knowledge about the market in question and then to determine what market research studies might be helpful in bringing him a more complete understanding of it.

When the contract for gin was signed, McPhael's first thought was to study the market for gin and develop an understanding of its characteristics and peculiarities, both absolute and relative to the standard whiskey brands. The first study that he commissioned was, therefore, a study of the characteristics of gin drinkers, Scotch drinkers, and bourbon drinkers. This enquiry was designed to determine the demographic characteristics —income, education, occupation, age, residence by geographic area, residence by city, and sex—of individuals who had had at least four drinks of gin or bourbon or Scotch in the past four weeks. Although such information might certainly be useful in making decisions about what advertising media to use in support of Old Carnaby Gin, McPhael felt that such information had a much more fundamental purpose. "When I think about marketing gin, I want to understand what those consumers out there who drink gin are like," he said with particular intensity to Conforte on the day he agreed to pay $22,000 (plus or minus 10 per cent, depending on the actual cost of field work, tabulation, and analysis) to the market research firm of Joshua Wubbener and Partners, Inc. for the carrying out of such a study. "I want to translate those numbers into people I see on the street and meet in our plants and at parties and on trains and all over. I have to feel the kind of people I'm working on, because then I'll make decisions in and for their interest and not what I think their interests are —and it'll all end up that you sell more of the stuff, Confy, lots more." Conforte shuddered ever so slightly under the blazing veneer of his best sales presentation smile.

Twenty weeks passed. It was then announced to key corporate officers and staff that the Wubbener firm would present the findings of its research on the following Monday afternoon at 1:15 P.M. in the Bourbon Brothers Board Room. If the fact that the meeting was to be held in the Bourbon Brothers Board Room was not enough, in itself, to impress its importance on the staff, the fact that old J. O. T. McPhael himself had accepted his son's invitation to attend was. If the content of the meeting promised to many a dull afternoon, the anticipation of the senior McPhael's reaction did not. Sparks might fly, and the possibility was too promising to resist. And so on the following Monday, Joshua Wubbener himself, natty and in extraordinarily professional form, took two hours out of the lives of seventeen Bourbon Brothers executives to reveal the demographic characteristics of recent drinkers of gin, bourbon, and Scotch.

The basic material presented by Wubbener is summarized in Exhibits 3–1 through 3–7. The audience reaction to this material was mixed. Old J. O. T. McPhael lasted about twenty minutes into the presentation and then went soundly to sleep. During the later years of his presidency the employees had all been aware of his tendency to nap in the afternoon meetings, and it had therefore become traditional to schedule important meetings, or any meeting that he might be expected to attend, in the morning hours in order to accomplish the business of the firm with the greatest expedition. But such traditions die easily if their reason for being disappears. Young J. O. T. was as vigorous after lunch as before, and suddenly, two years before, Bourbon Brothers had rediscovered that executive decisions could be made both before lunch *and* after lunch. So it was something of an embarrassment to all concerned that the old man's peculiarity had been overlooked, but everyone did his best to ignore his slumber, thanking a benevolent God that he did not snore. Young J. O. T. and two or three of his most admiring young henchmen sat bolt upright through the meeting, assiduously following Wubbener's every word, gesture, intonation, and implication. J. O. T., Jr. himself was deeply interested in the presentation and perhaps his close associates were too—if they were not, it was clearly considered by them to be desirable to appear to be.

But the bulk of the audience showed little signs of interest. They stared in glassy-eyed inertness at Wubbener, reacting little at all to his most telling marketing insights, ignoring his bon mots, giving very little if any suggestion of interested attention. And there was good enough reason for all of this, thought Wubbener, to whom such experiences were normal. After all, most of them don't understand what the abstract numbers are all about. And those that do understand couldn't care less, because in the end they know that J. O. T., Jr., and his entourage will make the decisions anyway.

And J. O. T., Jr., did. He concluded that the typical gin drinker was very different from the typical bourbon or Scotch drinker. He felt distinctly uncertain about his understanding of this new market because its composition was clearly different from that of the bourbon market— and the Scotch market too, for that matter.

When Wubbener finished his presentation, J. O. T., Jr. asked one or two questions, each of which was matched by rather insipid further questions by his close colleagues. J. O. T., Jr., then closed the meeting with gracious remarks about how incisive and helpful the presentation had been and asked Wubbener to come to his office for further discussion. J. O. T., Sr.,

[Text continues on p. 69.]

EXHIBIT 3-1

Specimen Data: Characteristics of Individuals Consuming Four Drinks or More of Gin, Bourbon, or Scotch in the Past Four Weeks by Income of Household in Which Individual Resides

TOTAL	DISTRIBUTION OF U.S. INDIVIDUALS 98,989,000 PER CENT	DISTRIBUTION OF INDIVIDUAL CONSUMPTION					
		GIN		SCOTCH		BOURBON	
		PER CENT	INDEX	PER CENT	INDEX	PER CENT	INDEX
Household income							
$25,000 and over	1.8	6.7	372	7.8	433	3.4	189
$15,000–$24,999	3.4	12.1	356	10.8	318	5.7	168
$10,000–$14,999	12.9	18.4	143	22.9	178	14.9	116
$ 8,000–$ 9,999	13.0	17.6	135	21.1	162	17.7	136
$ 5,000–$ 7,999	31.6	27.1	86	26.9	85	32.6	103
Under $5,000	37.3	18.1	49	10.5	28	25.7	69

SOURCE: Consumer Survey (Joshua Wubbener and Partners, Inc., 1955).

EXHIBIT 3–2

Specimen Data: Characteristics of Individuals Consuming Four Drinks or More of Gin, Bourbon, or Scotch in the Past Four Weeks by Education

TOTAL	DISTRIBUTION OF U.S. INDIVIDUALS 98,989,000 PER CENT	DISTRIBUTION OF INDIVIDUAL CONSUMPTION					
		GIN		SCOTCH		BOURBON	
		PER CENT	INDEX	PER CENT	INDEX	PER CENT	INDEX
Individual Education							
Attended college	23.6	36.4	154	39.9	169	29.2	124
Graduated, college	13.0	27.9	215	26.0	200	13.3	102
1 to 3 years college	10.6	8.5	80	13.9	131	15.9	150
Graduated, high school	27.7	21.2	77	30.5	110	28.1	101
Did not graduate, high school	48.7	42.4	87	29.6	61	42.7	88
1 to 3 years high school	17.8	6.7	38	12.5	70	26.2	147
Did not attend high school	30.9	35.7	116	17.1	55	16.5	53

SOURCE : Consumer Survey (Joshua Wubbener and Partners, Inc. 1955).

EXHIBIT 3-3

Specimen Data: Characteristics of Individuals Consuming Four Drinks or More of Gin, Bourbon, or Scotch in the Past Four Weeks by Occupation

TOTAL	DISTRIBUTION OF U.S. INDIVIDUALS 98,989,000 PER CENT	DISTRIBUTION OF INDIVIDUAL CONSUMPTION					
		GIN		SCOTCH		BOURBON	
		PER CENT	INDEX	PER CENT	INDEX	PER CENT	INDEX
Individual occupation							
Total prof., mgrs., etc.	17.1	37.2	218	34.5	202	40.1	235
Prof., tech., etc.	8.3	19.7	237	23.6	284	24.2	292
Mgrs., off. per.	8.8	17.5	199	10.9	238	15.9	181
Other employed	49.7	36.7	74	44.7	90	35.3	71
Clinical	12.7	14.1	111	11.6	91	17.7	139
Other	37.0	22.6	61	33.1	90	17.6	48
Not employed	33.2	26.1	79	20.8	63	24.6	74

SOURCE: Consumer Survey (Joshua Wubbener and Partners, Inc., 1955).

EXHIBIT 3-4

Specimen Data: Characteristics of Individuals Consuming Four Drinks or More of Gin, Bourbon, or Scotch in the Past Four Weeks by Age

| | TOTAL DISTRIBUTION OF U.S. INDIVIDUALS 98,989,000 PER CENT | DISTRIBUTION OF INDIVIDUAL CONSUMPTION | | | | | |
| | | GIN | | SCOTCH | | BOURBON | |
		PER CENT	INDEX	PER CENT	INDEX	PER CENT	INDEX
Individual age							
18–34	23.0	16.4	71	23.4	102	18.6	81
18–24	5.9	3.2	54	4.4	75	5.5	93
25–34	17.1	13.2	77	19.0	111	13.1	77
35–49	31.6	39.7	126	44.7	141	40.4	128
50 and older	45.4	43.9	97	31.9	70	41.0	90
50–64	26.3	33.7	128	23.7	90	28.4	108
65 and older	19.1	10.2	53	8.2	43	12.6	66

SOURCE: Consumer Survey (Joshua Wubbener and Partners, Inc., 1955).

EXHIBIT 3-5

Specimen Data: Characteristics of Individuals Consuming Four Drinks or More of Gin, Bourbon, or Scotch in the Past Four Weeks by Geographic Area

| | DISTRIBUTION OF U.S. INDIVIDUALS 98,989,000 PER CENT | DISTRIBUTION OF INDIVIDUAL CONSUMPTION | | | | | |
| | | GIN | | SCOTCH | | BOURBON | |
		PER CENT	INDEX	PER CENT	INDEX	PER CENT	INDEX
TOTAL							
Individual residence							
Northeast	25.3	61.7	244	51.2	202	32.9	130
Central	28.0	18.4	66	23.1	83	43.6	156
South	29.9	11.1	37	12.4	41	17.1	57
West	16.8	8.8	52	13.3	79	6.4	38

SOURCE: Consumer Survey (Joshua Wubbener and Partners, Inc., 1955).

EXHIBIT 3-6

Specimen Data: Characteristics of Individuals Consuming Four Drinks or More of Gin, Bourbon, or Scotch in the Past Four Weeks by City Size

TOTAL	DISTRIBUTION OF U.S. INDIVIDUALS	DISTRIBUTION OF INDIVIDUAL CONSUMPTION					
		GIN		SCOTCH		BOURBON	
	98,989,000 PER CENT	PER CENT	INDEX	PER CENT	INDEX	PER CENT	INDEX
Individual residence							
Total metropolitan areas	64.4	93.7	145	90.5	141	63.2	98
Metropolitan city	33.1	47.2	143	41.3	125	34.1	103
Metropolitan suburban	31.3	46.5	149	49.2	157	29.1	93
Nonmetropolitan areas	35.6	6.3	18	9.5	27	36.8	103

SOURCE : Consumer Survey (Joshua Wubbener and Partners, Inc. 1955).

EXHIBIT 3–7

Specimen Data: Characteristics of Individuals Consuming Four Drinks or More of Gin, Bourbon, or Scotch in the Past Four Weeks by Sex

| | DISTRIBUTION OF U.S. INDIVIDUALS | DISTRIBUTION OF INDIVIDUAL CONSUMPTION | | | | | |
| | | GIN | | SCOTCH | | BOURBON | |
TOTAL	98,989,000 PER CENT	PER CENT	INDEX	PER CENT	INDEX	PER CENT	INDEX
Individual sex							
Male	49.2	67.2	137	60.9	124	62.3	127
Female	50.8	32.8	65	39.1	77	37.7	74

SOURCE: Consumer Survey (Joshua Wubbener and Partners, Inc., 1955).

was still dozing placidly as all of this transpired. The meeting broke up quietly and, as in the old days, four or five of the most senior members of the audience remained in the Board Room, waiting for him to awaken to assure him that the meeting had just ended and that he had missed nothing of consequence during the short period in which he had rested his eyes.

J. O. T., Jr., meanwhile, expressed his feelings of uncertainty to Wubbener. "Josh, you've done a good job of telling me who these gin drinkers are, but I'll be damned if I know enough to really go after them with Old Carnaby. The study is fine—don't get me wrong—but what do these people do with gin, and when and where do they drink it anyway? What do they think makes gin brands different, and why? What do they think makes a good gin brand—is it proof, or aging, or color, or what? Do they think gin is gin, or do they think different brands taste different?"

Wubbener was slightly taken aback by this intense questioning. First of all, he believed that he had just made a fine presentation of a remarkably well-planned and well-executed study. He was proud of it and proud of the job that he had done. And he was not quite ready for such a listing of remaining unknowns—perhaps another five minutes of praise or chatter about baseball and politics would have been more in keeping with the moment. And he was also concerned because he hadn't the foggiest notion as to the meaning of the phrase that his Yankee ears heard from J. O. T.'s Southern drawl as "Oh Conny Bee." But as the monologue continued, he pulled himself together and realized that more business was standing there waiting to be taken home and that J. O. T. had most likely been talking about a type or brand of gin. This was enough for Wubbener, the consummate salesman and profit seeker.

"J. O. T., I know exactly what you have in mind. As I was analyzing the results I kept thinking that the bones need a little meat on them. Sure, you must know the characteristics of the buyers before you can do anything. You were smart as hell to ask for a demographic study *first*, but now we have to get inside those people's heads and figure what they think about gin and why they think it, right?" "Yeah," said J. O. T., Jr.

"I'll tell you, J. O. T.," said Wubbener, warming to his task, "there's a new approach to that kind of question. It's called motivational research. With a lot of firms it's still experimental, it's so new. But not with us. We've been at it for at least three years, developmentally. What it does is apply behavioral science techniques to what motivates people to buy products and select brands. Social psychology, anthropology, sociology—all the pertinent procedures and viewpoints come to bear. And, J. O. T., it's dynamite. Let me write you a letter describing how we go about it." "Yeah, Josh, you do that," said J. O. T., Jr.

And Wubbener had the following letter in the mail within forty-eight hours.

JOSHUA WUBBENER AND PARTNERS, INC.
Marketing & Motivational Research

January 27, 1955

Joseph O'Brien Toscano McPhael, Jr.
President
Bourbon Brothers Distilling Company
Crystal Springs
Kentucky
Dear J. O. T.:

It was great being with you and your group on Monday.

I particularly welcome the opportunity to write you about motivation research, the procedures we employ, and how they might be applied to give you greater understanding of the gin consumer.

A variety of different techniques and procedures are commonly used in motivational research. These include depth interviews; focused group interviews; Rosenzweig picture-frustration tests; thematic apperception tests; role playing; Rorschach tests; and many, many others. As I suggested in our conversation earlier in the week, we have been working experimentally with several of these techniques for the past three or four years—doing our best to find out which ones had real promise for generating material with immediate and practical application to marketing.

Our overall conclusion is that although almost every one of these procedures can make a contribution, some are more valuable than others and a great deal of experience is necessary to apply that technique with the highest promise of success in a particular situation. After discussing the gin problem, as you outlined it, with several of our senior staff people yesterday, we conclude that the focused group-interviewing procedure is best adapted to your immediate needs.

Focused group interviewing involves two elements. The first element is the respondents: a group of eight to twelve representative consumers are gathered together in the living room in a home in their neighborhood. These people have come to "discuss a topic which will be of interest to them" and have been promised a pleasant experience, a token gift, and refreshments.

The group interview situation permits respondents to relax, drop some of their defenses, and express their feelings and ideas relatively freely. Certain resistances to talking that are frequently encountered in individual interviews are reduced because of the conversational interaction and involvement that develops in the group situation. The motivation to share helpfully in the group conversation is typically high, as is the desire to make meaningful contributions before one's peers.

The second element in focused group interviewing is a trained social scientist. It is his job to carefully, unobtrusively, and scientifically make this group of "typical" respondents talk exhaustively about a particular subject. This social scientist works from a memorized topic outline. His role is to appear charming, to encourage all the respondents to talk freely, to establish and maintain significant rapport within the group, and to probe ruthlessly and extract the respondents' fundamental attitude patterns toward the subject under discussion.

All depends upon the group leader, his knowledge of the topic to be investigated, his skill in making people talk, and his quick ability to recognize important conversational strains and to capitalize upon them. Any uninhibited clod can sit in a room with a group of people and make them talk about a subject. A truly creative social scientist who is expert in human relations can establish rapport with groups, exhaustively explore the ramifications of the subject under investigation, and creatively synthesize the conversation that has developed.

To be properly done, the focused group-interviewing process cannot be completed in a session or two. It is necessary to conduct at least eight, and frequently more, sessions so that each developed hypothesis concerning consumer perception, behavior, and thought patterns can be tested and retested. The researcher does this by waiting for a particular topic to develop spontaneously in a particular session or by subtly introducing it into the ongoing conversational flow. In either event, the objective is the same: to assess and reassess dominant consumer feelings and attitude patterns and relate them back to the understanding of the researcher/ moderator as it develops and heightens from session to session with different people in different ways.

Out of all this comes a fundamental understanding of consumer reaction—to products, ideas, brands, whatever. The results are assessed in terms of the consistency with which all groups and members within groups react.

If a majority of members in a majority of groups reveal similar attitudes and behavioral patterns for the same reasons and within the same logic, no matter how the issue comes to the surface within a particular session and no matter how it is probed or presented or attacked by the moderator, one can be quite certain that these findings reflect the prevailing consumer motivational/attitudinal pattern. But if the consumers exhibit inconsistency or variety in their attitudinal and behavioral patterns and interactions, one cannot be sure about projecting the results to the broad middle majority of consumers.

Assessing these responses is, again, the responsibility of the trained social scientist who conducts the sessions. He studies and restudies the tape recordings that are made throughout the sessions. He remembers the way in which the consumers themselves acted and the emotional tone that prevailed as different conversational topics were touched. Insofar as is possible, he interprets the material and his own remembered involvement from the standpoint of psychological theory.

In the end, the analyst reaches judgments about the group consensus. The validity of his judgments about consumer attitudes toward, perceptions of, and motivations for using products and brands depends upon the quality and breadth of his experience, and, ultimately, upon the quality of his mind. In the final analysis, we want to know why people make product and brand choices and we want to use this knowledge as a basis for planning the marketing actions that will be most appropriate in directing their choices to our product and brands. If the moderator is equal to the task, this is exactly what his final report concerns itself with.

Experience indicates that it is a real advantage for the person who actually moderates the sessions to be responsible for writing the final report. There are no research middlemen in this process: the report writer has personally been exposed to everything in the research process. Yet the tape recordings are always available for independent review and appraisal in order to keep either bias or lack of marketing sophistication from seeping into the process.

In the case of investigating consumer attitudes toward, perceptions of, and motivations for using gin and particular brands of gin, it would be our proposal that twelve groups of consumers be subjected to this focused group-interviewing procedure. Four of these sessions would be conducted in and around Washington, D.C., four in and around New York City, and four in and around Miami, Florida. In each of these markets three of these sessions would be conducted with men who drink gin and one with women gin drinkers. The age range in each group would include respondents between thirty-five and fifty, and all of the respondents would come from the middle and upper-middle socioeconomic classes.

In setting these specifications for the composition of the consumer groups, we are attempting, within the broad framework provided by the recently completed usage study, to talk to representatives in those groups and geographic areas that are likely to be most sensitive to marketing and promotional activities in behalf of a specific gin brand. Thus, the proposed focused group-interview sample is at once more widely dispersed geographically than the bulk of the gin market and more concentrated by age than the bulk of the gin market. New York and Washington and their environs are major northeastern cities and crucial gin-consumption centers and are included in the sample because of their prominence and importance in gin consumption and gin marketing. Miami is in a low-consumption geographic area but is itself an important gin-consumption area. It is a different market by climate and consumer life-style, and we would expect that a comparison of the attitudinal, perceptual, and motivational patterns that exist in this market and those of the other markets—if, indeed, they differ—could contribute very substantially to our understanding of what really makes the gin drinker tick. As far as age is concerned, we ignore the old consumers, important as they are in terms of consumption volume, simply because our experience indicates that habit very largely takes over brand perceptions and choices in the post-fifty-year age group and that relatively younger groups of consumers are rather more likely to provide more vivid insights into their basis of brand choice.

Although we carefully introduce a series of specifications for the composition of our consumer respondent groups, our experience has most typically been that response from group to group is considerably more homogeneous than heterogeneous and that group differences usually tend to confirm the consistency of consumer response rather than its diversity. We are, after all, dealing with relatively simple choices in terms of both basic behavior and brand choice. These relatively simple choices tend to routinize into fairly simple and stable patterns and these routine patterns tend to reflect basic behavioral logic rather than widespread or exotic variations.

We would propose that Alexander Letvenoff, Ph.D., be responsible for the work on gin. His doctorate is in social psychology and his background is excellent. He has studied and taught for over fifteen years in schools that have pioneered in the academic and practical development of this kind of consumer research. Dr. Letvenoff has been on our staff for the past four years, and his only assignment has been to develop our expertise in motivational research applications. His work with us has been distinguished: I believe he is one of the finest commercial practitioners of motivational research in the country.

Our charge for this work as outlined above, through the final report and with the kind of postreport consultation that you typically require, will be $28,500. The project should not take more than fourteen weeks from inception to completion.

We would very much like to carry this important project forward for you.

Very truly yours,

/s/ Joshua Wubbener

The Wubbener proposal was accepted immediately and enthusiastically by McPhael and his advisers. In due course, the Wubbener research was completed and a final report presented to Bourbon Brothers executives. Excerpts from that document are presented in the following pages.

Consumer Attitudes Toward Gin

I. PATTERNS OF ALCOHOLIC BEVERAGE CONSUMPTION

Almost everyone has a favorite alcoholic drink. In fact, most people who drink with any regularity at all have not only a favorite drink, but a variety of favorites that cover three distinct drinking occasions: a light tall drink for summer afternoons and other occasions that entail relaxed conversation; a before-meal cocktail; and a drink, usually rather dry, that will sustain its drinker easily over the course of a party or a long evening. Some group members talked in terms of different favorites for each of these different occasions, and others categorized one drink as their favorite for two or even all of these occasions. But everyone appeared to distinguish the three occasions as unique circumstances that provoke unique contexts for the consumption of alcohol.

As group members said,

"I think of myself as a Scotch drinker as a general rule—it's what I'm likely to order in most circumstances, except before dinner I usually drink Martini cocktails to get the juices flowing. But after dinner or during the day it's Scotch." (MALE, Washington, about 35, lawyer.)

"I really don't drink that much, except I do like a drink before dinner sometimes and then I take a Daiquiri or a Rob Roy. After dinner it's got to be a longer drink, maybe a whiskey and Coke." (FEMALE, Miami, about 45 housewife.)

"At a party I mostly drink Canadian Club and water or soda. But before meals I'll have a Manhattan on the rocks. When I'm invited to someone's house and it's warm or I'm thirsty, then I'll ask for a Tom Collins or a gin and tonic, something bright and cooling, you know." (FEMALE, Miami, about 40, restaurant receptionist.)

"If it's early in the day, particularly if I'm around outside, then I like beer best. Before dinner I like a Martini or a dry bourbon Manhattan. After dinner—a tall drink of some sort—depends upon my mood and the weather and the kind of day I've had—maybe a gin and tonic or bourbon on the rocks or brandy straight." (MALE, New York, about 50, computer technician.)

But the *dry* evening drink appears to be the one by which the individual characterizes his drinking. Martinis and Tom Collinses are popular, for example, but virtually no one defines himself as a *gin drinker;* gin tends to be thought of as a component of various drinks and not as a liquor for which one has a specific taste.

Many group members believe that women prefer lighter or sweeter mixed drinks more often than do men. Men tend, on the other hand, to describe their drinking tastes in terms of a particular liquor such as bourbon or Scotch or Canadian, whereas women seem more likely to mention a particular drink as their favorite— whiskey sours or Tom Collinses, or screwdrivers or Daiquiris, or whatnot.

One group member had formerly worked as a bartender and he described the phenomenon as follows:

"Women drink colors. Give a woman a drink with a little color and a nice creamy head and she'll think it's delicious regardless of what went into it. At least that's the way with the women who aren't really drinkers. And when they order up they call for a drink by name—always a mixed drink, almost never for a liquor or a brand name. I mean a woman never says, 'Give me a Johnnie Walker Red and soda,' never." (MALE, Miami, about 45, taxi driver.)

As far as the long afternoon drink is concerned, it most often is associated with warm weather drinking situations—weekend afternoons in summer, or winter holidays in warm climates. It is most often made with gin and occasionally with rum.

"One of the things I like about gin—in a gathering, like a garden party or by the pool—most people will order a tall, cool drink, namely a Tom Collins or a gin and tonic, because it really is refreshing when you drink it. I'm pretty sure most people would agree with that, but the percentage of people who want a tall, cool drink will decrease as the night grows nearer and they retire to the air-conditioned rooms, and they'll want another drink, but not a cooler, but whiskey with water or soda, because they don't need that refreshing aspect when they're in out of the heat and the sun." (MALE, New York, about 50, broker.)

"I've always thought of Scotch or bourbon or rye as masculine drinks. Gin and Martinis and so on and so forth I've always classified as more liked by the feminine. This is the way I've always thought about it. And when I order a Tom Collins or a gin and tonic or like that it's because I don't want to indulge in any heavy drinking and I think it's just because a drink is offered to me or it's a tall drink and I don't want to become plastered." (MALE, Washington, about 35, economist.)

But most people, contrary to the preceding quote, do not think of the Martini as a feminine drink. The following exchange between two fortyish New York males reflects the more typical perception:

"Don't you find that, other than Martinis, the average gin drink is more in the woman's line of drinking, like a Tom Collins?"

"Yeah, maybe that is right, but I'll tell you one thing for sure and that is it takes quite a woman to handle Martinis; that's a man's drink."

The notion that gin drinks, such as the Collins and gin and tonic, are "more in the woman's line" is most often expressed by group members who appear to come from lower-middle-class backgrounds. The group participants of higher socio-economic status more often think of specific drinks in terms both of the occasion for drinking and the relative sophistication of the drinker. For the individual who "really likes to drink" an occasional Tom Collins may be all right but not when any more ambitious program of drinking is contemplated. It is not that the long, cool, gin-based drinks are especially feminine. Rather, they are casual and refreshing, frivolous rather than serious.

One's choice of favorite drinks seems to develop out of the continuous interplay of individual taste and reactions to alcohol on the one hand and social influences— particularly movement up through the class structure—on the other. First and most important in determining an individual's drink preference is his reaction to a particular kind of liquor because of its taste; many people distinctly dislike the taste of one or another kind of liquor and sometimes these dislikes are extremely intense.

Only vodka is perceived as lacking in any taste at all. Its lack of taste is to some a virtue because it mixes well with juices and has no distinctly "liquory" taste of its own. Those who dislike vodka say that they dislike it because it is uninteresting because of its lack of taste.

"Lots of people I know won't touch Scotch. And I agree with them. You couldn't force me to drink the stuff—I hate the taste and the way it smells and everything. It smells like Merthiolate to me." (MALE, Washington, about 50, accounting clerk.)

"Martinis—I can't stand a Martini. To me it's sour, and bitter and harsh, all in one. I like a sweeter drink like a Manhattan. They've got just as much power, but they're a lot better tasting." (MALE, Miami, about 40, transportation company supervisor.)

"I don't like the taste of bourbon or rye." (FEMALE, Miami, about 45, house-wife.)

"I like Scotch—Scotch and soda, or on the rocks. I really don't know why because it really tastes lousy. Maybe it tastes less bad than others. It's not sweet and I don't like a sweet drink. Scotch is a lot less sweet than bourbon or rye." (MALE, New York, about 40, city employee.)

"I drink vodka because it's a milder drink, even though it doesn't have any particular taste. I'm not crazy about the taste of liquor in general." (FEMALE, Washington, about 35, federal employee.)

"I doubt that a really serious drinker would like Vodka very much or drink it as a steady thing. My impression of the vodka drinkers is that they don't like liquor . . . don't like its taste, but want to be social and get a little buzz on and vodka's the easy way out." (MALE, New York, about 45, insurance salesman.)

As these comments indicate, taste is rarely put forth as a reason for liking a particular liquor. When asked why they like a particular kind of drink, group members tended to respond in terms of the drink's *effects:* they want a drink whose impact they can control and that will have no unpleasant aftereffects. Many people believe that both impact and aftereffects depend very much upon the individual's personal chemistry rather than the composition of the liquor itself.

"My wife is a bourbon drinker—when we are in a situation that calls for fairly constant drinking she stays with bourbon and water and says she really feels fine next day and I can tell you she can handle it too! Now with me it's different. I have three, four bourbons and I'm a mess and I feel lousy the next day too." (MALE, Miami, about 40, engineer.)

"I've talked to a lot of people about what they drink and why they drink what they do and all, and some of them say that they can handle one kind of drink and not another and others say the opposite. The only way to explain it is that it's definitely a personal characteristic. What they will drink throughout the night. I prefer gin and soda if I'm gonna be drinking for a while." (MALE, New York, about 40, department store buyer.)

"I can drink Scotch all night with almost no aftereffect—but Martinis! Wow! I can't drink them. Two Martinis and I'm gone. Scotch is different—just one after another." (FEMALE, New York, about 40, fashion illustrator.)

Beyond this belief that individual body chemistry strongly affects the impact and aftereffects of a particular liquor, there is agreement that some kinds of drinks tend to affect everyone the same way. Gin, for example, is believed to be more potent and immediate in its effect than bourbon and hence is thought to be appropriate for speedy relaxation before dinner but too strong for leisurely drinking in the evening. And, in general, sweet drinks are considered to have a speedy impact, because they often contain gin and because their alcoholic content is masked by mixes, so that one may be unaware of their intoxicating effect until too late. The richness of sweet drinks, in addition, is thought to increase the chances of unpleasant aftereffects. Bourbon, on the other hand, and to some extent Scotch as well, is believed to be slower in impact and sufficiently dry to prevent a hangover.

"A Tom Collins is something that a great many people who don't drink to any extent might take one of and that would be sufficient for the evening—whereas you don't consider a Tom Collins as an item that you would drink all evening long. As I just said, I feel that it has too much punch to it to drink any large quantity of. I think it hits you much harder than Scotch would—dry drinks as a general rule would be more acceptable for a normal drinking evening." (FEMALE, Miami, about 45, beautician.)

"Well, you see Scotch is a very good thing—or anything that you don't mix with anything but soda or water because you can have it after dinner; you're not mixing things up and you're gonna feel better in the morning." (MALE, Miami about 40, airline supervisor.)

"I think anything sweet in a drink will knock you out faster than drinking a whiskey with water or a Scotch with water." (MALE, Washington, about 45, tax accountant.)

These perceived variations in the impact and aftereffects of various drinks are often cited as reasons for changing one's preferred drink. Many of those interviewed, especially women, report that they were initiated into drinking via sweet drinks like a Tom Collins or a whiskey sour. People who drink irregularly, men or women, may stay with these or similar drinks, but those who drink regularly tend to shift toward something less sweet, often after having become ill or having had some other catastrophe as a result of drinking mixed drinks too heavily. This process of moving toward simple and less complicated drinks seems to the drinker himself to be one of increasing sophistication and expertise, often culminating in a preference for Scotch, which is commonly agreed to be an acquired taste and a "status" drink—something that, like Martinis, one "arrives" at, often in terms of social class as well as personal taste.

As one woman put it, and the rest of the group quickly agreed,

"I think we've probably all had the same experience, if we started out drinking rye . . . a few rye and ginger ales and slightly ill from them, while Scotch on the rocks or Scotch and water or soda, when you finally discover it, is really pretty safe." (FEMALE, Washington, about 45, housewife.)

Another woman put it this way:

"I've always thought of a Tom Collins as a young girl's drink, when you're first starting out to drink—I think sloe gin fizz and Tom Collins. Then as you get older you begin to think about moving up to Scotch or Martinis, and then you really begin experimenting to see what is best for you." (FEMALE, Miami, about 35, housewife.)

Although unpleasant experiences with the sweeter drinks may motivate experimentation and change, the drink one switches to is usually determined by social factors. None of our group members habitually experiment with new drinks on their own, nor do they know anyone who does. Nor do they browse among brands at liquor stores, except when shopping for wine.

As is suggested further on in this report, advertising may often determine their choice of brand in an unfamiliar kind of liquor if, for example, they are not bourbon drinkers but an expected dinner guest is. Most of our group members did not, however, think that ads would stimulate them to try some new kind of liquor. If one is motivated to change a preference in type of liquor, friends and acquaintances are most likely to determine the direction of the change.

"Five or six years ago I acquired a taste for Scotch. When I drank rye it seemed to disagree with me and the next morning I'd have a frightful headache from it. I happened to be going out with a fellow who was a Scotch drinker at the time and he told me I was foolish to drink rye when it gave me a headache and said I ought to switch to Scotch and got me started on it. Well, the first Scotch and water he gave me I told him tasted like iodine. I wondered what he was trying to do to me. But he said you have to work at it a little before you acquire the taste—you don't like Scotch right off the bat, the first time. He said it was worth the effort to feel clear next morning. So I kept it up for a while and had to admit he was right about the lack of hangover, and it really wasn't very long before I really began to like the taste of the stuff and I still do and that's what I drink now." (FEMALE, New York, about 35, housewife.)

Even if one is totally satisfied with his favorite liquor, social pressure can induce a change, although the change may be only temporary.

"I tried a new drink this weekend—vodka and orange juice, whatever it is called. I was down at a wedding in Chevy Chase and everyone at the table was ordering these things—screwdrivers—and I thought, why be different? So I tried it, and they were fine for a change. I'd prefer Scotch in the future, but here were all these red-coated, hunt-dressed people serving us and I just thought I'd have a screwdriver too." (MALE, Washington, about 35, federal employee.)

The very real nature of social pressure to drink a particular drink is clearly illustrated by the following remarks:

"I order a gin and tonic in the middle of the winter and everybody thinks I'm nuts—nobody else would *dare* to order a gin and tonic in the middle of the winter." (MALE, New York, about 45, garment executive.)

"I like a Daiquiri every so often and people often raise their eyebrows when I do. They look like they think that *nobody* drinks that anymore." (MALE, New York, about 40, insurance company auditor.)

"I got on to Scotch about the same way I started eating oysters. I lived for a while in Gainesville, where the thing to do was to eat raw oysters and you just weren't part of the crowd or you weren't very chic if you didn't have them or didn't like them. And I forced myself for a while and suddenly I found myself craving oysters. I didn't like Scotch much when I started, but everyone else seemed to and I forced myself to drink it and after a while it was really all I liked to drink." (FEMALE, Miami, about 35, housewife.)

Moving from region to region or from class to class may expose one to such social pressures; there is general agreement that regional differences in drinking habits are marked and even those who have not themselves made extensive moves across class lines are well aware of class differences in drinking tastes. A postal employee who had also been a part-time bartender summarized it this way:

"You see men that are like salesmen coming in. If they want to have a drink they'll come in and have a fast drink of vodka. Scotch and bourbon drinkers are both about the same, like office workers, I'd say. Then you get the laborer, he goes for the rye. Women are mostly gin, or even some vodka. But Martinis are a man's drink so I guess it would be right to say that men drink gin too—some of them a lot, too." (MALE, New York, about 50, postal supervisor.)

The role of status in influencing and establishing drinking patterns is verbalized in our groups in a variety of ways:

"If I'm with an acquaintance and he orders a very dry Martini, I think that this guy really knows what it's about and I'll order one too. It tastes like hell to me, but I don't feel comfortable unless I do." (MALE, Miami, about 35, salesman.)

"As you go on, you're offered a Scotch and soda—you gradually acquire a taste. It's also a very expensive drink and many people drink it to be part of the upper class. I have really found that to be true." (FEMALE, Washington, about 35, executive secretary.)

To summarize this discussion of how people choose the drinks they choose: First, the occasion has a great deal to do with the selection of the drink *type*—long and tall, short and potent, sweet or dry.

Second, the type of *drink*, rather than type of liquor, is most important in identifying an individual's relative drinking sophistication. For example, it is more sophisticated to drink Scotch than rye, Martinis rather than Tom Collinses; it is more sophisticated to drink straight liquor on the rocks after dinner than to drink whiskey with a sweet mixer like ginger ale. People often force themselve to acquire a taste for these relatively more sophisticated drinks when they begin to mingle with others who already have it.

Finally, as we will see in the pages to come, the popularity and prestige attached to a particular drink incorporating a particular liquor does not necessarily require that a particular brand of that liquor be bought and served.

II. CHOOSING BRANDS: A QUESTION OF QUALITY

Many people have a decidedly mixed outlook about their ability to discriminate by taste among different brands of liquor; to be able to do so is assuredly a mark of sophistication, our group members affirm, but because they are unsure of their own ability to do so, they tend to mistrust the claims of others. In every group session our respondents raised this issue spontaneously, asking each other if they thought they could tell one Scotch or bourbon or rye from another, and in virtually every interview anecdotes were told about fooling someone with pretensions to accurate tasting.

"I tried Johnny Walker Red and Old Dawson on him both ways—on the rocks and with water—and he really couldn't tell the difference. I was curious about these people with exquisite palates who can pick these thing out of the blue—this guy couldn't do it and I don't believe most of the others can either, regardless of what claims they make." (MALE, Washington, about 35, lawyer.)

One woman described gleefully how her mother had fooled a connoisseur uncle by mixing remnants of Scotch, bourbon, and rye in a premier-brand Scotch bottle and presenting it to him—he thought it was the "best Scotch he ever had." There appears to be a consensus that people who have consumed a particular brand for a long time may be able to distinguish it from others, but probably not in a mixed drink and definitely not after having several drinks. And differences in Scotches are thought to be relatively greater than in other kinds of liquors.

"There's a great difference in the weight of different Scotches. For instance, I can tell between Bell's or VAT 69 and Cutty Sark. Cutty Sark is in between the two and there's a definite difference in the taste." (MALE, New York, about 50 computer technician.)

As with flavor differences, differences in quality are not thought to be immediately obvious to everyone.

"When you have a party in the house and you have a bunch of women, they start drinking mixed drinks and all. You can give 'em a cheap rye and they don't know the difference no more than the man in the moon. Just put it in a decanter." (FEMALE, Miami, about 40, restaurant receptionist.)

"If you're going to have a big brawl, then you know that there's only going to be a small percentage that are really drinkers. The rest are just drinking to be sociable, and consequently you could give them an inexpensive gin, or vodka, or almost anything else, especially if they're going to drink it in some sweet mixer like ginger ale or Coke." (MALE, New York, about 40, department store buyer.)

In terms of taste, the sign of quality is agreed to be "smoothness." And this would be fine if people were confident of their ability to detect differences in smoothness or any taste indicator at all among different brands and levels of quality. Because they lack this confidence, they rely on a variety of indicators that they seem to feel are trustworthy.

"I buy bourbon by proof—100-proof bourbon, that's a better whiskey." (FEMALE, New York, about 40, fashion illustrator.)

"The older they are, the more aged they are, the easier they are to take, and the more enjoyable they are. A good vodka is as expensive as any other liquor, if it's a fine vodka and if it's aged long enough. The usual gin or vodka is an inexpensive brand; to me, it is nothing but something that just came out of a distilling tank, like moonshine." (MALE, New York, about 40, drug wholesaler.)

"Price is probably an indication of how many processes this goes through before it gets to the retailer." (MALE, Miami, about 50, dry goods retailer.)

"I always look to my husband for direction. I guess it's like other things—you get what you pay for. There must be something to that because the good ones are all much more expensive. And the imported brands are likely to be good because countries export their best, and they are more expensive too." (FEMALE, New York, about 40, housewife.)

Interestingly enough, given these different and often contradictory feelings and opinions about quality, none of our respondents felt that advertising could (or would) give them sound or dependable guidance in choosing between brands on the basis of quality or flavor claims. To our group, the function of advertising is to keep well-known brands well known. When one is unfamiliar with a particular type of liquor, however, the well-advertised, familiar names will be the ones chosen, if for no other apparent reason than that their continued advertising support suggests that others have found them to be quality products.

Women seem more interested in liquor ads than men, but they also agreed that in general it isn't the informational content or claims about the liquor's qualities that register: liquor ads sell "class," as several of the group agreed, by emphasizing glamor, candlelight, firelight, and the like. "It makes you feel elegant and sexy, which of course you want to be," as one Miami housewife put it. There was one exception to this general tone:

"Jack Daniels ads I'll read. They give you a little story, about way back down on the farm, something like that. How they hickory smoke it. I think unless they have some kind of a unique story to tell, even if it is kinda corn pone, that you're not really going to get all that involved." (MALE, Washington, about 50, accounting clerk.)

Both men and women referred to the importance of personal influence in determining switches or experiments in brand choice—the advice of friends, the urging of bartenders, the recommendations of their liquor dealer:

"I find that it you buy your liquor in the same place all the time, and you know the person, he might say, well, we have such and such on sale today. And I'll say well, you know, maybe it's not as good as this. And he'll say, oh, but it's very fine. Maybe the brand isn't as well known, but if he recommends it and I have confidence in him I might try it, just one bottle, and then I would take his word for it again." (MALE, New York, about 50, broker.)

" I'll tell you who pushes a brand, your bartender. I'm talking from experience now. You take a bartender when he gets a new brand in. I'd say five or six years ago Dewar's was unheard of and it increased in volume of sales terrifically. And why? Because they put it on the bars and the bartender pushed it. He says, 'Try this, it's mild, terrific Scotch.' You take a salesman pushing a new drink; there's a kickback in any business. Dewar's pushed Haig and Haig right off the counter." (MALE, Miami, about 40, bowling alley operator.)

Men and women do seem to differ somewhat in their reactions to packaging as a stimulus for experimenting with new brands. Women are more intrigued with the idea of buying collections of miniatures, either to sample themselves or to give as gifts; they may collect unusual bottles, and they tended to agree that at Christmas they were likely to buy different brands because of the wrapping or decanter. Men agreed, however, that handsome decanters do influence their choice of brands for Christmas presents.

In summary, just as personal taste and social influence combine to determine an individual's preference for types of drinks and types of liquor, social definitions of good quality and how it can be recognized seem even more important when it comes to brands. Brands, like drinks, have implications for one's acceptance as sophisticated and knowledgeable, but they are less readily recognizable on the basis of one's own taste. Therefore reliable symbols of quality like age, proof, price, ingredients, and the like assume importance. At least this is clearly true for whiskeys. The case of gin is somewhat different, as we shall see in the following pages.

III. THE COMPETITIVE POSITION OF GIN

As we have seen, gin has a rather stereotyped position in consumers' minds. It is the most popular component of tall summer drinks, but it is otherwise used mainly in Martinis, which are perceived as both potent and prestigious.

In tall summer drinks, gin is thought of as refreshing or, specifically, as cooling. But it is apparent that it is the gin drink rather than the gin itself that is really perceived as "cooling"—no one, for example, describes Martinis as cooling.

" I prefer a Tom Collins, especially in the summertime, when it's hot, because it's a nice, tall, cool drink. Far as I'm concerned, gin seems to have a cooling effect and it's got more of a cool taste to it. That's the only reason I drink it." (FEMALE, Miami, about 35, housewife.)

" My preference is gin, like all the rest of the fellas. It's a cooling drink in my estimation, although I do like bourbon. I prefer a gin rickey, though. There's nothing else I really care about. I particularly like it on real hot evenings, after you've already eaten—maybe a couple of hours later." (MALE, New York, about 50, broker.)

This quality of "coolness" is ascribed not only to the essential nature of gin itself but to the fact that gin is heavily advertised as a cooling summer drink. Whether gin itself is believed, at least by some individuals, to be intrinsically cooling or simply good in tall, cooling drinks, there is no doubt that gin is so strongly stereotyped as seasonal that a great many people drink it in the summer automatically, regardless of the actual heat.

"This gin business is very, very interesting. We went out to California last summer for a few weeks and set up a makeshift bar in our cottage and bought a bottle each of gin, of bourbon, of Scotch, and of vodka—many of our friends on the Coast are bourbon drinkers usually and some drink Scotch too, but not in the summer—summer in California, that is. We were there for five weeks and never broke the seal on that bottle of bourbon. Did they drink the gin! We bought it by the case. And it wasn't particularly hot—it was just summer, but people just guzzled gin." (MALE, New York, about 40, television producer.)

The typecasting of gin in mixed drinks—tall, cool ones in the summer and martinis—has an interesting consequence. Most people do not believe that there are significant differences in taste among different brands of gin.

"Is there any difference in gin? I thought gin was gin!" (MALE, Washington, about 50, accounting clerk.)

"I don't look for the same things in gin as I do, say, in Scotch. Getting back to the harshness and mellowness in a Scotch, I personally prefer a mellow drink— an aged Scotch—I enjoy it. But in gin, I feel frankly, I'm not as much of a connoisseur in gin, although I drink it, as I am in Scotch. Because I feel that almost any gin will serve its purpose in a Martini." (MALE, New York, about 40, salesman.)

"Most people that buy it will mix it in mixed drinks and everyone knows that it's not the gin taste at all but whatever you mix it with—so it really doesn't make any difference." (FEMALE, Washington, about 45, personnel worker.)

Most people, then, think there are no significant differences in tastes among gin or that those that may exist really don't matter. There are a few people who can or believe they can make taste discriminations. This seems to be particularly true of the hardened Martini drinker. They often object to the richness of the characteristic gin bouquet, though even this objection is not always strong enough to enforce brand sensitivity.

"There are some gins that have a more pronounced flavor or—what's that word that's commonly used when people evaluate gin?—bouquet, that's it— which I object to if it's too strong. Frankly, I can't name them. But I know it when I taste it or smell it; but by brand, I couldn't tell you." (MALE, New York about 45, architect.)

"Oh, I can tell the difference, all right. That Calvert gin that they brought out awhile ago has less of that essence that you get in gin, that flavor that I'm not too crazy about. And I can drink that where other gins I can't." (MALE, Miami, about 35, salesman.)

"That spice odor. Whenever I buy gin I always buy Gordon's but I have bought Gilbey's and that's comparable in price. It isn't a bad gin but I feel that Gordon's doesn't have that smell of the spices in it as much as Gilbey's." (MALE, New York, about 50, computer technician.)

There is considerable confusion about the significance of these variations in aroma or essence. To some they are simply variations among gins that appeal to different tastes, much like variations in the smoothness of Scotch. To others the aroma is a mark of high quality, and to still others it is an inherently unpleasant element in many gins that ought, if possible, to be removed during manufacture.

Only one person among all those participating in the group interviews considered himself primarily a gin drinker, made extensive taste discriminations, and enjoyed the variations he encountered.

"I love gin—I like the flavor. I'll drink it any way. I like the flavor of even different kinds of gins. My favorite drink is a Martini or a Gibson. Gilbey's definitely has a very pronounced difference . . . I can always tell Gilbey's. I can always tell Beefeater. Probably most of the time I can tell Gordon's. Gilbey's tends to taste a little sweeter; it doesn't make quite as good a Martini, but its interesting. I'll occasionally buy a bottle of Beefeater, but most of the time it's Gordon's or one of the others." (MALE, New York, about 40, television producer.)

Although there is some agreement, then, that gins vary in aroma and richness of flavoring, there is no consensus that aroma means quality and certainly no agreement that richness of flavoring is desirable. "Smoothness," which is itself inherently ambiguous, rather than taste may be emphasized.

"Your average gins, your good gins like Gordon's, what do you have, a fairly good gin, not like a greasy alcoholic mixture which doesn't have any taste at all except it tends to stick in your craw. But most of your gins taste just about the same. The good gins are smooth, the others raw, like raw wood alcohol going down. I think myself, when they make a gin, if they'd mix a little dash of lemon or lime into it, they'd have a better result." (MALE, New York, about 50, broker.)

Nor, furthermore, is there clarity about the qualities of gin other than "bouquet," "essence," and the like, which distinguish gins to a small extent at best. People frequently use contradictory or totally inaccurate terms in an effort to characterize a particular brand.

"Well, to me, Beefeater and Tanqueray are smoother, much smoother. The taste is better too. I think this is actually partly what I mean by smoothness, like Tanqueray I could drink on the rocks without any problem. It's very smooth and very thick. And it's very expensive, too. Tanqueray comes in a green bottle. It's a very smooth, light gin; it's almost a liqueur. It's heavy; you can drink it on the rocks. In fact, it would be a shame, I think, to mix it with anything. It seems heavy to me when you pour it. It's not sweet, though." (FEMALE, New York, about 40, fashion illustrator.)

"Bombay—I came across it on Fire Island—it's an English gin. It's a very smooth gin and extraordinarily dry, very, very dry." (MALE, New York, about 42, department store buyer.)

This general lack of clarity about the nature of gin's characteristics is matched by a lack of knowledge about how it is made. Whenever the question was raised, none of the group members knew what grains supplied the spirits for gin, nor even, indeed, were they always sure it is made from grain at all, or whether juniper berries supplied its characteristic flavor.

"What is gin distilled from? Nobody's ever told me. I was never curious and no one's ever been curious enough to ask me. Frankly, I don't know. I know what wood alcohol is and I know where whiskey comes from. What is the essence of gin? Is it a leaf? It's an alcohol and it must be mixed with something to give it that gin flavor but I don't know what it is." (MALE, Washington, about 35, lawyer.)

So it can be seen that, in general, gins appear to have none of the characteristics by which most people judge the quality of liquor. Differences in flavor are commonly thought not to exist or to be so masked by mixers as to be irrelevant. Where differences in taste are noticed they are not generally thought to be indicative of quality. No one seems to know how gin is made or what goes into it beyond the juniper flavoring. It isn't aged—or if it is, no one is aware of it—and consequently differences in age cannot be used to estimate quality. Furthermore, gin bottles tend to look alike and sometimes even like other liquors.

"If I was in the gin business, I think I'd put my gin in a colored bottle—just to make it different. I'd dress up the bottle by coloring it or making it fancy or distinctive somehow." (FEMALE, Miami, about 45, housewife.)

Finally, most gins are comparatively low in price. Gins aren't special. They are a commodity class rather than a collection of distinctive individuals. They are not, for example, ever thought of as potential Christmas gifts, and one gets the impression that if one were to receive a bottle of gin at Christmas, one would be as likely to take it as an offense as to welcome it.

"It's so low priced. I think they ought to jack up the price a little bit—I think they'd make it into more of a gift item." (FEMALE, Washington, about 35, federal employee.)

"Nobody seems to give gin and I was wondering why. I suppose because it's common like salt and pepper, not very elegant." (MALE, Miami, about 40, engineer.)

All of this seems to add up to the conclusion that gin cannot be sold to consumers on the basis of its inherent qualities. Gins do not differ significantly in ingredients, method of manufacture, age, or taste: "gin is gin." And the few differentiated brands are differentiated solely in advertising/price terms. Thus, Beefeater and Tanqueray are perceived as "the best," "prestige" brands that are especially good for Martinis. Gordon's and Gilbey's are not really in the same league—they are good standard quality brands.

The minority who perceive differences among gins have considerable difficulty in expressing in objective language the nature of these differences. There are more often than not references to gin aroma: a "spicy," or "perfumy," or "aromatic" essence that many people like and many people dislike. And among those who do identify this "essence," there is confusion about its source and its significance—to some it is a sign of product quality; to others it reflects a genuine product defect.

Questions for Case 3

1. Why is it important for the marketer to understand what the consumer thinks? Why is it important for the marketer to know the characteristics of consumers?

2. Describe the qualities of the data presented in the two studies summarized in this case. Can these studies both be used in the same way? Why or why not? Do you have more confidence in one study than in the other? Why?

3. Summarize the data presented in Exhibits 3–1 through 3–7. What implications for the marketing of gin do you derive from these exhibits?

4. Summarize the results of the qualitative research presented on pages 73–84. What implications for the marketing of gin do you derive from this research?

5. Consumer perceptions of gin appear to depend more upon brand price and brand advertising content than upon inherent product qualities. If gins vary little at all in product characteristics, is it not true that such differences caused by variations in advertising and price level add to consumer cost but make little valid contribution to society? Why is gin not marketed like coal or lumber or any other generic product?

CASE 4

The Determination of Sales Potentials

Cacaphony Sound Company and the Market Potential for Portable Color Television Sets

T HE CACAPHONY SOUND COMPANY is the world's largest producer of stereophonic sound systems. Cacaphony was started in 1962 by three young engineers who had worked together in the research and development department of Southeastern Electronics—a major supplier of electronic equipment to governmental agencies. These three young men—A. K. Erpff, G. N. Sternweiss, and L. P. Collins—had started, in their spare time, to develop designs for consumer electronic products. Their thought was that Southeastern Electronics must eventually face a day when the government market for electronic equipment dried up completely or became so competitive as to eliminate a flow of profits sufficient to subsidize sophisticated and broad-scale research and development activities. When this day came, they reasoned, a stake in the burgeoning consumer market for high-quality electronic systems might be essential to perpetuate Southeastern.

Or at least so their theory went. In fact, when Erpff, Sternweiss, and Collins presented a design for a very-high-quality table top FM tuner for home use and recommended that Southeastern enter the consumer market through this product, they were abruptly turned down. The Southeastern executive vice-president, A. E. Baker, to whom they proposed the new departure, remarked abruptly, after hearing the three men out, "You guys know as well as I do that we aren't in that business. We provide highly sophisticated electronic products for government use— as long as there is a government there'll be a Southeastern. We don't know anything about consumer goods, and furthermore, we don't want to know anything about them. You men should be out there doing your jobs, not daydreaming about things that won't happen, because they can't. I'm really disappointed in you."

Erpff, Sternweiss, and Collins felt, after joint consideration, that their design was worth pursuing regardless of Mr. Baker's sentiments. After a rather dispiriting period during which they tended to feel sorry for each other and resentful of Baker, they suddenly righted themselves and began to seek financial backing for their own company. The one area that Erpff, Sternweiss, and Collins had no knowledge at all about when they started was product distribution. They were fully confident that they could produce a superior product in any electronic product area to which they applied their expertise. But they had no idea of what to do with a finished product once they got it to their factory door.

Even before the three founders made the final decision to incorporate, they employed Artemas L. Schoonmaker, professor of marketing at a major business school in their immediate area. They asked Schoonmaker to consider how Cacaphony should distribute its product, assuming that the company would eventually be financed, that it would produce a line of consumer electronic products, and that it would have neither the desire nor the resources to develop an extensive in-house distribution capability.

Schoonmaker studied the problem at length and ultimately recommended that a network of manufacturers' sales agents be formed. He believed that several manufacturers of small electrical appliances had used manufacturers' agents in similar circumstances and that the better, more aggressive agents would welcome an opportunity to expand into this complementary field. Each of these agents would be assigned an exclusive territory and the company could develop its agent network as its capacity warranted, moving into full national distribution at its own pace. The agents would not take title to Cacaphony products but would sell them to some wholesalers, as well as directly to retailers, on terms dictated by Cacaphony. The agents would be reimbursed as they made sales but not until then.

This plan appealed to Erpff, Sternweiss, and Collins both for its simplicity and because it involved little additional financial risk to them. As soon as they incorporated Cacaphony, they retained Schoonmaker to specify the details of the sales agent agreements and to recruit and supervise the sales agents for them. (This put more than a little strain on Schoonmaker's time and he was shortly so involved with Cacaphony that it was necessary for him to choose between teaching and commerce. He chose the latter and became sales vice-president of Cacaphony and ultimately rich and relatively famous. But when the job was done, five years later, he felt himself at loose ends and so resigned and returned to teaching.)

The rest is pleasant history. Within a year the Cacaphony Model 100 FM tuner was the largest-selling radio in America. Cacaphony followed with a line of stereo systems based on stereo amplifying units of varying sizes and capacities, an AM/FM radio tuner, a phono–record-player, and several high-performance loud-speaker models. This line also became an overnight success and Cacaphony Sound came to dominate the consumer market for high-quality sound systems. Their success was based on product superiority, price, and design integrity. The three partners continued to do all the basic design work themselves, and it was characterized by simplicity, ease of maintenance, and remarkably high and consistent performance standards.

* *
*

Early in 1969 the partners decided to apply their expertise to portable color television sets. Their conception was that it might be possible to design a very-high-performance portable color TV, to manufacture it in Japan, and to market it in the United States at a price significantly below the price level for portable color TV sets that could be obtained in the United States market place. But in 1969, Cacaphony Sound was a rather different company than it had been when founded in 1962. The company now employed over eleven thousand individuals, and over the years the basic nondesign activities of the company had been delegated by the partners to line and staff personnel who were competent and well paid and who expected as a matter of right to participate in the affairs of the company. No longer could Erpff, Sternweiss, and Collins go into a huddle, develop a design, and simply start making it. There were meetings to be held, viewpoints to be aired, memos to be written, and decisions to be made.

In the case of the color television decision perhaps Erpff, Sternweiss, and Collins rather welcomed the workings of the bureaucracy they had created. They had a technical design that they thought was a beauty. And they had a commitment from Koga Industries of Japan indicating that the set could be made in Japan, shipped to the United States, and sold to consumers at a price significantly below that charged by the leading domestic marketers of color television sets. But Cacaphony Sound had never sold a television set, and the partners were willing to admit it and to admit that they themselves knew considerably less about television than they did about sound reproduction systems. And so they seemed rather less reluctant than usual when their president and chief operating officer, L. O. "Popeye" Shortstreet, suggested that a thorough study of the color television set market was very much in order before the final decision to market the new set was made.

Popeye Shortstreet had a deep professional respect for the Cacaphony market analysis department, which he had caused to be formed in 1967. His experience was that when properly and specifically directed, the market analysis section was excellent at identifying secondary sources, finding relevant information, and synthesizing it into cogent and succinct reports. Shortstreet asked A. M. Montmeat, manager of Cacaphony market analysis, to conduct a general study of the American market for portable color sets as it had developed to 1969 and as it could be projected to develop through 1974 and 1979. Montmeat in his turn assigned the color TV project to Alice McNair Whiteson, a senior analyst in his department. Ms. Whiteson spent about three months gathering, analyzing, and interpreting the basic available marketing data for the portable color TV set market. Her work was presented in a ninety-two-page report entitled "Opportunities for Cacaphony Sound Company in the Portable Television Set Market 1969–1974–1979." The findings from this analysis were condensed into a short summary statement (in accordance with the policy of the market analysis department) at the beginning of the report. Here is that summary statement:

1. Although the TV market as a whole is relatively stable, the so-called portable segment of the color TV set market is growing and it is growing very rapidly. Exhibit 4–1 shows the unit sales history of the TV set market since 1961, and indicates the composition of these set sales as between black and white on the one hand and color console and color portable TV sets. As this exhibit shows, the black-and-white set market has declined very significantly since 1961, although it still represents a significant share of the units sold. "Portable" color sets did not become significant until after 1965, but they now account for 38 per cent of all the units sold. Color console set sales grew year by year until 1968, reaching a peak of over 10 million units in that year. Even color console sales appear to be ebbing before the very strong trend in portable sets. Console sales were off almost 1.4 million units in 1969.

2. Although "portable" color sets do account for a majority of the color sets sold and although they do constitute the fastest growing segment of the television set market, their dollar significance is somewhat less than their unit significance. An analysis of 1969 unit and dollar sales (shown in Exhibits 4–1 and 4–2) shows, for example, that "portable" color sets accounted for 38 per cent of the units sold but 36 per cent of the dollar sales. Exhibit 4–3 reveals that the average color "portable" sold in 1969 for $57.35 less at factory than the average color console. This gap between the prices of console and portable sets has remained around $55.00 in recent years, after some instability in the

EXHIBIT 4–1
Specimen Data: U.S. Television Set Sales in Units—Selected Years 1961–69
(000 Omitted)

YEAR	TOTAL TV SETS SOLD	BLACK-AND-WHITE SETS SOLD	COLOR SETS SOLD	"PORTABLE" COLOR SETS SOLD	CONSOLE COLOR SETS SOLD
1961	12,427.6	9,821.3	2,606.3	—	2,606.3
1963	13,492.8	8,411.3	5,081.5	—	5,081.3
1965	16,475.3	6,210.8	10,264.5	982.7	9,281.8
1966	15,448.3	5,921.0	9,527.3	1,324.6	8,202.7
1967	16,981.4	4,721.6	12,259.8	2,631.3	9,628.5
1968	17,821.3	3,011.7	14,809.6	4,792.4	10,017.2
1969	16,781.6	1,692.4	15,089.2	6,441.2	8,648.0

SOURCE : Compiled from a variety of trade publications and sources.

first years of portable availability (1965–$40.14; 1966–$103.87; 1967–$56.92; 1968–$55.84; 1969–$57.35).

As portables move into a dominant position in the color set market, the net effect will probably be a lowering in the factory dollar return per set sold. Note, however, that the average price of color television sets sold *at factory* held stable at $313.01 in 1969 compared to $310.56 in 1968.

3. It is a little difficult to ascertain just why portable sets are called *portable* because they are to an important extent not portable at all, at least in any realistic definition of that word. A "portable" set may, in a few cases, literally mean a set that can be picked up and moved freely about, its power derived from self-contained batteries and (perhaps) alternatively from conventional 115-volt floor electric outlets. But in the vast majority of cases, a portable set is not portable—unless one happens to call "portable" a mechanism weighing anywhere from 75 to 125 pounds and totally dependent upon line-delivered 115-volt power. A "portable" set is, in reality, a set that maximizes its function of delivering television entertainment and minimizes its function as furniture. It is a set stripped of most exterior frills, although its design may have pleasing and integrable lines.

EXHIBIT 4–2
Specimen Data: U.S. Television Set Sales in Factory Dollars—Selected Years 1961–69 (000 Omitted)

YEAR	TOTAL TV SET SALES	BLACK-AND-WHITE SET SALES	COLOR SET SALES	"PORTABLE" COLOR SET SALES	CONSOLE COLOR SET SALES
1961	$2,484,369	$1,632,141	$ 852,228	—	$ 852,228
1963	2,947,138	1,421,362	1,525,776	—	1,525,776
1965	4,274,182	1,041,639	3,232,543	$ 273,812	2,958,731
1966	3,982,241	872,463	3,109,778	313,903	2,795,875
1967	4,316,346	624,781	3,691,565	674,808	3,016,757
1968	5,019,684	420,362	4,599,322	1,307,321	3,292,001
1969	4,924,234	201,132	4,723,102	1,804,418	2,918,684

SOURCE: Compiled from a variety of trade publications and sources.

EXHIBIT 4–3
Specimen Data: Factory Price Per Average Television Set Sold—Selected Years, 1961–69

YEAR	TOTAL TV SETS	BLACK-AND-WHITE SETS	COLOR SETS	"PORTABLE" COLOR SETS	CONSOLE SETS
1961	$199.90	$166.18	$326.99	—	$326.99
1963	218.42	168.98	300.26	—	300.26
1965	259.43	167.71	314.92	$278.63	318.77
1966	257.78	147.35	326.40	236.98	340.85
1967	254.18	132.32	301.11	256.45	313.37
1968	281.67	139.58	310.56	272.79	328.63
1969	293.43	118.84	313.01	280.14	337.49

SOURCE: Estimated from Exhibits 4–1 and 4–2.

EXHIBIT 4-4
Specimen Data: Estimated Advertising Expenditures for Television Sets in National Media—Selected Years 1961–69
(000 Omitted)

SET TYPES*	1961	1965	1966	1967	1968	1969
Total advertising expenditures	$9,200	$11,900	$11,500	$15,200	$15,800	$16,700
Black-and-white sets	7,800	6,000	4,200	1,500	1,000	800
Color sets	1,400	5,900	7,300	13,700	14,800	15,900
"Portable" color sets	—	—	1,200	2,800	4,900	7,800
Console color sets	1,400	5,900	6,100	10,900	9,900	8,100

* Distribution of expenditure by set type is estimated from Aesop & Acton Advertising Agency competitive copy analyses. In those cases where black-and-white and color or more than one type of color set is included in advertisements, space costs and/or broadcast costs are prorated on the basis of the space or time allocation by set type.

SOURCE : Trade sources and Aesop & Acton Advertising Agency.

EXHIBIT 4-5
Specimen Data: Demographic Characteristics of Television Set Purchasing Families, 1968

	ALL FAMILIES	TV SETS PURCHASED	BLACK-AND-WHITE SETS PURCHASED	COLOR SETS PURCHASED	"PORTABLE" COLOR SETS PURCHASED
Base					
Number	8,210	2,600	290	2,310	1,406
Per cent	100	100	100	100	100
Income					
Under $5,000	12%	6%	12%	5%	2%
$ 5,000–$ 7,999	30	32	24	33	28
$ 8,000–$ 9,999	24	28	28	29	32
$10,000–$14,999	18	22	16	23	29
$15,000–$24,999	10	10	12	10	7
$25,000 and over	6	2	8	1	2
Education of household head					
Grade school or less	10%	14%	8%	15%	12%
Some high school	18	22	28	21	24
Graduated, high school	36	35	32	35	36
Some college	21	19	24	18	17
Graduated, college	15	10	8	10	11
Age of household head					
24 or younger	26%	34%	28%	35%	39%
25–34	28	32	30	32	34
35–49	18	18	22	17	21
50–64	12	10	14	9	4
65 and older	16	6	6	6	2
Social mobility					
High mobility	33%	40%	34%	42%	38%
Moderate mobility	33	30	33	29	33
Low mobility	34	30	33	29	29

4. The distribution of advertising expenditures has followed the distribution of TV set sales by product type. Thus in 1969 "portable" and console color TV sets were supported by essentially equal amounts of advertising expenditure and black-and-white sets received only 5 per cent of total advertising outlays. In 1965, console color and black-and-white sets each received about equal amounts of dollar advertising support and "portable" color sets received no advertising support at all.

The level of advertising support for television sets has risen slowly but surely during the period. Thus the 1969 expenditure of $16,700,000 was 40 per cent higher than the 1965 level and 82 per cent higher than the 1961 level.

This increase in advertising expenditure reflects both inflationary forces in our economy and the steadily rising long-term dollar sales trend in the product category. But the increase is undoubtedly also attributable to the developing importance, first, of color television and, later, of the "portable" sets, as the decade progressed. These innovations in the basic television set products available in the marketplace required continued advertising pressure to inform and educate the consumer about the characteristics and performance of the available products. Whereas advertising expenditures increased 82 per cent from 1961 to 1969, the number of sets sold increased 35 per cent and the dollar sales of this industry almost doubled. Advertising expenditure increases thus proceeded in consonance with the dollar sales growth.

5. The bulk of color TV sets—both console and "portable"—are purchased by lower- and middle-income families whose heads are under forty-nine years of age and have not been educated beyond high school. The demographic patterns of purchasers for the "portable" sets is quite similar to that of all color set purchasers. Thus the "portable" purchaser is also predominantly in the demographic groupings of lower and middle income, age under forty-nine, and high school or less education. The market for color television sets is very clearly a mass market: the only demographic segments excluded are families with older household heads and very-low-income families.

6. Television sets imported from Japan are assuming a dominant position in the domestic television set market. As Exhibit 4–6 shows, virtually all black-and-white sets are now made in Japan and two thirds of the "portable" color sets are now made in Japan. The manufacture of console sets has remained totally in non-Japanese hands, and, in fact, we have determined that no consoles of any kind were manufactured outside the United States in 1969. In spite of

EXHIBIT 4–6
Specimen Data: Proportion of Television Sets Imported from Japan—Selected Years, 1961–69

	1961	1963	1965	1966	1967	1968	1969
All TV sets	0%	0%	2%	7%	15%	28%	35%
Black-and-white sets	0	0	5	18	44	92	97
Color sets	0	0	0	0	4	15	28
"Portable" color sets	0	0	0	0	19	46	66
Console color sets	0	0	0	0	0	0	0

S O U R C E :   Compiled from trade and government sources.

the fact that the Japanese are not exporting consoles, it is clear that they are a dominant factor and one of increasing importance in the fastest-growing segment of the color television set market. Certainly there is no suggestion in these figures that the American consumer is in any way prejudiced against either color or black-and-white television sets of Japanese origin.

7. Retail availability of various television set types follows factory sales patterns. As Exhibit 4–7 demonstrates, black-and-white television sets have dramatically declined in retail availability in the period 1965–69, and "portable" color TV set models were about three times as "available" in 1969, at retail, as they were in 1965. Console color TV set availability has declined marginally in the same period.

8. Half the households in the United States own a color TV set, and 96 per cent own either a color or a black-and-white set. (See Exhibit 4–8.) All of the households that currently have only black-and-white sets represent potential for color TV set sales. In addition, the households that currently own color sets continue to own black-and-white sets. In fact, as Exhibit 4–8 documents, there are more black-and-white sets (1.89) in the average color-owning home than there are color sets (1.23). Thus, it is clear that households that currently have color television sets represent significant potential for color set sales. Their black-and-white sets will presumably, in due course, be replaced by color sets.

9. As far as the future is concerned, we believe that the following factors will be dominant in determining the size and character of the TV set market in 1974 and 1979.

a. Total set purchases will depend upon the obsolescence of existing sets and the trends in multiple set ownership that develop. The record sales of the late 1960's reflect the conversion of black-and-white homes to color and the strong demand for second, third, and even fourth sets in at least a fraction of American homes. We believe that these trends will continue unabated throughout the 1970's. More and more homes will have more and more sets and existing black-and-white sets will continue to be replaced by color. The opportunity has already been identified in Exhibit 4–8 and text point 8, above.

EXHIBIT 4–7
Specimen Data: Television Set Model Availability at Retail by Set Type, 1965 and 1969

	NUMBER OF DIFFERENT MODELS ON DISPLAY IN AVERAGE APPLIANCE STORE, 26 MAJOR MARKETS	
	1965	1969
All TV sets	37.3	42.9
Black-and-white sets	21.1	6.2
Color sets	25.2	36.7
"Portable" color sets	5.8	18.2
Console color sets	19.4	18.5

SOURCE: Trade association study.

EXHIBIT 4–8
Specimen Data: Television Set Ownership Characteristics of U.S. Households, 1969

Households owning television sets	96%
Average number of sets per owning household	2.3
Households owning color television sets	49%
Average number of sets per color-owning household	3.12
Color sets per color-owning household	1.23
Black-and-white sets per color-owning household	1.89
Average number of sets per black-and-white–owning household	1.61

S O U R C E :   Trade association estimates.

b. Set purchase trends will ultimately depend upon the relative stability of technology. We believe there will continue to be a robust demand for television sets throughout the 1970's even if no major product innovation occurs. This demand could explode if some fundamental improvement or extension of television is made. Thus sets incorporating the capabilities of in-home TV tape-recording and video cassette playback are one example of such a potential breakthrough, particularly if such equipment can be sold at relatively modest increases over the cost of available color console sets. Radical improvement in color tuning, such as a tuning system that guarantees a perfect ghost-free picture, could also result in a sales explosion, particularly if such an innovation was accompanied by a significant decrease in price. But such innovations are not a prerequisite for booming sales: strong demand will occur in any event, and if the innovations come along, they will add really significant sales to an already prosperous market.

c. We do know that color television set sales are relatively sensitive to general conditions in the economy. If the economy is expanding vigorously, then this will have a positive effect on color television set sales, and on the other hand, if the economy slows down so will color set sales. But the basic demand trend, as we have just pointed out, is bound to remain strongly positive and will be the fundamental force, regardless of the cyclical economic fluctuations that embellish this trend from year to year.

d. The basic state of U.S. trade relations with Japan will also be an important determinant of total TV set sales. The Japanese have been very aggressive in the television set market in the 1960's and if trade with Japan continues to be relatively unrestricted in the 1970's, as in the 1960's, we can expect the Japanese to be an increasing dominant factor in this market. Of course, the signs are legion that trade restrictions of one kind or another will be important in the 1970's and these, as they unfold, may cause a decline in the importance of Japanese imports and a resurgence of domestically produced sets. The demand will be there in any event, and it is possible that policy decisions in the government sector will have at least a little to do with the distribution of set production between domestic and Japanese suppliers. We have both the sophistication and the domestic production know-how to shift to domestic production if Japanese imports are restricted significantly.

EXHIBIT 4–9
Specimen Data: Projected U.S. Television Set Ownership in 1974 and 1979*
Dollar and Unit Bases (000 Omitted)

	1974		1979	
	DOLLARS†	UNITS	DOLLARS†	UNITS
Total sales	6,160,000.0	22,400.0	7,314,000.0	27,600.0
Black-and-white	132,000.0	1,200.0	143,500.0	1,400.0
Color	6,028,000.0	21,200.0	7,170,500.0	26,200.0
"Portable" color	3,813,100.0	14,780.0	4,536,740.0	18,884.0
Console color	2,214,900.0	6,420.0	2,633,760.0	7,316.0

* Assumes no major change in economic conditions; relatively free trade with Japan; no significant product innovation.
† Dollar projections assume a continuation of U.S. dollar inflation at 5 per cent per year.
S O U R C E : Cacaphony Sound Econometrics Section.

e. Finally, we believe that a certain number of console and black-and-white sets will continue to be required by the market: neither of these set types will become extinct regardless of existing and emerging sales trends.

Given the statistical base developed in our work on this project (these statistics are only summarized and highlighted in this section) and these basic conclusions about the future of the market for television sets, we asked our Econometrics Section to provide estimates of color set sales in total and by the three subsectors of the market for the years 1974 and 1979. The Econometrics Section has generated these sales estimates using the methods of multiple regression. They have estimated sales in 1974 and 1979 dollars (assuming a continuing inflation of U.S. dollars at 5 per cent per year) and in 1974 and 1979 units in Exhibit 4–9. These projections are neither optimistic nor pessimistic: they assume a modestly increasing gross national product, relatively free trade with Japan, and no dramatic product innovation over the next ten years.

* *
*

On the basis of these analyses, Popeye Shortstreet reached the following conclusions regarding the nature of the marketing opportunity for Cacaphony Sound:

1. The color television set market was immense and it would expand continuously over the next ten years.
2. Cacaphony Sound was prepared to compete in this market in the next ten years. The Cacaphony "portable" color set design and the agreement with Koga Industries to produce it gave Cacaphony a solid basis for successful and profitable competition in the color TV market as it then existed.

3. If trade restrictions limited or made unprofitable the importation of Japanese TV sets, no U.S. company was better equipped to shift emphasis to domestic production.

4. The same Cacaphony distribution system that handled the radio tuners and sound systems was well suited to the distribution of color television sets.

Shortstreet therefore recommended to the managing partners that Cacaphony immediately enter the portable color television set business. This recommendation was accepted and the new MAXIHUE line of four models was introduced to the trade in May of 1970. Consumer advertising commenced the following September. The original line consisted of four models, ranging in suggested list price from $269.95 to $399.95. These prices were about $30.00 less than the prices of comparable competitive receivers. And the MAXIHUE sets were exceptional performers—each of the MAXIHUE models produced a picture that was clearly superior in color tones and definition to that produced by any competitive model. This product superiority plus the lower price combined to produce for the MAXIHUE line an astounding sales success. By 1971 the MAXIHUE sets were the third largest sellers in the United States, and it was clear to Cacaphony officials that they would be the leading seller if more retail distribution was obtained. Distribution had been limited in 1970 because KOGA Industries could not fulfill orders at the rate at which they were placed by Cacaphony in 1970. It was not until late 1971 that new KOGA manufacturing facilities made it possible to fulfill demand and develop the distribution system in depth.

Competitive set manufacturers tried to duplicate the MAXIHUE set performance. They were impeded in this effort by three key patents held by Cacaphony on elements in the MAXIHUE tuning system. Over the years most of the leading television set manufacturers had developed their designs at about the same pace and along the same lines, and the individual set manufacturers had not made any improvements in design that were so unique that they were patentable. Furthermore, many of the fundamental improvements stemmed from the innovations of suppliers whose work was fully available to all the manufacturers. This was true, for example, of the development of certain luminous phosphors by a leading chemical firm in 1967. These phosphors, when used in the manufacture of picture tubes, produced color hues of strikingly improved intensity, and the phosphors and the basic technology involved in their use were made freely available to all set manufacturers.

So the Cacaphony patents were an unusual element and for several years no competitor was able, without directly infringing the patents, to develop alternative tuning devices that did for their units what Cacaphony had done for theirs. Truly competitive tuning devices were not perfected until 1978, long after the events with which the case is concerned.

In 1970 and 1971, the Cacaphony share of the portable color TV set market held at about 18 per cent on a unit basis, hampered as it was by the restricted supply of product. When the production limitations were overcome in late 1971, and full distribution was subsequently achieved, the unit share of MAXIHUE portable color TV set sales jumped from 18 per cent to 40 per cent by 1973. This development is indicated in Exhibit 4–10, which also reflects the brand shares held by the major competitive firms not only in the color portable but also in the color console and black-and-white segments of the market. As Exhibit 4–10 indicates, the competitive impact of the Cacaphony Sound line of portable TV sets was felt most by Apex and SDB. The color portable share of Apex declined from 32 per cent to 22 per cent between 1970 and 1973, and the color portable share of SDB declined from 20 per cent to 14 per cent in the same period.

Early in 1972, as Cacaphony Sound continued to prosper beyond the wildest dreams of its founders, Popeye Shortstreet came to the conclusion that a further development of the Cacaphony marketing organization was imperative. In the late 1960's and early 1970's Shortstreet had literally run the operations of Cacaphony, aided by a vice-president for sales (E. G. "Taffy" Uelander), a vice-president for finance (Elmer P. Anthony), and a vice-president for manufacturing operations (Anthony A. Fiscigna). The three founding partners handled product development, public relations, some customer relations, and whatever else their effervescent and unbounded interests settled upon. Shortstreet did his best to keep the founders out of the actual running of the company and concerned only with product design, development and quality control. And he was fairly successful in doing this, thus protecting his vice-presidents from too great an intrusion into their affairs.

But as Cacaphony Sound gradually increased the length of their radio and sound system lines and then went into the marketing of television sets, Shortstreet became aware of a weakness in the organization. Cacaphony Sound products were not marketed in any organized way: they were simply released to a receptive public, apparently ever anxious to absorb them from the distribution system. Cacaphony products were so good that the lack of continuous professional marketing attention was not felt. It simply wasn't needed in the first ten years of the company because the competitors were outclassed.

Shortstreet knew that this state of affairs could not be expected to last indefinitely. And he began to feel the strain himself as the increasing complexity of Cacaphony operations threw up a multitude of marketing issues and decisions that only he and Taffy Uelander could make.

The situation came to a head in December of 1971, as the expanded facilities of Koga Industries suddenly began to gush forth MAXIHUE television receivers in sufficient quantity to fulfill the latent consumer demand.

Shortstreet and Uelander were eating a sandwich in Shortstreet's office, hurriedly, one noontime when Shortstreet suddenly said, "Taffy, what

EXHIBIT 4–10
Specimen Data: Brand Position in the Television Set Market—Selected Companies, 1970, 1972, and 1973

	1970	1972	1973
Total market	100 Per Cent	100 Per Cent	100 Per Cent
Color portable	(100)	(100)	(100)
Color console	(100)	(100)	(100)
Black-and-white	(100)	(100)	(100)
Cacaphony sound			
Color portable	18	32	40
Color console	—	—	—
Black-and-white	—	—	—
Apex			
Color portable	32	26	22
Color console	16	18	20
Black-and-white	28	29	36
SDB			
Color portable	20	18	14
Color console	29	30	35
Black-and-white	24	29	26
Nagami			
Color portable	18	16	15
Color console	—	—	—
Black-and-white	32	24	29
All other			
Color portable	12	8	9
Color console	55	52	45
Black-and-white	16	18	9

S O U R C E :   Estimated from trade sources and trade association releases.

are you doing about increasing distribution on MAXIHUE? The Japs will give us all we can sell now, so the ball is in our court to really increase volume, you know."

"Look, Pops, I'm with you, but we gotta have some help in sales. The company is getting too big. I can't make that distribution just happen, you know. It has to happen right and that takes time and lots of work with the agents. So let's think about some more people and no Yo-yos, really smart people who know the business."

This conversation started a sequence of events that finally produced a brand manager system for Cacaphony Sound. In developing a job description for these positions (there were to be three brand managers, one for each of the major product lines) Shortstreet and Uelander emphasized that the men selected would be responsible at least for evaluating sales agents; identifying those markets in which Cacaphony was at a distribution disadvantage relative to competitors; establishing specifications for Cacaphony retail outlets; developing goals and programs to improve Cacaphony retail distribution; studying competitive products and product lines; developing and analyzing competitive sales statistics; studying competitive pricing practices and trends; supervising advertising and public relations programs; and identifying potentially profitable areas for corporate expansion through either new products or line extensions.

With these job specifications established, a search for qualified men to fill the new product manager positions was initiated. First priority was to be given to men already working within the Cacaphony Sound organization. As events unfolded, two of the new men were recruited from outside of the company and one, the Cacaphony MAXIHUE television set product manager, came from the company's own sales department. He was August N. Schneider, age twenty-seven, and he had come to work at Cacaphony Sound immediately after his graduation from a large north-eastern graduate school of business (he had in fact been an outstanding student of Artemas L. Schoonmaker, and it had been Schoonmaker who originally introduced him to Cacaphony Sound).

Schneider's first assignment after a one-year indoctrination in Caca-phony selling practices and philosophies was to maintain contact with three of the Cacaphony Sound manufacturers' sales agents in the north-western United States. These agents were neither big, nor sophisticated, nor particularly important to the overall Cacaphony operation, but they were bona fide agents, and it was a place to start and really find out what went on in the field.

At the time of his appointment as MAXIHUE product manager, Schneider had worked for Cacaphony for three years, the last two of which had been spent contacting the northwestern manufacturers' agents. He had had no other experience of any kind in marketing manage-ment prior to his new assignment.

The field-sales contact work had made a very strong impression on young Schneider. As a result, he tended to formulate marketing problems in retail-sales–oriented terms. He thought in terms of achieved distribu-tion, individual market sales performance, retailer relations with manu-facturers' sales agents, in-store display, and trade promotion. He believed, as he moved from his sales contact work and into marketing management, that the dominant fact in electronic goods marketing was that the consumer could only buy what was available to him in the stores. He believed strongly that it was what happened to the consumer after entering the retail outlet that was decisive in determining exactly what brand and model he ultimately purchased.

Schneider approached his new job with a strong sense of humility. He knew that nothing in his background fitted him uniquely for the role of

MAXIHUE product manager. But he was also smart enough to realize that in spite of the formal job description there was no tradition of product managership within Cacaphony Sound. This meant that he had not only the opportunity but the responsibility to define the MAXIHUE product manager's job as he saw fit. He recognized also that he had been chosen as MAXIHUE product manager not because of his experiences in product management work but rather because of his potential ability to give some meaningful definition to this new organizational role.

With this understanding, Schneider decided that his first few months on the job would be dedicated to learning rather than operating. He took care to explain this view to Uelander to be sure that Taffy would not be surprised nor disgruntled by a seeming lack of activity on his part. And, he was delighted to discover that Uelander approved his approach enthusiastically.

"How could we expect you to know how to do this job, when nobody else has ever done it here?" was Uelander's reaction. "Take some time to find out what's important and what's not. Don't try to snow me by just running around the country on airplanes, because I know there's more to this job than that, if you do it right."

Schneider scoured the company files to learn everything that was known about MAXIHUE and about its sales patterns. He spent over a week talking to the founding partners, both individually and in a group, letting them tell him whatever they wished to about MAXIHUE but emphasizing his interest in learning how and why they had developed the TV set line just as they had, and why it was better than competitive sets, and how vulnerable it was to competitive innovation, and what the partners expected they could invent to improve MAXIHUE, and on and on. Schneider spent four weeks traveling about the country (ignoring Uelander's injunction, understanding the difference between purposeful and purposeless motion) talking to the twenty biggest Cacaphony Sound manufacturers' agents. He tried to understand from these men why they were successful in selling Cacaphony products and what kinds of problems they encountered in making additional sales and expanding distribution.

He was particularly interested in the manufacturers' agents' views about dealer collateral material (that is, descriptive literature and in-store display material made available by the manufacturer for dealer use). He wanted to know their views on manufacturer-sponsored sales events in which dealers from time to time were given price allowances that were, in turn, used by them as a basis for consumer "sales." He was interested in the importance of cooperative advertising allowances (that is, allowances by the manufacturer to dealers in support of their local advertising programs) and the degree to which such allowances affected the development of improved distribution and total line display within stores. He also wanted to know if and how much cooperative advertising allowances were used in support of periodic manufacturer's sales events.

In all of this he sought information about how well Cacaphony and its programs were accepted by the trade and how they compared with competitive programs or firms like Apex and SDB and Nagami. In addition, he talked at length to Uelander and Shortstreet and to other members of the sales department.

When two months had passed, Schneider felt that he finally had begun to achieve an understanding of the MAXIHUE business. As a result of this self-imposed indoctrination, Schneider had developed a great admiration for the accomplishments of Shortstreet and Uelander, a full appreciation of the Cacaphony network of manufacturers' agents, and an awe of the power of a truly superior line of products to make up for short-comings and lack of attention to basic marketing plans and programs. Not that Schneider thought that Shortstreet and Uelander should have done more—rather he began to understand how much a total marketing effort in the field of consumer electronics really required. And he came to appreciate how little time and attention a staff of the size of the Cacaphony sales department, given all of its other concerns and responsibilities, could allocate to such an effort. In short, Schneider came to realize the real nature of his job: he knew that there was a job to be done and he knew its dimensions and the opportunity that it represented.

His first real problem was to figure out just where to begin. He had determined that there was a lack of cohesive and imaginative planning of programs of collateral material; he knew that the Cacaphony cooperative advertising programs were overgenerous by competitive standards; and he knew that the special-selling-event programs were poorly conceived and not properly integrated with either the collateral material programs or the cooperative advertising programs.

He suspected that the company had got to the point of making relatively generous cooperative advertising payments because they were relatively easy and straightforward to administer and required almost no follow-through with the retailer. He also suspected that these cooperative advertising promotional expenditures were not distributed as efficiently among manufacturing agents and retailers as they might be if the effect of these expenditures on Cacaphony sales and profits was to be maximized. Cacaphony really had not made any attempt to work with the retailers in the past. They had been content to buy their support rather than earn it, and Schneider was pretty sure that they had had to pay more than the traffic would bear and probably more than once.

Cacaphony paid a standard cooperative advertising allowance per unit of media space or time. The retailers were expected to contribute an equivalent amount, with newspaper proof sheets and broadcast station affidavits as proof that the advertising had been purchased. The system was based on a standard cost for each unit of space or time and ignored media discounts. Thus, although the large retailers actually bought the same space and time units as the smaller retailers for significantly fewer dollars because of media discounts, Cacaphony Sound's cooperative advertising payments were at the same rate to all. This situation was complicated by the fact that Cacaphony would accept advertising claims without limit, as long as they were substantiated by proof of performance. The net effect of all this was to concentrate Cacaphony Sound cooperative advertising payments with large retailers, regardless of whether this was in the best marketing interests of Cacaphony or not. There was a certain logic to this, but in the gearing of cooperative payments only to retailer sales volume, it was possible that market potential might be overlooked. Thus, if two markets of equal size and potential had dramatically different retail structures, that market with one or two larger retailers would, under the existing system, receive considerably more cooperative advertising support than would the market with many smaller retailers. If this were the case, cooperative advertising dollars were spent because of retailer leverage rather than to generate the highest level of Cacaphony sales and profits.

The Robinson-Patman Act of 1938, amending the Clayton Anti-Trust Act, limits and controls manufacturers' programs directed at retailers that affect the price paid by retailers for the manufacturer's products. In general, this act specifies that a manufacturer may not charge one customer more than another for equivalent merchandise. The Act recognizes that the buyer (retailer) may provide certain services or facilities (such as cooperative advertising) to the seller (manufacturer) and that he may be compensated for them as long as the same rate of compensation is offered to all competing retailers. The Cacaphony Sound cooperative advertising program met this parity requirement of the Robinson-Patman Act and was similar in this aspect to the cooperative advertising of competitive manufacturers of color television sets. Schneider believed that the Cacaphony cooperative advertising allowance program, as well as other retailer-directed programs, could be improved if some device were found to permit more direct control of the allocation of marketing funds to retailers by Cacaphony. He recognized that the Robinson-Patman Act would not permit variations in program terms as between competing retailers, but he was advised by legal counsel that he could offer different programs in different geographic areas as long as all competing retailers within a particular area were offered equivalent programs. This suggested to Schneider that different programs might be offered in different manufacturers' sales agents' areas because every retailer dealt with only one manufacturers' sales agent and each of these agents operated in a geographically exclusive area. This approach could at least help to direct dealer programs along lines better oriented to Cacaphony Sound, objectives in the different manufacturers' agents' market areas. And to the extent that differences in retailer size varied by manufacturers' agents' market areas, some of the inequities in manufacturer support from this cause could also be overcome.

Schneider had no idea how to start to develop a program that would recognize the geographic inequities with the information that was readily at hand. In spite of his suspicions and theories he had no objective basis for determining in what geographic areas he might spend relatively more promotional dollars so that MAXIHUE sales would be maximized. As it was, he thought Cacaphony was spending too much in some markets and not enough in others, but he didn't know how great these inequities were, and he didn't know where the money should be spent even if he could find a way to determine its optimum amount.

No one at Cacaphony had ever made any consistent attempt to analyze the market-by-market sales pattern either for the company or for any of its lines. Nor had any attempt been made to combine Cacaphony sales statistics with sales data for complementary product categories and data on other factors that were causally related to color television set sales or consumer electronic set sales in order to develop an index of sales potential for MAXIHUE portable color television sets or other Cacaphony products on a market area basis.

Schneider expected to use an index of the sales potential of portable color television sets, once developed, as a continuing and basic tool for directing marketing operations. It would be the point of departure, he was certain, for rectifying the distribution of cooperative advertising dollars among manufacturers' agents' market areas; for developing and implementing special sales promotional events; and for redesigning the kind and distribution of collateral materials provided by Cacaphony. Schneider knew that whatever reforms he developed for the marketing of MAXIHUE would have a profound effect on the marketing programs for the other Cacaphony lines, but he decided to design a complete MAXIHUE program and then propose that the other product managers consider its implications for their own lines rather than attempt to solve all the marketing problems for all of the Cacaphony product lines at once.

Schneider called upon the Cacaphony Sound market analysis section to develop the necessary index for MAXIHUE sales potential. Alice McNair Whiteson was again assigned to the MAXIHUE problem. Ms. Whiteson had risen to the post of associate manager of the Cacaphony Sound market analysis department since her original analyses of the portable color television set market in 1969. She had, in the intervening years, become the market analysis department's principal sales analyst. She had had extensive experience with the development of sales potential indices in her work with a leading management consultant firm prior to joining Cacaphony in 1968. And so, although she had not previously developed sales potentials for Cacaphony products, she had done a lot of sales analysis in the consumer electronic field and she had experience in developing sales potentials in other product categories.

She recognized indices of sales potential as a valuable sales and advertising-management tool, even though they had many shortcomings. The general notion underlying the index of sales potential was that many market phenomena either caused or were associated with achieved sales levels in a particular product group. If those market phenomena most closely associated with the sales of a product could be identified, measured, and combined on a market-by-market basis, the resulting index could be used to direct marketing policy in support of the most productive markets and toward the exploitation of the under-developed markets.

Ms. Whiteson had found, however, that this general formulation of the development and use of market potential could not always be directly applied, without difficulties, to a particular case. The major problems that she generally encountered were summarized in a memorandum (from Ms. Whiteson to Schneider) discussing how an index of sales potential for MAXIHUE portable color TV sets might be developed.

Cacaphony Sound Communication

TO: August N. Schneider
FROM: Alice McNair Whiteson
SUBJECT: Developing an Index of Sales Potential for MAXIHUE

The purpose of this memorandum is to identify the problems associated with the development of indices of sales potential and to suggest how they may be handled in the MAXIHUE case.

1. We have found it difficult to identify all the market factors that cause or are associated with achieved brand sales. For example, we believe that it could be argued that the sales of substitutable product categories should be included in an index of sales potential. Thus, in constructing an index of sales potential for a portable color television set brand such as MAXIHUE, we might consider the inclusion of at least the following sales series because they are substitutable, in one way or another, for portable color television set sales: movie box office receipts; professional and amateur athletic receipts; athletic product sales; indoor and outdoor game sales; book and periodical sales; consumer electronic equipment sales; console television set sales; black-and-white television set sales; and so on.

Future sales of portable color television sets might derive, at least in some degree, from each of these sources, and thus all of them together should indicate at least a good part of the "potential" for portable color television sets sales. (In saying "all of them together," we do not necessarily mean that each should receive equal weight: the question of proper weighting is discussed below.)

But how far should one go? In a broad sense all forms of entertainment expenditures can be included in the potential from which portable color TV set sales might ultimately derive. Certainly, any specific form of entertainment item is substitutable for a portable color TV set, and thus it might be included in the measure of potential. But one must be reasonable: it is not realistic to predict a world in which all entertainment will derive from portable color TV sets. So all forms of entertainment do not, in any practical sense, constitute the "potential" for portable color TV sets.

The rule of thumb that we have developed is to consider for inclusion in our ideal potential measurement any product category that is directly substitutable for the category for which we are developing an index of potential. In this case we would conclude that the potential for portable color TV sets is the total television set market. Thus we are saying, in effect, that in the best of all possible portable color TV set worlds, no TV set would be sold except a portable color TV set.

Certainly, it is difficult to conceive of marketing means that would make this come true literally, but we can say that portable color TV set development will depend directly upon the total volume of portable color, black-and-white, and color console set sales. To put it in a different way, we believe that it is reasonable to assert that a marketing area in which a great many television sets are now sold on a per-capita basis must hold greater potential for MAXIHUE than a marketing area in which relatively few total TV sets are now sold per capita.

It might be argued that there is a relatively inflexible maximum number of sets that can be sold in any given market and that market-to-market variations in set sales simply reflect this maximum. This view would suggest that the notion of potential for growth in the TV set market is unrealistic: that is, once television set sales penetration has achieved maturity, market-by-market variations are relatively fixed, reflecting a stable equilibrium rather than a potential for growth.

There are, in fact, two basic limiting forces in the sale of television sets. The first of these is the average number of rooms per home. Presumably the number of television sets in use will never exceed the total number of rooms in a home, but, at least potentially, the usage of television sets is expandable up to the total number of rooms in the home. The second fact that limits the volume of television sets sold is the rate at which they become obsolescent. The more rapidly a television set wears out, or is replaced, the greater the sales volume for the industry.

The potential for increased sales in a market area is, therefore, regulated not only by the number of homes but also by the number of sets per home and the rapidity with which their owners consider them to have become obsolescent. It is the combination of these factors that is reflected in sales levels in individual markets and in market-to-market variations in these levels.

Therefore, we conclude that total TV set sales should be the first element in an index of potential for portable color TV sets.

2. A second kind of factor that we like to include in indices of sales potential is those standard economic series that seem causally related to sales in the product class we are studying. Market-to-market variations in the incidence of working women are, for example, highly correlated with the consumption of cosmetics, and if we were to build an index of potential for cosmetic consumption, we would try to include a measurement of the incidence of working women in the index of cosmetic sales potential for each market area.

As far as television set sales are concerned, the number of households in a market area is clearly and directly related to the number of television sets sold. The more households there are, the greater the potential for television set sales. One way to take this factor into account is simply to add a household series to the list of other factors to be included. Another and more popular method is to convert all of the other indices under consideration to a per-household basis so that the resulting data are directly comparable and combinable, as well as reflective of household population potential.

Perhaps income might also be used as a factor in the index of potential for portable color television set sales. There is some evidence that when color television was first introduced, the purchase of the product was associated with income. I am inclined to think however, that in the currently developed market state variations in portable color television set sales are not generally correlated with variations in income. Certainly the demographic data in our files reflect no such direct relationship (Exhibit 4–5). It is probably true that the existence of discretionary household income is a generally necessary condition for the purchase of a portable color television set, but not a sufficient condition. If this is so, income is causal of portable color television set sales, but wide variations in discretionary income would have no necessary relation to fluctuations in portable color television set sales. Perhaps it would be more reasonable to assume that whatever specific income influences are at work are most clearly reflected by the relative current penetration of black-and-white and color television sets in a market and that these series indicate most clearly the predisposition as well as the means to buy portable color television sets. We would therefore not recommend the inclusion of income in our index.

Finally, we might consider the use of some index of retail activity on a market-by-market basis. The thought underlying such an inclusion would be that some market areas generate a higher level of retail activity per household than others and that the potential for the sale of color television sets would naturally be higher in such markets than in others. There are at least three reasons why retail activity might vary from market area to market area.

a. First of all, there are market-by-market variations in income. As we have just discussed, variations in household discretionary income are probably not directly related to variations in the sales of portable color television sets, but variations in the overall level of income from market to market may be important. Areas of low economic development (Appalachia) are, for example, much less likely to generate portable color TV set sales than are areas with higher economic development (southeastern New England). These kinds of variations are reflected in differences in the levels of television set penetration as pointed out above, and there would be no reason to include an index of retail activity if it reflected only area-to-area variations in income level.

b. The second reason for area-to-area variations in retail activity is the tendency for retail establishments to cluster in population centers. This is particularly true of those kinds of retail establishments that primarily sell consumer durables like automobiles, furniture, and electronic equipment. Unlike consumer package goods, it is usually necessary or desirable for the potential purchaser of a television set to have to travel some distance on one or more occasions to find retail establishments that offer a selection of merchandise. The fact that such retail establishments tend to cluster in downtown urban shopping areas and suburban shopping centers leads to variations in market-to-market retail activity.

c. The final reason for variations in retail activity from market to market has to do with market or regional variations in life style. As a generality, the pattern of retail sales is different in California, for example, than in Vermont. Part of this difference is undoubtedly due to variations in income and to the variations in urban concentration of retail outlets, but some of it is also due to climate-based differences in life styles as, for example, between an area much dominated by coast and of relatively mild climate and an area that is landlocked and intemperate of climate. The people in Vermont buy different things in different quantity than people in California, and this difference in the way discretionary income is spent affects the retail activity in the two states.

3. An interesting question now arises about what index of retail activity might be used in our index. One possibility is to use total retail sales. Another possibility is to use the total number of retail establishments that might be expected to handle television sets. A third alternative is to use a combination of indices reflecting consumer durable goods sales such as sales in department stores, automotive dealers and furniture stores and household appliance stores. Finally, one might use a single index that could be expected to reflect television set sales more directly, like sales of household appliances, regardless of outlet type.

The question of which of these indices to use brings us to the third issue in constructing indices of sales potential. How does one decide what series or market estimate to use?

Ultimately, the analyst must depend upon his own judgment in selecting the factors in the index. When he has finished the job, he will have estimates by market areas that represent his best approximation of the value that he does not know: the potential for a product category in individual markets—portable color television sets in this case. The important point is that there is no independent estimate of this series of values and no mathematical or analytical means of constructing such a series independently of logic and judgment. So the basic process of selecting elements for an index must be judgmental: What elements seem to be most logically related to the end product desired? One way to aid judgment is to compute the simple correlation coefficients for pairs of factors that judgment suggests are related to the desired index of potential. It is possible, for example, to appraise the relevance of the four proposed indices of retail activity to our index through the method of correlation.

Exhibit 4–11 shows the simple linear correlation coefficients for two kinds of television set sales statistics and each of four retail sales series. Thus estimated total sales of portable color TV sets in each of Cacaphony Sound's thirty-nine manufacturers' agents' market areas were correlated with 1972 estimates of total retail sales, total retail outlets, retail sales in stores selling consumer durable goods, and retail sales of appliance merchandise lines, without regard to retail outlet type. The process is repeated for the estimated total sales of television sets and the four retail sales estimates in each market area.

The correlation coefficients in Exhibit 4–11 show an interesting pattern. First, as was certainly expected, it is clear that television set sales and retail activity are positively correlated, and at relatively high levels. Television set sales and the number of retail outlets are positively correlated too but at much lower levels than for the retail sales series. Thus the first conclusion that is drawn from the analysis is that retail store count can be dropped from consideration, accounting as it does for a relatively small proportion of the variation in portable color or total television set sales ($r^2 = 10\%$ and 13%, respectively).

Total television set sales show a generally higher correlation with the retail sales series than do portable color TV set sales. Yet when the most selective of the retail sales series—retail sales of appliance merchandise lines—is used as the independent variable, the correlation coefficients for total and portable color sales are virtually identical. These data suggest, but do not prove, that portable color TV set sales are more selective and are related to more specialized retail sales patterns.

EXHIBIT 4-11
**Specimen Data: Simple Linear Correlation Coefficients, Selected 1972
Television Set Estimates* and Proposed Indices of Retail Activity for
Thirty-nine Cacaphony Sound Manufacturers' Agents' Market Areas**

	DEPENDENT VARIABLES (Y)	
INDEPENDENT VARIABLES (X)	TOTAL PORTABLE COLOR TV SET SALES*	TOTAL TELEVISION SET SALES*
Total retail sales†	.68	.85
Retail sales in stores selling consumer durable goods‡	.75	.86
Retail sales in appliance merchandise lines§	.82	.81
Total retail outlets**	.31	.36

* The Cacaphony Market Analysis Section's market sales estimates are developed from a variety of sources but depend most importantly on the monthly competitive sales appraisals of Cacaphony television manufacturers' agents and trade association estimates.
† As available from the "1973 Survey of Buying Power," *Sales Management*, July 23, 1973.
‡ As available from the "1973 Survey of Buying Power," *Sales Management*, July 23, 1973, including the following series: furniture–household appliance store sales, department store sales; automotive dealer and store sales.
§ As available from the "1973 Survey of Buying Power," *Sales Management*, July 23, 1973: Major appliance merchandise line sales (without regard to retail outlet type).
** Compiled from the "1967 Census of Manufacturers" and updated by the Cacaphony Market Analysis Section.

An easy decision to make, on the basis of Exhibit 4–11, is to use the retail sales of appliance merchandise lines series to represent retail activity. One could argue that this index produces the highest correlation coefficient for total TV set sales. The retail appliance merchandise line series is apparently the most sophisticated of the series, too: it is after all, the most selective index and thus, perhaps, more closely aligned, theoretically, with the inherent characteristics of the demand for television sets in general, and for color TV sets as a kind of speciality subdivision of this market.

But on the basis of experience we would be inclined to stay with the series reflecting retail sales in stores selling consumer durables. This consumer durable series produces a somewhat higher correlation with total television set sales than does the appliance merchandise line series. And the *potential* for portable color TV set sales must lie at least as importantly with current TV set owners as with current portable color TV set owners. The whole object of this exercise is to develop a series that will indicate the potential sales of portable color TV sets; if the current sales of portable color TV sets would suffice for this purpose there would be no need to introduce additional variables into the analysis. Because we have decided to broaden our perspective in this way, it seems proper, on the basis of the correlation analysis and of judgment, to use the retail sales in stores selling consumer durable goods in our index construction. In addition, the retail sales in stores selling consumer goods durable series seems to be more consistent with the overall goal of reflecting retail activity in its relation to population, income, and life styles than do other retail sales series. This last point is more a matter of analytic taste

EXHIBIT 4-12
Specimen Data: Selected Sales and Population Statistics by Cacaphony Sound Manufacturers' Agents' Market Areas

SALES AREA	1971 POPULATION ESTIMATES* (000 OMITTED)	1972 TOTAL TV $ SET SALES† (000 OMITTED)	1972 $ RETAIL SALES IN CONSUMER DURABLES‡ (000 OMITTED)	1972 CACAPHONY SOUND $ PRODUCT SALES§ (000 OMITTED)
1. Portland/Augusta	310.9	26,326	52,160	12,743.2
2. Burlington	609.3	62,398	124,270	14,866.3
3. Boston	2,455.4	181,417	461,120	22,924.2
4. Hartford	1,489.7	202,015	502,170	26,754.0
5. Albany	794.1	78,475	156,270	16,752.3
6. Yonkers	2,355.7	137,859	374,460	20,222.8
7. Long Island	3,408.5	272,351	692,130	33,725.1
8. Brooklyn	930.4	136,753	272,260	22,724.3
9. Newark	2,968.1	98,571	296,230	18,642.1
10. Buffalo	2,649.3	136,753	373,210	20,794.3
11. Cleveland	3,246.7	237,233	572,210	27,783.6
12. Cincinnati	3,331.2	247,231	582,130	31,722.7
13. Philadelphia	3,586.8	321,390	699,920	35,876.9
14. Charlotte	2,601.6	59,057	224,160	13,722.3
15. Atlanta	3,163.6	184,582	472,210	22,325.1
16. Jacksonville	3,418.1	83,298	269,920	16,322.1
17. New Orleans	1,935.8	86,187	272,210	17,511.8
18. Nashville	2,018.3	42,252	84,120	13,007.9
19. Detroit	2,135.5	236,429	572,230	26,521.3
20. St. Louis	2,060.7	180,437	351,160	22,333.3

21. Chicago	2,391.1	198,976	521,070	29,765.2
22. Milwaukee	956.1	93,773	192,760	18,722.6
23. St. Paul	1,541.9	119,697	348,920	20,523.7
24. Bismarck	441.3	49,311	98,260	16,922.3
25. Omaha	858.0	87,870	174,920	15,986.3
26. Oklahoma City	841.6	93,497	186,630	18,722.9
27. Dallas	811.9	151,047	292,260	21,062.1
28. San Antonio	1,585.7	140,220	379,650	22,725.9
29. Phoenix	918.3	133,785	306,610	20,621.3
30. Denver	932.4	95,004	189,620	18,724.1
31. Salt Lake City	1,440.6	130,825	385,420	22,524.3
32. Seattle	876.4	88,824	176,960	18,721.3
33. Portland	401.2	53,355	106,230	13,249.6
34. Sacramento	1,030.7	133,337	265,490	21,472.8
35. Fresno	811.9	113,693	232,450	20,511.7
36. Pasadena	810.2	96,536	197,230	16,542.9
37. Los Angeles	2,163.6	272,326	692,240	37,246.3
38. Riverside	431.1	71,416	142,630	20,523.4
39. Hawaii/Alaska	167.6	15,600	31,020	4,722.6
TOTAL	64,881.3	5,150,166	12,324,920	816,566.9

* As available from the "1973 Survey of Buying Power," *Sales Management*, July, 23, 1973.
† As available from the "1973 Survey of Buying Power," *Sales Management*, July, 23, 1973, including the following series: furniture–household appliance store sales, department store sales, automotive dealer and store sales.
‡ Compiled from a variety of trade publications and sources.
§ Cacaphony Sound Market Analysis Section.

EXHIBIT 4-13

Specimen Data: Construction of Index of Sales Potential for Portable Color TV Sets in Cacaphony Sound Manufacturers' Agents' Market Areas

SALES AREA	(1) PERCENT U.S. HOUSEHOLD POPULATION %	CUM. %	(2) TV SET SALES PER HOUSEHOLD (US = 100)	(3) SALES IN STORES SELLING CONSUMER DURABLES PER HOUSEHOLD (US = 100)	(4) CACAPHONY SOUND PRODUCT SALES PER HOUSEHOLD (US = 100)	(5) PORTABLE COLOR TV SALES POTENTIAL INDEX
1. Portland/Augusta	0.48		106	88	326	173
2. Burlington	0.94	1.42	129	107	194	143
3. Boston	3.78	5.20	93	99	74	89
4. Hartford	2.30	7.50	170	177	143	163
5. Albany	1.22	8.72	—	104	168	132
6. Yonkers	3.63	12.35	74	84	68	75
7. Long Island	5.25	17.60	100	107	—	95
8. Brooklyn	1.43	19.03	185	154	194	178
9. Newark	4.57	23.60	42	53	50	48
10. Buffalo	4.08	27.68	65	74	62	—
11. Cleveland	5.00	32.68	92	93	69	85
12. Cincinnati	5.13	37.81	93	92	75	87
13. Philadelphia	5.53	43.34	113	103	79	98
14. Charlotte	4.01		28	45	42	38
15. Atlanta	4.88	52.23	73	79	56	69
16. Jacksonville	5.27	57.50	31	42	38	37

17. New Orleans	2.98	60.48	56	74	72	67
18. Nashville	3.11	63.59	26	—	51	33
19. Detroit	3.29	66.88	139	142	99	127
20. St. Louis	3.18	70.06	110	90	86	95
21. Chicago	3.69	73.75	104	115	99	106
22. Milwaukee	1.47	75.22	123	106	155	128
23. St. Paul	2.38	77.60	97	119	106	107
24. Bismarck	0.68	78.28	140	117	304	—
25. Omaha	1.32	79.60	129	107	148	128
26. Oklahoma City	1.30	80.90	139	117	176	144
27. Dallas	1.25	82.15	234	189	206	210
28. San Antonio	2.44	84.59	111	126	114	117
29. Phoenix	1.42	86.01	184	176	179	180
30. Denver	1.44	87.45	—	107	160	132
31. Salt Lake City	2.22	89.67	114	140	124	126
32. Seattle	1.35	91.02	127	106	170	134
33. Portland	0.62	91.64	168	139	262	190
34. Sacramento	1.59	93.23	163	136	165	156
35. Fresno	1.25	94.48	176	151	201	171
36. Pasadena	1.25	95.73	150	128	162	147
37. Los Angeles	3.33	99.06	158	168	137	154
38. Riverside	0.66	99.72	208	—	378	253
39. Hawaii/Alaska	0.26	99.98	117	97	224	146
TOTAL	99.98		100	100	100	

SOURCE: Computations based on Exhibit 4-12.

than either judgment or external evidence, but analytic taste is important in sales analysis too.

4. There is only one other factor that we would suggest be added to the index of potential, and this is current Cacaphony Sound sales in each of the manufacturer's agents' market areas. At first blush, this factor may strike you as totally unrelated to the problem because total Cacaphony Sound sales have nothing in particular to do with the sales of any portable TV set except Cacaphony's. But Cacaphony Sound sales by market area do reflect directly the overall success of our company and the general level of competence exhibited by the individual manufacturers' agents. And, we submit, the potential for any portable color TV set line marketed by Cacaphony Sound must reflect our overall company success as a marketer from geographic area to geographic area as this will, in turn, reflect the gross field sales pressure that is available to any company product in a particular marketing area.

5. The raw values for the three sales series (total TV set sales, retail sales in stores selling consumer durable goods, and Cacaphony Sound product sales) and the household totals for each Cacaphony Sound manufacturers' agents' market area are shown in Exhibit 4–12. The computational procedure is to convert each of the raw sales series into per-household figures by dividing each market area statistic by the appropriate market-area household-population statistic. This procedure produces a group of three sales-per-household statistics for each Cacaphony Sound market area: total TV set sales per household, retail sales in stores selling consumer durables per household, and Cacaphony Sound sales per household. The next step is to convert these three per-household sales statistics into index numbers by relating each market-area per-household value to the overall per-household value in the total United States. These final, converted, figures are shown in columns 2, 3, and 4 of Exhibit 4–13. For example, the retail sales in stores selling consumer durable goods per household in the Cacaphony Sound Portland/Augusta (Maine) area was $167.77 in 1972 and the average per-household retail sales in stores selling consumer durables in the total United States was $190.02. The index for the Portland/Augusta area is accordingly 88, with the total U.S. value taken as 100.

Once these index values have been computed, it remains to combine the individual indices into a final overall index of potential for portable color TV set sales. The simplest and most direct procedure is to average the three index numbers. We always recommend this approach unless a very strong case can be made in logic, or from other data, for assigning unequal weights to the individual indices. (For example, suppose that in our earlier discussion we had concluded that it was desirable to include movie box office receipts in the index on the assumption that movie going is basically the opposite of TV viewing and that high levels of movie going inhibit TV viewing and TV set sales and vice versa. And, suppose that it is known that the total current dollar sales of TV sets are only one third as great as total dollar movie box office receipts. Certainly, in such a situation it might be argued that movie box office receipts should receive a different weight in the final index than TV set sales. But what weight? Should movie box office receipts go into the index in exact proportion to the dollars they represent, that is, three times TV set sales? Or should it be argued that past TV set sales are a much more important determinant of the potential for future TV set sales than past movie box office receipts? If this second assumption is accepted, then one would assign a lesser weight to movie box office receipts—say, one third—than to television set sales. The exact weight assigned is in any event a matter of judgment; there is no divine law that gives direction in such circumstances. Fortunately, movie box office receipts were not deemed important enough to include in the index and the judgment concerning their appropriate weight need not be made.)

In any event, we can see no reason to recommend an elaborate weighting system in this case. We believe that the individual indices should be directly combined into the final index of potential.

If you agree with this analysis, and procedure, we will proceed with the computation of the final index.

An index of sales potential for portable color TV sets based on this procedure for Cacaphony Sounds' thirty-nine manufacturers' agents' marketing areas is presented in Exhibit 4–13, based on data presented in Exhibit 4–12.

Questions for Case 4

1. Do you agree with the logic of this method of index development? Do you accept the recommendation of the market analysis division that the index of potential for portable color TV sets be based on a combination of data for households: total TV sets sales, retail sales of consumer durable goods, and Cacaphony Sound product sales? If your answer is yes, tell why. If your answer if no, tell why not.

2. There are several holes or blanks in Exhibit 4–13. Make the appropriate computations to fill in these blanks.

3. How would you use the finished index of sales potential in allocating trade promotion expenditures among the Cacaphony Sound manufacturers' agents' market areas? Assume that it is your intention to concentrate trade promotional activities in that half of the total manufacturers' agents' market areas that have the highest potential for portable color TV set sales.

   a. What manufacturers' agents' market areas constitute the high-potential half of households?

   b. Suppose you wished to identify three very-high-potential areas and three very-low-potential areas in order to validate by a market test the notion that trade promotional expenditures produce greater results in high-potential areas than in low-potential areas. Which areas would you use for the test?

4. Assume a consumer advertising budget for Cacaphony Sound MAXIHUE portable color TV sets of $4.5 million. What principle should be used to allocate this budget among the various manufacturers' agents' market areas if

   a. $2 million were set aside for network television.

   b. The remainder is to be used to buy cooperative newspaper advertising in markets of high potential (that is, markets with potential in excess of 100). Assume that each market area receives its proportionate share (population basis) of the total network budget and compute a cooperative newspaper advertising budget for the Dallas, Albany, Detroit, and Philadelphia sales areas. Further, assume that no attempt is made within the high-potential sales areas to further vary cooperative advertising allocations according to individual market sales potential.

5. Is it realistic to assume that Cacaphony could allocate cooperative advertising funds *only* to markets of the highest potential (as in question 4)? Discuss the pros and cons of such a change in dealer promotional support. If you were a manufacturers' agent in an area where such support was withdrawn, what would your attitude be likely to be? If you believe such withdrawal of support to be realistic, tell why. If you believe such withdrawal of support to be unrealistic, describe two kinds of promotional programs that might be subject to such changes in factory policy.

6. Why is the use of an index of potential superior to judgment in the allocating of sales promotional or advertising expenditure budgets? (If you believe it to be inferior to judgment, state your reasons.)

7. To what uses other than those suggested in the case could Schneider put this index of potential for portable color TV set sales? Give at least two additional uses of the index.

PART TWO

Formulating
Marketing Strategy

CASE 5

Making Marketing Decisions

The Allgood Drug Company Develops a New Athlete's Foot Remedy

THE ALLGOOD DRUG COMPANY is a medium-sized manufacturer of staple and branded proprietary drug products. Allgood is also moderately prominent in the manufacture and marketing of cosmetic products through its wholly owned subsidiary, Effluvia House.

Allgood was established in 1903. In its early history it was especially known as a supplier of a gradually extending line of high-quality "wet" and "dry" generic drug items. Allgood manufactured and marketed products like boric acid, epsom salts, potassium permanganate, mineral oil, bicarbonate of soda, witch hazel, aspirin, calomine lotion, and so on. The composition of all these products was well known (most were described in the U.S. Pharmacopoeia) and the individual pharmacist was fully capable of compounding and/or packaging them himself.

The basis of the Allgood business was that it offered the individual druggist a line of "wets" and "drys" in consistent package designs, with assured high purity and quality. In addition, Allgood offered these items to the druggist in small quantities (as few as one-twelfth dozen) at a price lower than it would cost the druggist to produce them himself. Allgood could offer lower prices because of its ability to purchase in bulk. Thus the Allgood business was founded on lower prices and more convenience for the druggist, rather than on exclusive branded proprietary drug items.

During the early years, the Allgood Drug Company expanded in three ways: first, by developing exclusive selling agreements with an increasing number of druggists in the existing area of distribution; second, by expanding the distribution area; and third, by extending the number of products offered in the line.

By the early 1920's, the Allgood distribution area had been expanded throughout the eastern United States. In addition, Allgood had developed intensive coverage of druggists throughout the area in which the products were distributed. Allgood executives estimated that the line was represented on an exclusive basis in about one third of the drugstores east of the Mississippi and that these drugstores accounted for about 45 per cent of all drugstore volume in that geographic area.

By 1926 the Allgood executive group was faced with a major question of how to continue to increase sales volume. They generally agreed that territorial expansion west of the Mississippi would be ill advised. The population was too sparse and centers of population too widely separated for Allgood to expand profitably the kind of selling and distribution system that had been developed in the eastern part of the country.

In addition, the executives agreed that it would be very difficult for Allgood to increase its penetration of drugstores in the current area of distribution to any important degree. Strong competition for the Allgood line had developed over the years, and two competitive lines, Surepure and Drugall, now dominated those outlets in the eastern states in which Allgood did not enjoy a franchise. The Allgood sales manager was optimistic that his men could convert important fractions of the Surepure and Drugall exclusive franchises to Allgood. Realistically, however, the Allgood executive group was sure that such competitive conversions would be minimal and that the net gain to Allgood, after corresponding competitive losses to Surepure and Drugall, would be small.

Finally, it was clear that Allgood had gone about as far as possible in expanding its line of generic wets and drys. Allgood manufactured 138 separate items in 1926. Allgood salesmen had received only five isolated requests for items not in the Allgood line in the last six months of 1926.

Nevertheless, the Allgood Drug Company was accustomed to annual volume and profit increases averaging about 8 per cent. If the major historic sources of these increases appeared to be drying up, it was up to the management team to find new sources of additional business. Allgood executives toyed with this problem from mid-1926 through early 1927, but no new policy was developed. The operating results of the company for 1926, released on January 18, 1927, were especially disturbing. Sales were up only 2 per cent and profits were down a full 18 per cent. The profit decrease was largely due to higher costs of selling to Allgood drug outlets. These higher selling costs reflected intensified competitive pressure from Drugall and especially from Surepure. Early in 1926 Surepure salesmen started to offer ninety-day credit terms (instead of the thirty-day standard in the industry) and had lowered their minimum acceptable order from $7.50 wholesale to $5.50 wholesale. By the end of 1926, Allgood and Drugall had been forced to meet these competitive moves. Selling costs were accordingly increased, and profits declined.

The 1926 financial statement (Allgood did not begin the practice of quarterly financial reporting until 1947) forced the Allgood management to come to grips with the problem of finding profitable extra volume. The decision was finally made in June 1927 to begin the development of a small line of branded proprietary items with unique formulations. It was decided that each proposed new item must meet four criteria before it could be considered for inclusion in the new Allgood branded proprietary line.

1. First, the product must require no expansion of existing Allgood manufacturing facilities. All new product candidates must be produced in the Allgood plant without new capital plant expenditures.
2. Each new product must represent a new and unique formulation. Allgood would manufacture no products that were merely copies of products already on the market.
3. Each new product must have demonstrated efficacy; it must noticeably relieve pain, discomfort, or some minor illness and do so without side effects or other harm to the user.
4. Each new product must be safe for general, nonprescription usage.

This policy marked a milestone for the Allgood Company. Immediately upon its adoption a new products development laboratory was established at the Allgood plant in Dover, Delaware, and a small but exceptionally promising trickle of new products began to come before the Allgood management group for review. The final decision as to whether a new product would be introduced by Allgood was made by a new products review committee consisting of the president, the executive vice-president, the medical director, the director of new product development, and the director of chemical research.

Between 1927 and 1961, Allgood introduced seventeen new products. Of these, six were unqualified successes, six were not produced in 1961, and five were continued in the line as profitable low-volume items. The six successful products and their year of introduction were Pain-out Analgesic Compound (1928), Mono-lax Laxative Tablets (1931), Cherry Lime Cough Compound with Codeine (1937), Gong-Gong Hangover Remedy (1941), Histofull Cold Tablets (1952), and Super Histofull Cold Capsules (1960). Each of these products had been supported by a major advertising budget from the time of its introduction. The aggregate Allgood annual advertising budget in support of these products in 1960 totaled $32 million.

The history of Allgood sales and profits in the period 1925 through 1960 is shown in Exhibit 5–1. As the exhibit suggests, the 1927 decision to begin marketing branded proprietaries was a sound one. The decision anticipated a long-term decline in the wet and dry business, as these historically important remedies were gradually replaced with branded items specifically compounded to cure individual complaints. It is clear from Exhibit 5–1 that Allgood would probably have entered a long-term decline had the decision to manufacture branded proprietaries not been made.

During the period of vigorous growth based upon new proprietary product introductions, from 1928 through 1960, Allgood had followed a relatively informal new product development procedure. The areas in which new product development work was undertaken were decided by C. D. "Cap" Hunterdon, the director of new product development. He

EXHIBIT 5–1

Specimen Data: Sales and Net Profits Before Taxes—The Allgood Drug Company,* 1925–1960 ($ millions)

	1925	1930	1935	1940	1950†	1955	1960
Wets and drys	28.0	31.4	26.9	20.9	13.4	12.0	10.7
Pain-out Analgesic Compound		16.2	18.1	42.5	75.8	70.7	68.6
Mono-lax Laxative Tablets			32.8	30.6	26.6	20.1	18.1
Cherry Lime Cough Compound				14.7	22.2	26.4	28.2
Gong-Gong Hangover Remedy					17.1	24.3	32.4
Histofull Cold Tablets and Super Histofull Cold Capsules						42.8	87.7
All other branded items		6.7	12.4	13.3	12.3	18.4	10.6
Total sales	28.0	54.3	90.2	122.0	167.4	214.7	256.3
Net profits before taxes	6.2	10.1	17.4	22.6	35.3	38.4	47.6

* Not including subsidiary companies.
† 1945 is omitted because of distortion caused by World War II.

reported directly to the president of Allgood, and the ultimate measure of his success lay in the number and quality of new products that he and his new product development group perfected and presented to the new products review committee for approval to market.

On the record, Cap Hunterdon's activities had been immensely successfull during the thirty-five years following his appointment in 1928. A man of quiet, intense intelligence, Hunterdon's approach to the selection of fields or areas of development had been characteristically simple and direct. "Just picked an ailment that everybody has and made a good product that was hard to copy," said Hunterdon when asked in 1933 how he happened to develop Pain-out Analgesic Compound. And this philosophy led him successfully to the development of Mono-lax Laxative Tablets, Cherry Lime Cough Compound, Gong-Gong Hangover Remedy, and the Histofull Cold remedies. But if the Cap Hunterdon philosophy had been simple and to the point, he had exploited it with genius: no other drug company could match the Allgood record of successful new product development in the three decades following 1928.

In 1963, Hunterdon celebrated his sixty-fifth birthday, and reached the mandatory retirement age for Allgood employees. His apparent successor was Frederick Mount, Hunterdon's assistant for eighteen years. During his association with Hunterdon, Mount had come to respect and love the brilliant man who had done so much for Allgood Drug Company. As much as possible, Mount patterned his way of thinking and working after Hunterdon's, with the thought that he would eventually succeed him. But Mount was no Hunterdon and Hunterdon knew it.

Mount was dependable and basic in his approach to pharmacology but his thinking was systematic to a fault. In his attempt to emulate Hunterdon, Mount paid too much attention to his day-to-day ways of working and too little attention to the ways in which Hunterdon actually achieved his final goals. If Hunterdon was systematic and logical in his work habits, it was more to give an example of normality in his office-laboratory than to make the final leap to a new product idea. What Mount did not distinguish were the periods of extreme and absorbing concentration that overwhelmed Hunterdon when he was close to a breakthrough. For days and even weeks Hunterdon would become oblivious to the outside world, literally concentrating all of his intellectual and emotional resources on the single goal. In a sense, it could be said that Hunterdon forced solutions to outstanding problems out of thin air. He refused to relent after he sensed that there was or could be a way to a breakthrough on a new product formulation. His solutions seemed, more often than not, to be the product of an overwhelming willpower concentrated in an imaginative personality: in almost every case, the solutions were simply beyond the creative power of a trained pharmacologist merely playing out his daily destiny. But Mount missed all this. He believed that if he came to the office every day and systematically applied a reasonably well-rounded knowledge of pharmacology to a reasonably clearly stated problem it would in due course be solved. He believed this because that is the way it *seemed* to work for Hunterdon, if one did not understand the basic difference between perseverance and genius.

As Hunterdon's retirement approached, it did not even occur to him to consider Mount as a potential successor. Mount did what he was told and did it well, but he did nothing more. Hunterdon despised him for his lack of imagination and was astonished by his inability to become emotionally involved in the significant opportunities that surrounded him. If Hunterdon erred, it was because he made no attempt to find a better man than Mount to succeed him and made no effort to convey to Mount the degree to which he was incapable of succeeding him.

Hunterdon's evaluation of Fred Mount was shared by J. C. McPhee, president of Allgood. It was McPhee's opinion that Hunterdon might well be irreplaceable—that in his experience and special genius Hunterdon was virtually unique. McPhee asked Hunterdon to express his own thoughts on the future of new product development for Allgood. He wanted to know specifically whether Hunterdon believed that Allgood could find a qualified successor, or whether Hunterdon believed that some totally new organization form for new product development was required for the years ahead.

This was a difficult request for Hunterdon. His years of success had tended to make him something of an egoist and he genuinely doubted that his special knack could be found in any other person. But even if another Hunterdon existed, he was convinced that a fundamental change in the

Allgood procedure was called for. He recognized that a successful new product was one that was totally aligned to the needs of consumers. In the old days, consumers' needs tended to be obvious to the studious observer, but this was no longer necessarily so. And as technology in the medical and pharmaceutical fields became increasingly sophisticated, the variety of possible products was immense. The question was no longer to find what efficacious products might be profitably produced but to select from the almost infinite number of such products that could be produced those few that consumers would buy.

Hunterdon was also keenly aware that even he, with his enviable record, had had only one new product success in the past eleven years (Super Histofull Cold Capsules). So he wondered whether any single person, regardless of his special skills, could hope to be successful in future conditions. All these thoughts were finally expressed in a twelve-page memorandum on the history of his own work, the future of new product development in the proprietary drug field, and the future of branded proprietary drug development within the Allgood Drug Company. This fascinating and remarkable document was well summarized by a conclusion and recommendation section, in which Hunterdon made three major points:

1. The golden days in proprietary drug development are over. Good products exist for the relief or cure of almost every common ailment. Many of the new drugs that might improve these existing products are tricky, their efficacy for minor ailments is not well known, and their day-to-day use is at least likely to cause sensitization to effect and at worst likely to be extremely dangerous to the patient. Government regulation will increasingly reflect the hazards inherent in proprietary developments based on available new drugs.

2. The consumer is king. We must listen to him with much greater attention than we have in the past. Casual observation of ourselves and our families was enough to bring us to a realization of the widespread and common consumer need for a Pain-out or a Gong-Gong. But tomorrow's new products will not cater to universal ailments, and we will have to explore new ways of familiarizing ourselves with those segments of the population that suffer from these peculiar complaints.

3. One man will never know enough to build the new products that will be successful in the 1970's and 1980's. I don't know very much pharmacology and I know less chemistry. Our successful products have been relatively unsophisticated, just as my own knowledge is uncomplicated. This will not do for the future success of Allgood new product development. I, or a man with my training, would be a liability to Allgood as director of new product development over the next twenty or thirty years.

Hunterdon went on to recommend that an office of new product exploration and formulation be substituted for his job. He recommended that a marketing man be put in charge of this new department and that he be made responsible for directing specially created teams of research specialists whose job it would be to develop products to consumer specifications. Under the Hunterdon proposal, no new product research scientist would have the responsibility for initiating new product development work. Only the consumer could initiate such work through the medium of specific marketing research results.

The function of the product development research teams (to be composed of biologists, chemists, pharmacologists, and whatever other specialists particular developmental assignments required) was simply to solve the pharmacological problems posed by consumers. There was to be no lonely genius guiding the destiny of Allgood new products. On the contrary, the distinguishing feature of the new system, as envisioned by Hunterdon, was the fact that it was a *system* designed to convert consumer desires into finished products through the use of a combination of the best brains and skills that the resources of Allgood could bring together. (Hunterdon suggested that Frederick Mount be made principal pharmacologist for the company under the new organization.)

The only executive decision required by the proposed system lay not in the technical area but in the marketing area. Before a product was put under development the director of the new product exploration and formulation office was required to decide that an adequate potential for the product existed. As a rule of thumb, Hunterdon recommended that no product be developed unless a *total* market potential of $25 million in factory sales existed for it. This meant either that the current factory sales of existing products in the field amounted to $25 million or that it was reasonable to assume that an improved product would add sufficient volume to the field to bring total factory sales above the $25 million mark. Hunterdon did not, of course, expect that new Allgood products would achieve 100 per cent of this potential, but he did expect that they would be sufficiently distinct and efficacious to achieve at least one third of this potential in a reasonably short period of time. If a potential new product could not be expected to generate at least $8 million in factory sales within a two- or three-year period after its introduction, Hunterdon did not believe that it could be a profitable addition to the Allgood line of branded proprietaries.

The Hunterdon proposals shook the Allgood Drug Company to its foundation. In the cozy comfort of miraculously expanding sales and profits, with good old Cap upstairs bringing along the new products, the management atmosphere at Allgood had become conservative. No one within the Allgood executive group, except Hunterdon himself, had been trained to seek radical solutions to difficult problems. His brilliant solutions to the complex problems of product development had created the success for Allgood that left all its executives save Hunterdon ill prepared to deal with his retirement. In the end, President McPhee accepted the proposals in their entirety. Concurrently, McPhee accepted the resignation of two

members of the existing new products review committee: Angus Hainsohn, medical director, and Charles Evans Hughes Cooker, executive
vice-president. Hainsohn and Cooker were totally opposed to the Hunterdon proposals, but they were unable to offer any realistic alternatives. It
was clear to McPhee that Hainsohn and Cooker were fine custodians of a
successful business but totally unprepared either intellectually or emotionally to help guide a business along a new path. And so in 1965 another
new day dawned for Allgood.

The new product exploration and formulation office was formed on
March 15, 1965. It was turned over to Quincy Cornbusher, a veteran
marketing man who had spent twenty years with two companies: ten with
Drugall Drug Products, as a product manager, and ten with Bancroft and
Baylest Advertising Agency in account management work on packaged
drug and food accounts. When he was hired Cornbusher was given broad
authority by President McPhee and the newly constituted Allgood
executive committee. His only mandate was to put the Hunterdon proposals to work immediately and vigorously.

Cornbusher enthusiastically accepted the Hunterdon appraisal of how
new drug products should be developed. As soon as he began work, early
in 1965, he made a resolute attempt to get to know Hunterdon and to
familiarize himself with Hunterdon's current projects. He found Hunterdon to be both remote and self-effacing. On the one hand, Hunterdon
showed no special interest in talking to Cornbusher—the fact that Cornbusher was a marketing man rather than a pharmacologist seemed to
inhibit Hunterdon. But beyond this apparent disinterest in communicating with Cornbusher, when contact was established Hunterdon tended to
play down the impact of his past contributions and to deride the importance
of his work in progress. Perhaps, thought Cornbusher, it was because
Hunterdon was self-conscious about his recent lack of productivity. Or
perhaps he felt that what he was now investigating and the methods that
he was using were so totally unrelated to the new organizational structure
that they could only hinder future progress. Finally, Cornbusher wheedled
a list of some thirty-eight product categories out of Hunterdon that the
latter admitted he had been "looking over in the past ten to fifteen
years." But Cornbusher got only a list—he received no amplification of
of any kind that would suggest Hunterdon's own appraisal of the relative
promise of the various product categories. Cornbusher asked for such an
evaluation several times and finally Hunterdon snapped grumpily, "None
of them looks particularly good to me, but you never can tell when you're
going to get the idea that will solve the whole thing and win the ball
game. But so far I don't have anything good for any of them." And with
that, the subject was closed. Cornbusher shrugged his mental shoulders
and set forth on his own to initiate the new product development program.

Cornbusher decided that the general approach to the exploration and
formulation of new drug products should involve three phases or steps:

1. In Phase I, he believed that the tools of economic and market analysis should be used to identify those markets that seemed to have a high potential for new product development. Cornbusher reasoned that the most likely way to identify the areas of high potential was to examine closely the activities of competitive firms and the success of their products in the marketplace. Cornbusher also considered the use of exploratory marketing research in this phase in order to develop general insight into human ailments and proprietary drug needs in relation to these ailments, but he rejected this consumer-oriented approach for three reasons:

   First, he believed that most of the major human needs had already been identified and exploited in one way or another in the marketplace and that exploratory marketing research would merely confirm that this was so.

   Second, he had little confidence in marketing research "fishing expeditions" with vague objectives and nonspecific orientations.

   Third, he believed that, regardless of the potential value of marketing research in this kind of activity, the short-term interests of the company would be best served by a surveillance of the marketplace through economic and market analyses. Once this approach had identified the product categories of opportunity, it would be time enough for general exploratory marketing research.

2. In Phase II, after product categories of opportunity had been identified, Cornbusher believed that marketing research should be used to explore consumer attitudes toward the existing products in the identified fields and to probe for unsatisfied consumer desires in the identified product categories as well as to identify consumer dissatisfactions, if any, with the existing products. Cornbusher believed that the marketing research task in this second phase was a twofold one: first, to develop a general qualitative understanding of these vulnerable product categories as perceived by consumers; and, second, to develop a specific, quantitative picture of consumer attitudes, product usage, and product need patterns within the product categories.

3. Finally, when a clear understanding of the consumers' desires, practices, and dissatisfactions existed for the product categories of opportunity, it was time to start Phase III. In this phase, all the new knowledge developed by marketing research was turned over to the laboratory people, formed into specialist teams as envisioned by Hunterdon, who were specifically directed to develop a new product to satisfy the currently unsatisfied consumer needs and wants identified by marketing research in Phase II.

Cornbusher's plan was to initiate a Phase I study once every eighteen months or two years and use the results of this study to set marketing research and laboratory work priorities at least until the results of the next

Phase I study were available. The first Phase I study was concluded in February 1966. The results of this economic and market analysis indicated that there was a total of six ailment categories that clearly presented a minimum of $25 million potential and in which it appeared that the available over-the-counter remedies were vulnerable because they did not offer completely satisfactory relief. The six ailments were athlete's foot, sunburn, poison ivy infection, eye strain from distorted sunglasses, hemorrhoids, and bug bites. (Each of these six categories had appeared on the list turned over to Cornbusher by Cap Hunterdon.)

In the meantime, as the Phase I study was under way, Cornbusher negotiated an unusual long-term contractual arrangement with a leading marketing research firm, Fryberger, Kahn, and Krane Associates, Inc. The essence of this arrangement was that the Allgood Drug Company was to have at least one hundred days of Allen Krane's professional time applied against its problems each year. In addition, the agreement specified that two market research teams consisting of a project director, an assistant project director, a psychologist, and a statistician were to be set up by Fryberger, Kahn, and Krane to work exclusively on Allgood projects. The negotiated fee for professional marketing research time under this arrangement was $250,000 per year, Out-of-pocket costs for specific projects were negotiated as the individual projects were approved.

The first area into which Fryberger, Kahn, and Krane was asked by Cornbusher to launch an exploration was the market for athlete's foot remedies. The assignment was made in March 1966. The agreement specified that when a product category was turned over to Fryberger, Kahn, and Krane for exploration, the work would be carried out in two steps. The first step involved an exploratory study based on depth inter-views with seventy-five middle-majority users of products designed to produce relief or cure of the particular ailment under study. Next, with the results of this exploratory research in hand, a major attitude and usage study (Phase II) covering the product category and reflecting the major hypotheses developed from the exploratory depth interviews would be undertaken.

This attitude and usage study was to be used to help make a basic decision about whether or not Allgood would attempt to develop a product superior to those currently available for the treatment of the ailment. This decision basically depended upon two conditions: (1) that a broad potential existed for the new product (potential broad enough to generate product category sales of at least $25 million); and (2) that existing products did not satisfy consumer demand.

In principle, the first of these conditions was satisfied by the Phase I study, and the second condition was determined by the attitude and usage study. Cornbusher recognized, however, that it was possible that the results of the attitude and usage study might contradict the results of the Phase I study. If such a case were to arise, Cornbusher was inclined to accept the evidence of the attitude and usage study in preference to the Phase I study.

After the attitude and usage study was completed, and if it led to a decision to start product development work, subsequent marketing research was undertaken by Fryberger, Kahn, and Krane to test consumer reaction to alternative new product formulations, new product names, and new product package designs.

The depth interview exploration of the athlete's foot remedy market was begun in April 1966. Twenty-five depth interviews were made with athlete's foot sufferers in each of three markets (New York, Chicago, and San Francisco). In each of these markets about half of the twenty-five interviews were conducted with males and half with females, and half were conducted with individuals over thirty-five and half with individuals thirty-four years of age or younger.

These are the results of the depth interview research as summarized in a report written by Ludmilla Oppenheimer, the chief clinical psychologist of Fryberger, Kahn, and Krane, in July 1966:

---

1. Athlete's foot is a minor problem to people who suffer from it. When they do not have it they forget it completely, and when they do have the ailment they tend to view it stoically and with a certain resignation. They feel that there are minor steps that can be taken to facilitate its disappearance, but they are almost certain that it will come back and that the major factors determining this cycle are beyond the sufferer's control.

2. Sufferers are not aware that athlete's foot is more prevalent and more persistent in some seasons of the year than in others. From the sufferer's standpoint, when he gets athlete's foot, he's got it, regardless of the season. Yet many of our respondents expect, apparently on the basis only of logic, that population incidence of athlete's foot will be higher in the summer and that infections will generally be more severe then.

3. Most sufferers apparently use a branded powder specifically designed as an athlete's foot palliative or cure. Some sufferers use a branded ointment. No one in this sample reported the use of a liquid. Everyone in our sample reported using a specific athlete's foot cure; there was no reported usage of general nonspecific cures or of home remedies.

   The intensity of treatment varies, apparently, with the perceived severity of the ailment at a particular time. Multiple product use is most likely to occur when the infection is severe. Most of the respondents in this sample treated the ailment in the morning on arising, and only a few reported treatment in the evening before bed.

4. There does not appear to be a widespread belief that athletes are more prone to athlete's foot than anyone else. Some of our respondents understood that athlete's foot is caused by some sort of fungus infection, and many suspected that the most likely place in which to contract athlete's foot is in public places where people commonly walk barefoot. There was some feeling, following this line of thought, that younger people are more likely to get athlete's foot because they are more likely to be barefoot in public, that is, in public swimming pools, in military barracks, in YMCA or YWCA gymnasia, in school or college locker rooms, and so on.

5. Final cures are not expected. In the experience of these sufferers athlete's foot subsides temporarily but it almost inevitably recurs. (It should be noted that the sample is composed only of persons who claim to be current "sufferers." The sample is therefore relatively unlikely to include people whose athlete's foot has been cured or people who do not have athlete's foot or have not identified it when they do have it.) These sufferers genuinely do not expect a cure. One respondent pointed out, for example, that he had contracted athlete's foot from his father who had "picked it up" in France during World War I. Neither was cured, and neither expected to be.

6. Available over-the-counter athlete's foot remedies are seen as palliatives rather than cures. The existing products may encourage a quiescent state but they do not kill athlete's foot.

7. Athlete's foot is frequently considered serious enough by its sufferers so that medical attention and advice are sought. General practitioners, dermatologists, and school nurses were all mentioned as sources of such attention and advice. Almost all of the people in this sample had obtained professional counseling in respect to treating athlete's foot. People who had received such advice were no more sanguine about curing athlete's foot than those who had not.

On the basis of this report, Cornbusher immediately authorized Fryberger, Kahn, and Krane to proceed with a full-scale quantitative study of the general population's attitudes toward athlete's foot and practices concerning it.

The results of this study of athlete's foot incidence, practice in treating athlete's foot, and usage of and attitudes toward available over-the-counter athlete's foot remedies are summarized in Exhibits 5–2 through 5–11. Although the study itself yielded well over 150 separate tables, Allen Krane believed that these ten exhibits included all of the key findings that would determine the marketing action to be taken by Allgood. He summarized these central findings in the following six paragraphs:

1. Athlete's foot has a broad and relatively general incidence in the population as a whole. Athlete's foot is not restricted to an obscure or hard-to-reach group in the population.

2. Athlete's foot sufferers do not expect a cure. They seem to regard currently available remedies as palliatives.

3. Currently available athlete's foot remedies are not acceptable because they do not cure athlete's foot.

4. Athlete's foot is not regarded as a medical problem. By and large, sufferers are either self-diagnosed or diagnosed by nonprofessional friends, and sufferers do not go to doctors for a cure.

5. Athlete's foot remedies are mainly used at home. The form of a remedy is not restricted by a need for it to be portable or adaptable to out-of-home use.

6. Athlete's foot remedies are used more intensively by high-income sufferers than low-income sufferers; by sufferers who live in larger towns and cities than in small towns or rural areas; by males to a slightly greater degree than females; and by older sufferers to a greater degree than young sufferers.

EXHIBIT 5-2

Specimen Data: Incidence of Athlete's Foot and Use of Athlete's Foot Remedy in Past Year, by Sex and Age

INCIDENCE OF ATHLETE'S FOOT	ALL ADULTS	MALE ADULTS	FEMALE ADULTS	MALE				FEMALE			
				18-25	26-35	36-50	OVER 50	18-25	26-35	36-50	OVER 50
Number	8,099	4,362	3,737	572	822	1,432	1,536	546	645	1,200	1,346
Per cent	100	100	100	100	100	100	100	100	100	100	100
Now have athlete's foot	14%	16%	12%	9%	16%	17%	18%	2%	10%	15%	14%
Have had athlete's foot in past year	24	26	22	13	27	30	27	4	18	26	27
Have not had athlete's foot in past year	76	74	78	87	73	70	73	96	82	74	73
Have used athlete's foot remedy in past year*	18	20	16	9	19	23	22	3	12	20	20
Powder	10	10	10	8	11	11	9	1	7	11	15
Ointment	12	15	9	4	15	18	12	—	6	11	10
Liquid	3	6	2	2	3	4	10	1	—	—	—
Have not used athlete's foot remedy in past year	6	6	6	4	8	7	5	1	6	6	7

* Some respondents use more than one form.

EXHIBIT 5-3

Specimen Data: Usage of Athlete's Foot Remedy Outside Home, by Sex and Age

PLACE OF USE	ALL USERS*	MALE USERS	FEMALE USERS	MALE USERS			FEMALE USERS		
				UNDER 36	36-50	OVER 50	UNDER 36	36-50	OVER 50
Number	1,458	872	586	204	350	318	93	240	253
Per cent	100	100	100	100	100	100	100	100	100
Use remedy outside home	15%	15%	15%	13%	14%	17%	20%	16%	12%
School	3	3	3	13	—	—	19	—	—
YMCA	1	1	1	1	1	1	1	1	1
Club locker room	5	7	2	—	9	9	—	4	1
Other	6	4	9	—	4	7	1	11	10
Do not use remedy outside home	85	85	85	87	86	83	80	84	88

* A user is any person who reports using any athlete's foot remedy in the past year.

EXHIBIT 5-4
Specimen Data: Frequency of Athlete's Foot Condition in Past Year, by Sex and Age

ATHLETE'S FOOT CONDITION	ALL USERS*	MALE USERS	FEMALE USERS	MALE USERS			FEMALE USERS		
				UNDER 36	36–50	OVER 50	UNDER 36	36–50	OVER 50
Number	1,458	872	586	204	350	318	93	240	253
Per cent	100	100	100	100	100	100	100	100	100
Chronic	85%	86%	83%	88%	87%	84%	90%	82%	82%
Occasional	15	14	17	12	13	16	10	18	18

* A user is any person who reports using any athlete's foot remedy in the past year.

EXHIBIT 5-5
Specimen Data: Identification or Diagnosis of Athlete's Foot, by Sex and Age

PERSON RESPONSIBLE FOR IDENTIFICATION	ALL SUFFERERS*	MALE SUFFERERS	FEMALE SUFFERERS	MALE SUFFERERS				FEMALE SUFFERERS			
				UNDER 36	36–50	OVER 50		UNDER 36	36–50	OVER 50
Number	1,943	1,134	810	296	430	408		138	312	360
Per cent	100	100	100	100	100	100		100	100	100
Doctor or nurse	18%	19%	17%	19%	22%	16%		14%	18%	17%
Other person	42	40	45	41	45	34		48	46	42
Parent or relative	20	10	34	9	10	11		34	38	30
Friend	10	15	3	16	15	14		4	3	3
Stranger	6	6	6	6	6	6		6	4	8
Other	6	9	2	10	14	3		4	1	2
Sufferer	40	41	38	40	33	50		38	36	41

* A sufferer is any respondent who reports having had athlete's foot within the past year.

EXHIBIT 5-6

Specimen Data: Expected Cure of Athlete's Foot by Sufferers,* by Sex and Age

CURE EXPECTATION	ALL SUFFERERS*	MALE SUFFERERS	FEMALE SUFFERERS	MALE SUFFERERS			FEMALE SUFFERERS		
				UNDER 36	36-50	OVER 50	UNDER 36	36-50	OVER 50
Number	1,943	1,134	810	296	430	408	138	312	360
Per cent	100	100	100	100	100	100	100	100	100
Consider themselves cured	5%	4%	6%	4%	7%	1%	4%	6%	7%
Expect complete cure	17	16	18	20	12	17	24	17	16
Do not expect complete cure, only temporary relief	78	80	76	76	81	81	72	77	77

* A sufferer is any respondent who reports having had athlete's foot within the past year.

EXHIBIT 5-7

Specimen Data: How Users Now Using an Athlete's Foot Remedy Feel It Should Be Improved,* by Sex and Age

SUGGESTED IMPROVEMENTS	ALL USERS†	MALE USERS	FEMALE USERS	MALE USERS			FEMALE USERS		
				UNDER 36	36–50	OVER 50	UNDER 36	36–50	OVER 50
Number	1,458	872	586	204	350	318	93	240	253
Per cent	100	100	100	100	100	100	100	100	100
Available remedies should be improved	88%	98%	73%	79%	99%	96%	80%	69%	74%
Make it more effective	73	81	61	89	81	76	55	54	70
Add an ingredient to kill the fungus completely	42	54	24	56	54	53	24	26	22
Make it smell better	2	—	5	—	—	—	5	5	5
Make it in a more convenient form	6	6	6	4	5	8	6	6	6
Do nothing to improve it—it's OK now	12	2	27	1	1	4	20	31	26

* Some respondents gave more than one answer.
† A user is any person who reports using any athlete's foot remedy in the past year.

EXHIBIT 5-8

Specimen Data: Incidence of Athlete's Foot and Use of Athlete's Foot Remedy in Past Year, by Size of Market

INCIDENCE OF ATHLETE'S FOOT	ALL ADULTS	SIZE OF MARKET					
		2,000,000 AND OVER	1,000,000–1,999,999	250,000–999,999	UNDER 250,000	OTHER URBAN	RURAL
Number	8,099	1,944	899	1,539	729	1,215	1,863
Per cent	100	100	100	100	100	100	100
Now have athlete's foot	14%	18%	15%	14%	10%	10%	12%
Have had athlete's foot in past year	24	28	25	24	20	22	22
Have not had athlete's foot in past year	76	72	75	76	80	78	78
Have used athlete's foot remedy in past year*	18	24	23	22	17	18	7
Powder	12	16	15	16	10	12	4
Ointment	14	18	18	16	16	10	8
Liquid	3	6	2	3	1	1	2
Have not used athlete's foot remedy in past year	6	4	2	2	3	4	15

* Some respondents use more than one form.

EXHIBIT 5-9

Specimen Data: Incidence of Athlete's Foot and Use of Athlete's Foot Remedy in Past Year, by Geographic Region

INCIDENCE OF ATHLETE'S FOOT	ALL ADULTS	GEOGRAPHIC REGION			
		EAST	MIDWEST	SOUTH	FAR WEST
Number	8,099	2,268	2,349	2,268	1,214
Per cent	100	100	100	100	100
Now have athlete's foot	14%	16%	15%	12%	14%
Have had athlete's foot in past year	24	28	23	20	26
Have not had athlete's foot in past year	76	72	77	80	74
Have used athlete's foot remedy in past year*	18	20	20	14	18
Powder	12	14	10	12	12
Ointment	14	12	16	13	16
Liquid	3	3	3	3	3
Have not used athlete's foot remedy in past year	6	8	3	6	8

* Some respondents use more than one form.

EXHIBIT 5-10

Specimen Data: Incidence of Athlete's Foot and Use of Athlete's Foot Remedy in Past Year, by Income

INCIDENCE OF ATHLETE'S FOOT	ALL ADULTS	INCOME					
		UNDER $3,000	$3,000– $4,999	$5,000– $5,999	$6,000– $6,999	$7,000– $9,999	$10,000 AND OVER
Number	8,099	1,539	1,620	1,053	890	1,701	1,296
Per cent	100	100	100	100	100	100	100
Now have athlete's foot	14%	14%	12%	15%	14%	16%	13%
Have had athlete's foot in past year	24	25	22	22	23	25	26
Have not had athlete's foot in past year	76	75	78	78	77	75	74
Have used athlete's foot remedy in past year*	18	12	14	16	18	20	25
Powder	12	6	8	10	15	15	20
Ointment	14	6	7	8	17	19	29
Liquid	3	2	2	1	2	4	6
Have not used athlete's foot remedy in past year	6	13	7	6	5	5	—

* Some respondents use more than one form.

EXHIBIT 5–11
Specimen Data: Cross-Tabulation of Expected Cures of Athlete's Foot, by Sufferers Now Treating Athlete's Foot with a Remedy and Those Not Now Treating*

CURE EXPECTATION	ALL SUFFERERS†	SUFFERERS NOW TREATING ATHLETE'S FOOT‡	SUFFERERS NOT NOW TREATING ATHLETE'S FOOT§
Number	1,943	1,458	485
Per cent	100	100	100
Expect complete cure	22%	21%	25%
Do not expect complete cure, only temporary relief	78	79	75

* See Exhibits 5–2 and 5–6.
† A sufferer is any respondent who reports having had athlete's foot within the past year.
‡ "Now treating" includes all respondents who report having used an athlete's foot remedy within the past year.
§ "Not now treating" includes all sufferers who do not report use of an athlete's foot remedy within the past year.

Krane presented an exhibit summarizing salient market character-istics on the available brands (price, retail availability, package size, package type). This material is shown in Exhibit 5–12.

Krane also reported data from the survey on brand usage, although this information did not figure in the conclusions reported. (See Exhibit 5–13).

EXHIBIT 5–12
Specimen Data: Salient Marketing Characteristics of Athlete's Foot Remedy Brands

BRAND	PACKAGE SIZE—PRICE*					RETAIL AVAILABILITY†
	2 OZ.	4 OZ.	5 OZ.	8 OZ.	12 OZ.	
Senocuse Jr.						
Powder	—	$1.29	—	$2.39	—	Excellent
Ointment	$ .99	—	$1.98	—	—	Excellent
Amolee						
Liquid	1.35	2.00	—	—	—	Good
Ointment	1.50	—	2.75	—	—	Poor
Powder	—	—	2.95	—	—	Not seen
Stang ointment	.69	—	1.25	—	$2.49	Poor

* Suggested retail price.
† Based on observational visits to thirty large drugstores in each of thirty top markets.

EXHIBIT 5-13
Specimen Data: Last Brand of Athlete's Foot Remedy Used,† by Sex and Age

BRAND	ALL USERS*	MALE USERS	FEMALE USERS	MALE USERS			FEMALE USERS		
				UNDER 36	36–50	OVER 50	UNDER 36	36–50	OVER 50
Number	1,458	872	586	204	350	318	93	240	253
Per cent	100	100	100	100	100	100	100	100	100
Senocuse Jr.									
Powder	22%	20%	25%	20%	22%	18%	18%	23%	30%
Ointment	21	21	21	20	21	22	18	23	20
Amolee									
Liquid	8	10	5	9	9	12	—	6	6
Ointment	7	6	9	3	7	7	7	4	13
Powder	5	7	2	7	7	7	5	2	1
Stang ointment	2	3	1	3	3	3	1	—	1
All other									
Liquid	12	20	—	20	24	16	—	—	—
Ointment	11	11	11	12	10	12	7	10	13
Powder	8	7	10	9	6	7	5	10	11
Don't know brand	20	15	27	10	18	15	36	30	22
Doctor's prescription	6	7	4	8	6	8	11	4	2

* A user is any person who reports using any athlete's foot remedy in the past year.
† Some respondents mentioned more than one brand or form.

Cornbusher requested that Krane make a specific recommendation based on his findings. Krane then recommended that the highest laboratory priority be given to the development of a new athlete's foot remedy that would truly cure athlete's foot.

Questions for Case 5

1. Discuss the importance of the laboratory scientist in uncovering new products. Does the Hunterdon recommendation negate the insight and genius of the exceptional laboratory scientist? Is it practical to leave new product development work solely up to the marketing researcher and his methodical probing of consumers? Can it always be assumed that a team of laboratory scientists can always produce a superior new product in fields in which market research indicates a consumer need exists?

2. Evaluate the six product categories identified by Cornbusher's first Phase I study (i.e., athlete's foot remedies, sunburn remedies, poison ivy remedies, eye strain remedies, hemorrhoid remedies, and bug bite remedies) according to the four new product criteria set by the company in 1927 (see page 121).

3. Compare the conclusions of the exploratory depth interviews reported on pages 129–130 and the conclusions from the quantitative Phase II study reported on page 130. What is the significance of each of these statements? Which has greater import for marketing decision making? Why?

4. Identify the exhibits that serve as a basis for each of the quantitative conclusions reproduced on page 130.

5. Is Cornbusher's three-phase formulation of the new product development process consistent with Hunterdon's valedictory statement? Do you believe that Hunterdon would agree with Cornbusher's approach?

6. Describe the marketing model that underlies the athlete's foot attitude and usage study.

7. Do you agree with Allen Krane's recommendation "that the highest laboratory priority be given to the development of a new athlete's foot remedy that would truly cure athlete's foot"? If you agree tell why, and if you do not agree tell why not.

8. Assume that Cornbusher agrees with Allen Krane and authorizes high-priority product development work on an athlete's foot product. Also assume that an acceptable, effective product has been developed.
   a. Discuss the kinds of considerations that would be involved in setting the price for this product.
   b. Discuss the kinds of considerations that would be involved in determining distribution channels for this product.
   c. Discuss the kind of considerations that would be involved in deciding whether or not to advertise this product and at what level advertising support, if needed, should be set.

9. Comment on the question of time as it relates to marketing actions taken after the completion of a study like the athlete's foot market study. Is it necessary to move quickly once results like those in Exhibits 5–2 through 5–11 and 5–13 are in hand, or does it make no difference?

CASE 6

Elements of a Marketing Model

Home Products Universal Handsome Boy Cleaner Faces a Competitive Threat

HOME PRODUCTS UNIVERSAL is a small Midwestern manufacturer of soap, wax, and other cleaning and maintenance products for the home (see Case 1). The company is relatively small, its markets are regional, and its products are very similar to the leading products of the giant home products manufacturers. Home Products Universal has been very profitable throughout its existence because although its operations are modest in size in relation to the national companies, its marketing is aggressive, its product quality is high and its management is superb. Home Products Universal is extraordinarily cost-conscious, but it is not penny wise and pound foolish. It knows its costs and it knows how to minimize them while delivering solid value to the consumer.

In the scouring-powder product category, Home Products Universal markets a product called Handsome Boy. This scouring powder has been consciously designed to equal the market leader, Meteor, on six product characteristics considered crucial by the technical staff assigned to this product category in the Home Products Universal laboratories. These characteristics are percentage of synthetic detergent, concentrations of synthetic detergent, percentage of pumice, percentage of bleaching agent, concentration of bleaching agent, and percentage of inert material. Exhibit 6–1 summarizes recent laboratory analyses of Handsome Boy and Meteor on these six product characteristics. The Meteor products upon which these analyses were based were purchased in Minneapolis, Minnesota (Home Products Universal Region III) in high turnover supermarkets by representatives of the Home Products Universal sales staff. The Handsome Boy samples were drawn at random from the Home Products Universal production line.

A glance at the February, April, and June bimonthly data reveals the two products to be essentially at parity. There are minor variations in

EXHIBIT 6-1

Specimen Data: Laboratory Analysis of Two Scouring Powders, Meteor and Handsome Boy, 1972

	FEBRUARY 1972		APRIL 1972		JUNE 1972		AUGUST 1972		OCTOBER 1972		DECEMBER 1972	
	HB	M	HB	M	HB	M	HB	M	HB	M	HB	M
Synthetic detergent												
Amount (%)	2.0	2.2	2.1	2.0	2.3	1.9	2.1	2.1	2.2	2.4	2.0	1.9
Concentration	.72	.66	.77	.66	.72	.66	.73	.66	.74	.67	.77	.68
Bleaching agent												
Amount (%)	1.5	1.7	1.6	1.2	1.7	1.4	1.4	1.5	1.6	1.7	1.4	1.6
Concentration	.92	.99	.90	.96	.94	.92	.93	.97	.91	.94	.92	.95
Pumice amount (%)	12.0	11.0	12.0	13.0	12.2	16.0	12.1	20.0	12.0	20.6	11.0	21.0
Inert material amount (%)	84.5	84.1	84.3	83.8	83.8	80.7	84.4	76.4	84.2	75.3	85.6	74.5
TOTAL (%)	100.0	100.0	100.0	100.0	100.0	100.0	100.0	100.0	100.0	100.0	100.0	100.0

proportions (and concentrations) of ingredients from bimonthly period to bimonthly period in the first six months of 1972. But the laboratory people have assured Home Products Universal management that these variations are normal.

Suddenly, in the August analyses, a significant increase in Meteor's pumice level is observed—from 16 per cent in June to 20 per cent in August. It is also retrospectively noted by Home Products Universal management that the June level of 16 per cent was above the normal pumice level of Meteor as exemplified by the February and April levels of 11 per cent and 12 per cent, respectively. It is now recognized that the June pumice level may not have been a chance variation. The higher (about 20 per cent) pumice level for Meteor has now been confirmed in both the October and December analyses, too.

This change in Meteor's formula confounds the Home Products Universal laboratory people. They submit the following comments on the developing situation:

1. Pumice is a more expensive ingredient than inert material.
2. Meteor's mixing drums are of a modern high-dispersion, high-speed type and it is very unlikely that the pumice levels observed are due to a continuing malfunction of this equipment.
3. A level of 10 per cent pumice is essential to achieve the standard level of mechanical, abrasive effect in cleansers.
4. Industry opinion has agreed, historically, that pumice levels in excess of 15 per cent make a cleanser excessively abrasive and that this condition may lead to excessive porcelain wear in normal consumer home use.
5. In the opinion of the laboratory, the new Meteor high-pumice product would produce cleaner, brighter sinks faster than current Handsome Boy but would also, over a long term, produce faster deterioration in porcelain sink surfaces. "Over a long term" is defined by the technicians as a one-year decline in expected sink surface life for each four years a high-pumice product of the Meteor type is used in *thorough* cleaning at least three times a week. Low-quality porcelain surfaces were assumed in this estimate. No extended-usage test had been conducted by the laboratory.

The HPU management experience has been that such laboratory estimates are likely to be conservative and/or reflect abnormal or severe usage conditions.

A variety of additional facts, apparently bearing upon the developing competitive situation, were developed by the marketing research department of HPU and reported by Aloysius LaGrange, director of marketing research.

1. In 1970–71, 18.4 per cent of the adult married males in the country moved from one house to another house. This moving rate approximates the normal annual rate observed throughout the country since World War II.

2. An HPU Marketing Research Department study conducted in 1959 indicated that the average homemaker thoroughly cleans a kitchen sink two times per week with scouring powder. In that report, however, it was concluded that the household usage pattern of scouring powder was strongly skewed to a relatively small proportion of total homes, which in 1959 consumed a disproportionately high amount of household scouring powder. In this study it was found that 93 per cent of all homes purchased cleanser in a four-month period. This study identified 10 per cent of these cleanser-consuming homes as the heaviest consumers of household scouring powder: they consumed one third of all household scouring powder sold. In addition, the next 20 per cent of these cleanser-consuming homes also consumed 33 per cent of all scouring powder sold. Thus, the remaining 70 per cent of cleanser consuming homes were relatively light consumers of household scouring powder, and accounted for the remaining 34 per cent of all scouring powder sold. These data were interpreted in 1959 to mean that some housewives use household scouring powder continuously and perhaps even compulsively. At the other end of the scale was a large percentage of housewives who used scouring powder on an intermittent or occasional basis. No estimates of frequency of sink cleaning with or without scouring powder were available for the three analysis groups.

3. No information was available in the 1959 study regarding the home moving patterns of heavy cleanser users, medium cleanser users, or light cleanser users.

4. No information was available in the 1959 study for brand share by the three usage groups.

5. Exhibit 6–2 was prepared by the HPU Marketing Research Department showing Meteor and Handsome Boy market shares as reported by the A. C. Nielsen Company (specimen data) during late 1971 and 1972 by Handsome Boy marketing regions. This table indicates that Handsome Boy holds a 7-per-cent share of the market within its marketing area. This market share varies from region to region, and slightly from month to month. Meteor holds a dominant scouring powder franchise in the HPU marketing area. It held one third of the market in early 1971, and this share rose to a level of 41 per cent by late 1971. The major portion of these share increases occurred toward the end of the year in most Handsome Boy regions except Region IV and Region II. In Region IV, a sharp share increase for Meteor is seen in the November–December 1971 period. This share increase has been maintained and slightly improved during 1972. In Region II, no Meteor share change has been observed over the period reported.

It is now surmised by the HPU Director of Marketing, Arthur V. Pensa, that the major part of HPU Region IV was included in a Meteor test marketing of the high-pumice product during the late months of 1971. Although the share improvement for Meteor was noted in the bimonthly HPU Nielsen Analysis, prepared by HPU Marketing Research in early 1972, it was not recognized as a possible result of an improved product. In fact, the possibility of an improved Meteor product was first recognized by the HPU management with the recent release of the laboratory analysis confirming a higher pumice content (Exhibit 6–1).

Region IV is a relatively weak area for Handsome Boy. Its market share has fallen from 4 per cent to 3 per cent during the period in which high-pumice Meteor has been under test. Nielsen sales estimates in cases (upon which Exhibit 6–2 is based, but not shown) show a sales decline for Handsome Boy in Region IV from November–December 1971 to November–December 1972 of 31 per cent. There has been a case-sales decline for Handsome Boy in Regions I, III, and V, combined, of 3 per cent between July–August 1972

EXHIBIT 6-2

Specimen Data: Analysis of Nielsen Food Index Data Market Share of Consumer Dollars, Meteor and Handsome Boy, by HPU Regions, 1971, 1972

| | 1971 | | | | | | 1972 | | | | | | | | | | | |
| | JULY–AUG. | | SEPT.–OCT. | | NOV.–DEC. | | JAN.–FEB. | | MAR.–APRIL | | MAY–JUNE | | JULY–AUG. | | SEPT.–OCT. | | NOV.–DEC. | |
HPU REGION	HB	M	HB	M	HB	M	HB	M	HB	M	HB	M	HB	M	HB	M	HB	M
I	5%	37%	6%	36%	5%	37%	7%	37%	6%	37%	6%	38%	6%	38%	5%	42%	5%	46%
II	7	34	6	34	6	33	6	33	6	33	6	32	6	32	6	32	6	33
III	12	28	12	27	11	27	11	28	11	29	11	29	12	29	12	36	14	36
IV	4	41	4	43	4	50	3	51	3	51	3	52	3	52	3	53	3	53
V	8	27	8	26	8	26	8	26	8	26	8	27	8	27	8	37	9	37
TOTAL	7%	33%	7%	33%	7%	35%	7%	35%	7%	35%	7%	36%	7%	36%	7%	40%	7%	41%

S O U R C E : Modeled on the reports of the A. C. Nielsen Company.

and November–December 1972, according to Nielsen. But this case-sales decline of 3 per cent is difficult to interpret because of the seasonal and long-term growth trends in the scouring powder market. Total factory case sales are off 22 per cent in January 1973 versus a year ago, but HPU management believes factory sales data to be inherently volatile and unreliable bench marks over short periods (under three months).

Meteor has shown no share increase in Region II. HPU marketing management does not know whether this is because the Meteor high-pumice product has not been introduced in Region II or because, for some unknown reason, the high-pumice product has not yet been successful in Region II.

6. Exhibit 6–3 shows data on Meteor prices. Such observations on competitive pricing are routinely produced by the HPU Market Research Department for supermarket price levels in a leading city in each of the HPU regions. There is no indication in these price data that Meteor retail prices are increased when an increased level of pumice is added to the Meteor product. In its analysis of the price observation data, HPU Marketing Research pointed out that third-quarter (seasonal) price declines were common in the household scouring powder market because of an industry practice of allowing case-off allowances to retailers during summer months. Also HPU Marketing Research noted that regional differences in retail prices were common for all HPU and competitive lines because of differences in transportation and various retail overhead factors from region to region. The HPU Marketing Research Department analysis also pointed out that there had been no unusual price activity for other competitive brands of scouring powder during 1972.

EXHIBIT 6–3

Specimen Data: Spot Checks of Average Meteor Retail Prices in Twenty Supermarkets in Each of Five Leading Cities in HPU Regions, 21-oz Size, 1972

CITY	REGION	FIRST QUARTER	SECOND QUARTER	THIRD QUARTER	FOURTH QUARTER
Indianapolis	I	$0.23	$0.23	$0.22	$0.23
Denver	II	.24	.24	.22	.24
Minneapolis	III	.23	.23	.21	.23
Louisville	IV	.22	.22	.21	.22
Chicago	V	.23	.23	.21	.23

7. No changes in Meteor advertising *content* have accompanied the introduction of the changed Meteor product. Meteor has been promoted as "the leading household scouring powder" for several years. Meteor is said, in its advertising, "to make sinks and other surfaces cleaner and brighter than any other cleanser because Meteor contains *perboronal*, a miracle bleaching agent especially designed for household cleaning uses."

8. Exhibit 6–4 summarizes estimated Meteor and industry advertising expenditures for the last quarter of 1971 and for the first three quarters of 1972 by HPU regions. As the exhibit shows, there is a severe seasonality in advertising expenditures in this product category. This seasonal pattern takes the form of relatively high expenditure levels in the first and fourth quarters of each year, with relatively low expenditure levels during second and third quarters. It is traditional in the industry to reduce periodically the case cost to retailers of

EXHIBIT 6-4

Specimen Data: Competitive Advertising Expenditure Analysis,* Meteor and Competitive Spending by HPU Regions
1971, 1972

| | 1971 | | | | 1972 | | | |
| | FOURTH QUARTER | | FIRST QUARTER | | SECOND QUARTER | | THIRD QUARTER | |
HPU REGION	M	ALL OTHERS	M	ALL OTHERS	M	ALL OTHERS	M	ALL OTHERS
I	$81.6	$248.0	$72.3	$221.0	$41.6	$110.8	$30.1	$108.7
II	50.6	178.0	41.2	162.4	12.3	41.7	15.6	21.6
III	40.9	126.7	38.4	120.3	8.4	61.7	10.2	72.6
IV	276.4	313.4	201.2	309.6	113.6	93.8	101.4	86.6
V	129.1	279.6	126.2	274.4	70.2	107.3	66.3	72.4
Total	$578.6	$1,145.7	$479.3	$1,087.7	$245.1	$425.3	$223.6	$352.0
Total (Year Ago)	$471.7	$1,096.3	$326.3	$1,013.7	$185.1	$397.3	$172.7	$301.6

SOURCE: Supplied by HPU's advertising agency and based on industry sources.

household scouring powders, and these case allowances generally are reflected in decreased retail shelf prices during the summer months, as we have seen above.

Exhibit 6–4 indicates that the normal seasonal expenditure pattern was followed in total industry advertising expenditures, and by Meteor, except in HPU Region IV. In Region IV Meteor spent more for advertising in the last quarter of 1971 (normally a high spending season) and the first quarter of 1972 (normally a high season) and in the second and third quarters of 1972 (normally low seasons) than their share of business seemed to justify and more proportionately by a large amount than in any other HPU region. There was no reported change in the allocation of Meteor funds among the various advertising media. Arthur Pensa interpreted this table to mean that Meteor increased its level of advertising expenditure over normal coincidentally with the introduction of the high-pumice product in HPU Region IV.

Competitive advertising estimates become available only about three and one-half months after the end of the reporting period. Thus only the first three quarters of 1972 data are now available for review by HPU management.

9. A blind paired comparison product test between Meteor and Handsome Boy had been completed by the HPU Marketing Research Department in 1967. The laboratory analysis of the two products indicated no substantial change in the Handsome Boy and Meteor formulations from 1967 until the recognition of higher pumice content in Meteor in 1972. Company policy stated that consumer product tests need not be made between HPU products and leading competitors unless substantial changes in formulation were known to have taken place in the competitive product or a major change was contemplated in the HPU product formulation.

A summary of the results of the 1967 blind product test is presented in Exhibit 6–5. The HPU Marketing Research Department issued this summary table with a capsule analysis in 1967, as well as a detailed report. The capsule analysis made the following points:

1. Handsome Boy has achieved marginal consumer acceptance over Meteor. There is no reason to believe that consumers perceive Meteor as a superior scouring cleanser, when the two products are critically compared on a blind test basis.
2. There is some indication that the Meteor product has a marginally superior odor relative to Handsome Boy.
3. Handsome Boy is preferred over Meteor for its porcelain shining ability and, marginally, for its ability to make sinks white. It is possible, but cannot be demonstrated through this research, that the slight overall consumer preference for Handsome Boy is caused by its superiority over Meteor on these points.

The HPU marketing research department has a policy of destroying all copies of marketing research reports at least four years old, except for a master copy kept in the HPU marketing research department library.

EXHIBIT 6–5
Specimen Data: Summary 1967 Results, Meteor Versus Handsome Boy, Product Test

I.   Overall preference:
     Base: Total testers
          Number   312
          Per cent   100

          Prefer Meteor   38%
          Prefer Handsome Boy   44
          No preference   18

II. Reasons for preferring each brand:

Base: Those preferring each brand:	Meteor	Handsome Boy
Number	119	137
Per cent	100	100
Cleans well	58%	62%
Removes stains	39	31
Has pleasant odor	21	10
Not hard on hands	19	21
Shines porcelain	10	36
Makes sinks white	9	14
All other (not over 5%)	17	28

III. Expressed preference on key product characteristics:
     Base: Total testers
          Number   312
          Per cent   100

	Prefer Meteor	Prefer Handsome Boy	No Preference
Cleaning ability	46%	38%	16%
Stain removal	42	30	28
Not hard on hands	7	3	90
Makes sinks white	32	51	17
Shines porcelain	27	52	21

Unfortunately, the master copy of the 1967 consumer blind product test between Handsome Boy and Meteor was removed from the library in 1970 by an employee who subsequently left the company. No trace of the master copy of the complete report can now be found.

Aloysius LaGrange is not particularly concerned that the previous blind product test report is missing. Shortly after he joined HPU in 1968 LaGrange instituted a totally revised blind product test procedure. Its major difference from the former procedure is that consumers now use one test product alone for one week and then use the second product alone for a second week. Previously, the two products were used by cooperating consumers indiscriminately and without discipline throughout the two-week test period. A second major difference is that respondents are now asked to evaluate the test products against their regular brand, as well as against the paired-test product. Thus an overall preference is obtained against the regular brand *and* in relation to the second test product. Similarly, each test product is evaluated on specific product characteristics against both the regular brand and relative to the other test product. The use of the regular brand as an additional reference point binds the test to normality, at least as it is perceived by the respondent.

When this change in procedure was made, LaGrange released a staff memorandum, which said, in part,

---

The new rating procedure guarantees a balanced appraisal of product performance characteristics. On the one hand, a test product must perform at the level of expectation held by the respondent for the product category: it must perform at parity or better with her regular product. On the other hand, and in addition, the test product must perform at parity or better with a specific referrent—the competitive test product.

It is believed that this new procedure will provide laboratory personnel with considerably more sensitive direction in product development than has heretofore existed.

Can the previous consumer blind test work of the department be depended upon? How, and to what extent? It is the belief of the HPU Marketing Research Department that the results of consumer blind tests conducted according to previous procedures are totally reliable in respect to overall consumer preference expressions. We believe, however, that blind comparisons of performance characteristics on key product attributes cannot be reliably made on the basis of prior procedures and that conclusions on these points derived from prior tests must either be ignored or verified using the new procedure.

The Handsome Boy brand manager, Albert Manoir, asked the HPU marketing research department to develop a plan for a new blind consumer product test of Handsome Boy and Meteor. In asking for such a plan, Manoir reasoned that it would be premature to reach any conclusion about potential causes of the apparent market success of high-pumice Meteor until conclusive product test evidence was in fact in hand.

The plan for the Home Products Universal product test of household scouring powders was submitted to Manoir on February 19, 1973. He approved it, with minor revisions and recommended to Arthur V. Pensa, HPU marketing director, that the revised product test be undertaken on February 19, 1973. Pensa (who was on winter holiday during the last week in February and the first week in March) accepted the recommendation on his return from vacation. His written authorization to proceed was received by the marketing research department on March 12, 1973. No preparation of any kind had been made for the test by the marketing research department because it was a firm policy of HPU that no marketing research work of any kind could be initiated without written authorization of the marketing director.

Two weeks were required to organize and prepare materials for the study, prior to the actual beginning of field work. During this period the manufacturing department prepared unidentified (except for code letter) samples of Handsome Boy and repacked Meteor into the test cans. The marketing research department prepared the required questionnaires, recruited interviewers in the four cities in which field work was to be carried out, and made arrangements for the test product samples and questionnaires to be delivered to interviewer supervisors' homes by air freight in order that briefing of the interviewing staff could commence on March 26. Briefing and practice interviewing required three work days. Field work commenced on March 30. All product placements were completed by April 6, except in Rock Island–Moline, where spring thaw and flooding delayed the placement phase completion for a week, until April 13. All call-back interviews were completed by April 27, except in Rock Island–Moline, where the work was not completed until April 30. Coding and tabulating were accomplished in ten days and a final tabular report was presented to the marketing research analyst on May 11.

The key tables received by the marketing research analyst are reproduced in Exhibits 6–6 through 6–16. The cooperating consumers received test products identified only as "G" and "N." All the respondents

EXHIBIT 6–6
Specimen Data: Overall Comparison of Test Products with Regular Brand, 1973 Product Test

Self-administered questionnaire:
3. How does product G (N) compare with your regular brand?

	RATING METEOR	RATING HANDSOME BOY
Base: Total respondents		
Number	276	276
Per cent	100	100
Test product is		
Much better	22%	19%
Slightly better	19	16
About the same	37	37
Slightly worse	12	14
Much worse	6	11
No answer	4	3

received two cans of cleanser; half received Meteor marked "G" and Handsome Boy marked "N." The other half received Meteor marked "N" and Handsome Boy marked "G." This letter reversal was used to prevent any possibility of a bias toward or against one of the identifying letters from translating itself into a bias toward or against one of the test products. In the final tables the test products are identified as brands, and the letter reversal has been unscrambled in the tabulating process.

EXHIBIT 6-7
Specimen Data: Comparison of Test Product with Regular Brand on Specific Characteristics, 1973 Product Test

Self-administered questionnaire:
4. How does this product compare to your regular brand on each item below?

	RATING METEOR	RATING HANDSOME BOY
Base: Total respondents		
Number	276	276
Per cent	100	100
Cleaning power—test product is		
Much better	20%	22%
Slightly better	15	17
About the same	38	42
Slightly worse	12	7
Much worse	8	4
No answer	7	8
Cuts grease better—test product is		
Much better	22%	25%
Slightly better	15	13
About the same	34	39
Slightly worse	12	8
Much worse	8	4
No answer	9	11
Removes stains—test product is		
Much better	42%	20%
Slightly better	28	21
About the same	10	30
Slightly worse	12	16
Much worse	2	7
No answer	6	6
Does more household jobs—test product is		
Much better	21%	20%
Slightly better	13	12
About the same	42	36
Slightly worse	10	12
Much worse	5	9
No answer	9	11

EXHIBIT 6–7—continued

	RATING METEOR	RATING HANDSOME BOY
Gets sinks white—test product is		
Much better	18%	32%
Slightly better	13	10
About the same	40	30
Slightly worse	10	8
Much worse	10	12
No answer	9	8
Shines porcelain—test product is		
Much better	22%	31%
Slightly better	16	21
About the same	37	32
Slightly worse	9	10
Much worse	6	4
No answer	10	2
Mild to hands—test product is		
Much better	10%	21%
Slightly better	6	11
About the same	12	44
Slightly worse	33	5
Much worse	26	4
No answer	13	15
Pleasant odor—test product is		
Much better	35%	22%
Slightly better	21	18
About the same	25	35
Slightly worse	8	11
Much worse	6	10
No answer	5	4
Cleans with less rubbing—test product is		
Much better	15%	12%
Slightly better	23	28
About the same	51	50
Slightly worse	2	3
Much worse	—	—
No answer	9	7
Doesn't scratch porcelain—test product is		
Much better	24%	26%
Slightly better	18	18
About the same	35	29
Slightly worse	6	7
Much worse	7	12
No answer	10	8

EXHIBIT 6–8
Specimen Data: Cleaning Jobs for Which Test
Products Were Used, 1973 Product Test

Call-back questionnaire:
2a. Which can did you use in the first week?
2b. What cleaning jobs did you use this first product for?
2c. And which can did you use in the second week?
2d. What cleaning jobs did you use the second product for?

	METEOR	HANDSOME BOY
Base: Total respondents		
Number	276	276
Per cent	100*	100*
Cleaning floors	15%	18%
Cleaning sinks	92	94
Cleaning bathtubs	62	58
Cleaning porcelain tile	46	51
Cleaning ovens	14	12
Cleaning spots from walls	18	17
Cleaning pots and pans	36	37
Cleaning counter tops	81	79
Other uses	22	18
No answer	2	3

* Some respondents gave more than one answer.

EXHIBIT 6–9
Specimen Data:
Overall Preference for Products
Tested, 1973 Product Test

Call-back questionnaire:
3a. Taking everything into consideration, which of these two cleaners do you prefer?

Base: Total respondents	
Number	276
Per cent	100
Prefer Meteor	42%
Prefer Handsome Boy	43
Like neither	2
Like both	13
No answer	—

EXHIBIT 6–10
Specimen Data: Reasons for Preference for One of the Two Test Products
1973 Product Test

Call-back questionnaire:
3b. Why do you prefer that one?

	PREFER METEOR	PREFER HANDSOME BOY
Base: Respondents who preferred one of the test products		
Number	116	119
Per cent	100*	100*
Cleans well	47%	48%
Cleans well; good disinfectant; efficient; does a good job; liked how it cleans.	31	28
Powerful; cleans without scrubbing or rubbing; just once over; has strength	26	29
Cuts grease from cooking utensils; cuts grime.	12	10
Cleans fast.	4	7
Removes stains	52%	40%
Gets stains off sinks and other surfaces.	46	20
Removes stains fast from sinks.	13	12
Gets off discoloration.	17	9
Odor	45%	29%
Clean odor; disinfectant odor; no unpleasant odor; not too strong	31	22
Like bleach smell.	16	9
Makes porcelain shiny and white	26%	37%
Sinks and tubs shine after use; old dull color gone; porcelain looks like new again.	18	29
Sinks are white again; have a white glow.	10	14
Mildness	11%	22%
Doesn't seem to be harsh on hands; no irritation to hands.	2	20
Hands are smooth and clean smelling after use.	10	7
All other (no mention over 5%)	19%	12%

* Some respondents gave more than one answer.

EXHIBIT 6–11
Specimen Data: Preference for Test Products Based on Specific Product Characteristics, 1973 Product Test

Call-back questionnaire:
4. Some people prefer one product generally, but also like specific things about the other product. For example, which of these *two* products do you think:

Base: Total respondents
Number 276
Per cent 100

Has the most cleaning power?		Shines porcelain best?	
Meteor	35%	Meteor	38%
Handsome Boy	33	Handsome Boy	52
Both the same	30	Both the same	8
Don't know, no answer	2	Don't know, no answer	2
Cuts grease better?		Is milder to hands?	
Meteor	17%	Meteor	12%
Handsome Boy	14	Handsome Boy	38
Both the same	68	Both the same	45
Don't know, no answer	1	Don't know, no answer	5
Removes stains best?		Has most pleasant odor?	
Meteor	58%	Meteor	42%
Handsome Boy	32	Handsome Boy	46
Both the same	6	Both the same	12
Don't know, no answer	4	Don't know, no answer	—
Does more household jobs?		Cleans without rubbing?	
Meteor	12%	Meteor	38%
Handsome Boy	7	Handsome Boy	40
Both the same	80	Both the same	20
Don't know, no answer	1	Don't know, no answer	2
Gets sinks white best?		Doesn't scratch porcelain?	
Meteor	37%	Meteor	36%
Handsome Boy	50	Handsome Boy	38
Both the same	12	Both the same	20
Don't know, no answer	1	Don't know, no answer	6

EXHIBIT 6–12
Specimen Data: Overall Product Preference, by Intensity of Product Use, 1973 Product Test

Call-back questionnaire:
  3a. Taking everything into consideration, which of these two cleaners do you prefer?

	TOTAL	HEAVY CLEANSER USERS	LIGHT CLEANSER USERS
Respondents			
Number	276	140	136
Per cent	100	100	100
Prefer Meteor	42%	38%	46%
Prefer Handsome Boy	43	45	41
Like neither	2	4	—
Like both	13	13	13
No answer	—	—	—

EXHIBIT 6–13
Specimen Data: Overall Product Preference by Respondent Age, 1973 Product Test

Call-back questionnaire:
  3a. Taking everything into consideration, which of these two cleaners do you prefer?

	TOTAL	UNDER 25	25– 34	35– 49	50– 64	65 AND OVER
Respondents						
Number	276	34	89	69	61	23
Per cent	100	*	100	100	100	*
Prefer Meteor	42%	(10)	43%	45%	49%	(7)
Prefer Handsome Boy	43	(10)	47	45	43	(10)
Like neither	2	(2)	—	3	1	—
Like both	13	(12)	10	7	7	(6)
No answer	—	—	—	—	—	—

* HPU Marketing Research Department policy prohibits percentaging on a base of less than 50 cases.

EXHIBIT 6–14

Specimen Data: Overall Product Preference by Respondent Family Income, 1973 Product Test

Call-back questionnaire:

3a. Taking everything into consideration, which of these two cleaners do you prefer?

	TOTAL	UNDER $5,000	$5,000–$7,999	$8,000† AND OVER	REFUSED
Respondents					
Number	276	81	125	50	20
Per cent	100	100	100	100	*
Prefer Meteor	42%	46%	41%	48%	(4)
Prefer Handsome Boy	43	48	46	44	(1)
Like neither	2	—	1	6	—
Like both	13	6	12	2	(15)
No answer	—	—	—	—	—

* HPU Marketing Research Department policy prohibits percentaging on a base of less than 50 cases.
† Three income groups ($8,000–$9,999; $10,000–$14,999; and $15,000 and over) have been combined to provide an adequate base for percentaging.

EXHIBIT 6–15

Specimen Data: Overall Product Preference by Respondent Race, 1973 Product Test

Call-back questionnaire:

3a. Taking everything into consideration, which of these two cleaners do you prefer?

	TOTAL	WHITE	NONWHITE	NOT RECORDED
Respondents				
Number	276	224	50	2
Per cent	100	100	100	*
Prefer Meteor	42%	45%	28%	(1)
Prefer Handsome Boy	43	50	14	—
Like neither	2	†	9	(1)
Like both	13	5	50	—
No answer	—	—	—	—

* HPU Marketing Research Department policy prohibits percentaging on a base of less than 50 cases.
† Less than 1 per cent.

EXHIBIT 6–16

Specimen Data: Preference for Test Products Based on Specific Product Characteristics by Intensity of Product Use, 1973 Product Test

Call-back questionnaire:
4. Some people prefer one product generally, but also like specific things about the other product. Of these two products, which one:

	TOTAL	HEAVY CLEANSER USERS	LIGHT CLEANSER USERS
Base: Respondents			
Number	276	140	136
Per cent	100	100	100
Has the most cleaning power?			
Meteor	35%	33%	37%
Handsome Boy	33	35	31
Both the same	30	30	30
Don't know, no answer	2	2	2
Cuts grease better?			
Meteor	17%	18%	16%
Handsome Boy	14	13	15
Both the same	68	67	69
Don't know, no answer	1	2	—
Removes stains best?			
Meteor	58%	64%	52%
Handsome Boy	32	25	39
Both the same	6	7	5
Don't know, no answer	4	4	4
Does more household jobs?			
Meteor	12%	13%	11%
Handsome Boy	7	6	8
Both the same	80	79	81
Don't know, no answer	1	2	—
Gets sinks white best?			
Meteor	37%	32%	42%
Handsome Boy	50	54	46
Both the same	12	14	10
Don't know, no answer	1	—	2
Shines porcelain best?			
Meteor	38%	36%	40%
Handsome Boy	52	56	48
Both the same	8	7	9
Don't know, no answer	2	1	3
Is milder to the hands?			
Meteor	12%	6%	18%
Handsome Boy	38	44	32
Both the same	45	44	46
Don't know, no answer	5	6	4

EXHIBIT 6–16—continued

	TOTAL	HEAVY CLEANSER USERS	LIGHT CLEANSER USERS
Has most pleasant odor?			
Meteor	42%	41%	43%
Handsome Boy	46	47	45
Both the same	12	12	12
Don't know, no answer	—	—	—
Cleans without rubbing?			
Meteor	38%	36%	40%
Handsome Boy	40	44	36
Both the same	20	18	22
Don't know, no answer	2	2	2
Doesn't scratch porcelain?			
Meteor	36%	40%	32%
Handsome Boy	38	34	42
Both the same	20	20	20
Don't know, no answer	6	6	6

Questions for Case 6

1. A great variety of facts are presented in Case 6. Of all those presented, which five do you consider most significant?
2. Marketing models describe the interrelationship existing between various elements in a marketing situation. There are at least three marketing models implied by the facts in the case. One implies that consumer product preference causes brand sales. Another implies that advertising expenditures cause brand sales.
   a. What is the third implicit model?
   b. Comment on each of the three implicit models.
3. Marketing research has determined that household cleanser usage is heavily skewed toward a relatively few heavy-using households. Thus the 10 per cent heaviest-using households account for about one third of cleanser consumption and the next 20 per cent of these cleanser-consuming households (by volume) also account for about one third of cleanser consumption.
   a. What is the marketing significance of these heavy-using households?
   b. How would the marketer exploit these characteristics to make more sales?
   c. What additional information should the marketer have about the heavy-using households?
4. Two kinds of sales data are presented in the case: data generated from sample-survey retail-audit procedures by the A. C. Nielsen Company, and factory sales data. Contrast these two data sources from the standpoint of the marketing manager. Be sure to discuss the significance of a Nielsen share decline from 4 per cent to 3 per cent in one territory. Also, comment on the volatility of factory sales data.

5. The following conclusions are drawn from the 1973 Handsome Boy versus Meteor product test. Indicate the specific sources of these conclusions in Exhibits 6–6 through 6–16.
   a. There is no marked consumer preference for the new Meteor product.
   b. There is no evidence that the high pumice level dramatically improves Meteor performance.
   c. The product test results suggest that factors other than change in formula are responsible for improved Meteor performance in the marketplace.
6. Comment on the fact that no change in the content of Meteor advertising accompanied the increase in that product's pumice content.
7. It is suggested by some employees of Home Products Universal that a direct comparison should not be made between the consumer preference results of the 1966 and the 1973 product tests because they are based on a significant difference in methodology. They propose that a second product test be run in 1973 comparing old Meteor (that is, the low-pumice product) versus Handsome Boy. Discuss this proposal.
8. If you were president of Home Products Universal, when would you begin to become impatient with the events described in this case? Why?
9. Discuss the indicated increase in pumice level from the standpoint of new Handsome Boy product development. Are the facts presented totally consistent? Be sure you consider the questions of Meteor product test performance, Meteor pricing, Meteor advertising expenditures, and the cost of pumice in your answer. Should Handsome Boy household cleanser be reformulated?

Case 7

Product-Positioning Decisions

Effluvia House Cosmetics Introduces a New Deodorant

THE ALLGOOD DRUG COMPANY purchased Effluvia House Cosmetics Corporation in 1970. The purchase arrangement between the two firms called for a cash payment of $28.5 million as well as the transfer of 100 shares of Allgood common stock for each of the 3,826 shares of Effluvia House "A" common stock outstanding. The Allgood common shares were traded at a high of $37.35 on June 1, 1970, the date on which the actual stock transfer was made. Thus the approximate purchase price paid by Allgood was $42,790,110, or about fifteen times the Effluvia House 1969 profit after taxes of $2,722,681.

Under the purchase agreement, the president (founder and principal owner) of Effluvia House, Andrew A. Monroe (age fifty-two), was to remain as chief executive officer for a period of five years. In addition, two other Effluvia House officers, John A. Jacoby (aged fifty-seven) and Jennifer Briault (age fifty-eight) signed employment agreements with Allgood Drug Company covering a period of five years with the understanding that they would continue as executive vice-presidents in charge of sales, advertising, and promotion (Mr. Jacoby) and product development and production (Ms. Briault).

These three employment agreements were scheduled to expire on May 31, 1975. By that date, J. C. McPhee, president of Allgood, planned to have trained or recruited a new management team to replace the Monroe–Jacoby–Briault group. It was agreed that Allgood could terminate these employment agreements prior to May 31, 1975 at its discretion and upon payment in full of contract salaries through the end of the employment agreements.

McPhee spent a good deal of time during the two years following the acquisition of Effluvia House studying the workings of the organization. Effluvia House marketed a full line of facial cosmetics (powders, lipsticks, eye makeup, face creams and toners, and so on) and perfumes. The line was distributed through leading department stores and large drugstores. In all, Effluvia House maintained distribution in about 6,720 outlets—

6,300 drugstores and 420 department stores. Effluvia House maintained its own sales representatives (cosmeticians) in approximately 250 of the leading department stores and also maintained a department store training force of 15 women who traveled constantly, visiting those stores in which an Effluvia House sales representative worked, as well as those department stores in which the line was sold by employees of the stores. In addition, Effluvia House maintained a separate training force of 10 women who visited all the drugstores employing one or more cosmeticians.

McPhee discovered that about 45 per cent of sales came from the 250 department stores where Effluvia House maintained a sales representative. The bulk of the business in these outlets came from steady and dedicated customers. This clientele was maintained primarily by the expertness and service of the individual sales representatives and the competitiveness of the line. New customers were usually added on the basis of recommendations from existing customers, from response to direct mail solicitation of department store customers, and from "walk-ins" generated by Effluvia House's reputation for quality and excellence, as well as by its display advertising.

A less personal and long-lasting relationship was found between Effluvia House and its customers in the other department stores and in the drugstores. Marketing research demonstrated that customers in these "other" outlets tended to use other cosmetic brands as well as Effluvia House and to have used the individual Effluvia House products that they purchased for an average of 2.9 years. Customers in the major department stores, on the other hand, showed a marked tendency to be exclusive customers of Effluvia House and had purchased each product they used for an average of 7.2 years. The Effluvia House clientele in the major department stores also were, on the average, considerably older than the customers in the other outlets—the average age of the former was 53.4 years, whereas the average age of the latter was 40.6 years.

A major marketing objective of Effluvia House was to maintain a steady flow of new customers into their major department store accounts to offset normal attrition due to competitive activity and death. To this end, a good deal of direct mail advertising was directed toward the charge customers of the individual department stores. In addition, national display advertising was run with the dual objectives of maintaining the Effluvia House image of quality and excellence and of building a reputation for restrained and modest contemporaneity in product and shades. Effluvia House was not a high-fashion house and did not aspire to such a reputation, but it did not linger far behind the leaders; its customers had demonstrated a desire for modern but not bizarre facial cosmetics.

After two years of sporadic study McPhee came to the conclusion that the Effluvia House cosmetics business was totally alien to his packaged proprietary drug experience. The personal and relatively long-lasting relationships that existed between Effluvia House and its established department store customers were quite different from the fickle and transitory brand customer relationship that McPhee had experienced. And the whole manner of Effluvia House cosmetic marketing, from the policy of selective distribution to the employment of clerks to work in the stores of retailers, was totally alien to him.

By mid 1972, McPhee had reached several rather disturbing conclusions about Effluvia House. First, it was clear to McPhee that it would be impossible for him to become de facto president of Effluvia House and run it with his left hand when Monroe's employment contract expired in 1975. Second, he decided that it would be neither wise nor desirable to shift Allgood executives over to Effluvia House either for short terms or for more permanent assignments. He concluded that none of his men really had the right background for such work and that if he did shift them over, it would be necessary to leave them there more or less permanently, thus depriving Allgood of men thoroughly familiar with and assiduously trained in Allgood business methods. Third, McPhee's two-year surveillance had convinced him that there was no younger man in Effluvia House capable of handling the presidency. Finally, and most disturbing of all, McPhee could see no way of bringing the packaged-goods marketing capability of Allgood and the cosmetic-producing capability of Effluvia together to produce a successful line of mass-merchandised cosmetic products. They were two different companies, and all of the Allgood people thought and acted out of one set of perceptions and traditions and all of the Effluvia people thought and acted out of another.

And so McPhee turned to the management consulting firm of Kellner, Boudreau & Gordon and asked them to help. He made his decision with considerable reluctance. He believed that a successful executive should solve his own problems and especially the problems that were the fruit of his own previous decisions. But he needed help in finding a new chief executive officer for Effluvia and he knew that he would have to go out-side for this person. The only way he knew to find such a person was to do it through a solid management consulting firm that dabbled in "head hunting" (executive search and placement) on the side. He also needed help in figuring out how to attack the mass market for cosmetics and, again, he could only assume that this was the kind of activity at which good management consulting firms excel. And so Kellner, Boudreau & Gordon came into the picture with the specific assignments of finding a new president for Effluvia House and proposing a plan by which the expertise of the parent company and its subsidiary might be harnessed to reap the potential profits in mass cosmetic marketing.

Six weeks later Kellner, Boudreau & Gordon recommended that Ms. Renata Ellwood (age forty-eight) be hired as president of Effluvia House. Ms. Ellwood was employed at the time this recommendation was made as executive vice-president in charge of sales, promotion, and merchandising

of the House of Evangeline Finchley, a leading competitor of Effluvia
House. Ms. Ellwood had held this position for eight years. She had been
passed over three years earlier when a new president had been appointed
on the death of founder Evangeline Finchley. The new Finchley president
was Anthony E. F. Frederickson (age thirty-nine), who had been recruited
from the outside. There was no sign that Frederickson would do anything
except run Finchley competently for the next twenty years. Moreover, it
was clear that even if he did falter, Ms. Ellwood was not likely to be
selected by a board of directors that had once considered her qualifications
and then decided to choose someone else.

Ms. Ellwood had started in the fine cosmetics business in 1942 at the
age of eighteen as a sales representative for the House of Evangeline
Finchley in the leading department store in Providence, Rhode Island.
Young she was, but Finchley was glad to get what it could in the way of
employees for its non-war-related business at the height of World War II,
and Ms. Ellwood appeared considerably older than she was, had great
poise, was intelligent, and seemed doggedly determined to be a success.
In 1948 she became a department store traveller for Finchley, and after
eight years of this road experience she was brought to the Finchley offices
in New York City. She held progressively more responsible jobs in the
home office until, in 1966, she was appointed executive vice-president in
charge of sales, promotion, and merchandising.

If she was nothing else, "Natty" Ellwood was a determined and
aggressive woman. There were many things to which she would not
stoop, but at the same time her only goal in life had been, as long as she
could remember, to move constantly upward. On more than one occasion
in her career there had been at least a hint of ruthlessness in this pursuit.
When she was younger, Natty had been attractively chic. Now, in her
forty-eighth year, she weighed exactly 2 pounds more than in the 126
pounds she had carried with her to her first day of work in Providence.
But now the slickness had developed into a rather hard and brittle quality
that made her seem exceptionally businesslike in everything she did.

In the three years since Frederickson had become president of Finchley
a relationship of cool productivity had developed between the two. Natty
Ellwood did her job with total competence, as if to spite Frederickson
rather than to help him become more effective in his new role. But
beneath an exterior cold sweetness, "Miss Ellwood," as Frederickson
called her, was privately contemptuous of him. He was simply not as
good in the job as she would have been, and she knew it.

She was quite sure that her own humble beginnings in the company
were the major reason that the board of directors had not chosen her for
the presidency when it became available. The very fact that she had
started behind the counter in Providence and traveled for eight years in
the 1950's was the basic reason she would have been ideal for the presidency. But she realistically appraised the Finchley board as just a bit too

quietly genteel to consider having a former shop girl in the presidency of their prestigious concern. All these factors contributed to Natty Ellwood's potential availability, and when a discreet inquiry came from a man that she had met two or three times at cosmetic trade association meetings about whether she knew anyone who might be qualified to run a major fashion cosmetic house she hemmed and hawed a bit and then said that she really couldn't think of anyone except perhaps herself.

There followed a series of meetings with Kellner, Boudreau & Gordon executives and finally Ms. Ellwood was introduced to McPhee. They talked for several hours on four separate occasions. McPhee liked Natty all right and believed she could do a competent or better job in running Effluvia House, but he was concerned that she had no mass-marketing experience and could not, therefore, be expected to move knowledgeably into the kind of venture that he had in mind for Effluvia–Allgood. When they discussed this topic she pointed out that she had plenty of ideas about products for the mass market and he had plenty of people who knew the problems and limitations and opportunities in mass distribution outlets and that if she kept an open mind and his people did, there should be no insurmountable obstacles in the way as long as he, McPhee, was really interested in such expansion and was willing to invest as much money as would be required to make it come true.

McPhee procrastinated. He urged Kellner, Boudreau & Gordon to forward their own recommendations about how the assault on the mass market should be made. He wanted to know if a person with Natty Ellwood's background would be compatible with the organization proposed by the management consultants and refused to make up his mind about Ms. Ellwood until their recommendations were in hand. He soon had the following letter from Eldridge Gordon, the partner in charge for Kellner, Boudreau & Gordon:

Kellner, Boudreau & Gordon

348 Madison Avenue
New York City 10017

December 7, 1972

J. C. McPhee
Allgood Drug Company
318 Third Avenue
New York City, N.Y.

Dear J. C.:

You have asked us to study the question of whether Allgood and Effluvia House can effectively mass-market cosmetic products and, if so, what kind of organization should be developed to implement such a program.

We enthusiastically endorse the notion of melding the expertise of these two firms. There are very significant opportunities in the market for mass cosmetic products. Allgood has the marketing know-how to make mass market sales and Effluvia has the product-development–manufacturing know-how to make products that can be sold, and sold at a reasonable profit. So we say that this is a valid goal for your company and one that should be pursued with vigor. How to do it?

Let me list some assumptions, and the conclusions to which these assumptions lead us:

1. The products will be developed and produced by Effluvia House and this parentage will be acknowledged on Effluvia House packages, in advertising, and to the trade. Probably the products should not be attributed directly to Effluvia House but to a subsidiary of Effluvia House—e.g., the New Dawn Division of Effluvia House Cosmetics. (We have no particular interest in the name New Dawn—it is the best we can think of offhand, but we are not in the business of coining names for subsidiaries. No doubt you will have a dozen better ideas.)

   As long as Effluvia House is the source of the products there seems no reason not to acknowledge it as long as such acknowledgment will not lash back upon the image of Effluvia House. It is because of this latter possibility that we suggest that the source of the new products be a separate division of Effluvia House. This approval assumes that the new division will benefit from an overt association with Effluvia House but that its separate status will shield the parent company from the effects of its mistakes.

2. If it is a separate division of Effluvia House, its president, or general manager, should come from current Effluvia House personnel. The principle is a simple one: if the operation is to be a success, it must have superior products to sell and they must come from Effluvia House. The best chance of full Effluvia House cooperation is for a competent and well-respected Effluvia House employee to be promoted to general manager of the division. The person chosen should be relatively young and intelligent, have entrepreneurial instincts, and have a background that emphasizes the product development, manufacturing, and financial aspects of the business. We believe that Harvey Armbister Knowles is such a person: his personnel file is attached. He satisfies all the criteria except that he has had no direct product development experience although his work on the Bloom of Spring line of high-fashion cosmetics for females under twenty-five gave him plenty of exposure to the research and development people and certainly revealed an entrepreneurial bent. The general manager will report to the president of Effluvia House.

3. A senior product manager (or with a more expansive title perhaps) should come from Allgood Drug with responsibility for marketing all of the products developed by the new division. The products will be sold to the trade by the Allgood Drug sales force. We do not yet have a specific candidate for the position. The person finally chosen should combine significant knowledge of drug and food trade selling and merchandising as well as good experience in consumer promotion and advertising. He must be young, imaginative, and really capable of independent and aggressive thought. There will be plenty of people around telling this person what to do and he must be able to ignore this kind of well-meaning advice and plot his own course. He must know the Allgood sales organization, as he will depend upon it to do trade selling. Arthur Weiner and Scott Lampstonne are the candidates that we have found within Allgood, and we will shortly complete our further investigation of these two, as well as any other potential candidates that have not as yet come to our attention. The senior product manager will report to the general manager.

4. One key person should be recruited from the outside: he is the director of marketing research for the division. We must locate an experienced market researcher who has done outstanding work for a successful mass marketer of

cosmetic products. The one thing that neither of your organizations possesses is knowledge of the mass cosmetic consumer and how to extract new and pertinent knowledge from these ladies. The market researcher will have this role and he must have a strong enough background and personality to convince the other two that they are wrong and that he is right when his data contradict their individual or, worse, joint judgments or intuitions. We do not now have a candidate for this job, but it is an active assignment for us and we expect that two or three qualified candidates will shortly be engaged in our screening processes. The marketing research director will report to the general manager.

5. The group should be housed together and physically within the Effluvia House offices if this is possible. We do not envision a big organization at the beginning. Secretaries and perhaps a few assistants will suffice as a start and a great deal of space should not be needed. But the organization is, after all, a part of Effluvia House and it should be physically located at Effluvia House, close to all of the resources that it will have to exploit to the hilt if it is to be successful.

This is, in bare bones form, how we recommend that you proceed. Set up a separate division of Effluvia House, staff it with key personnel from Effluvia House, Allgood Drug, and outside, and make the president of Effluvia House responsible for its success.

We have discussed this basic structure with Renata Ellwood and she sees no reason why it should not be adopted—she is, in fact, enthusiastic about it and about the prospect of running it in your behalf.

We recommend therefore that this basic structure be adopted and that you offer Renata Ellwood the presidency of Effluvia House Cosmetics.

Very truly yours,

KELLNER, BOUDREAU & GORDON

/s/   (Eddy)

Eldridge Gordon, Partner

J. C. McPhee received this letter on a Friday morning in December. He read it through immediately upon receiving it and then put it away, planning to read it again on the following Monday, but letting his mind play with the problem in the meantime, reaching a subconscious conclusion, probably immediately, to be verbalized and confirmed on Monday. This was the way that he made important decisions: if he was still unsure of his course after the incubation period, he would call in one or two associates and discuss the problem with them, let it incubate again, and try to resolve it once more a day or two later.

His thoughts strayed to the Gordon letter several times over the weekend, each time with less skepticism and with greater favor, and finally on Monday, after a second reading, he decided to agree with its recommendations and proceed immediately on the path it outlined.

When the offer finally came from McPhee, Renata Ellwood did not hesitate a moment in accepting it. She became president of Effluvia House on February 1, 1973 with full executive authority to staff and run her business as she saw fit. Andrew Monroe continued as a full-time consultant to Effluvia House and John Jacoby and Jennifer Briault continued in their jobs until adequate replacements could be found for them.

Renata Ellwood had plenty of things to do in her new job, but one aspect of it to which she paid immediate and continuing attention was the formation of the subsidiary to develop and sell cosmetics to the mass market. She set June 15, 1973 as a target date on which the new subsidiary would become fully operational.

One of her first jobs was to find an acceptable name for the new enterprise. She talked to McPhee about this at some length because she realized, and pointed out to him, that only the chief executive officer of an organization really has the ultimate authority to decide what it or any of its subsidiaries will be called, and she wanted to be sure that he was fully in agreement with her choice before the final decision was made. They both agreed that the Kellner, Boudreau & Gordon suggestion—the New Dawn Division—was inappropriate and totally unsuited to Effluvia House. Finally, after considerable thought, Natty Ellwood recommended the name Miss Effluvia Division, and three days later, having given it thorough subconscious consideration in his decision-making fashion, McPhee approved and that was that.

Harvey Knowles was designated, as Kellner, Boudreau & Gordon had recommended, president of the new division, and Arthur Weiner was made its executive vice-president. Allison Marks Sappora was recruited from All-a-Glow Inc., a leading mass marketer of cosmetic products, as director of marketing research. Although Ms. Sappora was only thirty-one, she had developed an industrywide reputation as a market researcher and it was generally acknowledged, at least outside of All-a-Glow Inc., that her work had made a significant contribution to the success of that firm. But the officials of All-a-Glow seemed unaware of this, or if they were aware of it they seemed disinclined to compensate Ms. Sappora at her market value and she thus became available to Miss Effluvia.

Knowles and Weiner were in place by June 15 and Ms. Sappora joined them on July 5, 1973.

* *
*

Harvey Knowles's first approach to the development of new products was simply to discuss what the research and development people of Effluvia House had in mind and were anxious to work on. As he expressed it to Weiner, "Artie, you and I are going to have to work with these birds for a long time and they can make us or break us, so we better get off on the right foot with them, be a little permissive, at least to start. Maybe Allison won't like it, and I suppose we pay her not to like it, but she won't be here to worry about it until July and meanwhile we got a job of work to get started, right?" As Weiner was rather overwhelmed by the cosmetics business as a whole, let alone the prejudices and peculiarities of his new boss, he decided that he wasn't going to argue about anything for a while, let alone what products were to be developed, and he agreed amiably and with apparent enthusiasm.

The chief of laboratory research and development for Effluvia House was Igor Smetsky. Smetsky was a European and had been trained in France as a *parfumeur*, having learned enough chemistry along the way to handle all of the requirements of product development in a major cosmetics firm. He had for some years been toying with a new underarm deodorant product concept. Most of the common deodorants operated on a masking principle, that is, they eliminated odor by masking it, typically by substituting another, more pleasant odor to offset the unpleasant odor derived from the oxygen-activated bacterial odor of perspiration. This masking principle had three distinct shortcomings in the view of Smetsky. First, it was hard to maintain effective deodorizing activity over a period of time. Second, it was hard to deliver an even and extensive coverage of deodorizing material to all the underarm area from which odor might spring. Finally, he disliked the masking principle itself. It was rather chemically inelegant for a product to exist simply to blot out or overwhelm an undesirable odor; it would satisfy Smetsky's aesthetic sense to a much greater degree if a product could be developed that would stop underarm odor before it began. This would not only be more elegant but potentially much more efficient too: a new deodorant based on such a principle could probably also be designed to last longer and to go on evenly with ease, reasoned Smetsky as he set about to solve the problem in his spare time.

Because oxygen is the element that causes perspiration odor, Smetsky reasoned that a product that cleared the underarm area of the presence of oxygen would eliminate odor before it even became odor. This approach was certainly simple enough and it also appealed to his sense of orderliness and purpose. And so in the middle 1960's Smetsky began looking for a chemical that would absorb oxygen and keep it from entering the underarm pores. There are many chemical ingredients that transform oxygen into something else, but there is no element that Smetsky believed would do what he wanted. He began to work with various oxygen-transforming compounds. The problem was complicated by the fact that the desired material must have a very high oxygen-absorbing or oxygen-transforming capability per weight unit. Finally, in early 1970, Smetsky developed a compound that had exactly the characteristics for which he had been searching. He called it ZOT, which stood not for some complex combination of chemical components but, rather, for Zero Oxygen Transformation. And this is just what ZOT accomplished: it eliminated oxygen from the skin surface, and a very small amount of ZOT transformed very large amounts of oxygen into nothing. The next problem was to develop an acceptable form of ZOT (it was first synthesized as a coarse gray crystal that, when ground, was water soluble and miscible in water and other liquids). Smetsky first developed a liquid form of the product and subsequently a cream form. Both these product forms were excellent. They were, in fact, too good. The ZOT phenomenon could not be controlled: when applied under the arm the oxygen zero transformation occurred, immediately and totally for whatever quantity of ZOT product was applied. Oxygen rushed to the underarm area from the surrounding atmosphere in exactly the quantity required to exhaust the ZOT application. When more than a very small amount of ZOT was applied, the rush of air caused a discernible pop or bang in the underarm area and considerable skin irritation as the adjacent clothing was violently whipped across the surface, impeding as it did unleashed oxygen, yearning for ZOT.

This rather bizarre phenomenon had an altogether depressing effect upon poor Smetsky. He realized that he had solved the monumental problem brilliantly, only to be confronted with another problem of perhaps an even greater magnitude. He hoped that a microencapsulation-based, time-released product might provide a solution, but he knew nothing about the microencapsulation process and was somewhat reluctant, in his proper Middle European way, to reveal to his colleagues the nature of the problem that he had wrestled with and achieved such a peculiar victory over. Smetsky had rarely been laughed at in his whole life, and he had no intention of becoming a laughingstock now. And so he undertook to learn enough about microencapsulation-based time release to determine if that principle could be applied to ZOT. It took him two years to do it, but by April of 1973 he had not only satisfied himself that microencapsulation was the answer, he had also successfully microencapsulated ZOT in a pleasantly perfumed liquid that he had designed for use in an aerosol container. The product, as he had perfected it, was discharged from the aerosol can in a rich shaving-cream-like foam that covered the underarm easily and thoroughly.

And so on the eve of the formation of the Miss Effluvia Division, its potential success had already, unbeknown to McPhee and Natty Ellwood, been placed securely within their grasp. Smetsky had perfected a superior underarm deodorant that worked on a totally new principle and that lasted and covered the entire underarm easily and completely.

Smetsky might have his pride and he might seem to some to be a bit on the prissy side, but he could smell opportunity for himself as well as the next person. When he heard that Miss Effluvia was to be formed, that Harvey Knowles was to be its president, and that Knowles was anxious to have the cooperation of the Effluvia House research and development staff and when he was asked if he knew whether any of his people might have any interests that might be worth pursuing, he immediately presented himself in Knowles's office and put the whole story before him. Knowles was overwhelmed. He had believed that he might spend three or four years before developing a satisfactory product entry, let alone a totally new product that could clearly take over a very large and important market. Even if underarm deodorant was not quite what he had in mind for Miss Effluvia, who was he to care about that in the face of huge potential sales and profits?

As the full import of Smetsky's discovery washed over him, Knowles felt himself becoming increasingly relaxed and affable. To think that it was going to be this simple: little old Igor Smetsky, sitting right there under his nose all the time. Indeed!

As his mood brightened, he talked with increasing agitation to Smetsky about how they would move forward with the product together, for the glory of Miss Effluvia and the profit of Effluvia House. There had always been a bit of pomposity about Harvey Knowles, and although he had been reasonably successful in restraining it around the office, it occasionally seeped to the surface, generally during the office Christmas party when he, as an Effluvia House supervisory employee, was called upon to award service watches to his deserving employees. But there had never been a jingoistic note at Christmas time to match what now rolled forth around the watchful Smetsky. But Smetsky would have none of it. After all, he had developed the ZOT microencapsulated, time-released aerosol underarm deodorant (perfected ZOT) in his spare time and to satisfy his own curiosity and purposes. At the time of the inception of ZOT development, Effluvia House had not had the slightest potential interest in underarm deodorant, and Smetsky surely would have been chastised, if not fired, had he presumed to work on such a project on company time. If it had become known that he was doing it as a hobby at home in his spare time, there would have been raised eyebrows and his judgment would have been called into serious question. It was only with the formation of the Miss Effluvia Division that Effluvia House developed an interest in products like perfected ZOT. Had the Miss Effluvia Division not been formed, Smetsky would have had to look outside of Effluvia House for interest and for a purchaser or a royalty arrangement. As he said to Knowles, "So you see, Mr. Knowles, perfected ZOT belongs to me and not to Miss Effluvia. It is totally fortuitous that you are president of a new division that would like this product and that I have this product. The fact that I work for Effluvia House is not relevant to your interest. We are in every sense at arm's length, and we must proceed on an arm's length basis. I am sure that the company attorneys will confirm my view of this and advise you that it only remains for you to reach a compensation agreement with me. Because of my loyalty to Effluvia House, I will refrain from offering perfected ZOT to any other company. There will be no auction for this product, Mr. Knowles, but there will be equity."

This little speech deflated Knowles rather rapidly. "All right, Smetsky, if that's the way you feel, we have nothing more to talk about at the moment. I have no authority to negotiate with employees of other divisions and I'll have to see Mr. McPhee and the company's attorneys about it."

But Smetsky refused to let the meeting end on that note. Rather, sensing a very real possibility of victory over this unpleasant, sweaty bureaucrat, he proceeded to the next higher level of discourse. "But before you speak with both these men, Mr. Knowles, you should have some idea as to what is in my mind. Surely this is important to you. I would prefer a royalty agreement, Mr. Knowles. That is, I would prefer a payment of three per cent of the factory sales volume achieved by the product. This would apply not only to products manufactured by you that contain perfected ZOT but to any manufactured products based on licenses for the use of perfected ZOT granted by you to others. If you choose not to accept this royalty proposal, then a cash payment of two and a half million dollars would be required. In either event, I will turn over perfected ZOT to Miss Effluvia House Division in its entirety—the journals in which I recorded the developmental steps, the formulae, the problems and danger points, and my working diagrams and plans for manufacturing the product in quantities large enough for mass market consumption."

Knowles was out of his depth, and with every word spoken by Smetsky he seemed to get higher and higher up on the dry land. He could see no alternative but to accede to Smetsky's demand, assuming that the company attorneys agreed with Smetsky's appreciation of his own situation.

Knowles talked with McPhee immediately. He told him about Smetsky and perfected ZOT and about Smetsky's proposition. McPhee's reaction was predictable. "Suppose you tell him to chase his tail? Tell him we'll take him to court and win. He is, after all, an employee, and he does, after all, have certain loyalties to us." "You may be right about all of that, J. C.", said Knowles, "but I think we better check it out with the lawyers before we take any position that we might later regret."

McPhee didn't like that point of view and he didn't like it coming from his new divisional president, who at all times was supposed to pursue aggressively the interests of the company. But he reluctantly agreed that in his caution Knowles could just be right.

And so the lawyers were called in. Two weeks of conference and opinions and memoranda ensued. Much verbiage broke across the desks of McPhee and Knowles and much intensive and soul-searching conversation engulfed them. When all this stylized business had been completed, it was clear that the lawyers believed the following to be true:

1. It was unfortunate that Effluvia House had not signed an employment contract with Smetsky that anticipated and protected Effluvia House against just such a set of circumstances as those that had now evolved.

2. In the absence of such an agreement, it was risky to take Smetsky to court. He had at least a 50–50 chance of winning in court, perhaps better. In addition, there were other negatives about taking an

employee to court: the effect on the morale of other employees could for example, be incalculable.

3. The final and preferred option was to negotiate a settlement with Smetsky at terms more favorable to the company than those proposed by Smetsky. A royalty arrangement was preferable to an outright cash payment, because under a royalty agreement Smetsky didn't make any money until Miss Effluvia had actually developed an acceptable commercial product and offered it for sale in the marketplace. There were many potential slips between an apparently successful prototype and a market success, and Smetsky should be compensated only on the basis of achieved sales.

On the basis of this summary, Knowles and Elbreth B. Sommerset, general counsel of Effluvia House, negotiated an agreement with Smetsky giving him a royalty of 1.25 per cent on factory sales of all products containing perfected ZOT, including both those manufactured by Miss Effluvia and Effluvia House and those manufactured by other firms under license. In return, Smetsky assigned all of his rights in perfected ZOT, including his patent applications to Effluvia House. He also agreed to sell any other inventions or fomulations to Effluvia House at a royalty of .25 per cent of factory sales. In due course, Smetsky and his heirs were to become millionaires many times over as a result of this simple arrangement. But at this time the future was not at all clear and it was with considerable apprehension that Smetsky also agreed to resign his position as chief of laboratory research and development of Effluvia House and accept a new position as special consultant to the president of Miss Effluvia Division. His only assignment with Miss Effluvia was to supervise the readying of perfected ZOT underarm deodorant for commercial sale.

* * *

While all of this had been going on, Knowles had also been taking steps to ready his fledgling organization for the task of converting prototype products into entries into the commercial marketplace. He discussed this subject at considerable length with Arthur Weiner and Allison Sappora. They concentrated these discussions on an identification of the fundamentals of marketing new products, always assuming that acceptable products would be made available to them, particularly from the product development laboratories of Effluvia House. In their conversations they understood that the product development people might need prodding and direction, but they assumed that once an area of potential exploration had been identified, product development would provide an acceptable prototype that would compete technically with comparable products from the leading cosmetic firms. Sometimes, too, they expected that they would get lucky and receive unsolicited but superior new products from product development, like perfected ZOT.

But then what should be done? What were the essential issues that must at that point be resolved? As a result of this deliberation, the group decided that in the mass market for cosmetic products five issues held the key for marketing success:

Product positioning—that is, the purpose of the product in consumer terms. What the product does and how it does this both in terms of absolute performance and relative to other available competitive products.

Product pricing—that is, the price that should be charged to maximize sales and profits.

Product physical presentation—that is, how the product is formulated and how it is packaged, both aesthetically and functionally.

Product communication—including name, advertising, and promotion for the product.

Product economics—that is, the development of a structure of product income and product expense competitively consistent with maximum sales and guaranteeing a reasonable profit within a reasonable time.

(A consideration of product positioning for perfected ZOT constitutes the balance of this case, and the other elements, as well as product positioning, are treated in Case 8, following, which is concerned with market planning.)

It seemed to Knowles that marketing research might be expected to make a contribution in all of these areas. Nevertheless, he expected that the determination of the product positioning was perhaps the area in which marketing research could give the most significant help. Allison Sappora agreed that marketing research was crucial in helping to define how a particular product should be positioned. She suggested that two fundamental research steps should be undertaken. First, she recommended that a consumer motivational study be made. The following is a summary of her statement on motivational studies:

The purpose of motivational studies is to gain general insight into the way in which consumers perceive the product category; their patterns of usage; the needs the product fulfills for them; and the roles the product plays in their lives. The motivational work is designed to accomplish two objectives. First, it is designed to give marketing people a "feel" for the product category in terms of the way the consumer himself perceives the category and responds to it. Second, the motivational research is designed to provide a description of the way in which consumers might respond to new products in the category and specifically to a new product with the specifications of the product that has been developed for us by the product development people.

Second, she recommended that a consumer concept test be developed on the basis of the motivational study results.

The motivational study will suggest the ways in which the consumer will respond to the proposed product. Sometimes there will be several ways in which such an appeal might be made and sometimes only one or two. Meanwhile, there are a variety of competitive products and their positionings are also important because it is with these competitors that our neophyte will ultimately compete in the market if all else goes well. The concept test undertakes to rank-order and quantify the appeal of these various products to consumers. In the concept test the consumer is asked to evaluate two product descriptions and choose between them. Over a sample of consumers, a cumulative evaluation and choice produces, finally, an overall ranking of the test concepts, as well as an indication of the reasons for their strengths and weaknesses.

The first Miss Effluvia product to be selected for this purpose was perfected ZOT. At the time the motivational and concept work were done, no name had been selected for the product. (And, indeed, it was not for several weeks that a decision was made to call the product Miss Effluvia Miracle Foam Deodorant.) But it was not necessary, said Ms. Sappora, for a product to have been named prior to consumer research evaluation in the concept-testing procedure. It was, after all, the product attributes that served as the focus of attention, and the name could come along in due course.

And so a formal motivational study was undertaken for product B-17, a code name that had no significance at all except that it implied bigness to Knowles and mystery to Ms. Sappora. The research work was based on the focused group-interview method. In this method groups of consumers are gathered together for informal yet rigorously directed group discussions under the leadership of a specially trained social psychologist. Each such group consists of ten or twelve consumers with whatever consumption and demographic characteristics seem important to the investigator. In this study, all respondents were female users of deodorants between the ages of twenty-one and forty-five. A total of nine sessions were held, three each with users of the new "heavy-duty" liquid roll-on products, users of aerosol spray products, and users of conventional roll-ons and creams.

During the actual sessions, consumers are encouraged to relax and interact with each other. The group leader tries to foster this relaxed atmosphere, giving it gentle yet purposeful direction. In giving it such direction, he follows a prepared topic guide that serves as a kind of general outline within which considerable flexibility is allowed. The topic outline for this particular project covered three basic areas:

1. A general discussion of underarm deodorants, the way in which women use these products, and their general feelings about them and attitudes toward them.

2. A much more focused discussion probing into the whys of deodorant usage, perceptions of deodorant brands, and attitudes toward deodorant brands and types.

3. Finally, product B-17 was introduced into the sessions. At first, the women were encouraged to handle, release, and smell the product. Subsequently, the moderator described, in an unemotional way, the product characteristics of B-17 and how it could be expected to perform as an underarm deodorant.

The following is an excerpt from the "conclusions" section of the final report on this motivational research on underarm deodorants:

Seven conclusions with implications for marketing may be drawn from this research. They are

1. There are actually two distinct markets for underarm deodorant products. On the one hand are individuals who perspire modestly, particularly in the summer time, or during physical exertion. These individuals do not consider perspiration and its odor a major problem and they are casual almost to the point of indifference in their selection of deodorant brands. But these people do use deodorants regularly—even if they do not perceive an acute problem. They have become habitual users, presumably because such activity reinforces their self-image of fastidiousness.

    There is another group that views underarm perspiration and its odor in a considerably more serious way. For this second group (we have no idea how large this group is proportionately, but it is large and may be between 20 per cent and 40 per cent of all women) underarm perspiration is a continuing and annoying bother. Wetness and odor are their constant companions, and they are anxious to find a solution, switching from brand to brand, looking for a superior product that will finally give them significant relief and a sense of security.

2. There is no heavy-user grouping in the conventional sense in this market. All users, regardless of the kind of perspiration problem they have, seem to use a deodorant in a ritualistic, once-or-twice-a-day way.

3. The women with a severe perspiration problem require an antiperspirant and are, secondarily, anxious about deodorizing action. The women whose perspiration problem is less acute are relatively disinterested in antiperspirant claims, as such, but tend to be more responsive to deodorizing claims. Women understand that a variety of individual needs exist and expect, therefore, that a variety of brands should be marketed to meet this variety of needs.

4. B-17 is of particular interest to those women who feel the need of deodorant protection but are not concerned with a serious perspiration problem.

5. Women are distinctly uninterested in the mechanics of how oxygen works. Discussions of time-release mechanisms and oxygen transformation bore them to tears. This is particularly true of the women in this market to whom B-17 has its primary appeal, that is, the indifferently fastidious deodorant user. If B-17 were an antiperspirant, the group who need such a product and are distinctly more concerned with the entire product category might be more

interested in mechanics and transformations. They are the ones for whom these products are, after all, relatively important.

6. The product generates a great amount of excitement. The foam form is novel and interesting and its virtues in use are obvious. The thought that it is a significant new breakthrough and that it is based on a destruction rather than a masking principle seems to be intrinsically dramatic and interesting—forget about the details of how it works.

7. An unexpected finding was the unanimity with which women accepted the B-17 fragrance. It seemed to suggest a clean, natural kind of fragrance—one that would perpetuate and enhance the sensuous warmth of the finished bath. There was considerable interest among some of the group members about whether this fragrance was maintained over the effective life of the product under the arms or whether this fragrance was dissipated as the odor-killing activity of the product was unleashed.

* * *

The Knowles-Weiner-Sappora group digested these results, discussed them at length, and finally agreed that a successful exploitation of B-17 might involve several elements or combinations of elements.

In the first place, it seemed clear that the product could appeal only to the deodorant user—not to the woman who perceived her need to be for an antiperspirant. The deodorant user had several interesting characteristics that could well be mirrored in the positioning of the product. She was not seriously interested in deodorants: the product category fulfilled a need if not a preoccupation for her and she was not especially concerned with product differences or performance characteristics. By extension, it seemed reasonable to assume that the product positioning need not be heavy-handed or serious but could be light, gay, and feminine.

Secondly, the product itself had inherent interest. The key to its interest lay in the fact that it was new, looked new, smelled new, and operated on a breakthrough principle. Even though the details of the principle were irrelevant, the promise that the principle was totally new and involved the elegance of destruction rather than the hypocrisy of masking was of interest to the curious consumer, looking always for the next step toward perfection in every product category.

Third, there was enough brand switching and switching to new products to pose a considerable challenge to positioning. The product had to be sharply and clearly positioned with a distinct and easily discernible reason for being. It was easy to get lost in this category because of target-audience indifference, the proliferation of brands, and the history of introduction of "me-too," undifferentiated new products.

With these general thoughts in mind, Ms. Sappora set about developing a list of product descriptions. Each of these descriptions would spring from the research and would be designed to portray a unique and unambiguous deodorant product: one that might logically be found in the marketplace.

Here is the list that she developed:

DESTROYS OXYGEN

This new deodorant product is based on a totally different principle from all others. It destroys oxygen under the arm and thus perspiration odor. Perspiration odor cannot form without oxygen—this product destroys oxygen and keeps you odor-free for hours.

GUARANTEES SATISFACTION

This new deodorant product guarantees an end to underarm perspiration odor for hours after each use. It works on a totally new principle that destroys odor once and for all. This is the only deodorant product that can guarantee your satisfaction —no more perspiration odor. Be as lovely as you really are.

FOAMY FRESH PRODUCT

This is the first deodorant foam—so fresh, so effective. Apply it effortlessly and marvel at its bath-moist fragrance and freshness. It works as no other deodorant can work to bring you, in its foamy freshness, total deodorant protection for hours.

NEW, NEW PRODUCT

This is the first totally new deodorant product on the market in years. New in so many distinctive ways—works in a new way by destroying odor before it forms rather than merely masking it, comes in a new rich foamy form, with totally new bath-fresh odor. Keeps you odor-free for hours.

PROBLEM PERSPIRATION ODOR

Many women suffer from problem perspiration odor: constantly a problem, impossible to solve until now. This new product destroys problem perspiration odor totally and for hours with its completely new principle, which does not depend upon the weak masking action of all other leading brands.

When these alternative product-positioning statements were completed by Ms. Sappora, considerable thought was given to two topics. The first question was whether or not the statements captured both individually and collectively the overall insights into the consumer conveyed by the motivational research. Knowles felt that the statements tended to be too contentious and too rational, ignoring, in the process, the rather more fastidiously feminine characteristics of that key segment of the market for deodorant brands. Should there not be a lighter, more cosmetic orientation in the statements, he wondered. Ms. Sappora countered that a certain rationality was inherent in all such research, but that she believed that the compatibility of the various approaches with a distinct cosmetic orientation could be probed in the questions asked the respondents. In addition, she pointed out that any of the positions could be executed in communications with more rather than fewer trappings of femininity. Mr. Weiner was concerned that statements did not include those of competitive products. Ms. Sappora acknowledged this to be true but pointed out that the five positioning statements included all of the postures now taken by competitive products and included in addition the very strong distinguishing characteristics of B-17: the unique principle of its action, its new form and its fragrance. A competitive statement without these distinguishing characteristics would tend to sound rather hollow, reasoned Ms. Sappora, and she believed it would be unproductive to include them in the research. With these issues resolved, Ms. Sappora fielded a research project based on the following research design.

The concept test was conducted among a sample of one-thousand deodorant users (women who admitted a more serious perspiration problem were screened out of the sample). The field work was conducted in five markets: Atlanta, Boston, Cleveland, Jacksonville, and Denver, two-hundred interviews per market.

Each qualified respondent was shown two identical aerosol containers labelled "New Foam Deodorant." In addition to this generic description, each container was labelled with one of the product-positioning statements previously quoted. The respondent was told that the products were not currently on the market. She was asked to tell the interviewer which of the two products she would prefer and why. Next she was asked to describe what kind of women she thought would be most likely to use each of the test products. Finally, the respondent was asked, for both concepts to which she was exposed, if she had one question about each of the products, what the question would be.

The study was designed so that each respondent saw only two of the five product positioning statements. When each of the five concepts was paired with every other concept, a total of ten concept pairs resulted:

A. Destroys oxygen.
B. Guarantees satisfaction.
C. Foamy fresh product.
D. New, new product
E. Problem perspiration Odor.

1. A–B Destroys oxygen vs. guarantees satisfaction.
2. A–C   ,,   ,,   vs. foamy fresh product.
3. A–D   ,,   ,,   vs. new, new product.
4. A–E   ,,   ,,   vs. problem perspiration odor.
5. B–C Guarantees satisfaction vs. foamy fresh product.
6. B–D   ,,   ,,   vs. new, new product.
7. B–E   ,,   ,,   vs. problem perspiration odor.
8. C–D Foamy fresh product vs. new, new product.
9. C–E   ,,   ,,   ,,   vs. problem perspiration odor.
10. D–E New, new product vs. problem perspiration odor.

Because each positioning appeared as a contestant in four pairs, it was judged by a total of four hundred respondents, more or less, against the average strength of the other four positionings. The score for each product positioning was computed by division of the total number of respondents who saw each statement into the number of respondents who chose the concept.

Beyond the basic choice questions, a projective question was asked ("What kind of woman do you believe this product would appeal to?") to show the qualitative impact of each positioning. Finally, the respondent was asked what questions each of the positionings left unanswered in order to reveal the ways in which they seemed to the consumer to be incomplete.

Exhibits 7–1 through 7–18 summarize the data obtained from this study of perfected ZOT concepts.

EXHIBIT 7–1
Specimen Data: Overall Performance Ratings of Five Underarm Deodorant Concepts

CONCEPT	RESPONDENTS WHO PREFER CONCEPT	BASE
A. Destroys oxygen	63%	398
B. Guarantees satisfaction	47	392
C. Foamy fresh product	56	404
D. New, new product	40	404
E. Problem perspiration odor	44	394

EXHIBIT 7–2
Specimen Data: Preference Ratings by Individual Concept Pairs

CONCEPT PAIR	PER CENT	CONCEPT PAIR	PER CENT
A–B	67–33	B–D	56–44
A–C	73–27	B–E	53–47
A–D	53–47	C–D	82–18
A–E	60–40	C–E	62–38
B–C	47–53	D–E	50–50

EXHIBIT 7–3
Specimen Data: Per Cent of Respondents Who Prefer Concept by Age of Respondent

CONCEPT	OVERALL PREFERENCE	34 OR YOUNGER	35 OR OLDER
A. Destroys oxygen	63%	65%	61%
B. Guarantees satisfaction	47	49	45
C. Foamy fresh product	56	56	56
D. New, new Product	40	38	42
E. Problem perspiration odor	44	42	46

EXHIBIT 7–4
Specimen Data: Reasons for Preferring
"Destroys Oxygen" Positioning

Base: All who prefer "destroys oxygen"	
Number	251
Per cent	*100**

New way of working, new principle	72% √
Destroys oxygen, that's good	26 √
No more odor, at all	12
Works for hours	10
It's a scientific product, complicated product	6
All other	12

* Reasons add to more than 100 per cent because some respondents gave multiple answers.

EXHIBIT 7–5
Specimen Data: The Kind of Woman Who Would Prefer This Product—
"Destroys Oxygen"

	TOTAL	PREFER DESTROYS OXYGEN	PREFER OTHER POSITION
Base: Respondents exposed to "destroys oxygen"			
Number	398	251	147
Per cent	*100**	*100**	*100**
Women with scientific training	49%	22%	95%
Women like me	27	42	1
Professional women, working women	34	5	83
Any kind of women, can't say	21	27	11
All other	6	10	—

* Some respondents described more than one kind of woman.

EXHIBIT 7–6

Specimen Data: Additional Information Desired About "Destroys
Oxygen" Positioning

	TOTAL	PREFER DESTROYS OXYGEN	PREFER OTHER POSITION
Base: Respondents exposed to "destroys oxygen"			
Number	398	251	147
Per cent	100*	100*	100*
Why is oxygen important?	28%	10%	60%
How can oxygen cause odor?	16	5	35
Oxygen is pure not dirty?	10	3	22
Other information requested	20	25	11
No information requested	45	62	16

* Some respondents asked more than one question.

EXHIBIT 7–7

Specimen Data: Reasons for Preferring "Guarantees
Satisfaction" Positioning

Base: All who prefer "guarantees satisfaction"	
Number	184
Per cent	100*
I believe all products should guarantee results	62%
New principle is good, wonderful	27
A new product is usually worth trying, buying, etc.	12
Works for hours	8
All other	4

* Reasons add to more than 100 per cent because some respondents
gave multiple answers.

EXHIBIT 7–8
Specimen Data: The Kind of Woman Who Would Prefer This Product—
"Guarantees Satisfaction"

	TOTAL	PREFER GUARANTEES SATISFACTION	PREFER OTHER POSITION
Base: Respondents exposed to "guarantees satisfaction"			
Number	392	184	208
Per cent	*100**	*100**	*100**
Pennywise, good shopper, shrewd	39%	41% ✓	38%
Concerned about results	28	29	27
Woman like me	17	15	19
Any kind of woman, can't say	24	21	26
All other	16	18	14

* Some respondents described more than one kind of woman.

EXHIBIT 7–9
Specimen Data: Additional Information Desired About "Guarantees
Satisfaction" Positioning

	TOTAL	PREFER GUARANTEES SATISFACTION	PREFER OTHER POSITION
Base: Respondents exposed to "guarantees satisfaction"			
Number	392	184	208
Per cent	*100**	*100**	*100**
What is the totally new principle?	58%	50%	65%
What is guaranteed?	56	40	70 ✓
How can odor be destroyed once and for all?	22	8	34
Other information requested	6	4	8
No information requested	2	1	3

* Some respondents asked more than one question.

EXHIBIT 7–10

Specimen Data: Reasons for Preferring "Foamy Fresh Product" Positioning

Base: All who prefer "foamy fresh product"	
Number	226
Per cent	100*
Foam is a good idea	52%
Bath freshness, fragrance	48
Different from other deodorants	35
Works for hours	21
It would feel good	18
All other	31

* Reasons add to more than 100 per cent because some respondents gave multiple answers.

EXHIBIT 7–11

Specimen Data: The Kind of Woman Who Would Prefer This Product—"Foamy Fresh Product"

	TOTAL	PREFER FOAMY FRESH PRODUCT	PREFER OTHER POSITION
Base: Respondents exposed to "foamy fresh product"			
Number	404	226	178
Per cent	100*	100*	100*
A woman who enjoys being a woman	63%	64%	61%
Fastidious, fresh-looking woman	49	40	61
Smart, attractive woman	28	19	40
A woman like me	54	67	38
Any kind of woman, can't say	2	3	1
All other	6	5	7

* Some respondents described more than one kind of woman.

EXHIBIT 7–12
Specimen Data: Additional Information Desired About "Foamy Fresh Product" Positioning

	TOTAL	PREFER FOAMY FRESH PRODUCT	PREFER OTHER POSITION
Base: Respondents exposed to "foamy fresh product"			
Number	404	226	178
Per cent	100*	100*	100*
What does foamy fresh mean?	26%	18%	36%
What does product do, how does it work?	20	16	25
Sounds messy, is it?	8	2	15
Other information requested	16	10	24
No information requested	52	72	26

* Some respondents asked more than one question.

EXHIBIT 7–13
Specimen Data: Reasons for Preferring "New, New Product" Positioning

Base: All who prefer "new, new product"	
Number	162
Per cent	100*
Sounds like a genuinely new product	52%
Like the way it's supposed to work	37
Foam sounds good, like fun	16
Keeps odor free for hours	7
All others	12

* Reasons add to more than 100 per cent because some respondents gave multiple answers.

EXHIBIT 7-14
Specimen Data: The Kind of Woman Who Would Prefer This Product—"New New Product"

	TOTAL	PREFER NEW, NEW PRODUCT	PREFER OTHER POSITION
Base: Respondents exposed to "new, new product"			
Number	404	162	242
Per cent	100*	100*	100*
Smart, well informed	46%	42%	49%
The kind who are up-to-date, fad-conscious	27	29	26
Overdressed, over made up	13	2	21
A woman like me	21	14	26
Can't think what kind of woman, don't know	24	26	23
All other	12	10	13

* Some respondents described more than one kind of woman.

EXHIBIT 7-15
Specimen Data: Additional Information Desired About "New, New Product" Positioning

	TOTAL	PREFER NEW, NEW PRODUCT	PREFER OTHER POSITION
Base: Respondents exposed to "new, new product"			
Number	404	162	242
Per cent	100*	100*	100*
Don't trust new product, too many new products	35%	33%	36%
How is it new, what's new about it?	25	27	24
Sound messy, is it?	14	16	13
Other information requested	17	15	19
No information requested	10	9	10

* Some respondents asked more than one question.

EXHIBIT 7–16
Specimen Data: Reasons for Preferring "Problem Perspiration Odor" Positioning

Base: All who prefer "problem perspiration odor"	
Number	173
Per cent	100*
A product for problem perspiration odor is needed	37%
Good for too much perspiration, wetness	35
Interesting principle	14
Last for hours	16
All others	18

* Reasons add to more than 100 per cent because some respondents gave multiple answers.

EXHIBIT 7–17
Specimen Data: The Kind of Woman Who Would Prefer This Product— "Problem Perspiration Odor"

	TOTAL	PREFER PROBLEM PERSPIRATION	PREFER OTHER
Base: Respondents exposed to "problem perspiration odor"			
Number	394	173	221
Per cent	100*	100*	100*
Woman with problem perspiration	68%	67%	69%
Woman with trouble staying dry	24	25	24
Messy woman	25	27	24
A woman like me	2	2	2
Any kind of woman, can't say	20	18	22
All other	6	5	6

* Some respondents described more than one kind of woman.

EXHIBIT 7–18
Specimen Data: Additional Information Desired About "Problem Perspiration Odor" Positioning

	TOTAL	PREFER PROBLEM PERSPIRATION ODOR	PREFER OTHER POSITION
Base: Respondents exposed to "problem perspiration odor"			
Number	394	173	221
Per cent	100*	100*	100*
What is problem perspiration odor?	54%	24%	78%
How does problem odor differ from problem perspiration?	42	18	61
Other information requested	16	17	15
No information requested	21	42	5

* Some respondents asked more than one question.

Questions for Case 7

1. Evaluate the Kellner, Boudreau & Gordon plan for organizing the new Effluvia House subsidiary. Do you believe that it is the best organization that could be created to accomplish McPhee's marketing objectives?
2. How important is product positioning? Does it really make any difference in a situation like that described in the case, i.e., in the case of a new breakthrough product?
3. Is there a limit to the number of positions that can be developed for a product? Can you think of two additional product positionings that could be used for this new product?
4. Describe the rationale underlying the concept test. Do you agree with it or not?
5. How important do you believe Knowles's objection to the concept test research to be? Are cosmetic products well suited to this kind of testing? Why or why not?
6. Analyze the data provided in each of the Exhibits 7–1 through 7–18. Prepare a brief set of conclusions and recommendations based on this analysis.
7. Do men use deodorant products? Why have men been ignored by the Knowles–Weiner–Sappora team?

CASE 8

Marketing Plans

Miss Effluvia Prepares to Market Miracle Foam Deodorant

ARVEY KNOWLES was delighted with the outcome of the product-positioning work on Miracle Foam Deodorant (see Case 7). While this work had been proceeding, he, Arthur Weiner, and Allison Sappora had discussed at length the desirability of conducting a product test on new Miracle Foam Deodorant. Ms. Sappora was very much in favor of such a test: "After all, gentlemen, all we have is Mr. Smetsky's enthusiasm and our own trial of the product to go on."

Weiner had been captivated by the product when he used it in his home. And so had his wife ("Susan thinks the product is terrific, and she's never been wrong yet"). Susan Weiner's view in corroboration of his own seemed fully enough to Weiner, and the thought of the complicated paraphernalia of a consumer product test, which he neither understood nor trusted, put him off even further. (Consumer product tests had not been an important ingredient in Allgood New Product development.)

Knowles was too committed to Miracle Foam Deodorant to consider seriously the possibility that a product test result would cause him to withdraw his support of the product. This was not a matter of intellectual dishonesty. Rather, his view merely reflected his own conviction about Miracle Foam Deodorant and his own judgment of its potential in the marketplace. But he was not, by training, a marketing man nor, by experience, a consumer-goods marketing man, and this tended to give him pause. Perhaps he was wrong. Perhaps it would help to have substantive consumer testimony to support his belief. But his concern went beyond this, too. After all, Allison Sappora had been hired and it was not only her job to make research recommendations, but she had, in fact, been assured that her counsel in such matters would be taken. So, in equity, Knowles felt a responsibility to agree with Ms. Sappora and give her his support in the product test program.

In the event, the outcome of the product test was even better than Knowles had dared to expect. Miracle Foam Deodorant was a clear winner over the other leading deodorant brands, All Clear and Cream Puff. The basic findings of this research are summarized in Exhibits 8–1, 8–2, 8–3,

EXHIBIT 8–1
Specimen Data: Blind Product Test
Overall Preference—Miracle Foam Deodorant Versus All Clear

	TOTAL	ALL CLEAR USERS	NON-ALL-CLEAR USERS
Base:			
Number	400	102	298
Per cent	100	100	100
Prefer Miracle Foam Deodorant	71%	68%	72%
Prefer All Clear	22	18	23
No preference	7	14	5

EXHIBIT 8–2
Specimen Data: Blind Product Test
Reasons for Preference Among Those Preferring Foam Deodorant

	TOTAL	ALL CLEAR USERS	NON-ALL-CLEAR USERS
Base:			
Number	284	69	215
Per cent	100*	100*	100*
It works better	64%	66%	63%
Lasts longer	32	26	34
Better foam	30	32	29
Longer lasting, better scent	26	30	25
All other	10	8	10

* Some testers gave more than one reason for preference.

EXHIBIT 8–3
Specimen Data: Blind Product Test
Overall Preference—Miracle Foam Deodorant Versus Cream Puff

	TOTAL	CREAM PUFF USERS	NON-CREAM-PUFF USERS
Base:			
Number	406	126	280
Per cent	100	100	100
Prefer Miracle Foam Deodorant	82%	84%	81%
Prefer Cream Puff	17	13	19
No preference	1	3	—

EXHIBIT 8–4
Specimen Data: Blind Product Test
Reasons for Preference Among Those Preferring Miracle Foam Deodorant

	TOTAL	CREAM PUFF USERS	NON-CREAM-PUFF USERS
Base:			
Number	333	106	227
Per cent	100*	100*	100*
Better fresher scent	72%	76%	70%
Works faster	41	43	40
Stays fresh longer	39	38	40
Foam form better	21	6	28
All other	11	2	15

* Some testers gave more than one reason for preference.

and 8–4. The very favorable consumer reaction reflected enthusiasm not only for the form of the new product but also for the way it worked, its longer-lasting quality, and its scent.

So just as the product-positioning work indicated that an emotional, cosmetic positioning was best for the product, the product test indicated a strong consumer preference for it. The stage was now set for the actual process of marketing to begin. And Knowles was immediately confronted with yet another decision. Who should be responsible for bringing this product to market? Certainly not himself. He was, after all, *President* Knowles, and his job was to monitor and evaluate the work of others, not to be an initiator. The same was true of Weiner in his capacity as executive vice-president and marketing specialist. He had not been hired *to do*, but rather *to direct*, and although he might ultimately be held responsible for the success or failure of Miracle Foam Deodorant, it was not his job to bring the product to market. Nor was it Allison Sappora's job: she had been hired to do marketing research, not to become a director of a brand's destiny.

As he thought about it, it suddenly dawned on Knowles that what was needed was a product manager. Knowles had never known a product manager, but he had heard the title used and it was now clear what kind of work the title described. He checked this impression out with Arthur Weiner: "Arthur, we got a winner, but no one to manage it, is that right?" "Just so, Harv," responded Arthur, and that was that.

Kellner, Boudreau & Gordon strongly recommended that the product manager come from outside Effluvia House and Allgood. They argued that the person who was expected to manage a new consumer product in the cosmetic field in a company with no operational expertise in this field must, in fact, have significant experience in precisely this line of work.

In due course they identified Sherman L. Elmandorf, a senior product manager in the employ of the mass cosmetic producer L'amour de France.

Elmandorf, age thirty-two, had been with L'amour de France for six years, and prior to that he had been a field sales trainee for Allgood Drug Company. He had joined Allgood after graduating from a major Mid-western graduate business school in 1964. Elmandorf knew Allgood was a superb trainer of sales personnel and he firmly believed that a career in marketing could be based only on solid field sales training. He had had no intention of making a career with Allgood, although he did not mention that to the recruiter from Allgood personnel, who was delighted to find a student of Elmandorf's academic achievements who seemed so anxious to enter the field sales training program. Elmandorf was the star of his field training class and as his reward was assigned, after the completion of his training year, to a territory that included most of interior Virginia and West Virginia, an area that had over the years been particularly un-productive for Allgood. Part of this assignment reflected respect for Elmandorf's performance as a trainee, and part reflected simple vin-dictiveness.

Elmandorf's training supervisor was August J. Judson, one of the deans of the working Allgood sales force, self-taught, grade-school–educated, a semiprecious diamond in the rough if there ever was one. Judson made it a point to have those sales trainees considered to have outstanding potential assigned to himself for field training. He enjoyed showing the younger men some of the tricks of the trade and he enjoyed the feeling of superiority with which the student relation endowed him. And he genuinely liked field selling and loved to watch a fledgling with superior selling talent develop under his own hand. But he mistrusted education and detested product managers. It was not long before the combination of Elmandorf's lack of discretion and Judson's native horse sense in judging people brought him to the conclusion that young Elmandorf was too preoccupied with his educational attainments. Worse yet, Judson decided that Elmandorf had no interest at all in a sales career but was instead preparing himself for a career in product management. Elmandorf was a good trainee, all right, probably the best that Judson had ever seen. But the older man felt that he was wasting his time, because Elmandorf did not aspire to the career that he himself had chosen and more or less enjoyed over the years.

So there was a mixture of truth and guile in Judson's recommendation to assign Elmandorf to the interior Virginias: "Elmandorf is one of the finest sales talents that I have ever had the pleasure of training. He understands selling in a common-sense way, without complicating it with everything he learned in graduate business school. If he can't build up the territory of the interior Virginias, then no one can. We need the best young man out there we can find, and he is just what the doctor ordered for the job."

Elmandorf worked the interior Virginias for exactly one year. As the year progressed, he began to understand that his Virginia assignment was something less than he had earned and even vaguely perceived a bit of vindictiveness, without really understanding what Judson had to be vindictive about. He increased the aggregate sales of company products in the territory by 41 per cent in his first year and then, his purpose accomplished, wrote a letter of resignation and went to New York to look for a job in marketing management.

His story was credible, even on checking, and his background was excellent and within three weeks he was employed by L'amour de France as an assistant brand manager. From there on he moved slowly and steadily upward, although not as fast as he wished and without the level of compensation or the assurances of future position that he believed he had earned. So when Kellner, Boudreau & Gordon approached him he was ready, and when Harvey Knowles assured him that his past history with Allgood was totally irrelevant, he accepted a position as senior product manager with Miss Effluvia at a flat 50 per cent increase in salary, ready to go to work on Miracle Foam Deodorant and determined to make it a success. He joined the company on October 16, 1973.

* *
*

In their first meeting, Arthur Weiner outlined his concept of marketing planning as a first step in moving Miracle Foam Deodorant into the marketplace. First, he felt that there should be a formal marketing plan summarizing the marketing situation, opportunities, objectives, and financial framework within which this new brand would be developed. Second, he indicated the need for a formal outline of the steps that should be taken prior to the test-market introduction of the new brand. Weiner asked Elmandorf to proceed with both of these steps.

Elmandorf's first move was to develop a topic outline for the Miracle Foam Deodorant marketing plan. To an important degree, this outline followed the so-called approved outline that Elmandorf had used at L'amour de France. The "approved" outline was followed without question at L'amour de France, and although Elmandorf considered it rather cumbersome and redundant, he decided that the conservative approach that it represented was probably safer to pursue with the neophytes of Effluvia House than the shorter and more succinct plan outline that he might write if he were totally on his own.

Elmandorf realized that the L'amour de France outline had never been approved by anyone in that company and that instead it represented a series of viewpoints and prejudices of a succession of general marketing managers, which in its successive honings on the conventional wisdom of these men made it rather generally mediocre and, therefore, very defensible. When he presented this outline to Weiner, he found him in a contemplative mood. He studied the proposed outline at considerable length and then said, "This is a good outline, Sherman. It's too good. It's the kind of outline old, successful companies that have lead feet develop. Nobody reads plans from that kind of outline—they just look at their covers and know that everything is all right. But we don't have to be that way, Sherman. I think we'll be a lot more successful if we're not that way. Someday a long time from now someone will take the marketing plans that we write and think they're no good, and they probably won't be because by then we will have gotten lazy and used to the system we make. But let us make the system, huh, Sherman? Let us do it to satisfy ourselves. Take another crack at that outline and dumb it down. Make it shorter and slicker and take out all the junk, but make sure the meat's all in it and then it will be ours and we'll know what to do with it."

As he finished this rather remarkable monologue, Weiner walked out of his office and down to the parking lot, got into his car, and proceeded to his golf club, where he was seven minutes early for a golf date he had made two weeks before. As he drove along on a golf cart after teeing off at the first hole, he gave up thinking about Elmandorf. "I wonder what the kid will do now," he mused. "I hope it's good."

Elmandorf was rather overwhelmed by what had transpired in Weiner's office, and especially by the abrupt departure. "I wonder where he had to go?" thought Elmandorf as he proceeded to collect his thoughts and try to figure out what to do about the marketing plan outline. Exhibit 8–5 shows the summary outline of the 1973–74 marketing plan for Miracle Foam Deodorant as originally prepared by Elmandorf, and Exhibit 8–6 shows the revised summary outline that he presented to Weiner two days after the pregolf meeting.

As the exhibit shows, Elmandorf eliminated most of the historical analyses because they were not especially relevant in the case of a totally new product. But in addition, his revised outline seemed to suggest, if only by implication, that an acceptable marketing plan should be an analytical crystallization of the marketing issues facing a brand, rather than a dreary, even if well-organized, compendium of the marketing facts of the matter. This change in viewpoint is perhaps best exemplified in the treatment of competitive activity suggested by Elmandorf. He calls it "A Marketing Profile of Three Leading Competitive Brands." The title and outline suggest a sensitive description of the important competition and what they have tried and accomplished over the preceding period. The earlier outline merely provides for the detailing of the overt facts about competition rather than an analysis of their marketing significance. Instead of a never-ending recital of all the "facts," the Elmandorf outline suggests a movement toward a more vital interpretation of the facts.

Weiner appreciated this subtlety in the revised plan and applauded it: "That's it, Sherman. Let's dwell on the why and how and play down the who and what and where. We're marketers, not historians."

EXHIBIT 8–5
Detailed Outline for Miracle Foam Deodorant (MFD) Marketing Plan
(Based on L'amour de France)

A. Brand and Market Sales Trend
   1. The market, definition, development
   2. Market composition
   3. Seasonal trends
   4. Market distribution patterns
   5. Market pricing patterns
   6. Product forms and flavors
B. The Underarm Deodorant Consumer
   1. Usage patterns by demographics
   2. Usage patterns by product types
   3. Review of pertinent attitude and motivational studies
C. The MFD Marketing Concept and History
   1. The distinctive product features
   2. A historical review of its marketing opportunities
D. The Competition
   1. Competitors defined
   2. The distinguishing features of each competitor
   3. Apparent competitive marketing objectives
   4. Competitive advertising copy—past five years
   5. Competitive advertising expenditures and impressions delivered—past five years
   6. Competitive promotional history
E. Governmental Regulation of Underarm Deodorants—History and Prospect
F. The MFD Test-Marketing Plan—Objectives and Plans to Accomplish Them
   1. Problems and opportunities
   2. Marketing objectives
   3. Profit-advertising-promotion plans, national year one
   4. Test markets defined
   5. Profit-advertising-promotion plans, scaled to test markets for year one
   6. Advertising plans, national year one
      a. Copy
      b. Media
   7. Advertising plans, scaled to test markets for year one
   8. Pricing
   9. Measurement of test-market accomplishment
   10. Plans for expansion
G. Summary of anticipated national marketing income and expenditures for years one, two, and three
H. Summary of anticipated marketing income and expenditures scaled to test markets for years one, two, and three

---

"Incidentally, while you're at it, try to find out whether men use this stuff and whether it's important to them, will you? Our liberated lady down the hall seems to think that women are the only ones who buy the stuff and use it and maybe she's right, but so far the only males that have been involved in this have been Knowles and me—not one male consumer

EXHIBIT 8-6
Detailed Outline for Miracle Foam Deodorant (MFD) Marketing Plan
(Short Version Developed by Elmandorf)

A. Summary Plan
B. The Market for Underarm Deodorants
  1. Total market volume
  2. Brand share and brand prices
  3. Analysis of market volume by package types and sizes
  4. A marketing profile of three leading competitive brands
    a. Distinguishing product characteristic(s)
    b. Marketing share and distribution accomplishment
    c. Advertising stance and significant changes in past five years
    d. Advertising expenditures and a profile of media usage
    e. Promotional activities and estimated promotional expenditures
    f. Significant competitive pricing, packaging, and product developments in recent years
C. The Underarm Deodorant Consumer and Consumption Patterns
D. Miracle Foam Deodorant
  1. The MFD product
  2. Why consumers will buy our product
  3. Product weaknesses and plans to overcome them
  4. Advertising and promotion strategies
  5. Packaging
  6. Pricing
  7. Anticipated distribution
E. MFD Marketing Objectives
  1. National and test market
  2. The market test—criteria and plans
  3. National expansion—criteria and plans.
F. A summary of anticipated marketing income and expenditures
  1. Test-market years one, two, and three
  2. National expansion years one, two, and three
G. Summary statement by brand managers

---

has been included in any of the research, as far as I know. It might be important."

When he heard this remark, Elmandorf broke out into a cold sweat "OK, Arthur, I'll look into it," "Ye gods!" he thought to himself. "Haven't these Yo-yos looked into men? I hope they're not as important in this as they might be."

But beyond the possibility that a marketing blunder had been made, Elmandorf was concerned that it had been given to him to unearth the truth. If Weiner was right, then Elmandorf would be the instrument of discrediting Ms. Sappora as well as, by implication, Knowles himself. Elmandorf had no relish for the position he found himself in, and he was certain that he had no desire to become Weiner's cat's-paw. "But I'll worry about that later on," he thought. "Let's see if we can find out somehow what the facts are."

Elmandorf used every informal resource at his disposal: friends in other companies, independent researchers, library research, and off-the-record luncheons with the fashion editors of two of the largest women's service magazines. And from everything he could determine, men *weren't* important! The consensus seemed to be that women brought under-arm products into the home and men, without expressing any opinion at all, merely used whatever happened to be available in the bathroom. Perhaps this wasn't true for the heavily perfumed lesser brands, but it appeared that all the leading brands had perfected scents sufficiently bland to satisfy the male without bringing him out from under his seemingly indifferent shell of masculinity.

So men didn't count, unless your product (as opposed to its positioning) was so overtly feminine in scent that the male simply could not countenance it.

Elmandorf composed the following memorandum on the topic:

Miss Effluvia Memorandum

TO: Ms. Sappora
FROM: S. L. Elmandorf
DATE: December 4, 1973   cc: Arthur Weiner

It is quite clear that men exert a negligible influence on brand selection in the underarm deodorant field, at least on the basis of everything I can track down.

Just as insurance though, shouldn't we consider some sort of research to confirm this in our own terms and to our mutual satisfaction?

With this contretemps behind him, Elmandorf proceeded with the development of the marketing plan.

Here is the marketing plan as prepared by Elmandorf, in accordance with his second outline, and presented to Weiner on December 8, 1973.

PLAN FOR MIRACLE FOAM DEODORANT
Summary

The underarm deodorant market aggregates approximately $224,120,000 (at consumer prices) and it is split between three advertised brands (All Clear—40 per cent; Cream Puff—27 per cent; and Quiet Please—14 per cent). In addition to this deodorant market, there is the underarm deodorant-antiperspirant market, which accounts for another $120,000,000 in consumer sales. This second market is not considered in this marketing plan because Miracle Foam Deodorant is not an antiperspirant product.

The standard product forms are liquid roll-ons and aerosol sprays (exception: Quiet Please is available in roll-on and cream forms but not aerosol). Consumer prices average about 1.5¢ per application, but the larger the container, the lower the price per application. Each form is customarily marketed in two package sizes: a relatively large size of the particular form and a smaller size. All brands advertise in women's magazines, and the two larger brands use television. No important *consumer* promotions are used.

The Miracle Foam Deodorant overcomes the major weaknesses of the extant brands. It works longer because it is based on a totally new principle of deodorization, and it has a fresh, clean scent because it does not depend upon a strong masking perfume for product action.

Test marketing will be undertaken to assess consumer response under marketplace conditions: market shares of 20 per cent, 25 per cent, and 30 per cent are forecast for the first three marketing years respectively, based on excellent product test scores and the apparent opportunity in the marketplace.

On the basis of these share projections, profits are forecast as follows:

Introductory year	$0
2nd year	$6,868,330
3rd year	$9,064,555

The Market for Underarm Deodorants

TOTAL MARKET VOLUME

The sales volume for underarm deodorants (consumer) was $224,120,000 in 1971. Sales volume development in recent years is summarized in Exhibit 8–7. The market increased five times between 1955 and 1967 but has remained relatively static during the past four years.

EXHIBIT 8–7
Specimen Data:
Underarm Deodorant Sales (000 Omitted)
Selected Years—Consumer Dollars

YEAR	UNDERARM DEODORANT SALES
1955	$ 41,030
1960	162,110
1965	183,240
1966	191,280
1967	207,340
1968	224,210
1969	212,690
1970	214,230
1971	224,120

SOURCE :   Modeled on the reports of the A. C. Nielsen Company.

There is a marked seasonal pattern in consumer purchases of underarm deodorants. Considerably more underarm deodorants are used in the summer months than in the winter months. The monthly consumption indices are shown in Exhibit 8–8.

BRAND SHARES

Brand shares of the leading underarm deodorant products are summarized in Exhibit 8–9. All Clear was the first significant brand of underarm deodorant in the

EXHIBIT 8–8
Specimen Data:
Seasonal Patterns for Under-arm Deodorant Sales

MONTH	INDEX*
January	35
February	26
March	80
April	107
May	152
June	165
July	132
August	135
September	121
October	99
November	81
December	67

* Average month = 100, based on monthly consumer sales data in 1965, 1966, and 1967.
S O U R C E : Modeled on the reports of the Market Research Corporation of America.

EXHIBIT 8–9
Specimen Data: Underarm Deodorant Sales and Brand Shares, 1955, 1960, and 1965–71

YEAR	UNDERARM DEODORANT CONSUMER SALES ($000 OMITTED)	BRAND MARKET SHARES (PER CENT)			
		QUIET PLEASE	CREAM PUFF	ALL CLEAR	ALL OTHER
1955	$ 41,030	—	—	88	12
1960	162,110	6	—	74	20
1965	183,240	9	—	65	26
1966	191,280	13	—	58	29
1967	202,340	15	24	41	20
1968	224,210	13	26	44	17
1969	212,690	15	28	38	19
1970	214,230	15	26	42	17
1971	224,120	14	27	40	19

S O U R C E : Modeled on the reports of the A. C. Nielsen Company.

marketplace. Its sales accounted for 88 per cent of the total volume in 1955. By 1971 the market had increased five times and All Clear held 40 per cent of the total dollar volume. Its dominant position in the market ended during the mid 1960's as Quiet Please and miscellaneous smaller brands chipped away at the All Clear franchise. The Cream Puff brand was introduced nationally in 1967 and immediately took 24 per cent of the market. This Cream Puff share gradually increased in the late 1960's and early 1970's to its current level of 27 per cent of the market. All Clear has held about 40 per cent of the business since 1967 and the Quiet Please share has stabilized in the low teens. It is important to note that this stabilization of brand market shares in the late 1960's was accompanied by a relatively static sales volume in the total underarm deodorant market.

CONSUMER PRICES

The consumer prices for competitive underarm deodorant packages are summarized in Exhibit 8–10. In general, the consumer pays more than 1.2¢ and less than 2¢ per underarm deodorant application, assuming that one ounce of deodorant will yield about twenty applications in liquid roll-on and cream forms and about ten applications in aerosol form. As is true in other product categories, a consumer pays less in big stores than in small stores and less in metropolitan than in rural areas. However, these variations in store prices do not reflect differentiated factory prices to different classes of trade or different regional outlets, except insofar as regular volume discounts are earned.

The leading brands are available in three forms (aerosol, liquid roll-on, and cream) and eleven sizes. The relative market importance of these variations is shown in Exhibit 8–11. Liquid roll-ons are the most important form, comprising about half (49 per cent) of all dollar sales. The single most important package size is the 2-ounce liquid roll-on, which accounts for 35 per cent of all dollar sales. Aerosols have 22 per cent of the market and the smaller, 4-ounce size dominates with 18 per cent of the total.

All other brands account for one out of five sales dollars, and it is assumed that they are predominantly roll-ons and aerosols with their various form and size popularities consistent with those of the major brands.

A Marketing Profile of the Three Leading Competitive Brands

ALL CLEAR

All Clear underarm deodorant is the leading brand in the market. In form it comes in a typical aerosol spray and a pink roll-on liquid. The masking perfume is rather spicy, suggesting a sweet oil of cloves. Both versions have excellent shelf lives (three to four years). The aerosol version has some tendency to cake up on underarm clothing, and the roll-on version is, in the view of our product development people, rather syrupy. But all our evidence indicates that the product performs adequately for consumers and that, on a performance basis, there is no reason why it should not be a consumer favorite. Package graphics are attractively understated and the predominant colors are white background and purple shades of lettering.

CREAM PUFF

Cream Puff underarm deodorant is quite similar to All Clear. The aerosol is typical and the roll-on liquid is whitish pink. Its shelf life is excellent for both product forms (five to six years). The aerosol version has a heavy floral scent, reminiscent of lily of the valley, and the roll-on liquid has a somewhat lighter version of this scent—some of our perfumers find a hint of musk oil in it. The aerosol spray tends to cake up in normal use, but the roll-on liquid is distinctly nonviscous and even seems somewhat watery to many of our production people. We suspect that Cream Puff quality control procedures are not all they should be. We have found significant variations in scent concentration in various batches,

EXHIBIT 8–10

Specimen Data: Shelf Prices of Leading Underarm Deodorants as of March 1, 1971—Total, Outlet Type and County Size, Food and Drug Combined

	QUIET PLEASE · CREAM · 2 OZ.	QUIET PLEASE · CREAM · 4 OZ.	QUIET PLEASE · LIQUID · 2 OZ.	CREAM PUFF · AEROSOL · 4 OZ.	CREAM PUFF · AEROSOL · 8 OZ.	CREAM PUFF · LIQUID · 2 OZ.	CREAM PUFF · LIQUID · 4 OZ.	ALL CLEAR · AEROSOL · 4 OZ.	ALL CLEAR · AEROSOL · 8 OZ.	ALL CLEAR · LIQUID · 2 OZ.	ALL CLEAR · LIQUID · 4 OZ.
All stores	56.2¢	96.6¢	68.2¢	68.4¢	120.3¢	52.7¢	88.1¢	80.6¢	144.3¢	60.1¢	104.2¢
Outlet type											
Chain	52.7¢	97.7¢	64.7¢	66.9¢	114.9¢	48.8¢	86.0¢	76.7¢	135.7¢	58.1¢	99.7¢
Large and medium independents	56.1	97.1	67.9	68.1	120.0	52.6	88.3	80.1	144.9	59.9	103.9
All other independents	59.4	98.2	69.9	70.1	124.3	58.3	89.8	85.3	149.7	62.4	110.6
County size											
A	54.2¢	93.8¢	64.9¢	64.3¢	109.2¢	48.6¢	84.2¢	75.2¢	131.6¢	56.7¢	98.8¢
B	55.7	95.9	68.1	67.7	117.3	50.2	87.1	78.9	139.7	58.9	102.3
C	56.8	96.8	69.2	69.1	122.6	53.8	90.0	81.1	144.9	61.1	107.6
D	59.1	99.2	69.1	72.1	131.7	56.9	92.3	84.2	152.8	64.3	108.8

SOURCE: Modeled on the reports of the A. C. Nielsen Company.

EXHIBIT 8–11
Specimen Data: Underarm Deodorant Brand Sales by Package Size and Type, 1971

Total underarm deodorant sales	$224,120,000	
Per cent	100	
Aerosol containers		
4 oz.	18%	
All Clear		12
Cream Puff		6
8 oz.	4	
All Clear		2
Cream Puff		2
Liquid roll-on		
2 oz.	35	
All Clear		20
Cream Puff		11
Quiet Please		4
4 oz.	14	
All Clear		6
Cream Puff		8
Cream		
2 oz.	6	
Quiet Please		6
4 oz.	4	
Quiet Please		4
All other brands	19	

S O U R C E : Modeled on the reports of the A. C. Nielsen Company.

especially of the aerosol product. But product performance seems to be uniformly quite good. Consumers seem relatively well satisfied with this product. Its basic appeal is, as we shall see, in its pricing and it appears to be considered good value for the money. Package graphics are a little heavy-handed, depending as they do on a four-colour representation of what may be a moist powder puff. The blue lettering seems to us to be a little garish and not as feminine as it might be.

QUIET PLEASE

Quiet Please underarm deodorant is available in two forms: the roll-on liquid and cream. This is the only leading brand with a cream and the cream constitutes about two thirds of its total business (Exhibit 8–11). Quiet Please has maintained a relatively stable brand share in the low teens in recent years. This probably means that demand for the cream form is relatively stable, as the roll-on has not been particularly successful even though it has been in the Quiet Please line since 1966.

The product, in both forms, has almost no odor at all. How it works remains something of a mystery because there appears to be no odor with which to mask underarm odor. But work it does, and even though we do not know how, we do know that it is a technically mundane product, containing about the same ingredients as its major competitors. This product seems to suffer from unimaginative marketing as much as anything else. The lack of tangible odor can be construed as a plus to many consumers, and it is possible that if Quiet Please became aggressive, introduced in aerosol form and took its differentiating cream and low-odor stories to the marketplace, it could become a more important competitor than it now is.

MARKET SHARE AND DISTRIBUTION ACCOMPLISHMENT

The market shares of the three leading brands were discussed above and are shown in Exhibit 8–9. The distribution for these three brands in a recent typical period is shown in Exhibit 8–12. Achieved distribution is generally good and tends to follow the brand share levels. Thus the distribution leader is All Clear, the market leader. Quiet Please is second in distribution to All Clear; as a distinctive-cream-form it is a more logical second brand for retailers to stock than Cream Puff. But Cream Puff has good strength in food chains and in A and B counties, which is sufficient to generate the number two sales position that the brand enjoys.

All Clear has emphasized distribution on its best-selling liquid roll-on form, whereas the other brands have stronger distribution on other forms: Quiet Please with its cream and Cream Puff, surprisingly, with its aerosol. It is difficult to understand Cream Puff's relatively poor distribution for its liquid, considering the relative popularity of that form, and an expansion of Cream Puff liquid distribution could well represent a significant opportunity for that brand.

Our Market Research Department has chosen not to purchase Nielsen distribution data by package size. However, the Allgood field sales organization has been polled for impressions on the achieved distribution by package size of the leading competitive brands. As the market strength of the smaller sizes (Exhibit 8–11) would lead one to expect, distribution is generally excellent on the smaller sizes. It tends to fall off in the smaller stores and in remote areas, particularly in the larger package sizes.

ADVERTISING STANCE AND SIGNIFICANT CHANGES IN THE PAST FIVE YEARS

None of the three leading brands of underarm deodorant has developed a truly distinctive advertising stance. Quiet Please says it works better but makes no attempt in its consumer communication to relate this asserted advantage to either its unique form—cream—or its relative lack of overt masking odor.

Cream Puff and All Clear make no differentiating claims: their advertising is distinctive and competitive only in specific instances of the relative voluptuousness of models who smile out from the tube or the full page and assert directly or indirectly that their underarms are odor-free because of the use of a particular deodorant product.

It seems clear that a major opportunity for brand differentiation in advertising exists if a different and better product is available.

ADVERTISING EXPENDITURE AND PROFILE OF MEDIA USAGE

There is a clear and positive relation between the level of brand sales and the level of advertising expenditures in this market. Quiet Please, with annual sales in 1971 of about $31,400,000, spent $3,124,120 for an advertising-to-sales ratio of about .10 (Exhibit 8–13). Cream Puff had brand sales of $60,500,000 in 1971 and spent $8,426,310 in advertising, thus developing an advertising/sales ratio of .14. All Clear spent $12,240,000 on advertising on sales of $89,648,000 for an A/S ratio of .14. The data suggest that All Clear is quite willing to invest advertising dollars to protect its number one position in the market. They also suggest that an

EXHIBIT 8-12

Specimen Data: Achieved Distribution of Leading Underarm Deodorants as of March 1, 1971—Total, Outlet Type, and County Size, Food and Drug Combined

	QUIET PLEASE			CREAM PUFF			ALL CLEAR		
	ANY	CREAM	LIQUID	ANY	AEROSOL	LIQUID	ANY	AEROSOL	LIQUID
All Stores	92	84	61	73	60	24	99	65	88
Outlet type									
Chain	98	95	72	85	84	12	100	62	100
Large and medium independents	74	60	31	40	35	6	98	12	95
All other independents	38	24	21	12	8	6	73	2	71
County Size									
A	99	95	82	80	70	35	100	78	100
B	85	80	42	60	52	22	99	43	91
C	76	68	31	41	39	4	98	12	90
D	12	10	3	6	6	—	79	2	78

SOURCE: Modeled on the reports of the A. C. Nielsen Company.

EXHIBIT 8–13
Specimen Data: Advertising Expenditures of Leading Underarm Deodorant Brands, 1971

	QUIET PLEASE	CREAM PUFF	ALL CLEAR
TOTAL	$3,124,120	$8,426,310	$12,240,000
Advertising/sales ratio	.10	.14	.14
Network television			6,296,200
Spot television		3,162,070	
Network radio			
Consumer magazines	3,124,120	5,012,440	4,126,320
Farm magazines			297,320
Newspapers			
Outdoor			
Miscellaneous		251,800	520,160

S O U R C E :   Supplied by advertising agency.

introductory brand should expect to spend at least 14 per cent of its achieved sales in advertising on a long-run basis and that an introductory brand should be prepared to spend, on an investment basis, at least at the dollar level of the competitor that has achieved a market share of a magnitude that he covets.

Each of the leading brands uses consumer magazines: they constitute the only medium for Quiet Please, the dominant medium for Cream Puff, and one of the two dominant media used by All Clear. The larger the brand, the more likely it is to use television. Quiet Please uses no television; Cream Puff uses some spot television (in the top twenty markets) but depends on consumer magazines for national coverage; and All Clear spends more for television than for consumer magazines and spends it in network television for national coverage. None of these brands makes any expenditures of consequence except in television and in national magazines.

PROMOTIONAL ACTIVITIES AND ESTIMATED PROMOTIONAL EXPENDITURES

There is no evidence of consumer promotional activity of any kind for any of the leading underarm deodorant brands.

Neither is there any evidence of unusual trade promotional activity. From time to time the trade will be allowed a 7–10 per cent promotional allowance for special display or advertising, particularly by Cream Puff, but these allowances have not been made on any regular basis.

SIGNIFICANT COMPETITIVE PRICING, PACKAGING, AND PRODUCT DEVELOPMENT IN RECENT YEARS

All Clear seems to have paid considerable attention to the improvement of their scent over the years. Our Marketing Research Director has knowledge of a substantial scent-testing investment by All Clear in the winter of 1967–8, and in the fall of 1968 they announced "new improved scents" for both their product forms. These improved-scent products supplanted their existing products. When the new scents were introduced, the package graphics were also modernized. No abnormal increase in advertising expenditure nor change in advertising content was made at that time, and although the All Clear share of the market did not decline in the subsequent year, there was no important improvement in market position attributable to the combination of change in the product and the redesign of the package.

Cream Puff apparently attempted to improve its scent shortly thereafter in order presumably, to achieve parity with All Clear. We believe this to be true on the basis of information obtained from a former Cream Puff employee who is now employed by one of our advertising agencies. No public announcement or consumer communication was ever made to this effect, however.

Quiet Please introduced an aerosol powder in the Omaha market area in 1970. The deodorant itself was, in the judgment of our Effluvia House technicians, indistinguishable from that available from Quiet Please in alternative forms, except that it was quite distinctly apple blossom in scent. This aerosol product was priced at about 2.2¢ per application, or rather higher than regular Quiet Please or the other aerosol competitors. This product was a total failure in the test market, and it was withdrawn after six months.

THE UNDERARM DEODORANT CONSUMER AND CONSUMPTION PATTERNS

The demographic characteristics of year-round underarm deodorant users and seasonal deodorant users are shown in Exhibit 8–14. There are no reliable data

EXHIBIT 8–14
Specimen Data: Characteristics of Users of Underarm Deodorant, Seasonal and Year Round

CHARACTERISTIC	POPULATION	YEAR-ROUND UNDERARM DEODORANT USERS	SEASONAL UNDERARM DEODORANT USERS
Income			
Under $5,000	28%	6%	16%
$ 5,000–$7,999	32	24	28
$ 8,000–$9,999	25	39	34
$10,000 and over	16	31	22
Education			
Grade school or less	21%	8%	10%
Some high school	18	12	18
Graduated high school	35	40	36
Some college	16	18	21
Graduated college	10	22	15
Age			
24 and younger	26%	33%	32%
25–34	28	39	36
35–49	18	18	20
50–64	12	7	8
65 and older	16	3	4
Social mobility			
High	33%	48%	42%
Moderate	33	35	31
Low	34	17	27

SOURCE : Consumer survey, 1971.

concerning the volume importance of the year-round underarm deodorant user. A "year-round" user is simply defined as an individual who claims to use an underarm deodorant in every month of the year and the "seasonal" user as one who claims usage, but not in every month of the year. We know that there is a sharp seasonal pattern in underarm deodorant usage (see Exhibit 8–8) and we guess that the average year-round user consumes at least 50 per cent more, and perhaps twice as much, underarm deodorant as the seasonal consumer. This would mean that year-round users account for between 60 per cent and 70 per cent of deodorant sales.

The year-round underarm deodorant user tends to be younger, better educated, and more mobile and to have a higher family income than average. The seasonal underarm deodorant user tends to follow the same pattern but is less extreme: he is young but not quite as young as the year-round user; he is better educated but not as well educated as the average year-round user; and he is more mobile and has a higher income than the population as a whole, but he is not as mobile nor as well compensated as the year-round user.

EXHIBIT 8–15
Specimen Data: Frequency of Underarm Deodorant Usage

Base	3,206
Per cent	100
Applications per day	
Apply once a day	96%
Apply twice a day	3
Apply more than twice a day	1

SOURCE : Consumer survey, 1971.

Exhibit 8–15 indicates that the typical deodorant user makes one deodorant application per day. Exhibit 8–16 shows that the typical user applies an underarm deodorant every day of the week. A few users do not use the product on the early

EXHIBIT 8–16
Specimen Data: Reported Underarm Deodorant Usage by Day of Week

Base	3,206
Per cent	100
Use a deodorant on	
Monday	88%
Tuesday	86
Wednesday	88
Thursday	90
Friday	97
Saturday	90
Sunday	98

SOURCE : Consumer survey, 1971.

weekdays, but on each day of the week at least 86 per cent of all deodorant users use the product.

MIRACLE FOAM DEODORANT

Against this background, the following paragraphs outline the introductory marketing strategy for Miracle Foam Deodorant. The existing underarm deodorant market seems vulnerable, in many ways, to the introduction of a truly improved product and to aggressive exploitation. Miracle Foam Deodorant is, we believe, a truly improved product, and we believe we have found ways to exploit this superior product that will have maximum competitive effect.

THE PRODUCT

Miracle Foam Deodorant works better, is in a better form, and has a better scent than any competitor's product now available in the marketplace. This product superiority is documented, from the consumer standpoint, by our very conclusive product-test results relative to competitors.

The product is based on an oxygen-destruction principle. The product destroys the very element that causes underarm odor. It is the combining of bacteria and oxygen under the arm that causes the odor. If oxygen is removed from the underarm area then odor cannot form, and it will not form for as long a period as oxygen is prevented from emerging on the scene. The product represents a chemical breakthrough of the very first rank. For centuries, odor has been overcome through the masking activity of perfume: a new odor is introduced that is more blatant than the old odor. The old odor remains, but it is hidden under the perfume. Now the odor never forms at all! This remarkable product works for hours, is easy to apply in a shaving-cream-like form, and can be subtly scented to enhance the effect created in the first instance by the total absence of any odor at all.

WHY CONSUMERS WILL BUY OUR PRODUCT

Consumers will buy the Miracle Foam product because it is technically superior to competitive products and because, on the basis of our product test research, its superiority is totally evident to a strong majority of consumers. Our product works better and its superior performance is easily perceived by consumers.

PRODUCT WEAKNESSES AND PLANS TO OVERCOME THEM

This underarm deodorant has no weaknesses as a product. It is an ideal product in the sense that it is exactly the product one would attempt to develop if one were to set out to make the best underarm deodorant he could from a technical standpoint. As will be detailed below, the one limitation of this new product is that it costs considerably more than the competitive products now available in the marketplace. Our analysis indicates that competitive products cost on the average more than 1.2¢ and less than 2¢ per application. Miracle Foam Deodorant pricing is such that consumers will pay more: probably the average consumer will pay more than 2.7¢ and less than 3¢ per application of Miracle Foam Deodorant. The basic reason for this disparity springs from the product form. A can of aerosol foam simply yields about 40 per cent fewer applications than a comparably sized can of aerosol spray.

We assume that because the Miracle Foam Deodorant product is so obviously and demonstrably better than competitive products that a sizeable fraction of consumers will gladly purchase our product more frequently and thus pay a significantly higher price. But it is well to remember that this is at best an assumption, not a fact demonstrated in the marketplace. It is a question that must, and will, be resolved in our test markets.

One other shortcoming of the product should be mentioned in the interest of completeness. Miracle Foam Deodorant is a deodorant. It is not an antiperspirant. There is a fraction of all users of underarm products that require not only a deodorant but also an antiperspirant because of the nature and severity of their underarm problems. The market for deodorants is larger than the market for antiperspirant-deodorants, accounting for about $224 million of the $344 million total. Two of our leading competitors—All Clear and Quiet Please—have entrants in this parallel market.

ADVERTISING AND PROMOTION STRATEGY

The overall advertising/promotion strategy is simplicity itself: the strategic objective is to create awareness of Miracle Foam Deodorant among all users of underarm deodorants and especially among year-round users of this product category. Underarm deodorant users should become aware that odor problems are solved in a totally new and very pleasant way with Miracle Foam Deodorant. The atmosphere of the advertising is of gentle femininity, in accordance with the findings of the product-positioning research (Case 7.) It is believed that if underarm-deodorant–using housewives come to know what we want them to know about Miracle Foam Deodorant, trial will almost surely ensue and that product trial will almost surely ensure repeat purchase.

Two distinct approaches to the accomplishment of these strategic objectives have been developed. Plan A depends only upon advertising and Plan B depends upon a combination of advertising and promotion. Plan A assumes that our communications know-how is sufficient to implant the desired awareness of and desire to try the product solely through media messages. Plan B does not dispute this assumption but argues that a fraction of available funds should be devoted to product sampling in introductory and subsequent years. Thus Plan A spends all of the available dollars in consumer media and Plan B allocates 30 per cent of the available dollars to the sampling of the product through the facilities of Select-O-Samp, a service that identifies members of product category groups and sends samples of a variety of products to these users through the mail. The promotion specification would be to identify current all-year-round users of All Clear and Cream Puff brand aerosol-spray underarm deodorants and send them a two-ounce trial size of Miracle Foam Deodorant. It is our proposal to test these alternative strategy executions in the marketplace and to implement the more successful plan nationally in 1974–75. As the financial plans for the brand reveal, an advertising and promotion budget of $14,356,469 is projected for the introductory year. This provides adequate advertising under either Plan A (all of the $14,356,469 is allocated to advertising) or Plan B (70 per cent of the available budget, or $10,049,528, is allocated to advertising and 30 per cent, or $4,306,941, is allocated to a promotional sampling plan) to make Miracle Foam Deodorant the most heavily advertised/promoted brand in the market during its introductory year. The proposal under Plan A is to spend 60 per cent of the available money in daytime network television and 40 per cent of the available money in women's magazines. The spending proposal under Plan B is to divide the available advertising dollars equally between daytime network television and women's magazines.

A detailed proposal for both Plan A and Plan B is now under development by the advertising agency and will be available, with recommended creative work, in about three weeks.

PACKAGE

The product will be sold in four-ounce and eight-ounce aerosol foam containers. Because of the nature of aerosol foam formulations, these packages will yield about 40 per cent fewer applications than will competitive aerosol spray packages with the same ounce content.

Both the four-ounce and the eight-ounce containers will be packed twelve to the case.

PRICING

The product will be trade-priced so that the following average retail prices should be achieved (assuming about the same effect of discounting on shelf prices as for competitors):

4 oz. @ 82.5¢
8 oz. @ 147.5¢

It is believed that major retailers will feature the four-ounce container at about 75¢ some going to 69¢ and the eight-ounce containers at $1.35 some going to $1.29. Such price features will parallel those now found on competitive products and thus will not effectively offset the real price disadvantage of Miracle Foam Deodorant. Only consumer acceptance of our product as distinctly superior can overcome this de facto price disadvantage.

Although some consideration has been given to printing consumer prices on the packages, it has been decided to avoid this step because it will not improve our relations with the major trade elements, who will usually price below the preset retail price anyway and will antagonize smaller retailers who often tend to price items well above the average retail price set at normal trade margins if they feel the traffic will bear the load.

ANTICIPATED DISTRIBUTION

Distribution of our product should be fairly good. The product will be helped because it will be introduced by the Allgood Drug sales force, and they are experienced and generally successful in introducing new products to the trade. This is an exciting product, and the fact that it is the first fruit of the Allgood–Effluvia House merger will generate a good deal of trade interest and enthusiasm. And the promise of significant advertising/promotion support will help get distribution too: the trade will hardly dare not to have a product backed at this level of support on their shelves. It is therefore anticipated—given an enthusiastic and successful performance by the Allgood men—that the distribution for Miracle Foam Deodorant should surpass that of Cream Puff early in the introductory year and should approach the distribution level of All Clear by the end of the second year.

Marketing Objectives in the Introductory Year (1974–75)

PROBLEMS AND OPPORTUNITIES

The major problem facing Miracle Foam Deodorant is its price. Our product costs more per application than competitive products because it simply costs more to make. And even though the shelf price will be comparable to that of the market leader, All Clear, it won't be long before the consumer understands what's up and makes a conscious decision either for us or against us. We know of only one analagous situation in the history of underarm deodorant marketing. Quiet Please test marketed a relatively high-priced product in an aerosol can and as we have seen it was an abject failure. Our investigation indicates that the Quiet Please aerosol product was no more than marginally better than regular Quiet Please. We conclude that the consumer refused to pay a premium price for a parity product. But we do not believe that the Quiet Please experience is relevant to the Miracle Foam Deodorant situation, because our product is a clear innovation in the category.

In the end the Miracle Foam Deodorant opportunity exists because of the relative inferiority of existing products and the market stagnation that they seemingly have engendered. Our product is better than the competition and well worth the consumer price differential. It remains to communicate this to the housewife and to convince her that this is so, and that is the essence of the opportunity that presents itself to us now.

OBJECTIVES

1. To achieve a 20-per-cent share of the underarm deodorant market in the introductory year.
2. To sell $37,420,000 at factory of Miracle Foam Deodorant in the introductory year.
3. To achieve consumer awareness of the product equivalent to the current consumer awareness of the market leader All Clear. (All Clear is known to 53 per cent of all adult females and to 72 per cent of all those who use an underarm deodorant.) In addition, communicate detailed knowledge of Miracle Foam Deodorant's points of superiority (it is a superior product, with new form and scent) among half of those housewives who are aware of it.

These objectives will be subject to test in three test markets in the marketing year beginning September 1974. If the test is successful, national introduction is anticipated in September 1975.

A SUMMARY OF ANTICIPATED MARKETING INCOME AND EXPENDITURES

The financial projections for the introductory marketing of Miracle Foam Deodorant are shown in Exhibits 8–17, 8–18, and 8–19. These exhibits follow the standard test-brand financial procedures of Allgood Drug Company. [See Case 9 for a detailed statement of these procedures.]

Exhibit 8–17 projects annual sales of underarm deodorants for the first three years in which Miracle Foam Deodorant will be marketed. The base projection in Exhibit 8–17 assumes that the total for these products is essentially stagnant and that the actual sales achieved in any current year are a reasonably good estimate of sales in any near-future year. It is assumed that the new product introduction will produce an increase in total market sales of 10 per cent per year.

Consumer sales are converted to factory sales by the reduction of consumer sales by one third (multiplying by .67). This reduction reflects Allgood Drug Company experience that trade middlemen add 50 per cent to the factory selling-price for the distribution functions they provide. Factory sales of Miracle Foam Deodorant are projected at 20 per cent of the total market for the first year, 25 per cent of the total

EXHIBIT 8–17
Specimen Data: Sales Estimates for Miracle Foam Deodorant,*
Introductory Year, Year 2, Year 3

	INTRODUCTORY YEAR	YEAR 2	YEAR 3
Total market, consumer dollars	$246,530,000	$271,180,000	$298,300,000
Total market, factory dollars	162,710,000	178,980,000	196,880,000
Estimated factory sales for			
Miracle Foam Deodorant	32,540,000	44,750,000	59,050,000
Pipeline	4,880,000	—	—
TOTAL	$ 37,420,000	$ 44,750,000	$ 59,050,000
Cases of 12	4,990,000	5,967,000	7,873,000

*Assumptions: 1. Consumer sales in 1971 are used as a base in all calculations.
2. The introduction of a totally new and superior product will cause an expansion of the underarm deodorant market, for both direct and indirect reasons, of 10 per cent a year.
3. Miracle Foam Deodorant will achieve a dollar share of 20 per cent in its introductory year, 25 per cent in its second year, and 30 per cent in its third year.
4. Each case sold will return approximately $7.50 in factory sales. It is assumed that a case of 8-oz. cans will return $12.00 per case, that 4-oz. cans will return $6.00 per case, and that three times as many 4-oz. cases will be sold as 8-oz. cases.

EXHIBIT 8–18
Specimen Data: Computation of Costs and Dollars Available for Profit, Advertising, and Promotion, Miracle Foam Deodorant
Standard Case Basis*

Factory dollars received per case	$7.50000
Cost per case	
Manufacturing costs estimated by Effluvia House Production Department†	1.90320
Sales, distribution, and administrative cost (Standard percentage from Allgood Accounting Department: 12%)	.90000
Overhead (standard percentage from Allgood Accounting Department: 21%)	1.57500
Market research (percentage recommended by Ms. Sappora: 2%)	0.15000
Royalty to Igor Smetsky: 1.25%	.09375
Total cost per case	$4.62195
Available, per case	$2.87805

* The "standard case" assumes that 4-oz. cases will outsell 8-oz. cases in the ratio of 3 to 1.
† Production Department states that production cost per standard case is stable at $1.90320 at volumes up to 10 million cases per year.

EXHIBIT 8–19
Specimen Data: Computation of Available PAP Funds, Introductory Year, Year 2, Year 3—Standard Case Basis*

	INTRODUCTORY YEAR	YEAR 2	YEAR 3
Factory Sales: Dollars	$37,420,000	$44,750,000	$59,050,000
(Cases)	(4,990,000)	(5,967,000)	(7,873,000)
Direct and indirect cost of goods before PAP			
Manufacturing costs (1.90320)	$9,496,968	$11,356,394	$14,983,983
Sales, etc. costs (.90000)	4,491,000	5,370,300	7,085,700
Overhead (1.57500)	7,859,250	9,398,025	12,399,975
Market Research (0.15000)	748,500	895,050	1,180,950
Royalty (.09375)	467,813	559,406	738,094
Total Cost of Goods Before PAP	$23,063,531	$27,579,175	$36,388,612
Available for PAP	$14,356,469	$17,170,825	$22,661,388

* The "standard case" assumes that 4-oz. cases will outsell 8-oz. cases in the ratio of 3 to 1.

market for the second year, and 30 per cent of the total market for the third year. In addition, Allgood Drug Company policy allows 15 per cent of total projected introductory volume as an estimate of pipeline sales. ("Pipeline sales" are non-recurring sales to retail and wholesaler stocks to develop distribution availability.) Finally, these factory sales estimates are converted, in the exhibit, to twelve-pack "standard" cases. In computing the standard case, it is assumed that four-ounce cases will outsell eight-ounce cases by 3 to 1.

Exhibit 8–18 summarizes the costs per case assignable against Miracle Foam Deodorant. There are four standard costs assignable against a new product under Allgood Drug Company accounting procedures: three of these are arbitrarily set by prior accounting studies and apply to all brands (sales and administrative costs, overhead, and marketing research costs). Manufacturing cost is estimated by the Production Department on the basis of the materials required and the volume levels projected. One additional non-"standard" cost is involved in Miracle Foam Deodorant: it is the royalty payment to Igor Smetsky of 1.25 per cent of factory sales. On the basis of these costs, it is estimated that each case of the underarm deodorant will cost $4.62195 and that this will yield $2.87805 per case available for profit, advertising, and promotion (PAP). Exhibit 8–19 shows the detailed computation of dollars available for PAP for the introductory year, for the second year, and for the third year.

Strict Allgood rules determine how PAP may be allocated among its three constituents (see Case 9). In summary, these rules state that each brand may spend 60 per cent of PAP for advertising (40 per cent) and promotion (20 per cent) and 40 per cent must revert to the company as profit. A major exception to this rule obtains in the the case of new products: the company will invest normal profits in advertising or in promotion in the introductory year of a new product. This means that total PAP is available for the new product's introductory year but not subsequently. The impact of these rules is shown in Exhibit 8–20. Exhibit 8–20A

EXHIBIT 8–20A
Specimen Data: PAP Projections Under Advertising/Promotion Plan A

	INTRODUCTORY YEAR	YEAR 2	YEAR 3
Factory sales	$37,420,000	$44,750,000	$59,050,000
Available for PAP	14,356,469	17,170,825	22,661,388
Advertising	14,356,469	10,302,495	13,596,833
Promotion	—	—	—
Profit	—	6,868,330	9,064,555

EXHIBIT 8–20B
Specimen Data: PAP Projections Under Advertising/Promotion Plan B

	INTRODUCTORY YEAR	YEAR 2	YEAR 3
Factory sales	$37,420,000	$44,750,000	$59,050,000
Available for PAP	14,356,469	17,170,825	22,661,388
Advertising	10,049,528	6,868,330	9,064,555
Promotion	4,306,941	3,434,165	4,532,278
Profit	—	6,868,330	9,064,555

allocates PAP for the first three marketing years under Plan A (all advertising and no promotion in the introductory year, and 60 per cent advertising and 40 per cent profits in the second and third years). Exhibit 8–20B allocates PAP for the first three marketing years under Plan B (30 per cent promotion and 70 per cent advertising in the first marketing year, and 20 per cent promotion, 40 per cent advertising, and 40 per cent profit in the second and third marketing years). In both cases, the projected annual profit is zero in the introductory marketing year, $6,868,330 in the second year, and $9,064,555 in the third year.

The final topic on the short marketing plan outline was "Summary Statement by Brand Managers." Elmandorf forwarded the marketing plan to Arthur Weiner on January, 8, 1973. He did not include the final summary statement in the plan. Instead, he delivered with the plan the following memorandum:

Miss Effluvia Memorandum

TO: Arthur Weiner
FROM: Sherman L. Elmandorf
SUBJECT: Miracle Foam Deodorant Marketing Plan
DATE: January 8, 1974.

Here is the marketing plan for the introduction of Miracle Foam Deodorant. It details a national plan for the introductory year and includes profit projections for the second and third years. It is incomplete in two aspects.

First, it contains no specifics on test markets or description of how this national plan would be translated down to the test market level. All of this planning can be undertaken immediately upon approval of the basic plan; we would prefer to work out test market details with the agency only after the overall approach has been agreed to by all concerned.

This plan is also incomplete in that it contains no summary statement by the product manager. The balance of this memorandum might form such a section, but as it is essentially negative in character, I thought it best to cover it in a separate memo rather than incorporating it into the plan itself.

I do not recommend that the company proceed with the marketing of this product. I know that this is an unexpected recommendation and that it contradicts all the judgments that have brought Miracle Foam Deodorant to its present stage of development. Yet, as I have worked through the various elements of the marketing plan, I have become aware of several "holes" in the product and it is because of this that I now recommend against its introduction into test market.

The following paragraphs summarize these misgivings.

1. There is no hard evidence that underarm deodorant users are disenchanted with the currently available underarm deodorant products. It is one thing for us to identify a market weakness on the basis of logic and informed opinion and all, and it is quite another thing to project these insights to the ultimate consumer.

2. I am deeply concerned about the oxygen destruction principle of the proposed product. We don't know enough about the length of time that a single application is effective and the degree of variation in effectiveness among individuals. It is one thing to mask odor and it is another thing to remove its cause. Masking effectiveness is fairly predictable, but the removal of cause may very well be a much more unstable phenomenon than we assume. I would point out that this issue was not addressed at all in the product test and that we simply have no useful information from consumers on this topic. Smetsky tends to pooh-pooh the whole notion, but he does, after all, have a somewhat proprietary interest in this product. I have explained this principle to several consumers, and once they really learn the details of it, unlike respondents in the concept tests, they are almost universally negative because they don't know how long the product would work and what would happen when it failed.

3. We have no solid information on the shelf life of the new product. I believe that some sort of accelerated shelf life tests have been initiated by the research and development people, but they still have a month or two to run and I seriously question whether they can accurately predict what the real shelf life of the product will be in the stores. In digging around, I discover that shelf life predictions have not been the long suit of the Effluvia House research and development people. Two products—Subtle Sunset face cream and Fatal Nature perfume—have been withdrawn from the market by Effluvia House within the past five years because of short shelf life after long shelf life had been predicted by the research and development people. This scares me half to death because we don't want this kind of trade relations problem with our

very first entry into mass merchandising. Don't forget that all of our competitors have excellent to superior shelf-life characteristics.

4. Can advertising really convince underarm deodorant users that Miracle Foam Deodorant is superior to available products and worth the premium price? I admit that all my arguments are subjective, but in all my experience in the cosmetic business I have never seen an instance in which advertising worked as well as we had been led to expect that it would. I have often thought that the same amount of money spent on trade deals would go much farther than advertising. Supposing, for example, we offered a straight 20 per cent extra discount on all introductory Miracle Foam Deodorant orders of four cases or more—that would really get the consumer price down. Then the merchandise would really move out of the stores and our cost would be considerably less than for a broad-scale advertising campaign at the level proposed, even in Plan B. I have to admit that our price differential really scares me—I'd rather lower price through trade deals than spend on roundabout advertising to induce consumers to want to buy our product.

5. When all is said and done, our decision is based on about four hundred housewives who said they liked our underarm deodorant after trying it in the most artificial atmosphere of the in-home product test. I think it's reasonable to believe that these women are simply being nice to us in the testing situation. I believe that the evidence and points of view summarized in this memorandum can lead persuasively to this conclusion.

Arthur Weiner was as distressed by the memorandum as he was elated with the marketing plan. Elmandorf had done a first-rate job in bringing together and presenting material in the marketing plan while absorbing the appropriate policies and procedures and history from both the Allgood Drug and the Effluvia House organizations. Yet in Weiner's view the memorandum was naïve and immature and would in no way influence the marketing of Miracle Foam Deodorant. Weiner's major problem did not involve deciding what marketing action to take; rather, the question was how to convey gently yet firmly his disagreement with Elmandorf's assessment of the product to Elmandorf without dampening his enthusiasm. Weiner pondered the problem for four or five days, all the while avoiding Elmandorf and any situation that might lead to a premature discussion (from Weiner's standpoint) of whether and when Miracle Foam Deodorant would be test-marketed.

Finally, on January 16, 1974, Weiner called Elmandorf into his office. His desk was empty except for the Miracle Foam Deodorant marketing plan and the Elmandorf memorandum. "I've read these documents," began Weiner poking with a middle finger at the marketing plan and the memorandum in a jerky nervous way "and I find myself in a kind of funny situation. I like the marketing plan: it's first rate. Good job and much better than what I thought you'd do when I saw that history book outline. But I don't agree with this other paper." He punched the memorandum with the middle fingers of both hands in a swooping motion.

"Disagree. Everyone has a right to his own opinion around here, but in the end it's a matter of marketing judgment, right? In my opinion, the deodorant is a darb, a real winner. And we're going to market it. But I'm going to put this memo away for a year. Open the subject up again then, if you want to—see how it goes. When it's all done, I have to make the decision—but if I'm wrong, we'll know a year from now and talk about it then. Okay?"

Elmandorf followed this performance as closely as he could and really could not see what there was left for him to say. He had no idea how old Weiner was or what he had done, if anything, that had graced him with more marketing wisdom than he, Elmandorf, had. As always in his dealings with Weiner, he found himself, at the end of the encounter, exactly where Weiner wished him to be. This was discomforting, but it reflected both their relative status and Weiner's skill as well as his own clumsiness in these interpersonal relations. Whether or not Weiner had actually achieved marketing wisdom was beside the point and Elmandorf knew it. Weiner called the marketing shots and Elmandorf knew this and accepted it and that was that. So Elmandorf simply responded, "If that's the way you want it, Arthur, that's the way it is. When do we start into test market?" The questions raised in Elmandorf's memorandum were then closed, never to be opened again, and they both knew it.

* *
*

Weiner's first request to Elmandorf was that he develop a critical path analysis for the introduction of Miracle Foam Deodorant into test markets. This request followed Allgood Drug policy. All marketing introductions were made on the basis of critical path analyses so that the time required to bring a new product or other innovation into being would be clearly established and so that an orderly development procedure would be identified and agreed to from the beginning.

The identification of the critical path involves three basic steps. First, it is necessary to identify all of the activities in the particular marketing endeavor in question. Second, it is necessary to classify these activities with respect to time sequence and with respect to whether or not individual activities are sequentially related to other activities or concurrently related to other activities. Thus some activities can be carried out only before and/or after other activities (that is, sequentially), and some activities may be carried out independently of others, as long as they are accomplished within a generally defined time sequence (that is, concurrently). The third step is to relate all of the activities formally, one to the other, in an overt representation of the sequence in which the events will be undertaken. This representation can take the form of a diagram that plots all the activities and their temporal relationship. It is on this diagram that the *critical path* is identified, and it is defined as the chain of sequenced activities required to complete the launching of the marketing innovation or the new product. Time is explicit in the critical path, and the elapsed time required in progressing along the critical path is the maximum time needed for the project. The critical path, therefore, defines the duration of the particular project and identifies the sequence of activities that must somehow be shortened if the project is to take a shorter period of time. The major benefit of critical path analysis is that it distinguishes between events that must be scheduled sequentially and those that may be scheduled in a group of concurrent activities. A critical path analysis tends to eliminate the sequential scheduling of two or more events that may, in fact, proceed concurrently.

Elmandorf's first job was, therefore, to prepare a list of all the activities that must be completed before Miracle Foam Deodorant could actually be presented to the public in a test market. These activities are summarized in Exhibit 8–21. The exhibit shows for each activity the maximum length of time required to complete it and the most reasonable minimum length of time that the activity might be expected to require. These time estimates were developed, at Elmandorf's request, by the individuals in Effluvia House directly responsible for them.

Elmandorf then began to analyse each of the required activities, identifying its functional and temporal relation to all the other activities. The major conclusions of this analysis are summarized as follows:

1. Toxicity testing precedes all other steps because unless it is certain that the product is not toxic, company policy forbids further development work on it.
2. Four separate kinds of activities are involved in the development of the product.
   a. All activities directly related to the final production of the finished product.
   b. All activities related to the creation of advertising for the product.
   c. Stability testing.
   d. Development of public relations programs.

   The advertising materials must be ready before a test market is opened up, but their development has no relation to the final production of the finished product. The same is true of the development of the public relations program.

   Company policy does not require that stability testing be completed before the test market introduction of the new product. This activity is initiated promptly, but it does not restrict the test market introduction. The company has reached this stability testing policy because the length of time required by such testing is generally considerably longer than other developmental activities and because the stability characteristics of constituent ingredients used are generally well known, which means that the stability of the normal Effluvia House new product is totally predictable. (Nothing, of course, was known about the stability of perfected ZOT. Elmandorf

EXHIBIT 8–21
Specimen Data: Activity Analysis—Miracle Foam Deodorant Development for Test Marketing

ACTIVITY	BEST-GUESS TIME (WEEKS)	MAXIMUM TIME (WEEKS)
1. 4-oz. can label design	2	3
2. 8-oz. can label design	2	3
3. 4-oz. packing case design	3	4
4. 8-oz. packing case design	3	4
5. 4-oz. can package copy approval	1	2
6. 8-oz. can package copy approval	1	2
7. 4-oz. packing case copy approval	1	2
8. 8-oz. packing case copy approval	1	2
9. Estimation of test market product qualities	3	3
10. Place can orders for test market	7	9
11. Place packing case orders for test market	14	17
12. Order raw materials for test market	2	3
13. Conduct Type I stability test	13	13
14. Conduct Type II stability test	42	42
15. Conduct toxicity test	6	8
16. Plan fashion editor information program	3	5
17. Manufacture test market product	4	6
18. Fill test market aerosol cans	2	2
19. Manufacture Plan B sampling pack	6	6
20. Quality control approval of manufactured product for test markets	1	2
21. Review advertising plans	1	2
22. Approve advertising copy	1	2
23. Produce advertising	6	14
24. Make media purchases in test markets	1	2
25. Hold sales meeting	1	1
26. Ship product to test markets	2	3
27. Order packing equipment	4	6
28. Set up manufacturing line	1	2
29. Approve 4-oz. design	1	2
30. Approve 8-oz. design	1	2
31. Approve 4-oz. packing case design	1	2
32. Approve 8-oz. packing case design	1	2
33. Finalize quantity production formulation and procedures	1	4
34. Trade sell-in in test markets	4	5

was justifiably concerned about it and Weiner was willing to take a limited marketing risk.)

3. Several activities must be concluded before actual raw material and packaging orders can be placed. These include the development and approval of all package designs; the finalization of a product pro-

duction formula; and the estimation of product quantities required for the test market. Packing equipment should also be ordered in anticipation of eventual production.

4. The actual ordering of packages and raw materials follows. The production time can best be set up in anticipation of their delivery.

5. The remaining steps are all sequentially related: the product must be manufactured and approved by the quality control authority; the sales meeting must be held; the trade sell-in must follow; and finally, the product must be shipped in accordance with the trade orders that have been received.

These activities are shown graphically in this sequence in Exhibit 8–22. The direction of activities is from left to right. Concurrent activities are arranged vertically in the exhibit. The number of weeks required by each activity is shown in parentheses immediately after the activity. A single figure in parentheses denotes a single time estimate. Two figures separated by a slash indicate the minimum time estimate in weeks and the maximum time estimate in weeks.

Elmandorf presented the critical path analysis to Weiner on January 21, 1974, and a final approval to proceed with the project was given by Arthur Weiner on January 31, 1974.

Questions for Case 8

1. Why is it necessary to test-market Miracle Foam Deodorant?
2. Describe the functions of the principal marketing officer in a company. Should Weiner manage the Miracle Foam Deodorant brand? Can a marketing officer be successful if he has not had first-hand experience in brand management? Why?
3. Two promotional plans have been developed: one involves only advertising and the other involves advertising and promotion. Why is it necessary to test these alternatives? Why shouldn't Miss Effluvia both advertise at a high level and promote the new product to the consumer? Is it necessary to continue consumer sampling into the second and third marketing years?
4. a. Is it reasonable to assume that the underarm deodorant market will expand at 10 per cent per year subsequent to the introduction of the new Miracle Foam Deodorant? Why or why not?
   b. Why should the new Miracle Foam Deodorant product achieve market shares of 20 per cent, 25 per cent, and 30 per cent respectively in its first three marketing years? Do you believe these share projections are defensible?
   c. Comment on the Miracle Foam Deodorant profit projections. Why should the same profit be anticipated under both Plan A and Plan B?
5. What is the purpose of the marketing plan? How extensive must a marketing plan be to accomplish this purpose? Do you prefer Elmandorf's short (revised outline) plan to his original (long outline) plan? What realistic choices does Elmandorf have when he is asked to revise his original (long

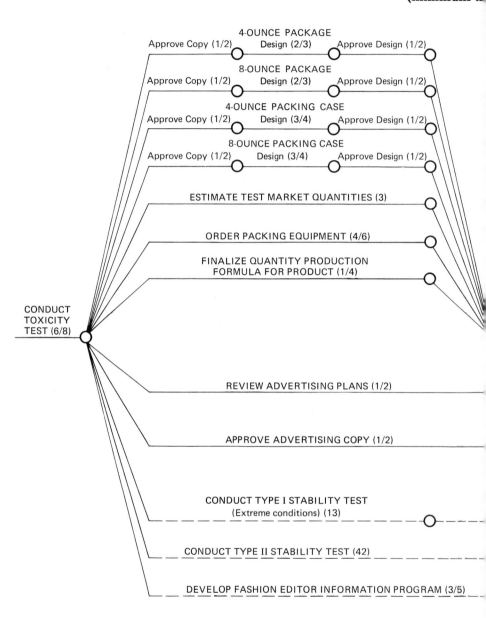

CONDUCT
TOXICITY
TEST (6/8)

4-OUNCE PACKAGE
Approve Copy (1/2)   Design (2/3)   Approve Design (1/2)

8-OUNCE PACKAGE
Approve Copy (1/2)   Design (2/3)   Approve Design (1/2)

4-OUNCE PACKING CASE
Approve Copy (1/2)   Design (3/4)   Approve Design (1/2)

8-OUNCE PACKING CASE
Approve Copy (1/2)   Design (3/4)   Approve Design (1/2)

ESTIMATE TEST MARKET QUANTITIES (3)

ORDER PACKING EQUIPMENT (4/6)

FINALIZE QUANTITY PRODUCTION
FORMULA FOR PRODUCT (1/4)

REVIEW ADVERTISING PLANS (1/2)

APPROVE ADVERTISING COPY (1/2)

CONDUCT TYPE I STABILITY TEST
(Extreme conditions) (13)

CONDUCT TYPE II STABILITY TEST (42)

DEVELOP FASHION EDITOR INFORMATION PROGRAM (3/5)

:
cle Foam Deodorant
imum time)

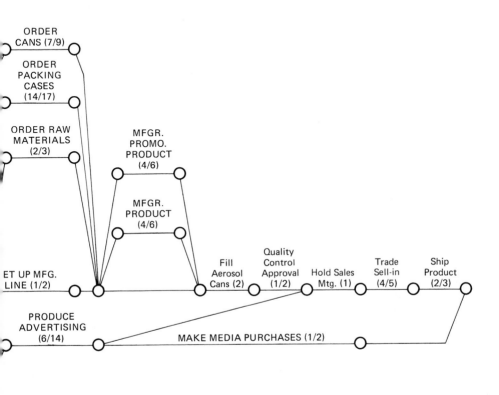

ORDER
CANS (7/9)

ORDER
PACKING
CASES
(14/17)

ORDER RAW
MATERIALS
(2/3)

MFGR.
PROMO.
PRODUCT
(4/6)

MFGR.
PRODUCT
(4/6)

ET UP MFG.
LINE (1/2)

Fill
Aerosol
Cans (2)

Quality
Control
Approval
(1/2)

Hold Sales
Mtg. (1)

Trade
Sell-in
(4/5)

Ship
Product
(2/3)

PRODUCE
ADVERTISING
(6/14)

MAKE MEDIA PURCHASES (1/2)

outline) plan? Under what circumstances might a company not need marketing plans?

6. Does Elmandorf present an acceptable case against the product in his memorandum of January 8, 1974? What role does marketing judgment play in Weiner's decisions? How does one acquire marketing judgment? Can marketing judgment be obtained without years of marketing experience? Could Miracle Foam Deodorant fail in the marketplace?

7. Define the critical path for Miracle Foam Deodorant. What is the minimum amount of time that will be required to introduce it into the test market? What is the maximum amount of time that will be required to introduce it into the test market? It is planned to start test market advertising on September 17, 1974. Assuming that the critical path is calculated on a starting date of February 13, 1974, will the product be in the stores, ready to sell, on that date?

CASE 9

Evaluating Marketing Plans in the Marketplace

Miss Effluvia Market-Tests Miracle Foam Deodorant

As PRODUCT manager Sherman L. Elmandorf developed the critical path analysis for Miracle Foam Deodorant, he also worked with the Miss Effluvia marketing research department in the development of test-marketing plans. (See Cases 7 and 8.) The basic purpose of test marketing is to subject a balanced and total marketing conception to the critical evaluation of the marketplace. All marketing research work that precedes test marketing is directed toward the appraisal of fractions of the final, complete marketing effort. Consumer response to the product or package or advertising or name or whatnot is tested. Such single elements from the marketing mix are tested—usually individually, but always artificially in the sense that the consumer is not asked to respond to the total product in the context of the marketplace. At the same time, marketing plans and projections are developed in terms of marketing experience that is never exactly congruent or relevant to the particular marketing situation at hand. Things continue to change and no single marketing plan is ever exactly like the ones that preceded it.

So neither marketing research nor experience offers an infallible guide in determining whether or not the particular combination of marketing elements will "fly" or not. Market testing is not, as we shall see, an infallible guide to ultimate national success or failure, but it comprises the first time the particular combination of marketing elements specified in the marketing plan come together with the consumer as a consumer. The consumer heretofore has been involved with the market planning more as a self-conscious research respondent, or as a reflector of the accumulated wisdom of the marketing past. But in the market test, this same consumer simply goes about his business as the maker of purchasing decisions involving his own money in real retail outlets.

Elmandorf had had plenty of test-marketing experience, and he knew how to write a test-marketing plan. But he continued to flounder in the rather loosely conceived Miss Effluvia organization, reflecting as it did the diverse and often conflicting views of three assertive personalities from totally different backgrounds. It was one thing to identify the kinds of skills needed to run a new organization and it was another to split them up among three rather different individuals and backgrounds, as had been done in the recruitment of Knowles (from Effluvia House with a heavy background in product development and manufacturing), Weiner (from Allgood with extensive experience in packaged drug goods marketing) and Ms. Sappora (from All-a-Glow with heavy experience in mass cosmetic marketing research).

With this variety of skills, it was always certain that there would be someone available to handle whatever problem happened to come up at a particular time. The difficulty was, rather, of the other kind: there was very likely to be too much talent available in any problem-solving situation rather than too little. Elmandorf knew that both Weiner and Ms. Sappora would have their own experience with and opinions about market testing, and whether Harvey Knowles knew anything about it or not, he would probably have a presidential opinion too, which, because it came from the president, was very likely to be controlling, right or wrong, half-baked or whole.

Elmandorf's reaction to these strong personalities in the organization was to let one of them take the lead in developing plans for market testing. Market testing was after all, reasoned Elmandorf, simply an extension of the marketing research work that had already been lavished upon this project. If market testing is the final evaluative step in the process that eventuates in the decision to make or not to make a national introduction, then let the marketing research group tell how it is to be done. With this thought, Elmandorf asked Allison Sappora if she could outline the basic guidelines to be followed in test marketing Miracle Foam Deodorant, paying particular attention to the experience and practices of Allgood Drug. (He was, it should be added, sure that Effluvia had never run a test market and suspected that Harvey Knowles wouldn't know one from a bale of hay.)

Allison Sappora was having her own troubles with the Miss Effluvia organization but she did not let them deter her. She had, after all, been hired to do a job; she would do it as well as she knew how, and if they didn't like it, she would find somewhere else to fry her fish. She was careful, however, to try to define just who "they" might ultimately be. That is, she gave a good deal of thought to the question of who might ultimately assess her work, both within Miss Effluvia and beyond. She concluded that she and Weiner had been brought into the company because there was no relevant marketing know-how in the Effluvia House organization and that, therefore, it seemed likely that she should look in the direction of Allgood procedures and prejudices for basic orientation rather than toward her own experience or toward Effluvia House.

Accordingly, Ms. Sappora got to know people in Allgood and in a relatively short period of time had developed sources of information within the company so that she could always find out how a particular marketing activity was handled in the parent firm or what the corporate viewpoint of a particular matter would be. This was important in two ways. First, it ensured that basic Allgood procedures would be reflected in much of the work of its subsidiary. Allison Sappora might not follow the Allgood way exactly when there were good mass cosmetic marketing reasons not to do so. But the basic derivation of her recommendations was usually clear, and this clarity tended to infuse a sense of propriety and continuity into the activities of the subsidiary, which helped give it both a sense of direction and ready corporate acceptance of its work. This acceptance was particularly valuable in those instances in which a Miss Effluvia plan involved effort on the part of the Allgood sales force. If Miss Effluvia required sales force effort of the same kind and magnitude as Allgood had in comparable situations, this acceptance helped matters considerably.

Secondly, Ms. Sappora's knowledge of and dependence upon corporate ways of doing things tended to be in her own best interest, too. If the ultimate appraisal of Miss Effluvia would be made in Allgood by Allgood people, there was reason enough to know what they liked and give them as much of it as was reasonable in the circumstances.

If Harvey Knowles, with his Effluvia House background, observed all of this, there was little enough that he could do about it. Ms. Sappora was, after all, politically sound and professionally correct, and Knowles either knew or would find out soon enough that this is a hard combination to beat. So when Elmandorf asked Ms. Sappora to supply a document outlining basic guidelines for market testing that took cognizance of Allgood experience and prejudices, she was both happy and ready to help. Over the next three weeks she delivered a total of three separate documents on this subject to him.

The first of these was entitled "General Considerations in Test Marketing" and provided a rather general, philosophic framework for test-marketing work for Miss Effluvia products. Second, Elmandorf received a research evaluation of ten "available" test markets, that is, markets that had less than two Allgood test products currently in test *and* were included among the basic augmented list of seventy-two acceptable Allgood Drug test markets. The general acceptability of a market for Allgood test-marketing activity depended primarily upon the general and media criteria for market selection outlined in "General Considerations in Test Marketing"; markets that obviously did not meet these criteria were automatically eliminated from the basic augmented list of acceptable markets.

The third document was called "Payout Planning for New Product Test Market Programs." It consisted of a series of basic guidelines for new product test market planning and contained a series of injunctions and rules for actually planning and evaluating a market test.

Here are these three documents:

GENERAL CONSIDERATIONS IN TEST MARKETING

This document has been prepared to help prevent test market failures.

Experience shows that test market failures are usually traceable to the planning and execution phase of test market programs. Such errors in planning and execution may lead to negative or inconclusive test market results in spite of the intrinsic merit of the product. Conversely, it is equally possible that poor planning and execution may lead to an apparently successful test-marketing of an inherently poor product with costly subsequent failure in national distribution.

This document specifically concerns itself with the test marketing of variations in marketing and/or advertising strategy for existing products, although the points made are also applicable to the test introduction of totally new products.

The Purpose of a Test Market Program

A test market program is designed to determine the potential sales success of an innovation in a product or an innovation in a product marketing or advertising program.

Thus the only objective of the test-marketing program is to provide new knowledge about the impact (if any) of the marketing or advertising innovation upon brand sales. This new knowledge should provide a basis for subsequently deciding whether the innovation may profitably be expanded beyond the test market itself.

This new knowledge should provide a predictably better basis for estimating the sales effect of the marketing/advertising innovation than the accumulated judgment of the marketeers involved in the project. If one cannot be sure that this will be so, then there is no need to go to the trouble and expense of market testing. But if certain basic standards are met, it is reasonably certain that test markets will provide new knowledge superior to a consensus of marketing judgments. If these basic standards are not met, it is almost certain that a consensus of good judgments will provide decisions that are at least as good as those based on inadequate market tests.

Standards for Testing Marketing Innovations

It is Allgood/Miss Effluvia policy to define a test market area in terms of the unduplicated television coverage area of the central city. This market definition is used because so many Allgood/Miss Effluvia brands are dependent upon the television medium and because such market areas are flexible and useful for test marketing even if the use of television is not itself a factor.

1. *Marketing or advertising innovations should be tested in several markets: at least two, and preferably three or more.* Different test markets invariably respond in different ways to different marketing or advertising innovations. It is impossible to select individual markets that are totally representative of the entire United States: individual markets differ from the United States as a whole and from each other. In practice, therefore, it is necessary to test in at least two and preferably three markets to ensure that the composite result stands a fair chance of being indicative

of the sales success of the marketing or advertising innovation in the whole United States.

It is naïve to believe that a few markets can be chosen that will consistently produce market test results projectable to the whole United States. However, if one views the market test as a test of a reasonable marketing hypothesis, then the research question is whether or not the marketing hypothesis can be proved in the market place. A favorable result in one market can occur by chance alone. But if a favorable result is obtained independently in three markets, the odds are 8 to 1 that chance factors are not responsible.

Some research practitioners argue that even three markets are not enough. But experience indicates that any result that holds in three independent test markets is likely to hold broadly throughout the country, *if the other standards of successful test-marketing have also been met*. Two out of three test market results in a single direction are less solid support for a decision: common sense and very close analysis of the results are needed in these cases, but even with such caution the final decision is chancier.

Note that if only two test markets are used in the first place, one's confidence in the result, whatever it may be, is disproportionately decreased. Two markets per innovation are a risky minimum for test market purposes: one always wonders what result might have been achieved in the third test market, had there been one.

2. *The test markets should be as widely dispersed geographically as possible.* Geographic dispersion is desired to control and to account as much as possible for the effect of geographic variation on test results.

3. *Each marketing innovation should be tested for at least six months, and even longer in some low-purchase-rate product categories.* Experience emphasizes that it takes *at least* six months to determine the likely sales result of a market innovation. Shorter periods may mislead because some marketing and advertising innovations are slow starters and catch on slowly, whereas others produce immediate sales spurts that subsequently fall off quickly. In the case of long-interval-between-purchase product categories, even longer minimum test periods should be used.

4. *Significant measurements must be chosen for evaluating the results of the test market.* Dollar sales are frequently chosen as the significant measurement for the appraisal of test results. Dollar sales to the trade (including retail and wholesale inventories) are available from company records. Dollar sales to consumers can be accurately measured in test markets if a fully projectable sample of retail outlets representing the entire test area is audited.

Market share is sometimes used as the single significant measurement for the appraisal of test markets. It is possible to make adequate estimates of changes in market share based on relatively less precise (that is, not projectable in the statistical sense) samples of retail outlets. For example, quota samples of retail outlets overweighted with high-volume outlets and concentrated in the principal metropolitan area in the test market are frequently used to obtain share estimates. It is considerably less expensive to set up such quota samples of retail outlets throughout the entire test areas. Even though such quota samplings do not necessarily reflect or project to overall dollar sales, they may produce adequate estimates of changes in market position. When such audits are confined to the major metropolitan area of a test area, it is important to be sure that this metropolitan area itself accounts for a substantial portion of the total test area.

Occasionally other indicators of the success or failure of test market innovations are used as a significant measurement for the appraisal of test results. Measures of changes in consumer knowledge, awareness, brand usage, repeat purchase, attitudes, intention to purchase, and so on are sometimes used in this way. These measurements are practical *in this usage* only if it can be demonstrated that they are themselves clearly related to sales or market share or some other objective of the market test for the particular marketing or advertising innovation.

Of course, such consumer measurements may be critically helpful in understanding the *reasons* for the particular test performance of an innovation (repeat-purchase data are an outstanding example) even if they are not used as a significant measurement for the appraisal of test results. Therefore, it is frequently recommended that such measures be made among consumers *coincidentally* with the market test in order to provide insight into why the test turned out as it did.

In general, it is Allgood/Miss Effluvia policy to develop both consumer-dollar-sales and factory-sales data for test market areas as a basis for appraising market tests. It is assumed by the company that no market tests will be undertaken that are not sufficiently significant to justify the expense of measuring dollar sales to consumers.

In general, it is also Allgood/Miss Effluvia policy to develop information concerning consumer awareness, knowledge (repeat-purchase patterns), and attitudes as supplements to the sales data in those instances in which this information can be expected to aid significantly in the appraisal of market test results.

The policy is one of liberality in authorizing measurement budgets in conjunction with approved market tests. Everything should be measured in test markets that will contribute to a correct final decision with respect to the national extension of the marketing variable under test.

5. *"Success" should be defined for every market test before the test begins.* It is important that results that will be interpreted to mean that the innovation tested is a success be specified before the test is undertaken. Similarly, the kinds of results that will be interpreted as a failure for the innovation should also be specified in advance. Success or failure will usually be defined in terms of the required number of dollars in sales, but they may also be in terms of the critical market share goal or whatever else is judged necessary for unambiguous success to be achieved from the marketing or advertising innovation. The standard of success must be set clearly and unambiguously in advance: if it is, the test results can be quickly appraised and evaluated. If the standard of success is not set in advance, the interpretation of results inevitably becomes compounded by the nature of the results themselves, and test effectiveness is almost always blunted by after-the-fact discussion of alternative interpretations of results.

There are two different types of analyses that are applied to sales results. First, in some situations the marketing innovation is introduced without extra or new marketing cost. The question in such cases is whether or not a change in sales trend follows the innovation, that is, whether the innovation leads to an increase in sales and profits or to a decline in sales and profits, with no change in marketing costs.

An example of such an innovation might be the introduction of a redesigned package, the reallocation of advertising funds to consumer promotional uses, or a change in advertising dollar allocation by media. If a change of this kind satisfies the rules of major innovation and practicality, the test is evaluated in terms of whether or not it changes the direction of the sales trend. Do sales grow faster than anticipated as a result of the innovation? Or do they grow more slowly than antici-pated as a result of the innovation? Or is there no appreciable change?

In the more typical case, however, a new marketing expenditure or an increase in marketing expenditure is involved, and a payout analysis is also required. Payout analyses relate the new or increased expenditures required by a marketing or advertising innovation to the extra sales produced by the innovation. When the new or increased cost has been recovered, the test has passed its success point, and only its *relative* profitability remains to be determined. Accurate measurements of dollar sales are needed to make payout projections and evaluations. The essence of the payout plan is the profit calculation: extra sales against new or increased costs. Payout calculations can be made whenever sales estimates, projectable to the entire test market, are available. Dollar sales to consumers should be the prime criterion for assessing payout because they reflect direct consumer response.

The Selection of Test Markets

Five basic standards for the selection of test markets are listed and discussed here. These standards give guidance in the selection of typical markets for use in test programs. In a specific test program, some of the standards may be more important than others; thus in a given test situation good judgment must be used in applying these standards to market selection.

SIZE OF MARKET

Ideally, test markets (already defined as the television coverage area of the central city) should range in size between 100,000 and 500,000 homes in the central city area. The objective is to eliminate very large central cities (such as New York, Los Angeles, and Chicago), which, because of their great size and complexity, are not typical, and to eliminate the very small markets, which do not reflect important buying power.

QUALITY OF MARKET

It is important that the test market be roughly average in terms of market quality. Specifically, this means that the purchasing ability of the residents within the test market should be about at the national average. The *Sales Management* Buying-Power Index is generally used to evaluate markets in terms of their basic quality. This index reflects the effective buying income in the market, the retail sales in the market, and the population in the market. These three factors are then related to the population size of the market in the computation of a quality-of-market index. Markets with relatively high and relatively low index levels are excluded from consideration as test markets on the basis of this standard.

MEDIA CHARACTERISTICS

The media facilities in the central city should be typical:

1. There should be at least two television stations.
2. There should be no single dominant radio station.
3. A local supplement offering four-color reproduction should be available.
4. Adequate daily and Sunday newspaper coverage should be available.
5. Local media rates should be at reasonable levels. (This factor must be appraised in terms of published rate cards; unpublished concessions cannot

be taken into account. It is possible that a market with seemingly high media rates based on rate cards may actually, in the event of purchase, be reasonable.)

6. Test markets should not receive dominant coverage from media facilities originating outside the test market. At the same time, it is important that the major portion of coverage for media originating in the test market be concentrated within the test market itself.

SALES PENETRATION

If sufficient data are available, it is important to evaluate individual test markets in terms of the success that specific brand and product groups have had in each market. Test markets should have average or better-than-average per-capita sales of test product groups and comparable company brands.

AVAILABILITY OF TYPICAL DISTRIBUTION FACILITIES

Test markets should be typical with respect to the availability of distribution facilities for specific product groups within the market. The typical distribution pattern for the product category should be mirrored within the test market.

The second document forwarded to Elmandorf was this memorandum:

Miss Effluvia Memorandum

TO: Sherman L. Elmandorf
FROM: Allison Sapora
SUBJECT: *Miracle Foam Deodorant Test Markets*

The attached table (Exhibit 9–1) shows ten Allgood/Miss Effluvia test markets that are available to Miracle Foam Deodorant for the immediate initiation of market tests.

As you know, Allgood Marketing Research has developed a basic list of fifty test markets, but because of the recent expanded market-testing activities of Allgood they have found it necessary to develop an augmented basic list containing an overall total of seventy-two test markets.

The basic list meets all the general criteria set out in "General Considerations in Test Marketing." That is, all fifty test markets meet size requirements, quality-of-market requirements, and major media requirements. Of the ten markets listed in the attached table, only Houston was on the original basic list. The other nine markets all fall down for one reason or another—usually because the television signals spill out far beyond the metro areas and into other, competitive, television markets. Frequently in these situations television rates may be based upon total coverage of homes rather than on the limited number of homes in the central city television area. We have usually believed that television advertising in these markets is over-priced. You may want to check this point with the advertising agency's media department.

You may think that Baltimore is too large and that Omaha and Bakersfield are too small. Or you may want to eliminate Bakersfield because it has no Sunday

EXHIBIT 9-1
Test Markets Available for Miracle Foam Deodorant: Data as of July 1972 Master Test Market Analysis Revision

MARKET	(1) TV TEST AREA HOMES (000 OMITTED)	(2) TV TEST AREA TV HOMES (000 OMITTED)	(3) % U.S. TV HOMES	(4) TV STATIONS VHF/UHF	(5) RADIO STATIONS AM/FM	(6) NEWSPAPERS DAILY/SUNDAY	(7) STANDARD METROPOLITAN STATISTICAL AREA BUYING-POWER INDEX	(8) STANDARD METROPOLITAN STATISTICAL AREA QUALITY-OF-MARKET INDEX
Houston	781.1	743.9	1.20	3/2	20/16	2/2	1.0068	100
Baltimore	721.6	680.8	1.10	3/1	22/17	2/2	1.0391	102
Buffalo	611.0	571.0	.92	3/1	13/12	2/1	.6617	101
Cincinnati	600.4	582.9	.94	3/1	11/8	2/1	.7017	104
New Orleans	457.5	423.6	.68	3/1	14/8	2/1	.4870	95
Dayton	404.6	396.7	.64	2/2	7/9	2/1	.4347	104
Portland (Ore.)	570.3	543.1	.87	4/–	17/10	2/1	.5325	105
Oklahoma City	430.3	394.8	.64	3/–	11/12	3/2	.3281	102
Omaha	281.6	276.1	.44	3/–	8/6	2/1	.2740	103
Bakersfield	91.2	85.2	.14	–/3	15/4	1/–	.1597	99

SOURCES:
1. TV Test Area Homes: Compiled from industry sources.
2. TV Test Area TV Homes: Compiled from industry sources.
3. % U.S. TV Homes: Compiled from industry sources.
4. Television Stations: Compiled from industry sources.
5. Radio Stations: Compiled from industry sources.
6. Newspapers: Compiled from industry sources.
7. Standard Metropolitan Area Buying-Power Index: As available from "Sales Management 1973 Survey of Buying Power," *Sales Management* July 23, 1973. (The buying-power index weights the market's effective buying income (5 times), retail sales (3 times), and population (2 times) to reach a single value reflecting the individual market's buying power.)
8. Quality-of-Market Index: Computed from "Sales Management 1973 Survey of Buying Power," *Sales Management* July 23, 1973. (The quality-of-market index relates the individual market's buying power to the percentage of U.S. population accounted for by the market.)

newspaper, specifically if print advertising is to be important. Anyway, we've put this table together to suggest the problems you may run into.

Our market recommendation from the available list is Houston, Cincinnati (TV rates are believed to be okay in both Cincinnati and Dayton but check with the advertising agency), and Portland, Oregon. You can assess the potential problems from the table and from agency comments: the point is that these markets are available and geographically dispersed.

The third document delivered to Sherman L. Elmandorf by Allison Sappora was entitled "Payout Planning for New Product Test Market Programs." It is a step-by-step primer in the company procedures and policies with respect to the test marketing of new products.

PAYOUT PLANNING FOR NEW PRODUCT TEST MARKET PROGRAMS: ALLGOOD/MISS EFFLUVIA COMPANY POLICIES AND PROCEDURES

The basic procedure for payout planning in a test market program for a new Allgood/Miss Effluvia brand consists of five specific steps. These steps are listed here, along with the company policy or policies applying to each step.

Step 1. A national sales estimate for the new brand must be made. This sales estimate involves four separate parts:

1. First-test-year case sales to fill the pipeline.
2. First-test-year factory sales.
3. Second-test-year factory sales.
4. Third-year factory sales.

Notes on Step 1

1. It is assumed that each test brand will make case sales in its first year that establish retail and wholesale inventories for the brand (that is, "fill the pipeline"). These case sales are considered nonrecurring and therefore should be isolated in the first-year sales estimates. It is company policy that such sales-to-pipeline estimates may not exceed 15 per cent of estimated total brand case sales in the first test year.
2. Case sales estimates should be based on: (a) projections of total market case sales for the product category and (b) projections of total market case sales for the Allgood/Miss Effluvia brand.
3. Allgood/Miss Effluvia brand case shares must be based on closely reasoned and logical evaluations of past sales performance. Allgood/Miss Effluvia policy does not permit share estimates in excess of 40 per cent in established competitive markets. Reasonable share estimates generally fall well below this figure and average about 20 per cent by the third year.
4. The established case rate for the brand developed in Step 2 (profit, advertising, and promotion) is applied to all shipments in all years, including the pipeline in the first test year.

Step 2. Determine amount available for PAP (profit, advertising, and promotion) in each year.

Notes on Step 2

1. The amount available for PAP is a residual figure. It is computed as follows. Determine the gross dollars received, per case, by the company. Deduct from this figure the manufacturing cost of goods per case plus allowance for sales costs, administrative costs, research costs, and overhead.
2. The manufacturing cost of goods per case is provided by the Production Department. Be sure to determine if these costs decrease with volume and reflect this in your estimates.
3. Sales and administrative costs are computed for the average company brand, and this percentage is applied, in accordance with company policy, to all test brands. The currently applicable sales and administrative cost percentage is 12 per cent of the gross dollars received.
4. Overhead is similarly computed and applied to test brands. The currently applicable overhead figure is 21 per cent of the gross dollars received.
5. It is Miss Effluvia policy to add 2 per cent to the manufacturing cost of goods plus sales and administration costs plus overhead to finance brand marketing research.
6. Company policy is to divide profit, advertising, and promotion 40 per cent–40 per cent–20 per cent. The profit percentage may not, under company policy, be changed on the basis of test market results.

Step 3. Develop a PAP payout plan for the brand.

Notes on Step 3

1. A payout plan involves the following elements: (a) a comparison of recommended promotion and advertising budgets with available PAP during each test year; (b) a statement about the ability of the brand to achieve its estimated sales so as to break even after the second year is complete, and provide full profit from the third year onward.
2. It is Allgood/Miss Effluvia policy that each test brand must pay out by the end of the test year. In practice, this means that each test brand is permitted to spend the available advertising, promotion, and profits in its first year in order to build a market franchise at predicted sales volume levels that can then be supported with the available advertising and promotion funds. Thus the brand is required to break even after one year, and full profit is returned to the company in the second year and henceforth. Profits in the first year are invested to build the market franchise.
3. It is Allgood/Miss Effluvia policy that certain advertising goals must be achieved within each of the three years. These goals relate to the introductory period (first six months of the first year); the postintroductory period (balance of the first year and all of the second year); the sustaining period (the third year and henceforward). The goals themselves are generally stated in terms of minimum market coverage by advertising (a minimum proportion of the brand target market that advertising must reach); minimum average frequency of exposure (the average time each market prospect is reached); and maximum media efficiency (the maximum allowable cost of reaching one thousand prospects).

4. It is Allgood/Miss Effluvia policy that the advertising agency is responsible for developing appropriate media plans for each test brand. These media plans are to state the minimum number of dollars required to accomplish the media goals. The Effluvia House brand manager is responsible for reconciling these media costs with available advertising, promotion, and (in the first year) profit dollars.

5. It is the general responsibility of the Effluvia House management to control cost elements throughout the company so that Effluvia House brands can be marketed at competitive prices, meet payout requirements, and yield adequate PAP margins.

6. Exception to policy: test market advertising costs may be budgeted above available PAP levels to make up for cost penalties incurred by the use of local media schedules for test purposes to simulate generally more efficient national schedules. In general, a 20 per cent premium is the maximum allowed. In any event the exact premium will depend upon agency estimates of local price variations.

Step 4. Decide whether test marketing is feasible under available dollars and payout policies. Recommend to management.

Step 5. If testing is feasible, choose test markets and translate the national base sales and media plans down to these test markets.

Notes on Step 5

1. Test markets must be chosen from lists supplied by the Marketing Research Department so that the total company testing program will be relatively equally divided among sales territories.

2. Test market advertising budgets are generally set by the metro-area *Sales Management* Buying-Power Index (Exhibit 9–1). This buying-power index times the total national advertising budget yields the basic test market advertising budget. This budget is subject to modification (see Step 3, Note 6).

3. Media translations from national plans to test market plans are made, in accordance with company procedures, by the agency media department.

Step 6. Develop alternative advertising and promotional plans. Recommend feasible alternatives for test.

Notes on Step 6

1. Alternative plans must represent real alternatives: substantial differences in marketing approaches must be reflected.

2. It is quite possible that feasible alternative plans do not exist. If this is so, Allgood/Miss Effluvia policy requires that the lack of such plans be documented.

Questions for Case 9

1. The Miss Effluvia marketing research department recommended Houston, Cincinnati, and Portland, Oregon as test markets for Miracle Foam Deodorant.

   a. Do you agree with these recommendations? Why or why not?

   b. If the data shown in Exhibit 9–2 are added to the pool of evaluative

EXHIBIT 9–2
Specimen Data: Estimated Underarm Deodorant Volume and Per-Capita Use in Dollars for Available Test Markets

MARKET	(2) ADULT POPULATION (000 OMITTED)	(3) DEODORANT SALES	(4) PER-CAPITA SALES	(5) INDEX TOTAL U.S. = 100
Houston	1,325.7	$2,644.6	$2.00	123
Baltimore	1,413.1	2,422.9	1.73	107
Buffalo	899.8	2,151.6	2.39	148
Cincinnati	913.7	1,994.7	2.18	135
New Orleans	684.4	1,277.5	1.87	115
Dayton	572.1	1,591.3	2.78	172
Portland, Ore.	721.1	1,949.8	2.70	167
Oklahoma City	445.2	1,322.3	2.97	183
Omaha	355.6	896.5	2.52	156
Bakersfield	215.6	336.2	1.56	96
TOTAL U.S.	138,393.4	$224,120.0	$1.62	100

SOURCES : 2. Adult Population: Estimated from industry and census sources.
3. Deodorant Sales: Estimated by Allgood econometric research section.
4. (2) divided by (3).
5. Index $= \dfrac{\text{Market value sales per capita}}{\text{U.S. value sales per capita}}$

information used in the selection of test markets, do you believe it would change the market selections made? Tell why. If you decide to stay with Houston, Cincinnati, and Portland, Oregon, tell why.

   c. What is the basic advertising allocation in each of the recommended test markets for the introductory year if the national advertising budget for that year is set at $14,356,469 (as in Plan A, Case 8)?

2. In the market introduction of a new packaged-good product, it is not unusual to spend $100,000 or more per test market in advertising alone. In light of this, is the point of view expressed on pages 230–231 about two versus three test markets reasonable? Why?

3. Define success for Miracle Foam Deodorant in each of the three test markets you have selected in Question 1.

Assume the following:

The national dollar sales estimates for Miracle Foam Deodorant are

Year 1	$37,420,000
Year 2	44,750,000
Year 3	59,050,000

The national case sales estimates for Miracle Foam Deodorant are

Year 1	4,990,000
Year 2	5,967,000
Year 3	7,873,000

Case costs for the first three marketing years are as follows:

	PER CASE	YEAR 1	YEAR 2	YEAR 3
Manufacturing	($1.90320)	$9,496,968	$11,356,394	$14,983,983
Sales, etc.	(0.90000)	4,491,000	5,370,300	7,085,700
Overhead	(1.57500)	7,859,250	9,398,025	12,399,975
Market research	(0.15000)	748,500	895,050	1,180,950
Royalty	(0.09375)	467,813	559,406	738,094

National advertising expenditures will be these (making Plan A assumption, Case 8, that is, no consumer promotion expenditures):

Year 1	$14,356,469
Year 2	10,302,495
Year 3	13,596,833

4. What is the dominant impression about Miracle Foam Deodorant that the advertising copy created for this brand should make? What criteria should Elmandorf use in evaluating copy presented to him by the advertising agency?

5. Some test market philosophies are based upon test markets that cover very broad geographic areas, such as states, groups of states, or Nielsen Food Index areas. Other test market philosophies including those of the Allgood Drug Company, are based on the use of smaller areas, such as the television market test area, which includes an unduplicated television coverage area of a central city. Still others are limited to standard metropolitan statistical areas or even inner city areas. What pros and cons underlie this choice?

6. On what basis would a policy prohibiting market share estimates in excess of 40 per cent be developed? How would such a policy cover the case of a totally new product like Miracle Foam Deodorant, without direct competitors? Do you agree with the policy or not? Why?

7. In cases in which market innovations are not likely to have a significant or decisive effect on sales, what other kinds of research information, if any, are needed to assess consumer response? Take as an example a major manufacturer of industrial lubricants who starts a modest advertising campaign in general consumer magazines to convey information about the company to the investment community and to opinion leaders. Should such a company "test-market" such a campaign, or should it depend upon some other means of appraisal? What other means of appraisal?

PART THREE

Choosing Alternative Marketing Tactics

C ASE 10

Industrial Marketing

The Catawba Electric Motor Company Expands Its Sales Organization

THE CATAWBA ELECTRIC MOTOR COMPANY has its headquarter offices and principal manufacturing facility in Spartanburg, South Carolina. The company was founded in 1934 by Edward Horton Goodfoile to make electric engines for use in a line of home washing machines produced by the Topjob Corporation of Louisville, Kentucky. Topjob had been formed a year earlier by Evan Hoopes. Hoopes had designed a simple and efficient home washing machine that performed at least as well as those of the leading competitors but was not, because of its design simplicities, as susceptible to breakdowns. Hoopes was a self-made authority on how to produce a foolproof electric clothes-washing machine: he knew nothing about electric motors except that whatever motor he put in his machine had to be both durable and foolproof.

Hoopes had attended high school with Edward Goodfoile in their home town of Spartanburg. Goodfoile had never been much of a student, but he was considered by most of his contemporaries to be sort of a mechanical wizard. He was forever designing and building labor-saving devices for his own home and for those of his cronies. More often than not these were electrically powered, and more often than not Goodfoile adapted or modified a small electric motor to make the particular Rube Goldberg-like device work.

After graduating from the Spartanburg high school, Goodfoile had settled into the rut of repairing the few electric appliances that had so far appeared in Spartanburg and making odd devices on a custom basis for various small manufacturing and commercial enterprises in the town. For example, he was making an electric pencil sharpener of his own design in 1924 and an electrically driven barbeque rig in 1929. Goodfoile had no noticeable ambition to do more than take care of Spartanburg's electric appliances and make a modest number of his own contraptions each year. This much work seemed to keep him happy and his family moderately well fed and that was enough for Ed Goodfoile.

Hoopes would have known nothing about this except that Goodfoile had married Hoopes's youngest sister, Caroline. The senior Mrs. Hoopes had never approved of Goodfoile at all, and the thought that he could be a potential son-in-law had never even occurred to her. But a son-in-law he, in fact, became, and Mrs. Hoopes never got over it. She viewed the rather shiftless, puttery Goodfoile existence as purposeless and tragic and took it upon herself to keep her six other children, who in her eyes had all done considerably better than Caroline in the way of matrimony, continuously informed about the weird soap-opera-like existence of the Goodfoiles.

Evan Hoopes saw Ed Goodfoile twice a year at the family gatherings at Christmas and the Fourth of July. Over the years they had come to know and like each other well enough and at least somewhat better than they liked any of the other members of the Hoopes clan. So on the Fourth of July 1934, the two of them found themselves talking about the new washing machine that Hoopes had developed and its need for an electric motor. Goodfoile grasped the concepts and the needs easily and almost immediately began to describe the design characteristics that the needed motor should have. Sometime later in the day Hoopes asked him casually if he thought he might be able to make such a motor in his shop and Goodfoile said he thought he might be able to make a good stab at it in a week or two, and he did.

That was the beginning of the Catawba Electric Motor Company. Goodfoile began to make motors for Hoopes, and as the Hoopes business expanded, so did that of Catawba Electric. In 1938, Hoopes managed to win a contract to produce electric washers for a leading mail-order merchandiser to feature in its own growing line of retail stores, and both Topjob and Catawba found, almost overnight, that it was necessary to quadruple their capacity. Hoopes and Goodfoile had arrived, as it were, and they were on the verge of becoming millionaires when World War II intervened.

Within a matter of months Hoopes found himself a prime contractor for 30-caliber machine guns and Goodfoile moved into the business of manufacturing electric propulsion motors for torpedoes. In the period just before the war, Goodfoile had hired Harlan J. Anderson as general manager of the plant that had grown so rapidly as a result of the Topjob contract with the mail order house. Anderson was an electrical engineer by training and an industrial designer by avocation. He and Goodfoile formed a formidable team, and as they worked through the problems of making torpedo propulsion systems and perfecting their quality control of these systems, they began to realize that they had created a production capability that far transcended the simple manufacture of electric engines for washing machines.

Washing machine motors were bread and butter, of course, but how about engines for other home appliances like refrigerators and air conditioners and dishwashers? And what about other electric motors that powered woodworking and metalworking equipment? The more the two of them looked the more they found places where electric motors were used, and the more they investigated the surer they were that they could design and make better and more versatile motors than were currently available.

While the war continued, they worked many nights and some weekends to make certain that the Navy's torpedoes ran fast and true, and they made a good deal of money under the cost-plus provisions of their war contracts. But in this space of time they planned ahead to the period after the war when they could see a rosy future, indeed, unfolding. (Old Mrs. Hoopes was dumbfounded by all of this and could hardly believe her ears when her son Evan remarked in the glow of the Fourth of July celebration in 1945 that her black sheep son-in-law would shortly make his second million dollars and that his future plans made that look like peanuts. But she never forgave Goodfoile, either for his early shiftlessness or for his later success, and she did not speak to him for the last five years of her life.)

The war finally did end, and within a year the Catawba business was growing by leaps and bounds. Catawba Electric Motor continued as a prime supplier of electric motors for the Topjob washer. By 1947 they were also supplying a line of specially designed motors to the second largest supplier of powered woodworking tools and also making motors for a small but growing manufacturer of window air-conditioning units. In 1948 Topjob contributed about 52 per cent of Catawba's volume, the woodworking tool manufacturer about 38 per cent, and the air-conditioning manufacturer the remaining 10 per cent. It was in 1948 that Edward Goodfoile approached Evan Hoopes about the possibility of expanding the Topjob line into other kitchen appliances like dishwashers and refrigerators.

"Evan, you know as much about making kitchen appliances as anybody else in the business. You've got the organization to do it and the sales force and the distribution. Now's the time to move. You wait and see, Evan, if you don't, in fifteen years those big guys like General Motors and General Electric and Westinghouse and who knows who else will be in your dealerships with full lines and good deals and trying to drive you and all the other single appliance makers right out of the door— you mark my words."

"You may be right, Ed," replied Hoopes, "and I'm pretty sure you are. But I like what I'm doing and I still make the best electric washing machine in the world. Now those other fellas can come in—and I'm not denying that they will—but they won't specialize on washers, and they'll have to be both good and lucky to beat me at the washer game. I don't think they can do it, and I do think I have enough customer and dealer loyalty to stay in business a good long time just by keeping right to my knitting. And besides, I don't know a thing about refrigerators or stoves or anything except washers and I don't know anyone who does, and I'm not sure I'd trust them to make as good a refrigerator as I make a washer even if I did."

"Okay, Evan, I'll accept that and respect you for it," replied Goodfoile, "but let me ask you a question. Would you object if I started selling refrigerator motors to some other company?" "No, Ed, I wouldn't object to that and, in fact, I couldn't. And I won't object if you sell motors to other washer makers just as long as they're not the same motors you sell me. I'd want them to look like different motors, and I'd prefer it if they didn't perform as well, too, but I don't know how I could get you to agree to that."

"I don't think you could, Evan," replied Goodfoile. "I'll make them in a different series, and I'll make them look a little peculiar, but a Catawba motor is going to perform like a Catawba motor, and there is no way I can make it not."

This is the conversation that was to make Catawba Electric Company over $200 million in sales in 1956 and that ultimately made this company the dominant producer of electric motors in America. It is also the conversation that transformed Catawba Electric's marketing efforts into a major company activity.

Up until 1946 there was really no need for any formalized marketing function with the company. Whatever marketing was needed was handled by Ed and Evan at Christmas, or on the Fourth of July, or in between, if necessary. Ed Goodfoile's male secretary-assistant handled the billing, and Evan Hoopes came over from Louisville whenever he wanted to change the performance or design specification of the motors supplied to him by Catawba Electric.

Beginning in late 1946, Goodfoile and his sidekick Harlan Anderson traveled together to approach makers of electric woodworking tools and air-conditioners about the possibility of Catawba Electric's supplying them with electric motors. Goodfoile and Anderson worked out their designs and cost estimates on the spot and either got the business or not before they returned to Spartanburg. The secretary-assistant continued to handle the billing and that was that.

But in the period between 1947 and 1956, Catawba expanded its operations far beyond the point where the brilliant team of Goodfoile and Anderson could do the marketing job.

In 1948 they decided that they would have to split the functions up, and from then on Goodfoile tended to the design and manufacturing operations and Anderson became Catawba Electric's first director of sales. He hired his first salesman in 1948 and his second and third in 1949, and by 1956 there was a total of thirty-seven Catawba Electric salesmen in the field, grouped in twenty-two districts and three divisions. In recruiting his sales force, Harlan Anderson had followed five fundamental principles:

1. *No one represented Catawba Electric but Catawba Electric employees*

trained personally by Harlan Anderson in the Spartanburg plant. Anderson refused to have anything to do with any kind of industrial middlemen. He believed that a middleman's loyalty was to himself rather than to the company he represented and that when a close decision had to be made, the company never won. Beyond this, he believed that no middleman could be given the breadth and depth of knowledge about the Catawba Electric line that he could give a salesman chosen and trained by himself.

He explained his reasoning in a memorandum to Ed Goodfoile when the latter inquired, early in 1951, how they could get quick sales coverage in the Pacific Coast area, an area that then did not enjoy the services of a Catawba Electric salesman.

C-E-M-C
MEMO

TO: Edward Goodfoile
FROM: Harlan Anderson   March 18, 1951

You have asked when we could get adequate sales coverage in the Pacific Coast territory. The answer is when I can find a qualified man and train him up.

Right now, we have eight salesmen operating in the northeast and north central areas. I believe we have an immediate need for three more men. Two of these should be sent to the South—one to Atlanta, and one to Texas, Dallas or Houston. A third man should be recruited and sent to the Far West.

When I get this sales organization job done, I want it composed of men whom I have chosen and trained. They all have to have high IQ's, they have to be mechanical or electrical (better) engineers, and they all have to know as much about Catawba designs and production capabilities as you or I do. And they have to get inside their customers' heads and do what they want and need and they have to know enough to know when they don't know the answer and come to you or me for help. I want dedication and I want brilliance, and I want Catawba to stand out in the field as the best motor because we've got the best sales force. That's why I won't go for brokers, or manufacturer's agents.

Brokers will handle anybody and are little better than central order takers. They know, at best, what's on the catalogue page, but they can't and won't create, can't and won't get into their customers' heads and find out what they need and what our capability might be in filling their needs, checking back here if they have to, making sure we only lose the business we can't make a profit on, and not because we didn't try.

Manufacturers' agents are better, and maybe we could train them up, but even if we can find ones with high IQ's and proper training they would still work for lots of other people besides us, and the better they are the farther they're stretched, and the less service and hustle we get.

Wait awhile Ed. We'll get the men, and once we've got the men, we'll get the business. But let's not jump into any halfway houses just because we're hungry.

Ed Goodfoile wanted more action than it seemed from this memorandum he was going to get. But he could not fault Anderson's reasoning nor the deep feeling for Catawba Electric Motor that his point of view reflected. And so he waited.

2. *In recruiting salesmen, Catawba insisted on hiring the best-qualified men they could find.* Anderson believed in brains and college education, and as a minimum he wanted men with an IQ of 120 and a college degree in either mechanical or electrical engineering. And he was willing to pay better than any of the other companies, direct competitors or not, to get the men he wanted. Over the years he developed cordial relationships with the heads of the electrical engineering departments in five large state universities spread geographically across the country.

"I find what I want in those state universities," he remarked to Goodfoile. "The kids that go there more often than not have learned to hustle; they don't come from your rich families and they've gotten their hands dirty, some place or other. And that's what I want. I spread it out geographically so when I need somebody to call in New England I can get somebody with pretty much the right accent who knows how to put chains on tires in the wintertime and won't catch pneumonia the first time there's six inches of snow. And when I need someone down south, I want someone who knows southern ways, and how to say no while he's smiling and saying yes, and knows that's what the other guy's up to when he does it."

Anderson discovered, over the years, that he was a shrewd judge of selling talent, and, even better, a shrewd judge of the kinds of young salesmen who would come and make a home, a career, and a substantial success with the Catawba Electric Motor Company.

3. *Anderson also believed that the only satisfactory basis for compensating salesmen was straight commission.* He recognized that a raw recruit had to be paid a salary while he was learning about the Catawba Electric Motor Company. And he knew that a totally new salesman, no matter how well trained, would require time to develop his territory and start the flow of orders coming in. So Anderson started all of his salesmen trainees at a relatively high salary and maintained that salary until a salesman's earned commission surpassed it. A Catawba Electric salesman could never earn less than his base salary (which was increased every three years he spent with the company) but he could always earn significantly more through sales commissions. Any salesman who consistently failed to earn commissions found himself under the close surveillance of Anderson. He explained this in his standard final speech to a sales trainee who had completed his in-plant training and was about to go out into the world of electric motors to make his way: "If you can't make commissions, then either we're wrong, or you're wrong. We can't train you any better than we have and we can't use more care and time in

selecting you than we did in the first place. If we're wrong, then we'll face up to it and fix it. But if we've done everything in our power to select you in the first place and trained you the best we know how, and the quotas are reasonable, then you must be wrong. You're a salesman all right, but if you don't make your commissions then you're not selling, you're dogging it. And we expect a Catawba Electric man to hustle, every hour, every day. If you're not hustling, then you're dogging it and if that goes on for very long, then you won't be a Catawba Electric man for very long."

Thus for Anderson the commission was the fundamental motivator, and whether a man earned his commissions or not was the only basis on which his performance was evaluated.

4. *Catawba Electric backed up their field selling organization with superior market information and superior quota determination procedures.* Anderson believed firmly that knowledge was the way to superior sales performance. He reasoned that the basic knowledge that is needed for superior sales performance is the identity, characteristics, and potential of all companies that might have a use for a Catawba Electric motor. And the identification of such potential Catawba Electric motor users was not limited to the electric motors already in the Catawba line. As Anderson saw it, Catawba had the capability to build an electric motor to satisfy any conceivable purpose. He expected his salesmen to call on any manufacturer that made a power-driven machine of any kind and do his best to find a way in which Catawba could develop a better motor for his purposes at lower cost than the product being supplied by competitors.

And, of course, once such potential users were identified, and their potential assessed, the basic information needed for the determination of sales quotas was also in hand. A distinction had to be made between potential that represented more or less routine use of Catawba motors and potential that required truly creative selling in the development and/or application of Catawba motors to an unprecedented use. But once methods were in hand for the development of such information and the salesmen understood it and accepted it, then the basis for acceptable sales administration and sales performance evaluation had been built.

Anderson hired the director of sales analysis from the Total Spark Company, a leading manufacturer of spark plugs, in 1953. This man was named Horace J. Quickley, and he was a trained botanist who had drifted into sales analysis when he could find no really acceptable way to put his skills as a botanist to use in the post-World War II economy. Anderson hired Quickley for two reasons. The first was that Quickley had a reputation as a genius for finding firms with potential capacity to use gasoline engines, which could, in turn, use spark plugs. Catawba had lost some business to Total Spark salesmen who had convinced users of Catawba Electric motors that they could save money and make a better product by converting to gasoline engines. The sales lost in these conversions (electric power saws and electric lawn mowers were the major categories) did not amount to a great deal of volume, but Anderson was intrigued by a competitor smart enough and aggressive enough to take business away from Catawba by substituting a competitive kind of motor. And when he investigated he discovered that it was Quickley who had identified the potential and sent the Total Spark salesmen to the Catawba customers.

So the first reason that Anderson hired Quickley was because he knew how to find particular kinds of manufacturers and direct salesmen to them. The second reason was that he was smart enough to figure out the kinds of firms that offered such potential to Total Spark in the first place. As Anderson put it to Goodfoile when he explained why he wanted to hire Quickley, "I don't know how much direction Quickley got from his boss over there at Total Spark, and I suspect we'll never find that out. But the way he tells it, he thinks it's fun to think of classifications of customers that might need gas motors and then find them and then send the salesmen out to nail them. The salesmen swear by him, according to my boys, and it occurs to me that that's just the kind of thing a crack botanist might do if he couldn't do botany. Anyway, with everything he knows about gas motors, it shouldn't be too much trouble to turn it all around and make it work for electric motors and for us." And so Horace Quickley was hired as director of sales information for the Catawba Electric Motor Company in 1953.

Quickley used three basic sources of information about companies that might provide potential for Catawba. These were the same three sources that he had used so successfully at Total Spark.

a. The first was the McGraw-Hill Plant Census, which provides up-to-date information on approximately seventy-five thousand manufacturing plants, including their location, their number of employees and the Standard Industrial Classification Code groups within which their manufacturing activities are concentrated.

b. Quickley also employed the services of a centralized newspaper reporting organization. This organization had come into being when a national wire service had gone bankrupt in the late 1940's. All that was left was a list of the part-time correspondents or "stringers" of that service spread throughout the country. These men and women were available, through the New York office of a former employee of the wire service, to perform reportorial and investigative tasks wherever such work was needed. Quickley used them in two ways. First, he paid a flat twenty-five dollars when supplied with the name and address, if it were new to him, of any manufacturing firm employing more than twenty-five people who used any kind of motor—gas, electric, or battery-operated—in their end product. Second, he sometimes contacted a representative in a particular city and asked him to ascertain the kinds of products made by a particular manufacturer whose name had shown up in the McGraw-Hill Plant

Census or had shown up in any one of the trade press publications that Quickley routinely monitored.

c. Finally, Quickley had two men on his staff who did nothing but travel to potential customers of Catawba and interview their purchasing agent or president or whoever was available in order to gather enough information about the company to determine whether it had potential for Catawba, what the nature of that potential was, and how great that potential was. Out of these detailed interviews came the raw material for quota setting and the salesmen's prospect lists.

5. *The Catawba Electric Motor Company sales force was subjected to a continuing flow of information about the products of Catawba, developments in industry that affected the demand for electric motors, and selling and sales techniques in general.* Anderson believed a well-informed salesman to be an effective salesman. He therefore initiated a biweekly newsletter for his sales force in 1951. This newsletter had only one objective: to give the Catawba Electric salesmen a continuing source of information that would make him a better salesman. It consisted of three basic kinds of material.

a. First, Anderson read every salesman's daily sales-call reports looking for opportunities that had been seized by a salesman in one area and that might be profitably exploited in other areas.

b. Second, every time a new Catawba product was developed to fill a customer's need, it was described in detail, and the exact circumstances and nature of the need it was developed to fill were also described.

c. Finally, Anderson reported as much information about competitor's activities and products as he could lay his hands on. Most of this came from the trade press, some of it came from his own salesmen, and sometimes Anderson picked up something from one of his informal industry contacts.

In addition to the biweekly newsletter, Anderson ran two national sales meetings for his sales force every year. These sales meetings were very carefully planned to communicate Catawba developments to the sales force. New products were unveiled at the meetings; salesmen's anniversaries and contest awards were made; promotions and retirements within the sales force were announced; and the company's promotional and pricing policies were introduced, demonstrated, and discussed at these meetings. In addition, Anderson believed very strongly in the use of sales meetings for enlightenment. He sought out interesting speakers from fields totally alien to electric motors—well-known newspapermen, writers, college professors, government people, and whatnot—and paid them whatever they asked to come and speak to his salesmen about their areas of expertise. Anderson believed that a successful salesman was a man of self-confidence and self-respect, and he believed that one way to build a salesman's self-confidence and self-respect was to treat him as a man of the world whom one could expect to be interested in the topics presented by these speakers.

Finally, a good portion of the time at the sales meetings was devoted unabashedly to fun and games. Anderson expected his men to want to shoot a round of golf, or spend a morning on the beach, or have a drink or two before dinner, and ample opportunity was provided for all of these activities.

Beyond the newsletter and the sales meetings, Anderson spent a part of every day on the long-distance phone, talking to his salesmen. Every man was required to supply a phone number at which he could be reached at a certain hour every working day of the year. Anderson made it a habit to speak to every salesman at least once a month, with no specific purpose except to chew the fat and keep in touch.

Under these policies, the Catawba Electric Motor Company sales force prospered. It was a small, cohesive organization, superbly trained and administered, and there is little doubt that there could never have been anything quite like it without Harlan Anderson and his unusual perception of what a sales force should be like and how it should be run. One of the reasons for its success under Anderson's design and direction was, of course, its relatively small size. Anderson could recruit and train every man in the force because the force never consisted of more than forty salesmen. Each of these men covered fairly broad geographic areas, it was true, but the average salesman had fewer than a hundred customers and the essence of his craft was to service each with devotion, care, and precocity. If there had been more customers there would have been more salesmen, and if there had been many more salesmen there would have been a need to have more formality and overt control and less of the relaxed and warm, yet demanding, administration of the Anderson regime.

If one had looked at this activity from the outside it is likely that its easygoing efficiency would have beguiled him into thinking that perfection had been achieved and that there would never be any need to change anything in the Catawba Electric sales organization. But such an assessment would have been based on two assumptions.

The first assumption is that Catawba Electric, its products, and its customers would go on forever pretty much as they were. As we will shortly see, this assumption is erroneous.

The second assumption is simply that Harlan Anderson was immortal. He was not immortal. He had, in fact, been thirty-two when he was hired by Ed Goodfoile in 1939 to help him make washing machine motors. By 1963 he was fifty-six years old and seemed a reasonable bet to be with the Catawba Company, functioning flawlessly and easily, at least until he was sixty-five and perhaps, if he wished (and no one could imagine that he would not wish) and God were willing, for a few years after that, on up to his seventies. But on his way back for the annual fall sales meetings in November of 1964, the airplane on which he was riding crashed while making an instrument approach through fog and haze into the Spartanburg airport, and Harlan Anderson, along with forty-two other unfortunates, did not survive.

At the time of the crash, Ed Goodfoile was on a trip to Japan. "Old Ed," as he was known affectionately to the Catawba employees, had been in semiretirement since 1960 and his sixty-seventh birthday and spent a good deal of his time traveling around the world with his devoted Caroline. Ed spent most of his time on these trips poking around, looking into the ways in which electric motors were made and used in remote corners of the earth. His wife spent most of the time sightseeing. They always had dinner together, occasionally breakfast, and it was their custom to sit next to each other on the airplane trips that connected one of their stops with the next.

While in Japan, Ed Goodfoile stumbled across a totally new kind of electric motor that had recently been developed by a giant industrial conglomerate for use in their clock division. Catawba had long since become a dominant supplier of the small electric motors used in electric clocks. But these motors had a certain minimum size—about fourteen cubic inches—and were dependent, of course, on 110-volt power supplied by their attached cord. Goodfoile had simply assumed that someday someone would make a smaller electric motor and had also rather vaguely understood that a fundamental change in motor design would have to precede such a development, because the standard clock motor design was based on physical laws that seemed, so far, impervious to any further miniaturization.

The thought of using batteries in such an application had not occurred to him because, for all he knew about batteries, it would require at least four good-sized dry cells to drive a clock motor, and they would create more bulk than might conceivably be displaced by the development of a smaller non-110-volt electric motor. Beyond these rather inconclusive and formless musings Goodfoile had never gone because the problem did not much interest him, and he really did not like to think of messy little batteries as a potential alternative to good old, line-fed, 110-volt current.

But the Japanese had not been anywhere near as inhibited in their thinking. They had developed a small dry-cell battery about one half the size of a standard flashlight dry cell, with about four times its power and about ten times its life expectancy. They had then designed a smaller motor with a very much greater relative efficiency (that is, a relatively greater capacity to transform a unit of dry-cell–produced electricity into productive work) than the conventional clock motor. This new motor could not only survive but thrive upon the energy input available from the new battery.

Semiretired though he was, and more concerned with making motors than selling them, Ed Goodfoile could still visualize potential when he saw it before his eyes. Clocks were one thing and children's toys were another, and beyond that were all kinds of potential industrial applications for this exciting new concept. He wondered whether he should try to design one of these motors himself or whether he should try to negotiate a license with the Japanese, and he called his lawyer to ask advice and found out that Harlan Anderson was dead, at age fifty-seven, of an airplane crash. He bought a dozen of the new clocks and headed for home, dragging Caroline on behind him.

* *
*

When Goodfoile arrived back in Spartanburg, he found the business in relatively good order, shocked at the death of Anderson, of course, but following along in the routines that had long ago been established and tested. The man in charge in the plant was Campbell G. Sturtevant, a veteran Catawba Electric employee, who had long before been selected by Goodfoile as his successor, with Anderson's enthusiastic approval. When Anderson's death became known, Sturtevant immediately asked the three Catawba Electric divisional sales managers to continue to tend to affairs in their divisions and, if any policy questions developed, to work out a joint recommendation among themselves for his review. Sturtevant believed that Jason W. Kanner, manager of the eastern division, was the logical choice to succeed Anderson, and in his informal contacts with the divisional managers themselves as well as several of the old pros in the sales organization, Sturtevant found that this was a decision that was considered both foregone and welcome by the sales people. But Sturtevant believed it best to await Goodfoile's return before making this important appointment.

Upon his return, Goodfoile agreed totally with the selection of Kanner and added one more, decisive reason: "He was Harlan's boy, you know, Campy— I think he thought of him as his successor from the first day he interviewed him up at the University of Massachusetts, and from what I know about it, Harlan was just as right about Jay Kanner as he was about everything else." And so the formal appointment of Jay Kanner as sales vice-president was made and he came back to Spartanburg to join the top management echelon of Catawba Electric.

He hadn't been in Spartanburg a week when he was summoned to Goodfoile's office. "Jay, there are one or two things that I think the two of us ought to agree on from the start," said Goodfoile. "First of all, you know and I know that there wasn't a person in the world that I was closer to than Harlan Anderson. We built this business together, and I have to think that he contributed more to it than I did. I know how to make those motors, but I didn't know a whit about how to sell them, and I'll tell you, you don't make money unless you figure out how to get people to want them and get people to know how to use them in their own products. But everyone makes mistakes and everyone tends to do a job his own way. I don't know if Harlan made any mistakes, and if he did, I'll be damned if I know what they were. But he ran it his way, and I expect you to run it your way. If there are things to be changed, change them and don't worry about your changing things that Harlan started, either because of the way I felt about Harlan or because of the way I feel about him now. I want you to be your own boss, is that clear?''

''That's clear with me, Ed,'' replied Jay, ''and I can't ask for anything more than that. But I am glad that you were thoughtful enough to say it, and it will make it easier for me to fit into things here in Spartanburg.''

''Okay, now that that's behind us,'' said Goodfoile. ''Let's get Campy in, because there's something that the three of us have to think about.''

At this point Goodfoile revealed the battery-powered electric clocks that he had discovered in Japan. ''There are two reasons for us to be interested in these things. The first is we do a lot of electric clock motor business and these things will compete directly with it. The second reason is that they represent a very new technology in electric motors. The batteries will get more powerful and smaller and last longer, and before we know it they will be competing in more and more of our areas of business. We're in the small-power-unit business, boys, and don't confuse that with only 110-volt line-fed electric motors—they're the past, but the future will be different. I've been talking with the lawyers about these Jap motors and they've looked into the patent area and they say that the idea of an electric motor isn't patentable. Probably the Japanese hold some internationally valid patents on four or five of the components, and maybe they don't. The lawyers think it's up to us. If we can design a smaller motor that performs better from scratch, they say go ahead and do it and forget the Japanese. We'll get our own patents. But if we can't come up with a better design, then they think we'd better get into a negotiation. The Jap batteries are going to be imported over here in the fall, and a couple of U.S. chemical companies have worked out licensing agreements for the batteries, because they apparently are based on some unique principle that does have patent protection.''

''You've been thinking about designing a motor for three weeks, Ed,'' said Campy. ''I know you won't want us to waste any of our time if you've thought out a solution.''

''I haven't, Campy,'' replied Goodfoile. ''I've got two or three thoughts and a lot of notes, but I haven't got a drawing, or any idea of what would go into a drawing, and you know that if I can't sketch it, I haven't solved it. So let's get some of your designers in and give them a crack at it.''

''And I know what you want from me,'' said Jay Kanner. ''You want to know if my boys can take that motor on or not, once you guys have figured out how to make it. Okay, I'll find out and give you a written answer, but I'll tell you now that forty guys, good as they are, can't begin to handle a motor with those characteristics and with that volume potential."

As it happened, it took Campbell Sturtevant and Ed Goodfoile and four employees of the Catawba Electric design and applications section three and one-half months to perfect the new motor. In the meantime, Jay Kanner had been hard at work. First of all, he had written the following memorandum to Horace J. Quickley.

C-E-M-C
MEMO

TO: H. J. Quickley
FROM: Jason Kanner
SUBJECT: *Confidential*   February 16, 1965

Mr. Goodfoile discovered a new, low-voltage, battery-powered electric motor when he was last in Japan.

He and Mr. Sturtevant and a group from D & A Section are working on a version to be marketed by us.

Assume that this motor will be powered by a 9-volt dry cell of relatively small size and that the combination will have the following characteristics:

1. The output of the motor will be relatively low. You can imagine the kinds of things a 9-volt motor will do:
   a. Drive electric clocks.
   b. Drive electric shavers.
   c. Power simple, small, light children's toys.
   d. Power simple, repetitive, low-power-utilization monitors and feedback devices in industrial and chemical applications.
   e. Power motion units for point-of-purchase displays.
   f. Use your imagination—it's better than mine.
2. The motor itself will be small, and even in combination with the battery it will be about one third the size of a very small line-fed electric motor.
3. The great virtue of this motor is not that it will outperform a line-fed motor: it simply will not. What it will do is supply a low-grade current over a long period of time for low-power usage applications. It is, in effect, a fourth-rate electric motor that is very cheap and very flexible and that will have an immense potential as its applications are, in fact, discovered.

Do not assume that I think that the marketing job on this product will be undertaken by the existing Catawba Electric sales force. I believe that this probably would be exactly the wrong thing to do because they don't know very much about the kinds of applications this thing will be good for, and beyond that, I suspect they will be contemptuous of them. And even if they are not contemptuous of them, they haven't been trained to handle this kind of item, which I assume will appeal to a lot of companies that we have never even heard of, let alone sold electric motors to. In this kind of situation, one of our other kinds of motors is going to get the sales force attention: I can't imagine our men preferring to sell this item to selling the bread-and-butter standard line items. And for all I know, this new motor may require a totally different and much more opportunistic kind of selling than our men—good as they are at what they were hired to do—are used to.

Anyway, all of this is just the rankest kind of speculation at the moment. When you deliver to us the data that describe the sales opportunity, we'll have a lot easier job of figuring out exactly what our boys can do and can't do for the new motor.

I'd like the following specifics from you:

1. An estimate of the number of firms, by industry, that manufacture the kinds of end products that are likely to have use for this motor.
2. An estimate of the volume, by industry, such devices are likely to generate, cumulatively, over the next five and ten years.
3. Any ideas that occur to you about other industries that might have applications for this kind of motor.
4. Any ideas you have about how we might proceed to market it.

About a month later, Kanner received the following communication back from Quickley.

C-E-M-C
MEMO

TO: Jason Kanner
FROM: H. J. Quickley
SUBJECT: *Still confidential*   March 18, 1965

We've taken a crack at answering the questions you've posed in your memorandom about the battery-operated, small-capacity motors. I say, "taken a crack" because you've given us a very, very tough series of questions and it may be totally impossible to generate really accurate answers to them.

Anyway, our answers are summarized in the attached exhibits (Exhibits 10–1, 10–2, and 10–3). We used our basic procedures in generating the estimate for 1965 in these exhibits and you know what they are (McGraw-Hill Plant Census, stringer network, home office interrogators). The procedures and assumptions used in reaching the estimates for 1970 and 1975 are detailed below.

I think we have a pretty good idea of the potential demand for the new motors as it stands today. The really troublesome thing is trying to work it out for five and ten years hence. The availability of these low-cost, low-capacity motors is bound to call forth literally thousands of new applications. Some of these new applications won't amount to very much in terms of volume, and others will probably be gigantic. But who's to know and who's to guess?

I suppose the development of these new motors will follow the classic S-curve that we know often reflects the growth pattern of a new innovation. But where are we on the curve now? At the bottom or halfway up?

The only realistic way out of this dilemma is to make some realistic guesses about how the S-growth-curve will unfold and the extremes within which the total volume might be developed five years from now and ten years from now and then to use these extreme estimates as a basis for reaching some realistic best guesses about the future.

EXHIBIT 10-1

Estimated Number of Firms That Will Utilize Low-Capacity, Battery-Operated Electric Motors, by Industry*

INDUSTRY	1965	1970			1975		
		LOW	MEDIUM	HIGH	LOW	MEDIUM	HIGH
Electric clock manufacturers	17	17	30	42	17	35	53
Electric shaver manufacturers	6	6	11	16	6	13	20
Children's toy manufacturers	120	120	210	300	120	249	377
Electric sensor, feedback mechanism, etc., manufacturers	10	10	17	24	10	20	30
Point-of-purchase–display manufacturers	475	475	829	1,182	475	980	1,485
All other	—	157	275	391	157	324	490
TOTAL	628	785	1,372	1,955	785	1,621	2,455

* See text for assumptions.

EXHIBIT 10–2
Estimated Unit Demand for Low-Capacity, Battery-Operated Electric Motors, by Industry, 1965, 1970, 1975*
(000 Omitted)

INDUSTRY	1965	1970			1975		
		LOW	MEDIUM	HIGH	LOW	MEDIUM	HIGH
Electric clocks	300	120	1,560	3,000	0	2,000	4,000
Electric shavers	100	50	175	300	0	200	400
Children's toys	1,200	6,000	8,000	10,000	7,500	11,250	15,000
Electric sensors, feedback mechanisms, etc.	50	3,000	6,500	10,000	4,500	9,750	15,000
Point-of-purchase displays	250	300	650	1,000	450	825	1,200
All other	—	4,945	5,973	6,885	10,750	12,775	14,624
TOTAL	1,900	14,415	22,858	31,185	23,200	36,800	50,224

* See text for assumptions.

EXHIBIT 10-3
Estimated Utilization Per Firm for Low-Capacity, Battery-Operated Electric Motors, by Industry*

INDUSTRY	1965	1970			1975		
		LOW	MEDIUM	HIGH	LOW	MEDIUM	HIGH
Electric clock manufacturers	29,400	7,100	52,000	71,400	—	57,000	75,500
Electric shaver manufacturers	16,700	8,300	15,900	18,750	—	15,400	20,000
Children's toy manufacturers	8,333	50,000	38,100	40,000	62,500	45,200	39,800
Electric sensor, feedback mechanism, etc., manufacturers	5,000	300,000	382,400	417,000	450,000	487,500	500,000
Point-of-purchase–display manufacturers	526	632	784	846	950	842	808
All other	—	30,538	21,700	17,900	68,400	39,429	30,200
TOTAL	3,025	18,363	10,500	11,692	29,544	22,702	20,500

* See text for assumptions.

We've made some fundamental assumptions in developing our various estimates and here they are.

1. We assumed, in Exhibit 10–1, that the low-capacity electric motor is an innovation that will catch on rather fast and that within five years most of the obvious uses for the gadget will have been found. But this growth can play itself out in a variety of different ways as far as projections of the number of adopting firms are concerned:

   a. First of all, it may mean that a lot of new companies will spring up, or it may mean that almost no new companies will emerge but that incumbent companies in the affected industries will adopt the new technology. In estimating the number of firms that will utilize the new low-capacity, battery-operated motors we have projected, as extremes, from these two opposite possible patterns of growth.

      i. Thus in projecting the "low" growth of firms utilizing the motor, we have simply assumed no change in the number of firms that will be operating in the affected industries as the low-voltage motor is adopted. For example, there are now 17 electric clock manufacturers, and under the "low" growth assumption we project 17 manufacturers in this category in 1970 and 17 in 1975.

      We do not, of course, assume that exactly the same 17 electric clock manufacturers will be operating in the field in 1975 as are operating now, but this assumption does proceed on the basis that the net impact of the new technology will be negligible in generating new firms and that those firms that cease to operate in the next ten years will simply be replaced by new firms on a one-for-one basis.

      ii. At the other end of the scale, we assume a high growth rate for new firms that proceeds at 120 per cent per year during the period 1966–70. That is to say, under the high growth assumption, new firms will come into being at the rate of 120 per cent per year over the number of the preceding year. The nature of the industrial adaptation to the innovation will be to increase the number of manufacturing units in each affected industry. By 1970, following the S-curve assumption outlined above, we believe that the bulk of the growth in each of these industries will have occurred. Of course, there will be growth in the period 1970–75, but it will not occur at the 1965–70 rate. It's hard to extrapolate growth rates five years from now when the growth rates of the intervening five years are only estimates themselves. We have arbitrarily assumed that 70 per cent of the growth of firms in each of these industries will occur in the early period and that 30 per cent of the growth will occur in the second five years. Thus, for example, in the electric clock industry, there are 17 firms in 1965. This 17 will grow at the rate of 120 per cent per year from 1966 through 1970.

      1965—17
      1966—20
      1967—24
      1968—29
      1969—35
      1970—42

The growth between 1965 and 1970 is a total of 25 firms. (That is, 42 firms in 1970 less 17 firms in 1965 = a growth of 25 firms.) This rate constitutes, by our assumption, 70 per cent of the total growth in the period 1966–75. Thus:

$$\frac{x}{25} = \frac{100}{70} = 36$$

The total number of firms in the electric clock industry is thus estimated, under the "high" growth assumptions, to be 53, or 17 plus 36.

iii. But these assumptions and calculations do not explain the way in which we have estimated growth in industries that cannot or do not currently appear to have any use for a low-voltage, battery-operated electric motor. We would call all of the industries that fall into this category "peripheral." They are peripheral relative to the basic industries listed by you in your memorandum. We can find no other industry that we are certain will be "basic," that is, certain to adopt the low-voltage motors. We agree with you that there is a great deal of potential beyond the "basic" industries, but we cannot build up an industry-by-industry estimate for it at this time. This is because we really have no idea what industries will surely adopt these motors, nor for what purpose or purposes.

Accordingly, we have simply assumed that the "all other" category will amount to a flat 25 per cent of the number of firms in the basic industry group regardless of year or growth rate assumption.

Thus, for example, in 1970 in the "low" growth rate assumption there is a total of 628 basic firms; 25 per cent of 628 is 157, and the total number of estimated firms on the "low" growth basis is 785 for 1970.

b. We have finally produced our "best" or "medium" estimate: a medium growth estimate that assumes that the two extreme estimates ("low" and "high") are equally wrong and that their average value is the most realistic projection of the growth in the number of firms in industries utilizing the low-capacity, battery-operated electric motor.

c. Exhibit 10–2 addresses itself to the next question that you posed: the unit demand for low-capacity, battery-operated motors by industry. In developing the data in this exhibit, we used rather different assumptions than those outlined above for estimating by industry the number of firms that will utilize the low-capacity electric motor.

A basic question in the estimating of unit demand for distinctly new product entries into product categories that have been relatively dormant is whether or not the distinctly new product (such as this motor) will become the dominant product within the industry or whether its use will be more in the nature of a fad. In one instance, we could assume that a very high fraction of total production in an industry would be shifted to the low-capacity electric motor. In the second instance we assume a short-term conversion to these new power sources and a subsequent decline in their usage.

But this reasoning works only with the relatively mature product categories. What about situations in which the availability of the low-capacity electric motor gives the promise of a fundamental expansion of an industry or a fundamental change in the nature of an established industry? For example, we believe that the low-capacity electric motor will lead to a vast expansion in the use of electrical sensor feedback mechanisms and the like for industrial purposes.

And we believe that the availability of these new motors will change, once and for all, the nature of the products manufactured in the toy industry and the point-of-purchase display industry.

Once again, these fundamentally different assumptions develop rather diverse "high" and "low" unit-volume estimates:

i. Our approach in estimating 1965 unit-volume potentials was to develop some idea about how many units in total would be manufactured in each of the basic industries in 1965. We then assumed that the low-capacity electric motor would achieve about 15 per cent of total unit capacity in the first year. This would mean, in the case of electric clocks, for example, a first-year (1965) demand of 300,000 units. Similar analysis developed the 1965 estimates for the other four basic industries.

ii. The "low" volume estimates for 1970 and 1975 differ markedly depending upon the industry that is under consideration. In the case of electric clocks and electric shavers, the estimate for 1970 assumes that products in these industries are at best fads and will fall below 1965 unit levels. It is then assumed, at the "low" level, that there will be no unit demand for low-capacity electric motors in these industries in 1975.

As far as the other three basic industries are concerned, it is assumed that major unit demand will develop, even at the "low" estimate level, in 1970, and that this volume will continue to expand at a somewhat slower rate through 1975.

iii. The "high" volume estimates assume that the low-capacity electric motors will become a significant factor in the electric clock and shaver industries and will, in fact, become the dominant product by 1970 and on through 1975. And for the remaining three basic industries, the "high" estimates merely assume a most optimistic unit-demand level in 1970 and an even higher level in 1975. Again, all of these "high" estimates are based on our analysis of the individual industries, and the different industry growth rates merely reflect our most optimistic appraisal of what will happen within these industries in 1970 and 1975.

iv. The totals for unit demand were computed on the basis of overall unit-growth estimates for the basic plus the peripheral "all other" industries. In the "low" volume unit estimate, it was assumed that aggregate unit demand would increase at a rate of 150 per cent per year for the first five years and that growth would proceed at a rate of 110 per cent in the second five years. These growth factors produced the following annual totals:

1965	*1,900,000* units
1966	2,850,000 units

1967	4,275,000 units
1968	6,413,000 units
1969	9,620,000 units
1970	*14,415,000* units
1971	15,856,000 units
1972	17,442,000 units
1973	19,186,000 units
1974	21,110,000 units
1975	*23,200,000* units

We then computed the unit demand from the peripheral, or "all other," industries by subtracting the projected demand of the basic industries from the projected total. Thus, for example, in 1975 the "low" projected demand for the basic industries was an aggregate of 12,450,000 units. The difference between the estimated total for all industries—23,200,000 units—and 12,450,000 units for the basic industries leaves 10,750,000 as an estimate for "all other" unit demand at the low level.

v. The totals for unit demand in the "high" volume estimate were based on growth rates of 175 per cent per year in the period 1966–70 and 110 per cent per year in the period 1971–75. These growth factors produced the following annual totals:

1965	*1,900,000* units
1966	3,325,000 units
1967	5,819,000 units
1968	10,183,000 units
1969	17,820,000 units
1970	*31,185,000* units
1971	34,304,000 units
1972	37,734,000 units
1973	41,507,000 units
1974	45,658,000 units
1975	*50,224,000* units

The unit demand for the peripheral, or "all other," industries was computed as in the case of "low" volume estimates:

Total units − basic demand = all other demand
50,224,000 − 35,600,000 = 14,624,000

vi. Again, the "best" estimate is the "medium" estimate, that is, the average between the "high" and "low" series in both 1970 and 1975. We believe that this average value is the best overall estimate of demand for the new electric motors on a unit basis.

d. Exhibit 10–3 is based on data for Exhibits 10–1 and 10–2. Total units per industry are divided by total firms per industry to yield an estimate of the number of low-capacity electric motors the average firm in each industry will require for its operations in each of the years and at each of the development levels for which estimates are made.

e. All of our estimates are based on the assumption that the level of technology in the industry will remain relatively stable over the next ten years. By this we do not mean that there will not be progress: the motors will become smaller and relatively more efficient, and the batteries will become stronger or longer-lasting or whatever. The low-capacity, battery-operated electric motor will become a better machine in the next ten years, but there will be no significant product breakthroughs in this period: the low-capacity, battery-operated electric motor will not be transformed into a realistic competitor with the 110-volt line-fed motor that is now the backbone of the Catawba business.

   f. We also assume that there will be no significant foreign competition during this period. It is so hard to anticipate the exact shape that foreign competition will take, I always prefer to assume that it will not develop. Even if one assumes no significant product breakthrough, foreign competition can upset the domestic market by making some small but significant innovation in price or quality or whatever. Undoubtedly we'll be able to meet it when it comes, but such unexpected intrusions frequently upset our volume projections, and estimates of producing firms, at least in the short run.

2. As far as "specific" ideas about the other industries that might have applications for this kind of motor are concerned, I believe I've outlined my views on this point above. Frankly, I believe that the gross volume will be significant from the non-"basic" industries, but I really have no idea just how it will develop or manifest itself and I don't want to give you a lot of fluff that may or may not work out to be true.

3. You also asked that I set out "any ideas" that I might have about how we should proceed to market the new motor. Frankly, I believe that the key to our success will be in the organization of the sales force. I don't believe that our estimates of the number of firms and the number of units that this industry will generate are literally correct, in any sense of the word. But I do believe that the general picture they convey is dead accurate and can give you a fundamental insight into the kind of selling job your men will be called upon to provide.

    Three of the basic industries are going to involve relatively small numbers of manufacturing firms. These are the clock, shaver, and sensor/feedback industries. The shaver industry will never generate really significant amounts of volume. The electric clock industry may generate a fairly sizable level of volume, and the sensor/feedback industry is going to be immense.

    On the other side, two of the basic industries will involve very large numbers of manufacturers. These are the children's toys and point-of-purchase industries. The manufacture of point-of-purchase material is now and is almost certain to continue as a kind of cottage industry—large numbers of small enterprises handling relatively small amounts of volume. The toy manufacturers are another dish of tea, however: even though there are lots of them, the average company is likely to generate significant volume and it is probable that ten or twenty top manufacturers will generate enormous volume. It should be noted, however, that this toy volume is not likely to be a steady affair from year to year. This is a feast or famine business and as one toy or another catches on with the kiddies of the country, it is likely that the demand will swing from one manufacturer to another.

    I really don't believe that I'm qualified to propose a sales organization structure that will be responsive to this industry pattern—but I am very sure indeed that the pattern portrayed in these figures is almost exactly the one that will develop in the next ten years.

When Jason Kanner received this communication he was impressed, as always, with the way in which Quickley responded directly to the issues that had been raised in his own request. Beyond this, he was quite certain that Quickley's analysis pointed precisely to the heart of the matter: How could Catawba Electric organize to meet the new challenge that lay ahead of it? And he was sure that whatever the solution to the problem, it would have a very significant effect on the sales organization that he had inherited. "Whatever I do with this motor," thought Kanner, "the current divisional managers should participate in the decision, and once they have been asked to participate we've got to try hard to make sure that the new plan doesn't either threaten or disgruntle either them or their men." With this thought in mind, Kanner decided to solicit the help of the divisional managers. He sent them the following memorandum:

C - E - M - C
MEMO

TO: A. B. Mellotone   (Western Division)
        N. L. Rearchos   (Central Division)
        E. R. Tuttle   (Eastern Division)
FROM: Jason Kanner
SUBJECT: *Very Confidential—Discuss Only with Me*   March 22, 1965

Mr. Goodfoile discovered a new, low-voltage, battery-powered electric motor when he was in Japan last year. I'm sure you know the general kind of device I mean: we had a general discussion of the principles involved in our spring sales meetings with Dr. Offenhauser of Ohio State University.

We have developed a Catawba version of this device, and we will shortly begin finalizing the basic introductory designs. You know what it means when designs get finalized: the boys in manufacturing will start making the things and everybody will start looking to us to sell them.

I'm enclosing with this memorandum a study by Horace Quickley, made at my request, of the potentials in this new adjunct to the electric motor industry. As you can see from Horace's data, we're talking about very large unit volume and, at least in some industries, very significant increases in the number of our customers. Of course, we know the electric clock industry pretty well, but the other four "basic" industries are really unknown to us, and heaven only knows where the so-called peripheral volume will come from.

One thing Horace didn't get into, which is important, is the relation—dollar-sales-wise—of this new device to our standard line-fed lines. We sold 22,283,611 electric engines last year at a gross sales volume of $457,821,344. That means that out typical motor sold for $20.55. We believe we had about 68 per cent of the line-fed electric motor business in this country.

If we take Horace's middle volume guess for 1970 and assume we'll get 68 per cent of it, that would mean about 14,600,000 low-capacity units. The hooker is that the Japanese appear to be manufacturing their units at about $4.22 each. Our D & A boys believe that at volumes in excess of 3,000,000 annual units, we will be producing our designs at $3.66 or less. If all those guesses are right, we're looking at a 1970 dollar volume of $53,000,000 or so—or about 15 per cent or 16 per cent of our 1965 sales volume. By 1970, $53,000,000 should be less than 10 per cent of our current sales volume.

I'd like your views on three matters:

1. I think it's clear that the Catawba Electric sales organization will have to change in one way or another to meet this new challenge. How should we change?
2. How can we minimize the overall impact of this change on our existing selling organization?
3. How can we minimize the cost of such a change?

Please be thoughtful about this, but be quick too. I'd like your replies within the next ten days.

Here are the responses received by Kanner to his request.

C-E-M-C
MEMO

TO: Jason Kanner
FROM: A. B. Mellotone (Western Division)
SUBJECT: *Confidential—Your Eyes Only*   April 1, 1965

Thanks so much for giving me an opportunity to respond to this new and exciting challenge to the Catawba Electric Motor Company sales force. I've studied Mr. Quickley's excellent analysis for some hours and I believe I have now mastered all of its many profundities and ramifications.

I come away with two fundamental conclusions based on this study. The first of these is that we are really talking about small potatoes: 15 per cent of our current business and 9 per cent or 10 per cent in the next five years.

My second conclusion is that we can do the job ourselves. As you know, I have a total of eighteen salesmen in my Western Division. Give me one or two more salesmen (that is the same percentage of my sales force that this new volume will constitute of company sales), and I'll give you twice as much new business as you're projecting. I'll get you all the low-capacity volume you project, and more on our standard items besides.

And Jay, I'm not going to question the wisdom of going into these Jap gimmicks, but you know the way I feel about the standard Catawba Electric 110-volt line-fed motor. That's what we know how to sell—not these things for clocks and toys.

But you give us the assignment, and another salesman or two, and we'll deliver the orders. Bank on it!

C-E-M-C
MEMO

TO: Jason Kanner
FROM: E. R. Tuttle   (Eastern Division)
SUBJECT: *What You Wrote Me About*   April 2, 1965

Let us handle the clocks, and the industrial sensors, feedbacks, and whatnot.
1. Not many firms.
2. We talk clock language and we know about industrial applications.

Find manufacturers' agents to handle the other applications.
1. Too many customers for us.
2. No need for in-depth continuing sales service.
3. The total units are small and the bulk (toys) comes from an unstable, high-credit-risk industry.

This way we keep our flanks covered in the electric motor business, but it doesn't upset the sales organization and we minimize cost. The manufacturers' agents get paid for what they sell.

These are my thoughts, Jay, but you tell us what you want us to do and we'll do it.

C-E-M-C
MEMO

TO: Jason Kanner
FROM: N. L. Rearchos   (Central Division)
SUBJECT: *Very Confidential—Your Eyes Only*   April 1, 1965

I am not sure I know what to recommend in reference to these new low-capacity, battery-operated motors. I am surprised that Mr. Goodfoile got interested in them because all the years we've known each other he hasn't mentioned much but line-fed 110-volt bread-and-butter items. Jay, being new on the job, are you sure you know his mind and Mr. Sturtevant's too?

My advice is don't get tangled up in these things. Let a good network of manufacturers' agents handle them, and if they don't want them turn them over to the brokers, even though Mr. Anderson used to say, all they do is send out catalogue pages and take orders.

But Jay, these things aren't our business: my boys wouldn't know what to do with them or for them. Our salesmen go out with their heads held up to sell something that's important, not little, junky, battery-operated motors for kid's toys.

I don't think this thing is for Catawba Electric and I think we should have a special meeting to talk it out, even with Mr. Goodfoile. That's what I think, but if you want my men to sell these things, we'll sell them, whatever we think of them.

Questions for Case 10

1. Is the marketing concept at all important in industrial marketing? Show how the situation in this case supports your answer.

is important for the user
consumer orientation take into account
1) make profits
2) competition
3) stability

2. Harlan Anderson makes a powerful case for the development and exclusive use of the company's own sales force. What are the flaws in Anderson's arguments? Under what kinds of circumstances would it be unwise to depend solely on a company selling organization?

3. The decision to plunge into the manufacture of low-capacity, battery-operated electric motors was made almost casually, without formal meetings, discussions, recommendations, or anything else. Is it a proper decision? What are two compelling reasons for Catawba Electric to move into this field? Of what value would marketing research be in making such a decision? Should marketing research have been undertaken by the Catawba Electric management? What would the purpose of such marketing research be?

4. The Catawba Electric salesman's compensation program is developed on commission over a minimum base salary. Commissions are awarded on the basis of performance against quota. Do you agree with Anderson's "either you're wrong or we're wrong" speech about commissions and quotas on pages 248–249? What are the weaknesses of a commission/quota system of the kind used by Catawba Electric? What are the strengths of such a system?

5. What does the phrase "this new motor may require a totally different and much more opportunistic kind of selling than our men are used to" (pages 256–257) mean? Do different customers require different kinds of treatment from a sales organization? What kind of electric motor customer would require full service? What kind of electric motor customer would require less than full service?

6. Of what use are the various estimates developed in Exhibits 10–1, 10–2, and 10–3? Would it be reasonable for Jason Kanner to proceed without such estimates? Explain why or why not.

7. What kind of sales organization should be established to sell the low-capacity battery-operated electric motors? Do you agree with the point of view expressed in one (or more) of the memoranda supplied by the three divisional sales managers? Analyze the content of each of these memoranda and tell why you agree or disagree with each one.

CASE 11

Package Design

A Test of Alternative Containers for Home Products Universal Handsome Boy Window Brite

T
HE PRODUCTS development laboratory of Home Products Universal perfected a new window-cleaning and polishing product in May of 1973. The laboratory believed that this product had three tangible consumer benefits. First, the product was designed to clean windows better than any competitive product on the market. Second, the product was easier to use than competitive products: it dried faster on the window and, once dried, was easier to remove. Finally, the new product had a unique chemical composition that caused a positive ionic charge to remain on the window surface after thorough cleaning. This positive ionic charge actually repelled dirt (at least under laboratory conditions) and thus reduced the need for frequent window-cleaning. In addition to these three product benefits, the laboratory found raw materials and developed manufacturing procedures that would permit the window cleaner to be manufactured at a price competitive with the price of the brands currently dominating the window cleaner market, yet still providing adequate margins for advertising, consumer and trade promotion, and profit.

Arthur V. Pensa, director of marketing, approved a standard consumer product test of the new product in July of 1973, as soon as sufficient product had been produced for this purpose. Meanwhile, because he was very encouraged by the enthusiasm for the new window cleaner expressed by Allen R. Scala, director of product development, Pensa directed Albert Manoir to assume immediate responsibility for the market planning for the product. Pensa specifically suggested that Manoir take responsibility for appraisal of the consumer product test results, initiate a search for suitable names for the new product, and commission the package design consultants to Home Products Universal (Bastion, Ferragher, and Alfredi) to develop suitable containers for the new product. (The normal Home Products Universal practice was to appoint a product manager, initiate a name search, and commission container designs only after the successful completion of a consumer product test.)

Albert Manoir asked the company legal department to advise him of any names owned by Home Products Universal that might be appropriate for use with a window cleaner. They reported that Home Products Universal was sole owner of the name Window Brite, having acquired it with a small independent soap company that had been purchased in 1938. Although other names were owned by the company that were not inappropriate for a window cleaner and although it was probable that totally new names could be developed, it was Manoir's judgment that Window Brite was an excellent name. He believed it to be so good that he recommended to Arthur Pensa that it be adopted for the product forthwith, without further creative or legal search for a name and without consumer research of any kind. Pensa accepted this recommendation, and from that point on the product was called Handsome Boy Window Brite.

Shortly thereafter, Manoir met with Allen Ferragher, representing the package design firm of Bastion, Ferragher, and Alfredi. Manoir described the basic characteristics of Window Brite and outlined the following specifications for a Window Brite container:

1. The container should cost no more than the containers of the two leading competitive products. (One competitor uses a standard glass bottle with sprayer attachment and the other a standard plastic bottle with a squeeze-spray opening.) These containers are relatively low in cost considering that both have the self-contained spray.
2. The container should have a self-applicating orifice, probably a spray of either the mechanical or squeeze type.
3. The container should be developed in a common and readily available packaging material, such as plastic, iron, aluminum, or glass. The Window Brite formula is completely stable and is noncorrosive to any of these materials.
4. The container should, preferably, be nonbreakable, although glass may be used if there is some other good reason for it.
5. The container should be developed with maximum label display surface.
6. The container should be inherently "handy" rather than cumbersome. It is important to remember that window cleaning is often done in awkward physical circumstances, and the container should, as much as possible, ease the awkwardness rather than add to it.
7. A minimum of four containers should be developed to meet these specifications.

Ferragher accepted these specifications without substantial question. They seemed to him to be both reasonable and correct, and without further commotion the firm of Bastion, Ferragher, and Alfredi proceeded to work on the container designs. They promised to be back with four prototype designs within three weeks.

In anticipation of these finished prototypes, Albert Manoir contacted Aloysius LaGrange, director of marketing research for Home Products Universal. He explained to LaGrange that normal Home Products Universal practice was to be ignored in this case and that a successful product test result was being anticipated by Arthur Pensa. Accordingly, Manoir continued, a product manager assignment had already been given to himself, Window Brite had been selected as a name, and container development work was now under way. Manoir explained that he now believed it to be time to draw up a specific plan to evaluate the alternative container designs under development by the package design house. He therefore requested a specific research proposal for testing these new containers. He suggested that LaGrange assume that only two of the four or more designs that would come from Bastion, Ferragher, and Alfredi would be selected, on the basis of creative and engineering judgment, for final consumer testing. He indicated that five men would make this screening decision: Pensa, Manoir, Scala, Allen Heamstead, director of engineering services for Home Products Universal, and LaGrange himself.

Aloysius LaGrange was an extremely competent research professional. Given a research problem, he was excellent at cutting through to its essentials and at thinking through and drafting a research plan to yield maximum and reliable pertinent information at minimum research cost. But the give and take of day-to-day management in Home Products Universal tended to make LaGrange nervous. He needed a stable platform from which to launch his marketing research projects, and whenever management seemed indecisive or whenever established practice or policy was subverted, LaGrange tended to become indecisive himself and frequently shied away from the research projects that these situations generated.

Manoir was fully aware of LaGrange's peculiarities. He emphasized that Window Brite was real, that LaGrange was to act with the same enthusiasm and productivity in behalf of Window Brite and the research on its new container designs as he would on problems of any established Handsome Boy product. Through all of this LaGrange acted as if he were two totally different people. It was clear that, intellectually, he understood the situation exactly and totally. But he seemed incapable of carrying the work ahead. Manoir waited in vain for two weeks for a brief outline of marketing research to test consumer reactions to the new containers.

Finally, in desperation, Manoir took three steps to force LaGrange to develop promptly the plan for consumer testing. He first mentioned to Arthur Pensa his intention to review the plan for marketing research on the new packages at the meeting at which the prototype containers themselves would be ready for review. Second, he called that meeting for a Wednesday afternoon six days hence and indicated to LaGrange that Pensa expected container testing plans at that meeting. Finally, Manoir wrote a memorandum to LaGrange outlining general thoughts about the container test. Although he did not intend this memorandum to constitute a formal research plan, Manoir did try to write it in a way that would encourage LaGrange to produce his own container test plan quickly if he in any way disagreed with Manoir's general ideas. A copy of this memorandum was then sent to Arthur Pensa. Here is the memorandum.

HPU INTERNAL COMMUNICATION

TO: A. LaGrange
FROM: A. Manoir
cc: A. Pensa   DATE: August 17, 1973

This memorandum summarizes some general thoughts that have occurred to me as we have discussed a container test for Handsome Boy Window Brite. As you know, Bastion, Ferragher, and Alfredi plan to expose four prototype containers to us next Wednesday, August 22.

1. First of all, I believe that it is safe to assume that we will be able to eliminate two of the four designs. If such an elimination can safely be made, the container test will be limited to two alternatives and this will save us both time and money.

2. I see no reason why a direct head-to-head comparison and choice between the containers cannot be made by consumers. I suspect that you will want to get fancy and attempt to conceal from consumers that we are in fact conducting a container test. But I believe that a simple, straightforward choice is as good as some more complicated research design.

3. I see no reason to conduct such a test in more than one market. This too, will save us both time and money.

Anyway, I hope that we will be able to discuss the test plan next Wednesday when the Bastion, Ferragher, and Alfredi people are here. If you agree with any of this, will you be prepared with alternative suggestions on that date?

LaGrange was furious when he received the memorandum. His immediate temptation was, as he expressed it to his wife the evening of the day the memorandum arrived, "to walk into that young smart aleck's office and punch him in the nose." But he did not do that, nor did he write a scathing memorandum back to Manoir to teach him, in a sarcastic tone, the research facts of life. Rather, he immediately drew up a research plan and attached to it a memorandum that he hoped would rebut, in a moderate way, the snide naïveté of Manoir's proposal. Here are LaGrange's memorandum and research plans.

HPU INTERNAL COMMUNICATION

TO: A. Manoir
FROM: A. LaGrange
cc: A. Pensa   DATE: August 21, 1973

Attached is the Marketing Research Department plan for a consumer test of two newly designed containers for Window Brite. In considering this test, it would be well to keep the following points in mind:

1. The plan assumes that it will be necessary to consumer-test only two of the four designs that will be proposed by Bastion, Ferragher, and Alfredi. We do not object to this assumption, and, in fact, we note that it is totally in accord with previous company experience. Nevertheless, we point out that there is no inherent marketing research reason for limiting the test to two designs: it is completely within our capability to extend the test to four or more containers.

2. There is an abundant literature suggesting that it is improper to ask consumers to make direct paired-comparison choices between alternative container designs. In our own experience there have been several instances in which consumers chose different containers in a head-to-head test than in a test that developed an indirect measurement of consumer preference. The head-to-head or paired-comparison method (also called "show" test) tends to put the consumer into the role of a package design expert, which he is most assuredly not. The indirect method is outlined in the attached plan and it is this department's standard testing procedure. It merely assumes that the consumer will develop a preference between containers when he has had a chance to use them but that this preference is most precisely measured when the consumer is not put in the position of verbalizing it as a conscious choice between containers.

3. It is department policy to conduct consumer container tests in three geographically dispersed markets.

It might be added that it is the policy of this department to plan container tests only after the prototype designs are available. We have adopted this policy because it is impossible to develop a final research plan until after the individual peculiarities of the test containers are totally known. Therefore, the attached plan is incomplete in that a questionnaire has not yet been designed. It will be designed when the containers are available and chosen.

We will be prepared to discuss these points and the attached plan Wednesday.

A PLAN FOR CONSUMER TESTING OF
HANDSOME BOY WINDOW BRITE CONTAINERS

Home Products Universal Marketing Research Department
August 21, 1973

Purpose

The purpose of this research is to identify which of two alternative container designs for Home Products Universal Handsome Boy Window Brite is superior from the consumer standpoint.

Method

This research will be based on the standard Home Products Universal method for testing containers with consumers. Here, in brief, is a description of this method.

The prospective consumer is approached as if she were being asked to participate in a Home Products Universal *product* test. First, she is qualified as a user of the product category under consideration. Next, she is told that a leading manufacturer has developed two new products in the test product category. Finally, she is asked to cooperate in the test, following the standard sequential monadic procedure. Under this procedure she is asked to use one test product first, usually for one week; to complete a questionnaire about it; to use a second product following the first, usually in the second week; to complete an identical questionnaire about it; and, finally, to submit to a call-back interview.

Under normal product test conditions the products under test are different, and everything else, including containers and packaging materials, is the same except for rotated identifying marks. When this procedure is applied to container testing, the two packages under test are different, and everything else, including the product is the same (again excepting rotated identifying marks). A direct question comparing the test containers is asked at the end of the call-back questionnaire, and container items are included in the scale question series. But the overall decision with respect to the preferred container is made on the basis of the preferred product in the product test.

The purpose of this procedure is to divert the consumer's attention from the container test as such. The container is perceived by the consumer only incidentally, and totally within the context of product usage. We believe that this procedure more closely parallels actual awareness and evaluation of various container designs.

In the case of the test of alternative Handsome Boy Window Brite containers, we would propose that respondents not only be qualified as users of branded window cleaners but also that the respondents agree to clean at least five windows with each of the test products. In this connection, we believe it undesirable to conduct this test in the dead of summer. We would prefer to wait instead until mid or late fall because we believe that a much higher proportion of qualified respondents will agree to test the products after the weather has become cool and consumer thoughts turn to storm windows. Finally, we would propose that in this test the two test containers be filled only one third full rather than to the top. It is our observation, although we unfortunately have no hard evidence, that spray orifices are most likely to malfunction after the container to which they are attached is partially empty.

Sample

The standard sample size for container tests of this kind is three hundred completed cases. Because we anticipate considerable difficulty in obtaining complete questionnaires from respondents who say they will cooperate but do not in fact satisfactorily complete the product use task, we would recommend that six hundred placements be made for this test. It is our intention to conduct the test in suburban areas of New York City, Columbus, Ohio, and Atlanta, Georgia. The standard modified-probability sample design with interviewer selection of respondents within predesignated blocks will be followed. The interviewers will be instructed to skip at least five houses between product placements.

Product Requirement

The Market Research Department will require a total of seven hundred each of the alternative new Window Brite container designs packed one-third full. One half of each of the new containers should be marked "F" and one half should be marked "H." These test containers should be available in shipping cartons at least two weeks prior to the estimated starting date for field work.

Timing and Cost

This research will take approximately twelve weeks to complete following the initiation of field work. The cost will be $7,500, plus or minus 10 per cent.

The meeting to review the proposed containers and discuss the research plans was held on the afternoon of Wednesday, August 22, 1973. Allen Ferragher presented four containers for Handsome Boy Window Brite cleaner to Messrs. Pensa, Manoir, LaGrange, and Heamstead of Home Products Universal. Allen Scala, the Home Products Universal director of new product development, was on holiday in Europe and was therefore unable to attend the meeting. Everyone present came to regret his absence as the afternoon wore on. Scala, more than anyone else in the company, exercised a benign influence upon Arthur Pensa. Pensa was generally conceded to be a competent if not brilliant marketing director. But he was given to moods of irascibility and stubbornness.

On this particular afternoon Pensa refused to choose two designs for testing from the four presented by Ferragher. Included in these designs were two with a conventional push-spray top and two with an aerosol release system. Both the push spray and the aerosol containers were executed in metal and in plastic. The metal containers were standard cylinders in both cases, and the plastic containers had been designed to fit snugly into the hand with what Ferragher described as a barrel-shape, finger-snub, ripped-grip design. The aerosol containers were about 30 per cent more expensive than the nonaerosol containers, and the plastic containers were about 30 per cent more expensive than the metal containers. The cost relatives are shown in Exhibit 11–1.

EXHIBIT 11–1
Specimen Data:
Cost Relatives for Four Alternative
Handsome Boy Window Brite
Containers

CONTAINER TYPE	COST RELATIVE
Metal spray	100
Metal aerosol	130
Plastic spray	130
Plastic aerosol	169

Pensa first expressed his annoyance at being asked to make a selective judgment between containers of differing costs: "I can't figure out which of these is better and why. I like the plastic aerosol best and the metal spray can worst, but I don't know if I like it enough more to cover the price spread." Then no one said anything at all for four and one-half minutes. Pensa broke the silence finally by pointing out acidly to Manoir that he believed that the design house should have been given explicit instructions to develop totally different designs at virtually equal prices. Manoir was rather taken aback when Pensa ignored his protestation that he had, in fact, asked the package design house to do just that. Instead of responding to Manoir, Pensa turned to LaGrange and said, "Supposing we're stuck with all four designs, can you find a way to assess the differential values to the consumer?" LaGrange said he did not understand the question. Pensa now addressed him as if he were an adolescent child: "I mean, can you ask the consumer if a package that costs me more is worth more to her, and if so, how much?" LaGrange replied rather grandiloquently that suitable procedures had not yet been developed to his knowledge but that important work on value perception and discrimination was being carried out in the psychology departments of several prominent universities.

At this point, Manoir recovered some of his composure and said, "But if we test them only for preference, we will know if consumer preferences follow the price differences and perhaps get some idea about whether the expensive containers are really preferred. We shouldn't assume that the more expensive containers will automatically win." "So," said Pensa, "you are recommending that we test all four?" To this Manoir said, "No, not necessarily," and LaGrange said, "Yes, of course." The divergent viewpoints were expressed simultaneously. "I vote for testing all four, but figure it out for yourselves, boys," said Pensa as he got up calmly and left the meeting.

The other participants were, at this point, left in a moderate state of confusion. No one said anything when Al Ferragher asked what the next move was. No one paid any attention when Allen Heamstead spoke up for the first time all day to make an inane remark about a recently completed trade between two professional football teams. Finally, Manoir said to Ferragher, "I guess we test all four." Then to LaGrange, "Al, can you whip up a plan to test the four containers, and do it pretty quickly?"

HPU INTERNAL COMMUNICATION

TO: A. Manoir
FROM: A. LaGrange
cc: A. Pensa   DATE: August 24, 1973

You have asked the Marketing Research Department to amend its plan to test two alternative proposed Handsome Boy Window Brite containers so that four alternative containers may be included in the research.

We would use the same basic method as outlined in our previous plan dated August 21, 1973. However, we would introduce the rotated paired-comparison procedure in which each test container is compared with each other container in 75 cases, yielding a base of 225 cases for each alternative container against the average of the other three test containers. You are familiar with this design from other work that we have done (see Case 7). The pairs are as follows:

75 cases	1 vs 2		75 cases	2 vs 3
75 cases	1 vs 3		75 cases	2 vs 4
75 cases	1 vs 4		75 cases	3 vs 4

As you can see, a total of 450 completed interviews is required by this design, or only 50 per cent more than would be necessary if two rather than four containers were tested.

We would propose no other changes in the plan except that a total of 550 containers of each design variation will be required. One quarter (112) of each should be labeled "E," "F," "G," and "H."

The estimated cost of this work is $12,000. The estimate of twelve weeks elapsed time following the initiation of field work remains unchanged.

Pensa approved the revised plan in mid-September. He did this with a certain ill grace, insisting that Manoir write him a detailed memorandum explaining why it was necessary to test all four designs, before giving his approval. The work was finally initiated in mid-October because everyone seemed to agree with Al LaGrange's concern over hot weather and window cleaning. LaGrange presented a set of five summary tables on January 14, 1974. They are reproduced in Exhibits 11–2 through Exhibits 11–6.

EXHIBIT 11–2
Specimen Data: Overall Consumer Preference Among Four Alternative Handsome Boy Window Brite Containers—Product Performance Basis

CONTAINER PREFERENCE	PER CENT	BASE
Metal spray	42	218
Metal aerosol	54	238
Plastic spray	48	212
Plastic aerosol	58	220

EXHIBIT 11–3
Specimen Data: Results of Two-Scale Questions Concerning Container Characteristics

		SCALE POINTS					
SCALE ITEM	CONTAINER	STRONGLY AGREE	AGREE	NO PREFERENCE	DISAGREE	STRONGLY DISAGREE	BASE
This product is	Metal spray	35	30	1	14	20	218
easy to apply	Metal aerosol	67	22	3	4	4	238
	Plastic spray	42	25	4	10	19	212
	Plastic aerosol	85	6	2	3	4	220
This product	Metal spray	14	10	2	35	39	218
container is	Metal aerosol	20	22	4	30	24	238
easy to handle	Plastic spray	25	32	2	21	20	212
	Plastic aerosol	42	37	2	15	4	220

EXHIBIT 11–4
Specimen Data: Reasons for Disliking Alternative Handsome Boy Window Brite Containers—Product Preference Basis

	DID NOT PREFER			
	METAL SPRAY	METAL AEROSOL	PLASTIC SPRAY	PLASTIC AEROSOL
Base: Nonpreferrers of each package				
Number	126	109	110	85
Per cent	100*	100*	100*	100*
Miscellaneous reasons associated with product performance: doesn't clean as well, etc.	23%	25%	72%	76%
Miscellaneous reasons associated with product characteristics: don't like the smell, don't like the color, etc.	41	46	12	12
Hard to get all the cleaner out of the container	38	14	21	27
Container is cold, slippery	26	26	3	—
Doesn't fit in hand very well	19	27	4	2

* Some respondents gave more than one answer.

EXHIBIT 11-5

Specimen Data: Results of Two-Scale Questions Concerning Container Characteristics Analyzed by Container Preference

SCALE ITEM	CONTAINER	PREFERRED	STRONGLY AGREE	AGREE	NO PREFERENCE	DISAGREE	STRONGLY DISAGREE	BASE
This product is easy to apply	Metal spray	Metal spray	47%	36%	—	7%	10%	92
		Other	26	25	2%	20	27	126
	Metal aerosol	Metal aerosol	75	20	1	2	2	129
		Other	59	24	5	6	6	109
	Plastic spray	Plastic spray	50	29	2	6	13	102
		Other	34	21	6	14	25	110
	Plastic aerosol	Plastic aerosol	96	2	—	1	1	135
		Other	67	12	5	7	9	85
This product container is easy to handle	Metal spray	Metal spray	20%	15%	—	25%	40%	92
		Other	10	6	3%	42	38	126
	Metal aerosol	Metal aerosol	30	26	2	22	20	129
		Other	8	18	6	39	29	109
	Plastic spray	Plastic spray	40	30	1	15	14	102
		Other	11	34	3	27	25	110
	Plastic aerosol	Plastic aerosol	52	42	1	2	3	135
		Other	26	29	4	35	6	85

EXHIBIT 11–6

Specimen Data: Overall Consumer Preference Among Four Alternative Handsome Boy Window Brite Containers—Product Preference Basis Analyzed by Number of Windows Cleaned

PREFERENCE CONTAINER		TOTAL	TEN OR MORE WINDOWS	NINE OR LESS WINDOWS
Metal spray	Per cent	42	35	52
	Base	218	69	149
Metal aerosol	Per cent	54	61	50
	Base	238	90	148
Plastic spray	Per cent	48	29	57
	Base	212	71	141
Plastic aerosol	Per cent	58	71	55
	Base	220	41	179

Questions for Case 11

1. Do you agree or disagree with the decision to accept the name Window Brite, out of hand, without any search for another, perhaps superior name? What kinds of criteria might be developed for the selection of a name for a new product? Should a new name be subjected to consumer research before final adoption?

2. Evaluate Albert Manoir's strategy for forcing Aloysius LaGrange to produce a research plan promptly, before the alternative container designs were available.

3. Prepare a memorandum from Albert Manoir to Arthur Pensa explaining why it is necessary to test all four of the container designs, as requested on page 278.

4. The firm of Bastion, Ferragher, and Alfredi was asked to develop a container that cost no more than the containers of the two leading competitive products. Discuss the importance of competitive container costs. Does Manoir know how to interpret the research results presented in Exhibits 11–2 through 11–6? What additional information might he need?

5. Analyze the data presented in Exhibits 11–2 through 11–6. On the basis of this analysis, write a recommendation as Albert Manoir to Arthur Pensa concerning which proposed container should be adopted by Home Products Universal. Of what significance is the fact that the consumer price for Window Brite will vary depending upon which container is ultimately chosen?

6. Why would the Home Products universal marketing research department prefer to see the proposed container designs before writing a container research proposal?

7. Why does the Home Products Universal marketing research department anticipate relatively heavy noncompletion rates among respondents in this particular container test?

CASE 12

Distribution Channel Decisions

New Orleans Jazz Preservation Recordings, Inc. Selects a Distribution Channel to Reach Phonograph Record Collectors

NEW ORLEANS Jazz Preservation Recordings, Inc. was founded by Bartholomew A. Bellamy in the fall of 1973. Bellamy had long been an enthusiastic supporter of New Orleans jazz and a keen fan of the handful of great New Orleans musicians who were still performing in public. The impetus for the formation of New Orleans Jazz Preservation Recordings, Inc. came when Bellamy met Aldo "Peanuts" Dubois, the venerable virtuoso New Orleans trumpet player. Dubois and a group of his peers were appearing for a limited engagement in a New York jazz club. Bellamy was introduced to him at a small reception and cocktail party held in honor of the musicians by a leading New York restauranteur who specialized in Creole cooking.

Dubois at the age of sixty-seven was spry and canny. He wanted to make recordings and he managed to get around to this topic in every conversation that he held with New Orleans jazz fans during his trip to New York. Everyone else had brushed by the topic, rushing on to some other matter of greater interest—everyone, that is, except Bart Bellamy. He was genuinely interested. He had no idea how phonograph records were created or produced, let alone what costs were involved. Dubois, on the other hand, knew his way around the recording business. For years, in every band in which he performed, he had assumed the role of de facto business manager, and in the process had built up a complete knowledge of the ins and outs of making records. He assured Bellamy that great New Orleans recordings were within his grasp. He, Dubois, would be honored to record for the Bellamy label, and he felt confident that he could entice other renowned veteran New Orleans musicians to record with him.

Almost before he knew it, Bellamy had formed New Orleans Jazz Preservation Recordings and had obtained a recording license from the American Federation of Musicians to make records under the NOJ label. In the first days of the company Bellamy was much more concerned with making records than with the question of how he might distribute them. After all, Bellamy consoled himself, he did know something about marketing (he was director of marketing planning for the Vandalia Tire and Tube Company, Inc., specialists in the fabrication of tires and tubes for bicycles, tractors, wheelbarrows, and other nonautomotive vehicles). And Bellamy had plenty of friends active in marketing, and if among them, they couldn't figure out how to sell enough records to break even, then they didn't deserve to be in the record business in the first place.

By early February 1974, Bellamy owned a master tape-recording that was to become legendary among New Orleans jazz enthusiasts when it was released on the NOJ label as "Stomps and Rags," featuring the Peanuts Dubois All Stars with vocalist Etta Rombeaux.

Bart Bellamy had reached a place where few other jazz enthusiasts and record collectors had ever been before: he was a record producer, writer of liner notes, intimate of celebrated jazz musicians, and darling of the thirty-eight other collectors of New Orleans jazz recordings that he knew. Also, he owned two thousand copies of "Stomps and Rags" by the Peanuts Dubois All Stars and had invested $4,832.12 in the project. He had neither sold, nor did he know how to sell, his first record.

It was, Bart Bellamy decided, a time for sober reflection and analysis. His first task was to identify and appraise the market he was trying to reach, and his second task was to isolate alternative distribution and communication channels to reach that market.

Bellamy could find no marketing research studies of the number or characteristics of the purchasers of New Orleans jazz recordings. Nor could he find anyone who could even hazard an educated guess as to who these people were or what they were like. The only hard knowledge available was the generalization that most jazz records sold about two thousand copies and only a few releases sold as many as five thousand. This information had come to him as hearsay from a distant cousin who dated a young accountant who, in turn, numbered among his clients a modestly successful producer of bebop recordings. Bellamy decided, therefore, that he must infer for himself the dimensions of his market and then set out to exploit that market himself.

Bellamy guessed that there were, as a generality, three distinct types of persons who might buy a copy of "Stomps and Rags." First was the individual who acquired records to play on his phonograph without discrimination of any kind, a person who bought whatever was popular, or whatever he thought he liked, and whose accumulation of recordings showed little discernment and less imagination. Bellamy was quite certain that this market represented a very substantial potential sale if only he could find ways of making it want his records. It was with this vast group that hits were made; they formed the target for the vast promotional apparatus of the record industry. But Bellamy thought it would be a miracle if he happened to tap this market. His product was, after all, of limited interest; it was conceivable that he might find a novelty among the tunes that Dubois had recorded that would spark a response from this general public, but he seriously doubted it. Dubois had, after all, recorded similar material many times before for bigger and more commercially sophisticated recording companies than New Orleans Jazz Preservation Recordings, and he had never achieved a truly popular success. In addition, Bellamy knew full well the kind of investment in promotion that would be required to stimulate a popular response to the Dubois material, and he rejected it as totally beyond his means. So, both because his taste was not the taste of the general public and because he did not have the capital to attempt to educate the public to appreciate New Orleans jazz, Bellamy concluded that he would have to seek his market elsewhere.

The second kind of individual who might buy "Stomps and Rags" was the general collector of jazz records, the person who had at least some interest in all jazz styles and periods and who was anxious to have outstanding examples of each in his collection. Bellamy guessed that this was a fairly limited group. He knew only that the circulation of *Down Beat*, the leading general jazz magazine, was about 70,000. He suspected that the jazz record collector group was larger, if only because all of his own jazz-record-collecting friends did not subscribe to *Down Beat*. He therefore estimated, on no more extensive information, that there were 150,000 jazz record collectors in the country who bought at least a few jazz records of one sort or another each year. Bellamy suspected that his product would be at least acceptable to a substantial proportion of these collectors, if their tastes were, in general, rather catholic with respect to the various jazz styles. In addition, he knew that a substantial fraction of total jazz record sales to this group moved through a relatively small number of record stores that specialized in jazz releases. There were not more than thirty of these specialist stores, and they were concentrated in the larger population centers. Bellamy believed that it would be possible for him to make sales to this group if he achieved distribution in the specialist record stores, if he undertook a communications program by sending review/promotional copies of "Stomps and Rags" to leading jazz critics with a request for review, and if he advertised his product in jazz record magazines.

The third kind of individual to whom the record was likely to appeal was the dedicated collector of New Orleans jazz records. Bellamy guessed that many of these collectors could also be included within the second group of more general jazz collectors. This third group, thus consisted, in part, of the hard-core New Orleans enthusiasts included within the larger group. In addition, the New Orleans collector group undoubtedly included some narrow specialists like Bellamy himself who would have nothing to do with anything except the traditional and unexpurgated playing of the New Orleans greats. Bellamy had no idea how many New Orleans collectors there might be; he guessed ten thousand, but this guess was more in defense of having spent almost $5,000 to produce "Stomps and Rags" than based on any rational estimating procedure. Bellamy guessed that these hard-core collectors were spread all over the country, and on the evidence of a fairly substantial amount of mail solicitation he had received from specialist record suppliers, he guessed that many of these collectors obtained at least some of their records from out-of-the-way suppliers by mail, rather than in record stores. Some of these hard-core collectors could certainly be reached through the major jazz record stores, but it might be just as easy to reach this group plus those others who lived in areas remote from the major jazz retail outlets by mail. Bellamy was certain that he could sell his product to these hard-core collectors; his problem was to find them and tell them about "Stomps and Rags" with as little unproductive promotional expense as possible. Bellamy was especially intrigued with this third market because he suspected that, once he established contact with it, there was a strong possibility that the business from it might become self-perpetuating. He suspected that the New Orleans specialist might buy every New Orleans record he could get his hands on if he had at least some assurance that a minimum level of taste and production quality was being maintained. Thus, the New Orleans specialist could be depended upon for a significant number of repeat purchases if he were satisfied with the NOJ product. Bellamy began to think of this third market in terms of an accumulated list of names that could be expected to generate repeat sales over the years.

Bellamy knew that inherent in this conception was the need for further investment on his part, both to build such a list of names and to produce enough additional record releases to establish himself and his NOJ label as an important element in the New Orleans jazz field. Bellamy concluded that he should be able to smoke out one thousand or two thousand hard-core fans in a reasonable period of time if there were as many as five thousand such fans in total and if he could produce three or four high-quality releases.

One other important consideration occurred to Bellamy. He was sure that it would be difficult, if not impossible, to pursue both the second and the third distribution approaches simultaneously. That is, he was sure that one could not develop a serious direct mail business and maintain distribution through the major jazz outlets at the same time. Bellamy believed that it would be impossible to develop direct mail orders from the New Orleans specialists who regularly shopped in the major jazz outlets unless they became convinced that the NOJ label was available only by mail. These specialists had come to expect that every jazz release, no matter how obscure, would be available to them through the major jazz retail outlets. And because of this experience, they would expect NOJ records to show up in due course in the racks of their favorite jazz record store. For the direct mail strategy to work, it would therefore be imperative that no NOJ release ever find its way to these retail outlets, for if it did, it would simply reinforce the expectation of these collectors and reassure them that it was unnecessary to go to the trouble of breaking their established purchase pattern to buy by mail. (But the reverse was not true. Even if Bellamy aimed at the jazz record collector and emphasized the jazz-retailer distribution channel, he could expect a certain number of direct mail orders from those New Orleans jazz record fans who lived in remote areas and could not habitually shop in the jazz shops of the larger cities. But to accommodate these collectors through direct mail would not be the same as to adopt the direct mail distribution strategy.)

Another important ingredient in the direct mail strategy was a continuous promotional campaign directed at the New Orleans specialist reminding him of the excellence and availability of NOJ recordings, but only by mail. Part of this campaign could be accomplished through good reviews (if the product earned them) from the critics; part of it could be accomplished by small-space reminder advertising in the jazz magazines; and part of it could be accomplished through direct mail solicitation of jazz enthusiasts, if lists of such enthusiasts were available.

A final element in direct mail distribution, reasoned Bellamy, would be the maintenance of the NOJ retail price. Direct mail's most significant potential advantage was the fact that the direct mail seller achieved significantly greater revenue from each sale without incurring important additional costs. The assumption about not incurring significantly increased costs rested upon the availability of high-yield direct mail lists, the efficiency and efficacy of small-space advertising in jazz magazines, and critical support. But the assumption about holding costs down was meaningless unless revenues were higher because the established retail price was maintained. If direct mail offered Bellamy a significantly higher return per record sold than alternative distribution methods, then it was reasonable to substitute direct mail solicitation for the more normal channels involving distributors and/or retailers. If this did not prove to be the case, there was no compelling reason to consider direct mail.

In spite of his emotional attraction to the direct mail method of distribution, Bellamy realized that he should make a more thorough and mature analysis of the three distribution methods before reaching a final decision. Emotions are one thing, Bellamy admitted to himself, and profits are another. Accordingly, he proceeded to develop a cost and break-even profile for each of the available methods of distribution. His work to this end is summarized in Exhibits 12–1 through 12–8. Exhibit 12–1 recapitulates the major characteristics of each of the three marketing approaches.

EXHIBIT 12–1

Specimen Data: Alternative Markets, Distribution Channels, and Consumer Communications

	POPULAR RECORD BUYERS	JAZZ RECORD COLLECTORS	NEW ORLEANS JAZZ RECORD COLLECTORS
Channel	Direct to large retailers Distributors to small retailers	Direct to major jazz retailers Accept mail orders	Mail order only None
Retail availability	General availability in record outlets	Available in jazz record retail shops	None
Consumer communication	Mass media advertising	Media advertising in jazz magazines	Small-space advertising in jazz magazines Direct mail solicitation of jazz collectors
Trade communication	Trade advertising to retailers and disc jockeys	None	None
Sales promotion	General distribution of promotional copies to jazz critics and disc jockeys	Limited distribution of promotional copies to general jazz critics and jazz disc jockeys	Intensive distribution of promotional copies to jazz critics and disc jockeys featuring New Orleans recordings

Exhibit 12–2 shows the various costs associated with each of the distribution channels. The costs are broken down into fixed costs and variable costs. The fixed costs are those that are constant regardless of how many records are produced. They include the cost of the recording session (payments to musicians and studio rental), the manufacture of pressing masters, jacket design, promotional copies to critics, and advertising. The expenditures for recording session, pressing masters, and jacket design are constant regardless of what distribution method is used. More advertising is required if the first distribution channel is used rather than the more limited channels. The advertising figure shown represents a minimum expenditure for each channel—more advertising money can be spent if sales are good and appear to respond to advertising. The cost of distribution to critics declines progressively as the scope of distribution is decreased.

EXHIBIT 12–2
Specimen Data: Cost Analysis for Alternative Distribution Methods for NOJ Records

COSTS	CHANNEL 1: POPULAR RECORD BUYERS	CHANNEL 2: JAZZ COLLECTORS	CHANNEL 3: NEW ORLEANS COLLECTORS
Fixed costs:			
Recording session	$2,500	$2,500	$2,500
Manufacture of pressing masters	130	130	130
Jacket design	200	200	200
Promotional copies to critics	450	250	150
Advertising	8,000	2,000	2,000
Total fixed costs	$11,280	$5,080	$4,980
Variable (per M) costs:			
Manufacturing records	$ 370	$ 370	$ 370
Manufacturing jackets	250	250	250
Royalties	160	160	160
Direct mail distribution		72	380
Direct mail solicitation per 2,000 pieces (production included in advertising)			150
Variable cost per M	$ 780	$ 852	$1,310

The variable costs include the cost of actually making finished records and jackets—the royalties to holders of copyrights of the tunes recorded; direct mail distribution (second and third channels); and, in the case of the third distribution method, the cost of direct mail solicitation. Production costs vary directly with the number of records pressed, except that custom record and jacket producers typically require a minimum order of one thousand. Thus a commitment for at least one thousand records and jackets is required, and costs are shown on a per-thousand basis. Most music publishers require royalty payments for records *pressed* (rather than for records *sold*) when dealing with small record producers. Thus royalty payments are shown as a variable cost per thousand records pressed. The $160 figure assumes that eight tunes will be included on each record; the statutory royalty payment is 2¢ per mechanical reproduction (or pressed record) per song. Thus royalty payments for a record containing eight songs would be 16¢ per record or $160 per thousand records pressed.

The cost of mailings to prospective buyers are not related in any way to the cost of the records produced. The more mailings made, the higher the cost, and the converse. Bellamy has decided arbitrarily to mail two thousand pieces per one thousand records pressed. He hopes to generate a 30 per cent response from this first mailing and to sell enough additional records to break even from critical reviews and advertising. With subsequent releases, at least some of the mailings will be made to individuals who have previously purchased a recording, and the response should therefore be considerably higher—perhaps up to 75 per cent. If the cost analyses are based on the lower response rate to direct mail—that is, on the response rate to prospect mailings rather than to buyer mailings—a conservative estimate of mailing cost factors is automatically used.

Costs of direct mail distribution—mailing cartons, processing, and postage—vary directly with records sold. These costs are 38¢ per record or $380 per thousand. It is assumed that 19 or 20 per cent of all sales through the second channel will be made by direct mail, and accordingly $72 per thousand sale is estimated for this expense.

Exhibit 12–3 shows cumulative costs at various levels of record production for each of the distribution channels. This exhibit starts with the fixed costs of Exhibit 12–2 and adds the variable cost per thousand records at each production level.

Exhibit 12–4 gives an analysis of revenue for the alternative distribution methods. These data reflect the net yield to the record producer from the various distribution channels. Whenever a record producer sells a record either directly to a larger retailer or through a distributor for distribution to nondirect retail accounts, he will net about 50 per cent of his list price.

EXHIBIT 12–3
Specimen Data: Cumulative Costs for Alternative Distribution Channels for NOJ Records

NUMBER OF RECORDS	CHANNEL 1: POPULAR RECORD BUYERS	CHANNEL 2: JAZZ COLLECTORS	CHANNEL 3: NEW ORLEANS COLLECTORS
Fixed Cost	$11,280	$ 5,080	$ 4,980
1,000	12,060	5,932	6,290
2,000	12,840	6,784	7,600
3,000	13,620	7,636	8,910
4,000	14,400	8,488	10,220
5,000	15,180	9,430	11,530
6,000	15,960	10,192	12,840
7,000	16,740	11,044	14,150
8,000	17,520	11,896	15,460

Additional retailer/distributor discounts generally come into play for especially large or unusual orders, but the NOJ label need not anticipate them in a revenue forecast for its records, given their relatively limited appeal. The NOJ record list price is $5 per record. Therefore, NOJ revenue will amount to $2,500 per thousand records distributed solely through the retailer/distributor channel (Channel 1).

The mixed retailer/direct mail channel (Channel 2) revenue yield will vary depending on the exact mix of sales through the two channels. Each record sold through retail/distributors will yield $2.50, and each record sold by mail will yield the list price of $5. If it is assumed that 20 per cent of total sales in Channel 2 will be by direct mail and 80 per cent by retailer, the yield per thousand records will be $3,000 (800 × $2.50 + 200 × $5.00). It is hard to predict what the exact mix of business through the two channels will be, but an arbitrary 80–20 seems reasonable if it is assumed that most serious New Orleans record collectors must have established at least some tenuous contact with a major jazz retailer, if they are adequately to service their collections. Therefore, it is assumed that Channel 2 direct mail sales will be made, at least in the beginning, primarily to those collectors who find it especially difficult to maintain such retail contacts.

EXHIBIT 12–4
Specimen Data: Revenue Analysis for Alternative Distribution Channels for NOJ Records*

	CHANNEL 1: POPULAR RECORD BUYERS	CHANNEL 2: JAZZ COLLECTORS	CHANNEL 3: NEW ORLEANS COLLECTORS
Revenue yield per M	$2,500	$3,000	$5,000

	ACCUMULATIVE REVENUE		
SALES	CHANNEL 1	CHANNEL 2	CHANNEL 3
1,000	$ 2,500	$ 3,000	$ 5,000
2,000	5,000	6,000	10,000
3,000	7,500	9,000	15,000
4,000	10,000	12,000	20,000
5,000	12,500	15,000	25,000
6,000	15,000	18,000	30,000
7,000	17,500	21,000	35,000
8,000	20,000	24,000	40,000

* Record list price is $5.00

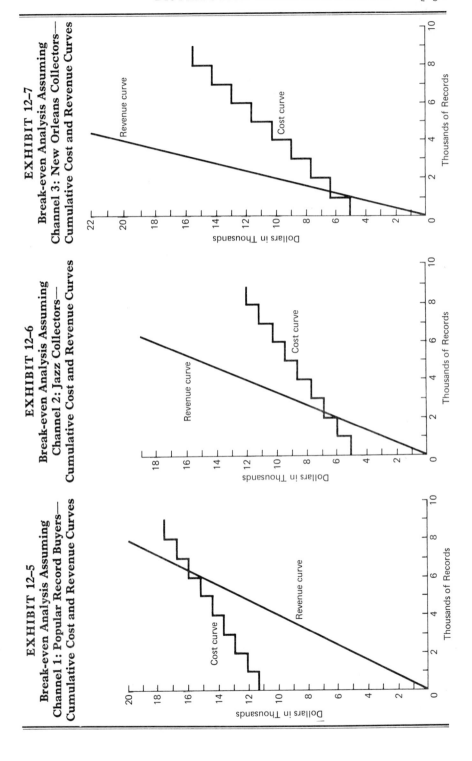

EXHIBIT 12-5
Break-even Analysis Assuming
Channel 1: Popular Record Buyers—
Cumulative Cost and Revenue Curves

EXHIBIT 12-6
Break-even Analysis Assuming
Channel 2: Jazz Collectors—
Cumulative Cost and Revenue Curves

EXHIBIT 12-7
Break-even Analysis Assuming
Channel 3: New Orleans Collectors—
Cumulative Cost and Revenue Curves

The revenue yield through Channel 3 will be $5 per record, because all sales will be made by mail. Thus Channel 3 will yield $5,000 in revenue per thousand records sold.

Exhibits 12–5, 12–6, and 12–7 present plots of the cumulative cost and revenue data from Exhibits 12–3 and 12–4 for each of the alternative distribution channels. These plots show the record sales volume at which each of the alternative methods of distribution breaks even. Thus Exhibit 12–5 shows the cumulative cost and revenue curves and break-even point for distribution Channel 1; Exhibit 12–6 shows the same curves and break-even point for Channel 2; and Exhibit 12–7 shows these curves and break-even point for Channel 3. The cost curve in each exhibit is shown in the form of a series of ascending steps to reflect the assumption that records will be produced in groups of one thousand and that all variable costs will be incurred at the time of production. The point at which the cost curve intersects the vertical axis is, in each exhibit, the level of fixed costs for the particular distribution method.

If these three exhibits (that is, 12–5, 12–6, and 12–7) are compared, distinct trends in the cost and revenue curves are apparent as the record producer considers increasingly more selective methods of distribution. Thus, as one moves from general to selective distribution of phonograph records, the fixed costs decline and the variable costs per record increase. Similarly, as one moves from general to selective distribution of phonograph records, the revenue yield per record increases.

These overall trends are summarized in Exhibit 12–8, which shows projected profit or loss for New Orleans Jazz Preservation Recordings, Inc. at different sales volumes and through the alternative distribution channels.

Channel 1 will not show a profit until 7,000 records have been sold. Channels 2 and 3, on the other hand, are profitable at much lower

---

EXHIBIT 12–8

Specimen Data: Profit and Loss Analysis at Various Sales Volumes in Alternative Distribution Channels

SALES VOLUME OF RECORDS	CHANNEL 1: POPULAR RECORD BUYERS	CHANNEL 2: JAZZ COLLECTORS	CHANNEL 3: NEW ORLEANS COLLECTORS
1,000	($9,560)*	($2,932)	($1,290)
2,000	($7,840)	($ 784)	$2,400
3,000	($6,120)	$1,364	$6,090
4,000	($4,400)	$3,512	$9,780
5,000	($2,680)	$5,570	$13,470
6,000	($ 960)	$7,808	$17,160
7,000	$ 760	$9,956	$20,850

* Figures in parentheses represent losses.

volume levels. Channel 2 will show a profit at a sales volume of 3,000 records, and Channel 3 will show a profit after 2,000 records have been sold. There seems to be no question that Channel 3 will be more profitable, particularly if Bellamy is correct in believing that a maximum jazz record sale is about 5,000 records.

But the fundamental question is whether Bellamy will find it as easy to sell 2,000 records by mail as he will to sell 7,000 records at retail. To take a pessimistic view, it may be easier to sell 5,000 records at retail than to sell 500 by mail. If this were the case, the net loss to Bellamy will be less if he adopts Channel 1 ($2,680 loss) than if he adopts Channel 3 ($3,600 loss). Bellamy now realizes that if he is to make an intelligent channel choice he will have to have some idea about how many records he is likely to sell given his planned promotional expenditures through each of these channels. No matter how potentially profitable a particular channel of distribution may appear, it is profitable only if it will generate sales at a level that will produce the potential profits.

But how will Bellamy estimate the sales volume through each of the channels? He knows of no other company that has ever undertaken an experiment to determine the sales-producing power of the alternative channels and, for that matter, he knows of no other company that has ever tried a direct-mail-only channel of distribution. So there is no experience available to Bellamy to indicate which channel is most potentially profitable or least potentially unprofitable. The sales projection is further complicated by the fact that individual phonograph records have different sales potentials. "Stomps and Rags" featuring the Peanuts Dubois All Stars may be an especially good or a rather poor seller, regardless of distribution channel. Another record with different New Orleans performers might have considerably greater or lesser sales potential as a record, again independent of the chosen channel. Bellamy must therefore factor into his sales estimates for each channel of distribution some value for the individual sales potential of "Stomps and Rags."

Bellamy believes that the only way in which the variation in sales potential for individual records can be accounted for in his channel sales projections is to anticipate the production of enough different records so that sales results will reflect an average performance for the records that he is capable of producing. Such an average performance will therefore reflect the kinds of artists that Bellamy chooses and that will consent to record for him, the quality of the studio facilities that he uses, the tunes that he and the artists choose to record, and so on.

Implicit in this notion of "the average sales performance" is that Bellamy will choose one channel of distribution and produce at least four or five different records for sale through that channel before he is able to assess realistically the average sales performance of a particular channel of distribution. Before Bellamy can reach a conclusion about the profitability of any one channel, he must use it four or five times so that its average

performance may be assessed. But of course Bellamy has already concluded that it would be necessary to release at least four or five records to
assess the feasibility of the direct mail distribution channel anyway, that
is, to assess whether or not the jazz record collector will adapt his record
purchasing to only-by-mail availability. Thus the real significance of the
notion of "the average record" and of the need to market at least four or
five different records through a particular channel in order to account for
variations in record popularity is that regardless of the channel one selects
a minimum of four or five different records must be marketed. Direct
mail is not the only channel, therefore, that requires several records
before its potential can finally be assessed.

Bellamy can now look at these various issues and factors as a decision
problem, which he can formulate in one of two kinds of payoff analyses.
If he can make some sort of reasonable projection of the sales he will
achieve with an average record in each of his distribution channels, he will
be able to formulate the decision problem under the rules of decision
making under risk. If he cannot make realistic sales projections for the
alternative channels, the decision problem must be formulated under the
rules of decision making under uncertainty.

Exhibit 12–9 shows estimated payoffs computed from the rules of
decision making under risk. In this exhibit, Bellamy has *guessed*[1] that a
sale of 1,000 records is the most likely sales outcome; that it will be three
times as hard to achieve the sale of 2,000 records; and that it will be nine
times as hard to achieve a sales response of jazz hit proportions (over 6,000

EXHIBIT 12–9
**Specimen Data: Decision Making Under Risk—Estimated Payoffs for
Alternative Distribution Channels**

	LOW SALES RESPONSE	MODEST SALES RESPONSE	JAZZ HIT
Probability	.692	.231	.077
Sales in records	1,000	2,000	6,000
Channel 1 (ES_1)	($9,560)*	($7,840)	($960)
Channel 2 (ES_2)	($2,932)	($784)	$7,808
Channel 3 (ES_3)	($1,290)	$2,400	$17,160

$ES_1 = (\$9,560)\,(.692) + (\$7,840)\,(.231) + (\$960)\,(.077) = (\$9,145.16)$
$ES_2 = (\$2,932)\,(.692) + (\$784)\,(.231) + \$7,808\,(.077) = (\$1,599.82)$
$ES_3 = (\$1,290)\,(.692) + \$2,400\,(.231) + 17,160\,(.077) = \$983.04$

---

* Figures in parentheses represent losses.

---

[1] Bellamy has at least one theoretical alternative to guessing the sales response
to the three distribution methods: he could market-test each. See Question 7 at
the end of this case.

records). He has converted these guesses into probabilities that reflect the relative chance of achieving various sales levels. Thus, he considers the probability of selling 1,000 records to be about nine times as great as selling 6,000 records and three times as great as selling 2,000 records. Accordingly, he assigns a probability of .077 to the sale of 6,000 records; a probability of .231 to the sale of 2,000 records; and a probability of .692 to the sale of 1,000 records. Arithmetically: .077 + 3(.077) + 9(.077) = 1.000. The expected dollar return from each of the three distribution channels (strategies) can then be computed using the formula:

$$ES_n = P_{1p_1} + P_{2p_2} + P_{3p_3} \cdots P_{np_n}$$
ES = the payoff of the n_{th} strategy
P_1, P_2, P_3 = the payoff under each sales result
p_1, p_2, p_3 = the probability that a particular sales result will occur

The payoffs from the particular sales result are obtained from Exhibit 12–8. The computation of ES_1, ES_2, and ES_3 are shown in Exhibit 12–9. As the exhibit indicates, producing jazz records is at best a risky business. Neither the retail-only channel nor the mixed retail/mail channel can be reasonably expected to yield a profit, and the mail-only channel will yield an expected profit of less than $1,000 per release.

Exhibit 12–10 is derived from Exhibit 12–9. It shows the payoff matrix for each of the crucial sales results without any guesses about the probabilities with which these results will occur.

EXHIBIT 12–10
Specimen Data: Decision Making Under Uncertainty—Estimated Payoffs Under Different Sales Response Assumptions (1,000 Records)

	LOW SALES RESPONSE	MODEST SALES RESPONSE	JAZZ HIT
Channel 1	($9,560)*	($7,840)	($960)
Channel 2	($2,932)	($784)	$7,808
Channel 3	($1,290)	$2,400	$17,160

* Figures in parentheses represent losses.

Questions for Case 12

1. List possible channels of distribution for NOJ records other than those considered in the text of the case. How would one decide whether or not to use some of these other distribution channels?

2. How feasible is marketing research in a market when sales average between 2,000 and 5,000 units?

3. Is mail order the only channel through which New Orleans jazz record collectors can be reached? If the target market is these collectors must one restrict oneself to the mail-order-only channel? Analyze the differences in anticipated communications and sales promotion programs under the jazz retailer channel and the direct mail channel.

4. In the exhibits Bellamy seems to have made his market definitions synonymous with distribution channels. What distinction should be made between a market and the distribution channel that reaches it? In what way do they differ?

5. Compute the profit generated from each of the distribution channel alternatives on the assumption that 25,000 records are sold. Comment on the result.

6. Do NOJ records fulfill a clear consumer need? Will the marketplace always respond to a fine product? Can a superior product always be sold if the right marketing approach is used?

7. Dependence upon direct-mail-only assumes that regular customers of jazz specialty shops will change their habitual purchase patterns. Is this a realistic assumption? Is it possible to test this assumption in the marketplace? Is it possible to undertake the test marketing of any of the alternative distribution methods? Why or why not?

8. On the basis of Exhibit 12–10, what channel would you choose under the maximin decision criterion (that is, the criterion of pessimism)? What channel would you choose under the maximax decision criterion (that is, the criterion of optimism)? What channel would you choose under a coefficient of optimism of $\frac{1}{10}$? What channel would you choose under the LaPlace criterion of rationality? Discuss the choices you have made under each criterion and relate them to the analysis presented in Exhibit 12–9. What conclusions do you reach about decision theory in situations of the kind presented in the case?

CASE 13

Pricing Decisions

Allgood Drug Company and Pricing Policy for Pain-out Analgesic Compound

HE ALLGOOD DRUG COMPANY began to develop branded proprietary drug items as a result of a basic policy change made in June 1927 (see Case 5). The first product to be marketed under the new policy was Pain-out Analgesic Compound, which was introduced by Allgood in February 1928. For some years thereafter Pain-out was the only important analgesic compound in the proprietary analgesic market. It qualified as a compound because it contained five grains of aspirin plus phenacetin and a buffering agent. This combination of ingredients could be shown, under certain, limited, clinical conditions, to produce an adequate level of analgesic in the bloodstream faster than a simple aspirin pill containing five grains of aspirin. Although the combination of aspirin, phenacetin, and a buffer was not unknown in medical circles, Pain-out was the first branded proprietary to offer such a combination and it was the first and only product of this specific type to receive substantial advertising support.

In the early years, Pain-out's only advertised competition was Purity First aspirin, a five-grain aspirin pill product that contained no additional ingredients. In 1955 Addington Labs introduced a new proprietary analgesic called Buffer King with Caffeine and supported it with advertising expenditures at the same level as Pain-out and Purity First. Buffer King contained five grains of aspirin, as well as a buffering agent, phenacetin, and caffeine. This formulation permitted Buffer King to make advertising claims competitive with those of Pain-out and Purity First, and Buffer King quickly achieved a substantial share of the proprietary analgesic market. Exhibit 13–1 shows total proprietary analgesic sales as well as the brand share of the three leading advertised brands from 1950 through 1974. As Exhibit 13–1 indicates, Buffer King achieved virtual brand share parity with Pain-out and Purity First by the early 1960's. Nevertheless, Pain-out absolute dollar sales held up fairly strongly during the period in spite of the lost share primarily because of the substantial growth in the total market. For example, Pain-out dollar sales in 1950 were $75,800,000, and in 1974 they were $92,124,000.

The proprietary analgesic market settled into relative competitive equilibrium in the early 1960's, and as Exhibit 13–1 illustrates, there were no significant changes in brand shares of the three leading brands over the ensuing several years. Purity First was the market leader, followed closely by Buffer King and Pain-out. As the market settled down, a well-defined and relatively limited arsenal of competitive tactics came to be used in behalf of each of the brands. This arsenal consisted primarily of three kinds of activity: consumer advertising, product line innovations, and variations in brand pricing. (Direct consumer promotion—except advertising—was restricted by an informal agreement among the major manufacturers through their trade association code of good practice.)

EXHIBIT 13–1
Specimen Data: Total Market Proprietary Analgesic Sales and Market Shares of Pain-out, Buffer King, and Purity First—Dollar Basis

YEAR	TOTAL MARKET CONSUMER SALES ($000,000)	SHARE OF MARKET (%)			
		PAIN-OUT	BUFFER KING	PURITY FIRST	ALL OTHERS
1950	172.4	44	—	48	8
1955	194.6	36	8	42	14
1960	251.7	27	22	39	12
1965	272.8	26	26	37	11
1970	294.6	26	30	31	13
1971	306.7	27	29	33	11
1972	314.8	28	31	32	9
1973	324.3	27	31	34	8
1974	341.2	27	30	34	9

S O U R C E : Modeled on the reports of the A. C. Nielsen Company.

The consumer advertising for the various brands was distinctive more for its volume than for its creativity. The exact content of specific advertisements was limited by the claims inherent in the products themselves and these were closely monitored by the Federal Trade Commission, individual competitors, the commercial continuity clearance personnel of the television networks, and the legal and medical departments of the sponsoring drug companies. The net effect of this system of controls and checks imposed by the government, the media, the competitors, and the sponsors themselves was to give the resulting advertising a certain deliberate and assertive stridency. It was, therefore, rather seriously insignificant in its final tone. But whatever its fundamental character, there was plenty of it; the combined advertising expenditures for Buffer King, Purity First, and Pain-out were over $90 million in 1974.

There was a continuing and serious effort on the part of each of the major advertised brands to develop distinctive advertisements, and effective new creative approaches were in fact brought forth from time to time. The industry marketing leaders agreed, and sales studies confirmed, that proprietary analgesic sales were responsive to such new advertising approaches if they were truly distinctive and if they did differentiate the advertised brand from its competitors. But the advantages based on creative innovation rarely lasted because competitors quickly responded either imitatively or with an equally differentiating counterclaim. Advertising constituted a major competitive arena for these products. If the net result of the advertising thrusts of the individual brands was inevitably to draw an effective parry from competition, this result was due only to the general level of advertising skill available to each of the brands. The specter hanging over them all was that their periodic advertising thrusts would be uninspired or that their specific advertising parries would be deflected.

Product line innovation was largely limited to a proliferation of package sizes. Exhibit 13–2 shows the variety of package sizes marketed by each of the three leading brands in 1955, 1965, and 1970. All the brands increased the number of different package sizes in which they were marketed during this period. The typical pattern was to add one or more larger package sizes. In addition, both Buffer King and Purity First added an intermediate size as well. Buffer King also added a liquid product in 1963, marketed in a six-ounce size equivalent to eighteen single-pill doses. In general, the three leaders tended to match each other on a package-size basis. By 1970 each of them marketed a very small size, two or three intermediate sizes, and one or two larger sizes. An exception was the liquid product marketed by Buffer King. This product surely seemed to be a legitimate line extension but did not generate enough sales volume to be considered more than a novelty item (see Exhibit 13–11).

The third area in which there was substantial competitive activity was that of pricing. Although the proprietary analgesic manufacturer has relatively little control over the exact price charged by the retailer, he does have competitive tactic options that permit him to influence the average level of retail prices and to influence some retail price movements in the short term. Beyond this, the drug manufacturer does set the price and discount structures under which his product is purchased by the trade and thus he can regulate, through his trade pricing policy, the gross returns available to retailers and wholesalers from his brands over the longer term.

Because the retailer has latitude within this framework to set the exact price paid by consumers, the opportunity to develop totally different styles and conceptions of consumer service is offered to the individual retailer. The net effect created by this freedom over the whole range of consumer

Exhibit 13–2
Specimen Data: Package Sizes Marketed by Leading Brands of Proprietary Analgesics, January 1, 1955, 1965, and 1970

BRAND	JANUARY 1, 1955	JANUARY 1, 1965	JANUARY 1, 1970
Pain-out Compound			
12-pill	x	x	x
30- "	x	x	x
90- "	x	x	x
150- "		x	x
Buffer King with Caffeine			
12-pill	x	x	x
24- "		x	x
50- "	x	x	x
100- "	x	x	x
300- "			x
6-oz. liquid		x	x
Purity First Aspirin			
12-pill	x	x	x
36- "	x	x	x
75- "		x	x
120- "	x	x	x
300- "		x	x
500- "			x

packaged goods—both food and drug—is that a wide variety of retailing patterns can emerge, ranging from the retailer who offers full marketing services (credit, delivery, clerk service, automobile parking space, air-conditioning, attractive store decor, store amenities, and so on) to the limited-service, aggressive, mass-merchandising price-discounter.

Each of the proprietary analgesic manufacturers establishes, as a matter of policy, a consumer list price for each package size in its line. The practical effect of this established consumer list price is to set a maximum retail price that is rarely exceeded by any of the retail outlets, no matter how extensive their consumer service or affluent their clientele. (Pain-out and Buffer King preprint this established retail price on the individual consumer packages, and Purity First does not.) Meantime, this established consumer list price constitutes the departure point for price discounting and all the non-list-price retailers compete with each other on a price basis beneath this established retail list price ceiling. The effect and extent of such discounting is suggested in Exhibits 13–3, 13–4, and 13–5, which contrast the weighted average price per pill on an established retail list price and on the actual price paid by the consumer for the three leading advertised brands.

EXHIBIT 13–3
Specimen Data: Weighted Average Prices for Pain-out Analgesic Compound, 1970–74

TWELVE MONTHS ENDING DECEMBER 31	ESTABLISHED RETAIL LIST PRICE PER PILL		CONSUMER PRICE PAID PER PILL	
	CENTS PER PILL	INDEX	CENTS PER PILL	INDEX
1970	0.7672	100	0.6142	100
1971	0.7548	98	0.6098	99
1972	0.7842	102	0.6139	100
1973	0.7963	104	0.6244	102
1974	0.8527	111	0.6642	108

S O U R C E :   Modeled on the reports of the A. C. Nielsen Company.

EXHIBIT 13–4
Specimen Data: Weighted Average Prices for Buffer King with Caffeine, 1970–74

TWELVE MONTHS ENDING DECEMBER 31	ESTABLISHED RETAIL LIST PRICE PER PILL		CONSUMER PRICE PAID PER PILL	
	CENTS PER PILL	INDEX	CENTS PER PILL	INDEX
1970	1.0095	100	0.9324	100
1971	1.0301	102	0.9466	102
1972	1.0421	103	0.9672	104
1973	1.0962	109	1.0177	109
1974	1.1544	114	1.0842	116

S O U R C E :   Modeled on the reports of the A. C. Nielsen Company.

EXHIBIT 13–5
Specimen Data: Weighted Average Price for Purity First Aspirin, 1970–74

TWELVE MONTHS ENDING DECEMBER 31	ESTABLISHED RETAIL LIST PRICE PER PILL		CONSUMER PRICE PAID PER PILL	
	CENTS PER PILL	INDEX	CENTS PER PILL	INDEX
1970	0.6496	100	0.6124	100
1971	0.6694	103	0.6138	100
1972	0.6985	107	0.6244	102
1973	0.7342	113	0.6782	111
1974	0.7560	116	0.6991	114

S O U R C E :   Modeled on the reports of the A. C. Nielsen Company.

Beneath the de facto price ceiling, the proprietary analgesic manufacturers contribute to periodic price fluctuations in actual retail price by their periodic trade pricing promotions, which offer trade discounts below normal margins if certain conditions are met. Descriptions of three common types of such trade promotions follow:

1. *Promotional discounts are frequently granted for a minimum purchase.* A short-term commitment to purchase one or more promotional deal "packs" constitutes a popular form of the minimum-purchase commitment. In addition promotional discounts are frequently offered to retailers who will contract to purchase a minimum quantity of one or more of the manufacturer's brands over a longer specifed period, such as a year or 18 months.

2. *A second kind of promotional discount is called dating.* This practice permits the retailer to order specified merchandise now against a billing date 30, 60, or 90 days in the future. In essence, dating offers the retailer a limited amount of interest-free working capital because it assumes that a significant fraction of the merchandise purchased under dating will move through the retail outlet before the invoices covering the merchandise become due.

3. *Superimposed upon periodic promotional discounts of the deal-pack and dating type are occasional changes in the established consumer list price.* The effect of an increase in consumer list price is twofold. First, such increases always involve an increase to the manufacturer in the revenue derived by him from the trade. Second, they almost always are used as a short-term price promotion because the trade is inevitably permitted to buy at the old price for a period of time or for a specified number of orders after the new higher price to the trade (and new consumer list price) has been announced.

All these promotional devices tend to increase trade inventories. Such dealer "loading" creates its own pressure to move merchandise off the retail shelves, and this pressure in turn frequently builds short-term retail price cuts, which tend to absorb some or all of the increased margin inherent in the trade promotion offer. In some cases retailers may even lower their prices to levels that cut into their normal profits to flush out the increased inventory. The net effect of such promotion is greater manufacturer volume at lower than normal revenue per unit and a correspondingly higher retail volume at profit levels that may be either above or below normal depending upon the retailer's pricing response to the promotion.

Beyond his pricing response to short-term promotions, which load his inventory, the retailer must also reformulate his retail pricing structure when a long-term increase in the price he pays for a product (and in the established consumer list price) takes effect. He is faced with the alternatives of passing along some, none, or all of the price increase to his customers. Thus, for example, when the Buffer King established consumer price on the fifty-pill size was increased from 49¢ to 57¢ in mid 1971 (see Exhibit 13–8), the basic trade price was increased coincidentally from $3.96 per dozen to $4.65 per dozen. The question posed for the retailer is how much of this price increase should be passed along to the ultimate consumer. To cover the increase in his cost, the retailer would pass along at least 4¢ per unit. To maintain his profit percentage he would have to pass along somewhat more than 4¢ to the consumer. He also has the alternative of increasing his retail price by a full 8¢ per unit, regardless of whether or not his basic selling price had, in the past, been the full 49¢.

As Exhibits 13–3, 13–4, and 13–5 indicate, there is usually a lag between the imposition of a new higher price and an increase in the actual price paid by consumers. But the consumer price does tend to move up in due course. In addition, there may be an increase in the consumer purchase of larger package sizes at a lower price per unit in a market that is characterized by increasing prices.

From the manufacturer's point of view, the determination of individual prices is a complex problem with a far from predictable outcome. When a manufacturer increases his price the following may occur:

1. In the short term a price increase will stimulate dealer loading at the previous price level if advance notice of the price increase is given. In the long term, dealer purchases will depend upon consumer response to the pricing situation at the retail level as it develops.

2. Over the long term, a price increase may have one of several effects on the consumer. If the retailer passes the price increase along to the consumer in whole or in part, the consumer may buy no less than previously, buy larger sizes at a lower price per unit, or buy less of the product. If the retailer does *not* pass the price increase along to the consumer, the consumer may buy the same amount as previously. In addition, if there is a long-term trend toward the purchase of larger package sizes at lower per-unit cost, the average consumer may buy in larger package sizes in spite of the fact that the price increase has not been passed along to him.

To the manufacturer, a price increase offers several potential outcomes. First of all, his revenue will increase if the price increase does not have the effect of reducing demand, and this increase will lead to extra revenue. If the price increase has the effect of accelerating the shift to consumer purchases of larger sizes, his overall revenue will increase, at least in the short term, but his revenue per pill will decrease. Whether the revenue per pill decreases below the average revenue per pill prior to the price increase will depend upon the interrelation between the changes in price by package size and the new volume levels for each package size. To the extent that a higher price tends to increase the amount per unit available to the manufacturer for promotional activities, a price increase tends to give the manufacturer greater potential flexibility in short-term promotional policy because, *if volume is maintained,* he will generate a larger promotional fund. Thus if volume is maintained after a price increase there will be more to spend on advertising, and/or his trade deals can be more frequent or more attractive. The important point about potentially increased promotion and advertising funds is that their theoretical existence after the price increase often provides a justification for deciding to make the price increase because increased advertising and promotion will provide the impetus for maintaining volume. This reasoning may be recognized as specious if carried to its extreme, but it may nevertheless become an important argument in favor of relatively small sporadic price increases.

Against these potential advantages, the manufacturer must weigh the fact that he cannot control the final average retail price charged to the consumer and that he cannot predict what the effect of this final average retail price will be on consumer volume.

One final issue often faces the manufacturer. It is unusual for every package size in a manufacturer's line to generate the same profit per unit as every other package size. Variations in price per pill tend to reflect the higher unit cost of small sizes but they may not make up all of the difference, which may be reflected in lower profit per unit on smaller sizes. Similarly, competitive price pressure on a particular size may force down profit margins. Thus, in determining his pricing policy, the manufacturer will be concerned with the overall effect on profits that may result from shifts in package-size sales mix due to changes in the pricing structure. Exhibit 13–6 shows the variations in profitability by package size for Pain-out as of January 1, 1974.

EXHIBIT 13–6
Specimen Data:
Profitability* by Pack-
age Size for Pain-out
Analgesic Compound—
January 1, 1974

PACKAGE SIZE	PER CENT
12-pill	26
30-pill	27
90-pill	24
150-pill	32

* Gross profit after allowance for advertising and promotion selling, research, and administrative expense.
SOURCE: Allgood Drug Company Accounting Department analyses.

The determination of price policy is thus difficult and tricky. The manufacturer has difficulty predicting what exact effect a price increase will have because of the cross-pressures that work upon the consumer, the retailer, and himself whenever a price increase is announced. The net effect is that a uniform conservative pricing pattern has emerged in the proprietary analgesic market. Under this pattern all firms make relatively small price increases across individual package sizes every two or three years. These increases are generally below 10 per cent (except on the smallest sizes), and price increases larger than 15 per cent are virtually unheard of. Exhibits 13–7, 13–8, and 13–9 trace the pricing histories on individual sizes of Pain-out, Buffer King, and Purity First over the period 1970–74. Exhibits 13–10, 13–11, and 13–12 show the tablet and dollar business held by each package size of Pain-out, Buffer King, and Purity First respectively for the year 1970 and for the year 1974.

Ronald Dutschman, director of marketing for Allgood Drug Company, turned his attention to pricing early in 1974. Dutschman had little taste for pricing decisions. His experience taught him that such decisions involved the emotions and professional predispositions of a broad range of company officials. Because the subject was so complex and subtle and because the results of pricing decisions were so hard to predict, the subject had become a management football at Allgood. Everyone but the night elevator man seemed to have an opinion and no reluctance to discuss it forcefully and at length. From time to time the Allgood operations

EXHIBIT 13–7
**Five-Year Pricing History for Pain-out Analgesic Compound—
Established Consumer Price As of January 1, 1970–1974.**

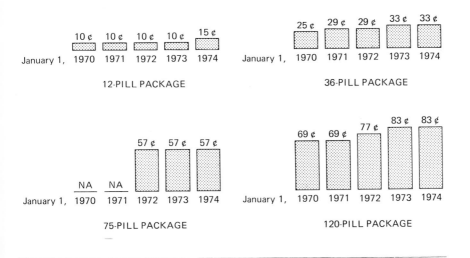

EXHIBIT 13–8
Five-Year Pricing History for Buffer King with Caffeine—
Established Consumer Price As of January 1, 1970–1974

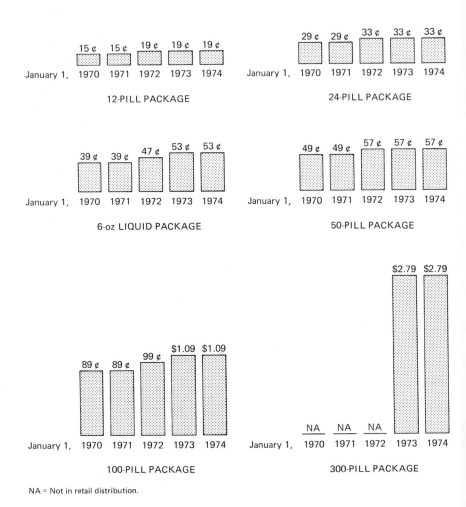

NA = Not in retail distribution.

EXHIBIT 13–9
Five-Year Pricing History for Purity First Aspirin—
Established Consumer Price As of January 1, 1970–1974.

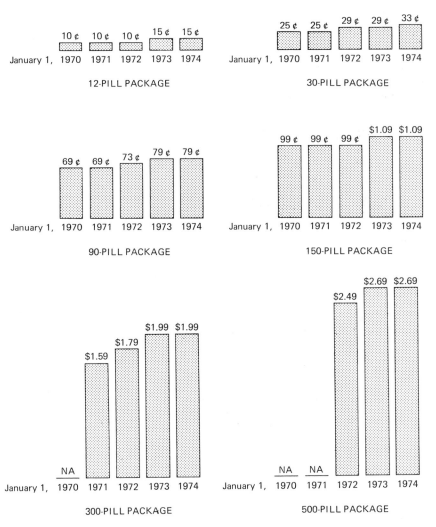

12-PILL PACKAGE

30-PILL PACKAGE

90-PILL PACKAGE

150-PILL PACKAGE

300-PILL PACKAGE

500-PILL PACKAGE

NA = Not in retail distribution

EXHIBIT 13–10
Specimen Data: Consumer Volume Contributed by Various Package Sizes of Pain-out Analgesic Compound—1970 and 1974

	YEAR ENDING DECEMBER 31, 1970		YEAR ENDING DECEMBER 31, 1974	
PACKAGE SIZE	CONSUMER DOLLARS	PILLS	CONSUMER DOLLARS	PILLS
12-pill	3%	3%	2%	1%
30-pill	12	11	8	6
90-pill	78	78	65	63
150-pill	7	8	25	30

s o u r c e :   Modeled on the reports of the A. C. Nielsen Company.

EXHIBIT 13–11
Specimen Data: Consumer Volume Contributed by Various Package Sizes of Buffer King with Caffeine—1970 and 1974

	YEAR ENDING DECEMBER 31, 1970		YEAR ENDING DECEMBER 31, 1974	
PACKAGE SIZE	CONSUMER DOLLARS	PILLS	CONSUMER DOLLARS	PILLS
12-pill	1%	1%	1%	1%
24-pill	4	3	3	3
50-pill	46	47	40	41
100-pill	39	44	37	38
300-pill	Not available		11	14
6 oz. liquid (18-pill equivalent)	10	5	8	3

s o u r c e :   Modeled on the reports of the A. C. Nielsen Company.

EXHIBIT 13–12
Specimen Data: Consumer Volume Contributed by Various Package Sizes of Purity First Aspirin—1970 and 1974

	YEAR ENDING DECEMBER 31, 1970		YEAR ENDING DECEMBER 31, 1974	
PACKAGE SIZE	CONSUMER DOLLARS	PILLS	CONSUMER DOLLARS	PILLS
12-pill	12%	7%	3%	2%
36-pill	45	43	27	24
75-pill	Not available		22	22
120-pill	43	50	38	40
300-pill	Not available		6	7
500-pill	Not available		4	5

s o u r c e :   Modeled on the reports of the A. C. Nielsen Company.

research group had been asked to analyze pricing in various markets in which the company marketed products. These requests inevitably involved the hope that the operations research people would be able to develop a model of expected market response to alternative pricing strategies. But, so far, the operations research people were frank to admit that they had simply had no luck at all. They continued to devote time and energy to the problem, but the market responses that they found formed no pattern, and they held out little hope for any quick breakthroughs.

So although he felt obliged to study the subject of Pain-out pricing, Dutschman dreaded it. He admitted that in the end the policy would be determined on the basis of management consensus and in difficult compromise and that no available analytic procedure could do much to provide any alternative means of reaching decisions in this area.

Dutschman knew that his advertising manager, Harvey Hendon Hill, and his sales director, E. G. "Slats" Appleyard, held violently different attitudes about pricing policy. Because Hill believed that the Pain-out franchise ultimately existed only in the minds of consumers, he believed that no amount of promotion at the trade level could to much to help sales, and he tended to lump all price manipulations into the general category of trade promotion. Although he recognized that increased prices would ultimately mean larger advertising budgets, his experience indicated that the resulting advertising-budget increases rarely amounted to much in spite of the anticipations of increased revenue advanced when price increases were discussed.

Appleyard, on the other hand, believed that the only way to move merchandise was to offer concessions to the trade. The more flexibility he was allowed in pricing, the more merchandise Appleyard believed he and his salesmen would move. Slats Appleyard was no philosopher. He dropped out of high school after his sophomore year, knocked around as an itinerant fruit picker for seven years during the Depression, and joined the Allgood sales force in 1946 after four years in the infantry, where he rose from a private to a field-commissioned second lieutenant and was discharged as a captain. Appleyard was a diamond in the rough, a vigorous salesman who took things as they came, living his business life from day to day without much regard for the future. To him, any price increase offered an opportunity for an immediate increase in sales as the trade added to inventories before the price change became effective. He could never recall any sluggishness or decline in consumer sales after a price increase, and he believed that so many other trade and competitive factors were involved in the ultimate consumer movement of Pain-out that he should be permitted whatever flexibility in the pricing area he felt he needed to keep the pressure on the trade. And if in the final analysis it became clear that the pricing policy had been too aggressive, he preferred to worry about that when it happened.

Dutschman decided to ask each of these men to write a memorandum to him suggesting a pricing strategy for Pain-out Analgesic Compound for 1975 and 1976. Here are these memoranda.

ALLGOOD MEMORANDUM

TO: Ronald Dutschman   2/3/75
FROM: E. G. Appleyard

I have your request of 1/22/75 for a statement of my feelings about Pain-out pricing. As you know, I have some pretty violent feelings on the subject. I think we should increase price at least as frequently as our competition and that our prices should be closer to Buffer King than to Purity First. I have no quarrel with our recent policy of moving prices up from time to time, with about the same frequency as our competition. My major objection is that we are so far below Buffer King. We're a compound, aren't we? Tell me why we shouldn't have the same general pricing level as Buffer King?

So my recommendation would be to make the following price increases immediately: 12-pill to 19¢; 30-pill to 39¢; 90-pill to 99¢; and 150-pill to $1.39. I'm sure we wouldn't want to make all these moves at exactly the same time. Spread them out over a year—but give them to me and I'll make your head spin at the amount of merchandise we move.

You may say that such a program will overload the trade. But all of our major accounts could be counted on to cooperate. I guarantee it! They will see the wisdom of getting our pricing up to the level of the other compound. They will understand that Pain-out deserves equality with Buffer King. They will absorb enough merchandise at the protected price before invoice increases to guarantee a gradual price increase to the consumer. We'll work with our major accounts to guarantee a smooth transition at the consumer level and a fat profit on the goods they take on before the price goes up.

Another thing is that it's a scandal that we don't have a longer line on Pain-out. Everytime I make a retail call, I get sick. There we are with four shelf sizes with Pain-out, and Buffer King and Purity First have six—50 per cent more. There's been a lot of talk here that we'll get as many shelf facings with our four sizes as the others get with their six, but that is just not so. We don't get as many facings, even in stores where we sell more. We need a bigger size—perhaps a 300—and it should be better still if we had two new sizes—a 300 and a 450 or 500. Don't worry about distribution—we'll get a big size into the stores and we'll get it in in quantities that will make your mouth water.

We joke about my beliefs about some things we should do to make this business go, but I'm deadly serious about the price increases and the extra sizes. We win or lose in the stores and I need more ammunition than I'm getting now to keep the trade happy and move that old merchandise.

ALLGOOD MEMORANDUM

TO: Ronald Dutschman   2/3/75
FROM: Harvey Hendon Hill

You asked for a thoughtful memorandum on the general subject of price increases for Pain-out.

I am opposed to any important change in our creeping price increase policy. We try to move our prices along at about the same rate as the rest of the market and I believe this to be prudent from a marketing standpoint. Let me enumerate my reasons for believing this to be so.

No one really knows much about the demand elasticity of proprietary analgesic products. Even if we could predict the exact effect on consumer price caused by an increase in price to the trade, there is no theory available to tell us what the ultimate consumer response to the final price might be. Nor do we really have adequate market data to assess the impact of price increases on consumer movements. We content ourselves with competitive reports on the *dollar* movement of our own product and those of our two principle competitors. But we know little about the dollar volume of individual other brands, including those with lower prices, and we know nothing about their unit volume. My own analysis reveals that the per-capita consumption of Pain-out pills is declining as our dollar sales volume per capita increases (see attached table [Exhibit 13–13]). Some may attribute this to greater competitive product differentiation, to less self-medication, or to other factors. I tend to attribute it to a negative consumer response to our price increases; I believe that consumers buy fewer pills when we raise price and that price increases inhibit the development of our brand. Our reliance on dollar sales figures obscures this. Thus I would submit that if we had had no price increases at all, although we would have had a lower level of revenue and profit, our tablet per-capita volume would not have declined.

EXHIBIT 13–13
Specimen Data: Trend in Adult Per-Capita* Consumption of Pain-out Analgesic Compound

YEAR	PILLS PER CAPITA
1970	100
1971	99
1972	99
1973	98
1974	97

* 100 equals pills per capita in 1970.

You will correctly point out that the long-term inflationary trend forces us to have some increases in price if we are to stay even from a cost/profit standpoint. I agree with this, but we should be careful not to lose volume to the price brands in the process.

Every time we have a price increase, we anticipate extra revenue, and I am promised extra advertising dollars. It is then assumed that we will be able through advertising, in concert with trade inventory pressure generated by the price increase, to raise ourselves up by our own bootstraps. I have always regarded this as wishful thinking, but that is neither here nor there. What is important is that I rarely see any extra advertising dollars; they always seem to be dissipated in gimmick promotions to the trade to work off the inventories absorbed by the trade as a result of the buying induced by the price increases.

What this all deteriorates into is a complicated shell game played between us and the trade. We push them as far as we can with various promotions and pricing gimmicks in the hope that we will reap a volume advantage in the process. But we ignore the consumer in the meantime. He stands innocently on the sidelines unaware of our machinations and those of our "friends" in the trade, trying to decide which proprietary analgesic to buy.

We depend ultimately upon what the consumer thinks of us. This is our only asset in a competitive market where most advertised products undoubtedly deliver perceptually equivalent relief. In this situation I fear a price increase unless it is made in tandem with our major competition. If we proceed alone and if we increase our prices significantly and without regard to the market, we may, on the one hand, lose significant numbers of customers to Purity First because it will be distinctly lower in price yet have an excellent consumer reputation. On the other hand, we may also lose significant numbers of customers to Buffer King, because we are no longer at a price advantage relative to that brand. In either event the price increase may upset the competitive edge in the minds of consumers that our advertising effort has given to us.

You know well enough that I hold no particular brief for the status quo in most circumstances, but I believe that in this instance we should proceed slowly and with great caution.

Specifically, I recommend no price increase on the 30-pill package in 1975–76,

EXHIBIT 13–14

Specimen Data: Total Market Proprietary Analgesic Market Shares of Pain-out, Buffer King, and Purity First, Consumer Dollar Basis and Pill Basis 1970–74

	1970 MARKET SHARES	
	CONSUMER DOLLAR BASIS	PILL BASIS
Pain-out	26%	28%
Buffer King	30	20
Purity First	31	33
All others	13	19

	1974 MARKET SHARES	
	CONSUMER DOLLAR BASIS	PILL BASIS
Pain-out	27%	30%
Buffer King	30	21
Purity First	34	36
All others	9	13

SOURCE: Modeled on the reports of the A. C. Nielsen Company.

and no price increase on the other sizes unless and until competition moves upward on its comparable sizes.

Questions for Case 13

1. Why does the text say "the proprietary analgesic manufacturer has relatively little control over the exact price charged by the retailer" (page 299)? How can a manufacturer lose control over the prices that his consumers pay? To what extent does the pricing of competitors restrain the manufacturer? The retailer? What kinds of leeway does the retailer have in setting prices? Is this leeway desirable from the manufacturer's standpoint?

2. Comment on Dutschman's concern because Pain-out price policy was more likely to be established by executive consensus than by rational analyses. Do you believe that this is the case in most corporations? What other marketing decisions do you suspect might be made in the same way?

3. In this case there appears to be little uniformity in either the absolute or the relative size of the price increases made within a particular line of products. Comment on this. Do you think it might be better to have prices increased by relatively the same amount on all sizes when price increases are made? Why or why not?

4. What issues would affect the timing of a price increase? Would it be better to institute a price increase on some package sizes in a brand line, or should a manufacturer increase prices on all items in the line at once?

5. There seems to be something of a paradox in Appleyard's feeling that a price increase will lead to an immediate sales increase: "Give them [i.e., consumer established price increases of 4¢ on the 12-pill size; 6¢ on the 30-pill size; 20¢ on the 90-pill size; and 30¢ on the 150-pill size] to me and I'll make your head spin at the amount of merchandise we move" (page 310). Common sense would seem to indicate that unit sales of a product should decline as the price increases. This is also the usual assumption of the classical economists. Comment.

6. What is the marketing significance of increasing the number of items in the Pain-out line from four to six as Appleyard suggests (page 310)?

7. Discuss the relative importance of trade relations and consumer reputation for a brand like Pain-out. Which of these objects of marketing effort should receive more attention? What considerations should guide the allocation of marketing money between trade promotional and consumer advertising expenditures?

8. What price increases would you recommend for Pain-out Analgesic Compound in 1975 and 1976? In your answer be sure to consider the viewpoints expressed by Appleyard and Hill. Is either one totally right in your view?

9. Why is there a lag between the imposition of a new higher price by the manufacturer and a corresponding increase to consumers? What likelihood is there that a manufacturer might be able to reduce this time lag or eliminate it?

CASE 14

Achieving and Evaluating Physical Distribution

The Annual Review of Handsome Boy Cleanser Distribution

Hᴏᴍᴇ Pʀᴏᴅᴜᴄᴛꜱ Uɴɪᴠᴇʀꜱᴀʟ manufactures a complete line of household detergents and cleaning products. Cases 1, 6, and 11 have described marketing situations involving three of these products: Handsome Boy Dry Bleach, Window Brite, and Handsome Boy Cleanser. This case is concerned with the evaluation of the relation of consumer sales to product distribution.

It is an established HPU policy to conduct an annual review of achieved distribution for each of its individual brands. The purpose of this annual review is to make sure that long-term trends in brand distribution patterns are isolated, analyzed, and understood at the brand management level.

HPU management makes a basic distinction between the purpose of these annual reviews and the day-to-day activities of marketing and sales personnel designed to improve the distribution picture for individual brands. The day-to-day activities are always aimed either at increasing the distribution of the individual brands or at improving the efficiency with which these brands are distributed. Thus brand managers will be involved with projects and activities designed to increase the total number of stores in which specific HPU brands are available to consumers or the total number of stores in which particular package sizes or types of these HPU brands are available to consumers. And they may also be attempting to withdraw specific brands or particular package sizes or types from particular kinds of distribution outlets or channels that have been identified as inefficient to maintain.

All these activities can be carried on in an operational way with little reference to long-term distribution trends, if any, that are developing in the marketplace. But HPU management is firmly committed to the notion that day-to-day operational practices must be based on policies developed with deep knowledge of the overall market situation. And they believe that the market manager can become so totally immersed in his day-to-day operations that he is likely to ignore or misinterpret these broad trends unless a conscious effort to analyze and interpret them is built into the company procedures. For these reasons HPU conducts an annual review of achieved distribution for each of its individual brands.

The basic data source for this review is the reports of the Nielsen Food Index, whose data are developed from the store audit method. The store audit generates data from observation and secondary data analysis in a panel of retail stores. It has two fundamental objectives: (1) to determine the quantity and quality of sales to consumers out of retail stores; and (2) to describe the conditions within the retail stores that contribute to or impede sales to consumers.

The store audit reports actual sales to consumers in units (or pounds, gallons, ounces, and so on) and in dollars. These reports are made both in total and in accordance with analytic breakdowns such as package size and type, package promotions, geographic area, county size, store size, outlet type, and so on. These reports include both the manufacturer's own brands and his competitor's brands. The data on sales are customarily reported both in absolute terms (dollars, cases, ounces, pounds, quarts, or whatever) and in relative or market share terms on the base of absolute dollars or units. Item or brand distribution (physical availability in the retail outlet) is reported for all brands included in a product group. This product distribution may be reported either for the brand line as a whole or for individual constituents of the line. In the latter instance, individual brand line constituents might include individual package sizes or types, or individual promotional packs. And product distribution may also be reported for the same analytic breakdowns as consumer sales—geographic area, county size, store size, outlet type, and so on.

In addition to product distribution, other in-store observations are made relative to the presence or absence of display materials, special display areas, actual shelf selling prices, and the like. Again, these observations can be reported, where appropriate, by package size and type, by promotional packs, by geographic areas, by county size, by store size, and by outlet type.

In general, data on product distribution may be reported on one of two bases: in terms of the proportion of outlets stocking or in terms of the proportion of total sales volume represented by the outlets stocking. When product availability is reported in terms of the proportion of outlets stocking (or on a "store count" basis), each outlet counts as one, regardless of what sales volume potential is represented. Thus on a store count basis the largest food supermarket and the most modest "mom and pop" store receive equal weight in the computation of product availability.

When product distribution is computed in terms of sales volume of the stores stocking, each outlet is weighted according to its sales volume. Many sales volume alternatives are theoretically available to the marketer for such weighting purposes. For grocery stores, for example, he may prefer that each store be weighted by the total volume of the store; by its packaged grocery volume (excluding fruits, vegetables, meats, and sundries); by its dry packaged grocery volume; by its food volume; by its nonfood volume; by individual product category volume; by product class volume; or by some other factor. In fact, the most common weighting base is total store sales volume. The Nielsen Company uses such a weighting base and calls it "all commodity volume." The use of all commodity volume has the virtue of providing a common weighting base across all product categories; thus the marketer who is interested in diverse product categories is assured that a common weighting base has been used in computing achieved product distribution from category to category.

The individual subscriber to a store audit service such as the Nielsen Food Index has considerable flexibility in determining the exact data that he will purchase. Of course, the basic measurements are inflexible; the actual determination of consumer sales, product availability, and so on in individual stores is made according to predetermined specifications and standards of the research supplier. And the research supplier frequently specifies the reporting period for which the data are available. The Nielsen Company's Food Index, for example, reports on a bimonthly basis and this is the standard reporting period offered.

But there is complete flexibility for the manufacturer in determining the competitive brands that will be reported; the competitive brands that make up the total market for a product class; the specific geographic areas by which the sales, product availability, and so on will be reported; and the detail in which individual measurements will be reported and cross-tabulated.

Thus in buying a store audit service, the manufacturer's management needs professional guidance from his marketing and marketing research personnel in specifying the kind and detail of information that is needed to guide marketing decisions above the minimum data package offered for sale by the research supplier.

The package purchased by Home Products Universal is reflected by the data in Exhibits 14–1 through 14–10. It represents a typical selection of information of the type provided by the Nielsen Company.

A Description of the Store Audit Measurement Procedure

The basic store audit procedure used to estimate consumer sales is quite straightforward. For sales to be estimated, it is necessary to make audits for two separate points in time. These separate points in time bound the period for which sales are to be estimated. At the beginning of the sales measurement period, the researcher counts the total number of brand units within a defined product class that are physically available in a store. By "physically available" is meant both merchandise on the shelf and merchandise available for sale to consumers, as well as merchandise in inventory within the store itself but not actually on the shelf available for sale to a consumer. This count of available merchandise establishes a base measurement against which to estimate sales to consumers.

At the end of the sales measurement period, a second store visit is made in which two separate kinds of determinations are made. First, another complete inventory count is taken of brand units within the defined product class. Second, a record of the merchandise received or purchased by the store, within the defined product class, is completed.

Total unit sales to consumer in the defined product class for the sales measurement period are then defined as merchandise units physically available at the beginning of the sales measurement period, plus units of merchandise in the product class received by the store during the measurement period less merchandise units physically available in the store at the end of the measurement periods. (In the case of Nielsen audits, the measurement period covered is usually bimonthly.) In addition, it is customary to subtract estimates or actual counts of units lost through spoilage or breakage (and in some cases pilferage) during the sales measurement period in order to reflect most accurately the merchandise actually sold to consumers.

The computational formula is as follows:

$$
\begin{array}{l}
\text{Sales for} \\
\text{a product} \\
\text{class in} \\
\text{measurement} \\
\text{period A}
\end{array}
=
\begin{array}{l}
\text{Product units} \\
\text{available in} \\
\text{store inventory} \\
\text{at beginning of} \\
\text{period A}
\end{array}
+
\begin{array}{l}
\text{Product units} \\
\text{received} \\
\text{during} \\
\text{period A}
\end{array}
$$

$$
-
\begin{array}{l}
\text{Product units} \\
\text{available in} \\
\text{store inventory} \\
\text{at the end of} \\
\text{period A}
\end{array}
-
\begin{array}{l}
\text{Units spoiled} \\
\text{broken (or} \\
\text{pilfered) during} \\
\text{period A}
\end{array}
$$

Note that this basic formula can be used not only to determine unit sales for a particular product class but also to determine unit sales for each individual brand within a product class. It may also be used to determine unit sales for individual package sizes or promotional packs within an individual brand. The formula, as it is presented, is used for determining unit sales. In order to convert unit sales into dollar sales, it is necessary to multiply unit sales in each different price category within each brand by its store shelf selling price and add the results within brands to compute brand dollar sales and across brands to compute product class dollar sales.

Product availability or "distribution" measurements are derived directly from the store audit itself. That is, to compute sales, it is necessary to ascertain the presence or absence in the store of each item being audited. Consumer prices are recorded in the store, as is the presence or absence of displays.

The store audit method can be used in the estimating of consumer sales for the nation as a whole, as well as in individual regions, states, counties, standard metropolitan statistical areas, or whatever. The accuracy and precision of consumer sales estimates will depend directly upon the nature and size of the probability sample of stores within which the store audit method is applied and the accuracy of the audit itself. (Stratified probability sampling is frequently used in store audit work with strata being established for individual outlet types. Outlet types are used as a basis for stratification because of the wide variation in unit volume that is associated with individual outlet types.)

When less accuracy is required and the major emphasis is upon the competitive impact of a change in marketing strategy, the sample of audit stores is sometimes limited to a panel of large-volume supermarkets. When this nonprobability sampling simplification is followed, the assumption is made that the marketing strategy change can be evaluated on the basis of brand share changes in the panel stores and without precise projections of total consumer sales in the test-marketing area. (Such service is not offered by the Nielsen Company but is available from other research suppliers.)

General Definitions of the Common Store Audit Terms

CONSUMER SALES IN UNITS OR DOLLARS

Total sales to consumers for a given product class or brand or brand type (package size, promotional pack, price class, and so on) in a stated reporting period and in a stated geographic area. Total sales are projectable to the stated geographic area when a probability sample of outlets is used. When a probability sample is not used, sales projections to a geographic area cannot be made; the total sales measured in a group of stores represent only these stores.

SHARE OF CONSUMER SALES

The proportion of unit or dollar sales held by a particular brand or brand type in a stated geographic area during a stated period of time. Shares are based upon reported unit or dollar sales. Shares are projectable to a total geographic area when they are based upon data derived from a probability sample. When shares are based upon data derived from a non-probability sample of stores, they refer only to the stores in which measurements have been made.

STORE INVENTORY IN UNITS OR DOLLARS

The total inventory on hand in retail outlets on the date of audit. The inventory includes stock in place on shelves available to customers and reserve stock, that is, stock in storage within the store but not available to customers. Inventory figures may be expressed either in units or in terms of the total dollar value at consumer prices.

AVERAGE MONTHLY SALES PER STORE HANDLING IN UNITS OR DOLLARS

Monthly sales of each item in the average store in units or dollars. When total sales are reported for a two-month period, as in the case of A. C. Nielsen data, the average sales per store are divided by two to produce an average monthly sales figure.

MONTH'S SUPPLY

The relation between the inventory on hand in the average store handling and the monthly sales in the average store handling. In this computation, the inventory on hand is divided by monthly sales to derive an estimate of the supply on hand in terms of average store sales per month.

AVERAGE CONSUMER PRICE

The composite price charged on the date of audit, weighted by the actual item volume at each of the observed store-shelf prices. The average consumer price will reflect variations in the shelf price during the time period. If a probability sample of stores has been selected and if a probability selection of observation times within stores is realized, the average consumer price will be projectable to the market area represented by the audit stores.

MAXIMUM DISTRIBUTION

The percentage of stores, each weighted by its individual commodity volume, handling a particular item at any time during the audit period. Maximum distribution includes individual stores that do not have the item in stock and available to customers on the actual audit date, yet carry or have carried the item at some time during the audit period.

OUT-OF-STOCK

The proportion of stores, each weighted by its individual commodity volume, that handled the item at any time during the audit period but do not have it available for customer sale on the date of the audit. In some cases this may represent out-of-stock for any one of several reasons reflecting inadequate inventory or inventory control. In other instances, an item may have been discontinued by the store's management during the audit period. In the case of such discontinuance, the store is shown as included in maximum distribution during the period (because the item was carried during the audit period), and the item is shown as out-of-stock on the audit date if this is indeed the case. In the next audit period, if the item's discontinued status has not changed, the stores previously handling it would not be included in maximum distribution, nor would these stores be counted as out-of-stock.

NET EFFECTIVE DISTRIBUTION

Maximum distribution less out-of-stock yields "net effective distribution" as of the audit date. In this computation it is assumed that the commodity volume of individual stores has been used as a weight in determining *both* maximum distribution and out-of-stock.

STORE DISPLAYS

The proportion of stores, each weighted by its individual commodity volume, in which a brand display was observed by the field auditors. If a probability sample of stores in the marketing area has been achieved, then the reported store display percentages reflect display exposure for the entire marketing area.

AUDIT PERIOD

The "audit period" is the elapsed time since the previous audit. In this usage it is implied that post facto audit measurements of elapsed events are made regularly but not continuously. In the measurement of consumer sales, for example, after an initial audit is made, the second audit plus the merchandise-received records will give a basis for estimating total sales during the intervening period, regardless of how long the period has lasted.

The projectability of all audit results assumes a random distribution of store audit visits in time, if all the auditing is not done on a single day, and a constant interval between audits in each store. Such randomness and control are achieved in the scheduling of the work of the field audit force.

Exhibits 14–1 through 14–10 show a basic set of sales and distribution data for Handsome Boy Cleanser. These tables have been prepared according to an agreed-upon format by the HPU marketing research department for use in the annual review of achieved distribution.

EXHIBIT 14-1

Specimen Data:* Consumer Sales of Handsome Boy Cleanser and Leading Competitors, in Home Products Universal Marketing Area—1955–72 ($000)

PRODUCT	1955	1960	1965	1966	1967	1968	1969	1970	1971	1972
Handsome Boy	1,046	1,575	1,521	1,339	1,672	1,702	1,717	1,758	1,794	1,842
Meteor	7,973	8,268	7,690	7,732	7,654	7,982	8,087	8,036	9,480	11,051
Kitchen Cleanser	4,829	4,733	5,433	6,311	7,022	6,544	6,822	7,221	6,224	5,892
Ebony	1,692	1,962	2,113	3,112	2,963	3,211	3,411	3,062	3,117	3,211
All others	1,892	3,147	4,968	3,817	4,761	4,877	4,467	5,035	5,087	4,315
Total market	17,432	19,685	21,725	23,311	24,072	24,316	24,504	25,112	25,702	26,311

* Modeled on the reports of the A. C. Nielsen Company.

EXHIBIT 14-2

Specimen Data:* Consumer Sales of Handsome Boy Cleanser and Leading Competitors, by Home Products Universal Regions—1965, 1971, 1972 ($000)

HPU REGION	1965					1971					1972				
	HB	M	KC	E	AO	HB	M	KC	E	AO	HB	M	KC	E	AO
I	164	1,208	1,011	189	700	292	1,516	1,243	291	796	224	1,960	1,131	294	670
II	338	1,642	1,732	422	695	361	1,986	2,061	635	979	385	2,120	1,972	631	1,324
III	545	1,272	966	606	1,155	547	1,395	1,158	936	939	767	1,845	1,093	975	441
IV	213	2,182	1,321	175	1,430	190	3,255	1,580	310	1,039	195	3,569	1,477	270	966
V	261	1,386	403	721	988	404	1,328	182	945	1,334	271	1,557	219	1,041	914
Total	1,521	7,690	5,433	2,113	4,968	1,794	9,480	6,224	3,117	5,087	1,842	11,051	5,892	3,211	4,315

* Modeled on the reports of the A. C. Nielsen Company.

EXHIBIT 14-3

Specimen Data:* Consumer Sales of Handsome Boy Cleanser and Leading Competitors, by Outlet Type—1965, 1971 and 1972 ($000)

BRAND	TOTAL	CHAIN FOOD STORES	INDEPENDENT SUPER MARKETS	LARGE AND MEDIUM INDEPENDENTS	REMAINING INDEPENDENTS
1965 data					
Handsome Boy	1,521	842	243	267	169
Meteor	7,690	3,832	1,344	1,324	1,190
Kitchen Cleanser	5,433	2,040	1,924	1,466	3
Ebony	2,113	542	481	772	318
All others	4,968	3,584	729	499	156
TOTAL	21,725	10,840	4,721	4,328	1,836
1971 data					
Handsome Boy	1,794	936	275	290	293
Meteor	9,480	4,326	1,572	1,822	1,760
Kitchen Cleanser	6,224	2,244	2,117	1,585	278
Ebony	3,117	633	779	899	806
All others	5,087	3,612	910	462	103
TOTAL	25,702	11,751	5,653	5,058	3,240
1972 data					
Handsome Boy	1,842	1,031	312	300	199
Meteor	11,051	6,522	1,531	1,724	1,274
Kitchen Cleanser	5,892	2,389	1,311	1,672	520
Ebony	3,211	713	724	906	868
All others	4,315	3,043	856	355	61
TOTAL	26,311	13,698	4,734	4,957	2,922

* Modeled on the reports of the A. C. Nielsen Company.

EXHIBIT 14-4
Specimen Data:* Consumer Sales of Handsome Boy Cleanser and Leading Competitors, by County Size—1965, 1971, and 1972 ($000)

BRAND	TOTAL	COUNTY SIZE A	COUNTY SIZE B	COUNTY SIZE C	COUNTY SIZE D
1965 data					
Handsome Boy	1,521	749	426	306	40
Meteor	7,690	2,962	2,182	1,569	977
Kitchen Cleanser	5,433	2,321	1,211	1,011	890
Ebony	2,113	851	468	436	358
All others	4,968	1,856	1,367	1,170	575
TOTAL	21,725	8,739	5,654	4,492	2,840
1971 data					
Handsome Boy	1,794	796	498	347	153
Meteor	9,480	3,788	2,640	1,888	1,164
Kitchen Cleanser	6,224	2,472	1,845	1,266	641
Ebony	3,117	1,272	966	607	272
All others	5,087	2,401	705	979	1,002
TOTAL	25,702	10,729	6,654	5,087	3,232
1972 data					
Handsome Boy	1,842	870	521	366	85
Meteor	11,051	4,796	3,066	2,211	978
Kitchen Cleanser	5,892	2,366	1,692	1,208	626
Ebony	3,211	1,177	968	677	389
All others	4,315	1,269	1,256	304	1,486
TOTAL	26,311	10,478	7,503	4,766	3,564

* Modeled on the reports of the A. C. Nielsen Company.

EXHIBIT 14–5

Specimen Data:* Consumer Sales of Handsome Boy Cleanser and Leading Competitors, by Package Size—1965, 1971 and 1972 ($000)

BRAND	TOTAL	14 OZ.	21 OZ.	SHAKER 6
1965 data				
Handsome Boy	1,521	726	795	—
Meteor	7,690	3,722	3,968	—
Kitchen Cleanser	5,433	3,416	1,880	137
Ebony	2,113	1,258	855	—
All others	4,968	3,995	973	—
TOTAL	21,725	13,117	8,471	137
1971 data				
Handsome Boy	1,794	706	1,088	—
Meteor	9,480	3,512	5,656	312
Kitchen Cleanser	6,224	2,960	3,138	126
Ebony	3,117	1,158	1,959	—
All others	5,087	4,732	355	—
TOTAL	25,702	13,068	12,196	438
1972 data				
Handsome Boy	1,842	652	1,190	—
Meteor	11,051	3,406	7,148	497
Kitchen Cleanser	5,892	2,170	3,494	228
Ebony	3,211	962	2,249	—
All others	4,315	3,981	334	—
TOTAL	26,311	11,171	14,415	725

* Modeled on the reports of the A. C. Nielsen Company.

EXHIBIT 14-6

Specimen Data:* Maximum Distribution and Out-of-Stock for Handsome Boy Cleanser and Leading Competitors, by Package Size in Bimonthly Periods—1965, 1971 and 1972

BRAND	1965						1971						1972					
	J/F	M/A	M/J	J/A	S/O	N/D	J/F	M/A	M/J	J/A	S/O	N/D	J/F	M/A	M/J	J/A	S/O	N/D
Handsome Boy	98_2	99_0	96_1	97_3	99_0	100_1	96_2	97_3	98_2	99_1	97_3	94_2	99_1	98_7	96_0	99_3	100_2	99_4
14 oz.	96_3	95_4	96_3	96_4	98_2	96_4	87_6	84_3	85_6	87_2	84_1	88_3	87_1	83_4	80_7	81_5	82_5	80_4
21 oz.	71_6	73_2	72_6	75_4	72_1	74_2	89_3	88_4	90_1	92_6	93_6	98_1	97_3	98_2	94_1	99_3	98_1	97_5
Meteor	99_2	99_4	100_2	98_6	97_5	99_0	98_3	99_4	97_2	100_2	99_1	96_2	98_3	99_4	99_5	99_0	99_1	98_3
14 oz.	95_2	94_3	92_7	99_6	93_6	94_5	90_1	89_2	87_3	88_5	84_6	87_1	85_4	81_0	82_6	83_1	79_6	85_0
21 oz.	62_4	67_2	66_4	68_1	70_0	72_1	95_1	94_2	96_3	92_0	93_1	93_2	94_2	98_8	94_0	92_6	95_1	94_3
Shaker 6	—	—	—	—	—	—	12_2	14_3	16_2	15_3	20_1	14_2	17_3	15_2	20_1	19_2	17_1	18_6
Kitchen Cleanser	96_2	94_1	93_1	95_2	97_3	92_1	99_1	97_0	96_3	94_1	95_0	99_0	92_1	93_0	94_3	97_1	96_3	99_0
14 oz.	84_2	83_2	84_2	87_1	88_3	82_1	72_6	73_4	75_1	72_4	76_0	77_3	72_1	74_0	75_2	76_3	72_1	74_3
21 oz.	68_1	69_2	73_2	70_4	75_1	73_2	85_2	88_7	90_2	82_1	83_2	90_1	92_1	90_3	91_2	94_3	95_1	91_2
Shaker 6	8_2	12_4	11_1	6_2	6_2	7_4	15_1	17_2	25_0	24_1	23_2	24_1	26_2	27_1	22_3	23_1	22_1	23_0
Ebony	75_1	76_3	70_2	74_3	72_1	70_3	75_2	74_2	73_2	74_6	73_5	72_0	71_1	73_2	74_6	70_0	75_0	73_1
14 oz.	75_1	76_3	70_2	74_3	72_1	70_3	75_3	74_1	72_0	74_5	73_2	71_0	70_2	70_4	73_5	70_0	75_6	72_5
21 oz.	75_2	74_6	70_3	74_3	70_1	70_1	72_4	74_1	73_3	72_6	72_1	72_1	71_1	73_2	72_4	69_1	74_2	72_6

* Modeled on the reports of the A. C. Nielsen Company.

EXHIBIT 14-7

Specimen Data:* Retail Prices and Month's Supply for Handsome Boy Cleanser and Leading Competitors by Package Size in Selected Bimonthly Periods—1965, 1971 and 1972

BRAND	RETAIL PRICES									MONTH'S SUPPLY								
	J/F 65	M/J 65	S/O 65	J/F 71	M/J 71	S/O 71	J/F 72	M/J 72	S/O 72	J/F 65	M/J 65	S/O 65	J/F 71	M/J 71	S/O 71	J/F 72	M/J 72	S/O 72
Handsome Boy	.214	.201	.216	.226	.215	.227	.231	.210	.227	2.1	2.4	2.3	2.0	2.4	2.1	2.1	2.1	2.3
14 oz.	.166	.162	.169	.181	.176	.182	.186	.183	.187	1.0	2.8	2.9	2.9	2.8	2.1	2.2	2.1	2.4
21 oz.	.234	.228	.241	.248	.233	.242	.254	.223	.247	1.5	1.4	1.6	1.7	1.9	1.8	1.7	2.0	1.8
Meteor	.219	.206	.221	.233	.221	.233	.236	.214	.229	1.3	1.4	1.5	1.4	1.8	1.6	1.2	1.8	0.8
14 oz.	.171	.165	.174	.186	.181	.187	.187	.182	.189	2.2	2.3	2.2	2.2	2.3	2.4	1.6	2.1	1.7
21 oz.	.239	.231	.247	.254	.239	.249	.262	.230	.249	0.6	0.7	0.4	1.1	1.5	0.9	1.1	1.2	0.8
Shaker 6	.182	.189	.181	.196	.197	.199	.202	.204	.202	3.1	3.2	3.6	3.4	3.2	3.3	3.1	3.2	3.0
Kitchen Cleanser	.174	.169	.174	.192	.188	.192	.194	.190	.194	1.7	1.8	1.6	1.9	1.8	1.9	1.5	1.9	1.8
14 oz.	.143	.141	.143	.162	.155	.158	.164	.157	.160	2.0	2.0	2.0	2.1	2.0	2.4	1.8	1.0	1.8
21 oz.	.189	.187	.192	.210	.204	.209	.210	.206	.211	0.6	1.4	1.2	1.6	1.7	1.7	1.2	1.0	1.4
Shaker 6	—	—	—	.194	.193	.192	.198	.197	.199	2.4	2.2	2.4	2.3	2.2	2.3	2.9	2.0	2.8
Ebony	.182	.181	.183	.208	.207	.208	.210	.211	.211	2.6	2.4	2.8	2.5	2.6	2.7	2.4	2.2	2.7
14 oz.	.152	.151	.152	.172	.171	.173	.173	.171	.172	1.7	1.9	1.8	1.9	1.9	2.0	1.9	1.6	1.8
21 oz.	.204	.203	.204	.227	.226	.288	.229	.231	.231	2.0	2.7	3.0	2.9	2.0	3.0	2.3	2.5	3.0

* Modeled on the reports of the A. C. Nielsen Company.

EXHIBIT 14-8

Specimen Data:* Handsome Boy Distribution and Out-of-Stock by Package Size, in Territories, by County Size and by Outlet Type, Average Bimonthly Period—1965, 1971, 1972

TERRITORIES

PACKAGE SIZE	HPU REGION I			HPU REGION II			HPU REGION III			HPU REGION IV			HPU REGION V		
	1965	1971	1972	1965	1971	1972	1965	1971	1972	1965	1971	1972	1965	1971	1972
Handsome Boy	94_2	93_3	93_1	98_2	97_1	99_3	99_2	98_3	98_1	94_2	93_2	94_1	90_2	91_3	90_2
14 oz.	90_1	84_2	81_2	94_1	90_2	89_1	96_4	94_1	93_1	92_1	85_1	80_1	87_3	89_2	76_4
21 oz.	68_2	85_2	91_4	82_1	93_2	96_4	85_1	92_1	96_3	42_1	75_2	91_4	59_1	90_1	85_4

COUNTY SIZE

	A			B			C			D		
	1965	1971	1972	1965	1971	1972	1965	1971	1972	1965	1971	1972
Handsome Boy	96_3	97_2	99_4	94_1	97_1	96_3	94_2	90_3	90_1	73_2	78_3	76_1
14 oz.	94_1	96_2	98_2	94_1	90_2	93_1	85_2	84_1	94_2	40_1	38_2	45_2
21 oz.	85_2	89_1	99_6	80_1	78_3	80_2	69_1	73_3	72_3	45_4	46_1	53_1

OUTLET TYPE

	CHAIN FOOD			INDEPENDENT SUPER MKTS.			LG. AND MED. INDEPENDENTS			REMAINING INDEPENDENTS		
	1965	1971	1972	1965	1971	1972	1965	1971	1972	1965	1971	1972
Handsome Boy	98_2	99_1	99_6	90_1	91_1	93_2	77_4	89_1	91_2	69_4	73_4	84_6
14 oz.	96_2	94_1	98_2	90_1	90_1	91_3	72_1	87_3	79_3	39_4	49_2	49_7
21 oz.	85_1	89_2	99_4	68_4	62_4	91_6	54_1	48_2	82_1	42_2	52_1	83_1

* Modeled on the reports of the A. C. Nielsen Company.

EXHIBIT 14-9

Specimen Data:* Handsome Boy Retail Prices by Package Size, in Territories, by County Size, and by Outlet Type, Average Bimonthly Period—1965, 1971, 1972

TERRITORIES

	HPU REGION I			HPU REGION II			HPU REGION III			HPU REGION IV			HPU REGION V		
	1965	1971	1972	1965	1971	1972	1965	1971	1972	1965	1971	1972	1965	1971	1972
Handsome Boy	.212	.220	.222	.210	.218	.220	.214	.222	.224	.213	.221	.223	.214	.223	.226
14 oz.	.164	.178	.179	.162	.176	.177	.166	.179	.181	.165	.178	.179	.166	.178	.179
21 oz.	.229	.242	.244	.227	.240	.242	.231	.244	.246	.230	.244	.246	.233	.246	.250

COUNTY SIZE

	A			B			C			D		
	1965	1971	1972	1965	1971	1972	1965	1971	1972	1965	1971	1972
Handsome Boy	.208	.216	.218	.212	.220	.223	.214	.222	.224	.217	.225	.227
14 oz.	.160	.174	.175	.165	.179	.180	.166	.180	.181	.165	.179	.179
21 oz.	.225	.238	.240	.228	.241	.243	.231	.244	.246	.236	.249	.252

OUTLET TYPE

	CHAIN FOOD			INDEPENDENT SUPER MKTS.			LG. AND MED. INDEPENDENTS			REMAINING INDEPENDENTS		
	1965	1971	1972	1965	1971	1972	1965	1971	1972	1965	1971	1972
Handsome Boy	.207	.215	.217	.212	.220	.222	.215	.223	.225	.218	.226	.230
14 oz.	.159	.173	.174	.164	.178	.179	.167	.181	.182	.170	.184	.186
21 oz.	.224	.237	.239	.229	.242	.244	.232	.245	.247	.235	.248	.252

* Modeled on the reports of the A. C. Nielsen Company.

EXHIBIT 14–10

Specimen Data:* Handsome Boy Displays by Home Products Universal Regions, Bimonthly Periods—1965, 1971, 1972

HPU REGION	1965						1971						1972					
	J/F	M/A	M/J	J/A	S/O	N/D	J/F	M/A	M/J	J/A	S/O	N/D	J/F	M/A	M/J	J/A	S/O	N/D
I	3	4	6	6	4	2	3	5	7	7	6	5	2	3	5	5	3	2
II	7	8	9	9	5	1	6	9	9	9	4	2	7	9	10	9	9	2
III	2	5	8	9	9	5	3	6	10	12	10	8	4	5	10	10	8	4
IV	2	4	3	3	4	2	1	2	1	1	—	2	2	1	1	—	4	—
V	2	4	5	5	3	2	10	13	15	15	14	8	3	5	4	4	1	2

* Modeled on the reports of the A. C. Nielsen Company.

Questions for Case 14

1. Why is achieved physical distribution a matter of concern to the marketer? How does the marketer go about increasing a brand's level of physical distribution? What kinds of activities lead to the loss of achieved physical distribution?
2. Why is it necessary to undertake a store audit program when factory sales are available for analysis by marketing personnel?
3. Analyze the data presented in Exhibits 14–1 through 14–10. On the basis of this analysis, prepare (a) a summary of major findings; and (b) recommended distribution guidelines for Handsome Boy Cleanser.
4. Which of the data reported should reflect consumer promotional activity?
5. Which of the data reported should reflect trade promotional activity?
6. The following data have been developed in a sales audit of a probability sample of stores in Fort Wayne, Indiana. The first audit was taken on March 15, 16, and 17, 1974, and the second audit on May 15, 16, and 17, 1974.

	CANNED SOUP	CAMPBELL'S SOUP	CAMPBELL'S CHICKEN SOUP WITH RICE
March inventory in cans*	15,729	10,810	758
Shipments to stores in cases*	689	563	72
May inventory in cans*	14,211	8,725	421
Estimated March–May			
Pilferage in cans	100	95	6
Breakage in cans	—	—	—
Spoilage in cans†	50	30	1

* Assume that 36 cans equal 1 case.
† Labels lost.

a. What are the canned-soup sales in the store panel between mid-March and mid-May?
b. What are the Campbell's Soup sales in the store panel in the same period?
c. What are the Campbell's Chicken Soup with Rice sales in the store panel in the same period?
d. What is the Campbell's Soup share of soup sales in the panel stores in the same period? What share of the total market and of Campbell's Soup sales did Campbell's Chicken Soup with Rice hold in this period?
e. Assume that the store panel accounts for 20 per cent of the total commodity volume in Fort Wayne. What are the projected total soup sales, the total Campbell's sales, the total Campbell's Chicken Soup with Rice sales, the total Campbell's share, and the Campbell's Chicken Soup with Rice share of total soup sales and Campbell's Soup sales in Fort Wayne during the audit period?

CASE 15

Government Regulation

Cacaphony Sound Advertising Is Reviewed by the Federal Trade Commission

THE EARLY sales performance of Cacaphony Sound's MAXIHUE portable color television sets was hampered because the Japanese supplier, Koga Industries, did not have adequate production facilities (see Case 4). In late 1972, new Koga manufacturing facilities became operational. From that time on, Koga had no trouble supplying Cacaphony Sound with as many MAXIHUE television sets as could be sold. With the improved availability of the product, Cacaphony Sound began aggressively to market MAXIHUE television sets in 1973.

The first move undertaken by MAXIHUE product manager August N. Schneider was to develop a program of incentives for the manufacturers' sales agents to increase distribution. Basically, this program involved additional discounts on sets sold to new MAXIHUE retail outlets, as well as additional discounts for exceeding overall sales quotas for 1973. The new 1973 quotas assumed that 1973 sales would be very much higher than 1972 sales because there would be no shortage of MAXIHUE sets. But if the new higher quotas were exceeded, the manufacturers' sales agents received significant new discounts on all of their 1973 sales as well as generous discounts on that portion of their sales attributable to new retail outlets.

Schneider was convinced that this discount structure would provide the manufacturers' sales agents with adequate incentives to increase sales very significantly.

But he realized that pressure on the retail sales organization from the manufacturers' sales agents was only part of the total required marketing effort. Advertising pressure on consumers would create a heightened consumer awareness of MAXIHUE portable color television sets and their very tangible price and performance characteristics relative to competitive television receivers. When supplies of MAXIHUE receivers were limited, Schneider believed there to be little reason to enhance consumer demand through consumer advertising. And so he had rejected all suggestions that a consumer advertising campaign in support of MAXIHUE be launched. But now that there were plenty of sets to be sold, he strongly believed that a consumer advertising program should be initiated.

When he had reached this decision, he realized that his most urgent need was to find an advertising agency that would help him in the development of an appropriate advertising program. Schneider had, among his prerogatives as product manager, the right to choose whatever advertising agency he wished. And, because MAXIHUE portable color TV set sales would, Schneider estimated, move from $1,024,000,000 in 1972 to $1,400,000,000 in 1973, he knew this volume level would generate a dollar advertising expenditure level great enough to be of interest to any advertising agency. So Schneider was faced with the question of whether to seek out a new advertising agency for the MAXI-HUE line of television receivers or to give the business to Aesop & Acton, the agency that handled all of the other advertising activity for Cacaphony Sound products.

There was a great deal to be said for finding a brand new agency. First of all, it would staff and organize itself to handle the MAXIHUE line without reference to the staffing and organization that already existed for the sound systems and radio accounts. Secondly, a new agency would be appointed only if and only because Schneider wished it to be. It would thus owe its loyalty to him and to no one else in the Cacaphony Sound organization. Finally, a new agency would approach the MAXIHUE assignment with a freshness and an enthusiasm that would be difficult to generate, Schneider guessed, within the incumbent agency.

But if there was much to be said for finding a new agency, there was a great deal to be said for giving the new assignment to Aesop & Acton. Any new agency would, after all, be an unknown quantity. It might, before the actual test of performance, promise anything. But the proof of performance would depend upon the work that was finally produced, and if one could not predict this from a new agency, it was certain that the work of Aesop & Acton had been, over the years, thoroughly satisfactory, if somewhat lacking in final brilliance. Secondly, Schneider knew that it would take a significant amount of time to screen qualified agency candidates and find one that seemed to fill the bill. Once the candidate was screened and chosen, additional time would be required to acquaint the new agency with Cacaphony Sound and with the MAXIHUE line of portable television receivers. No matter how experienced the agency might be with consumer entertainment systems and no matter how quickly they could find experienced and competent personnel to work on the Cacaphony account, it was certain that the familiarization and indoctrination period would add at least six weeks and perhaps as much as two months to the total period required before new advertising would be presented to Schneider and his colleagues.

Schneider was sorely tempted to find a new agency to do the job. He had no special fondness for Aesop & Acton and its executives. They had made no attempt to know him or his division even though they had continuously wooed Stevenson L. Wittrich, the product manager for the new home protection systems line, who had been appointed at about the same time that Schneider had received the MAXIHUE product manager's assignment. "Why do they wine and dine Wittrich and ignore me?" wondered Schneider to himself. He didn't particularly care whether the "double A boys" (as Aesop & Acton executives were known around Cacaphony Sound) took him to lunch or not, but the fact that they didn't was kind of a public pronouncement by the agency that he, Schneider, was not important, or at least was less important than Wittrich.

Beyond this purely personal reaction to Aesop & Acton, Schneider knew that to appoint them was the easy way out. They were already in place, they were accepted as competent throughout Cacaphony Sound, and no one from top to bottom in his organization would question a decision to appoint them. To go to another agency was risky, all right, but it was a way of attracting the attention of Cacaphony Sound to himself with the potential benefit of enhancing his own reputation very considerably, if the new agency did a good job and especially if it seemed to do a better job than might have been expected from Aesop & Acton.

In the end, Schneider took the easy way out. He appointed Aesop & Acton to handle the advertising for the MAXIHUE line of portable television receivers. Much as he wanted to find a new agency, he finally decided that he could not afford either the risk or the extra time that such a course of action would involve.

But in appointing the incumbent agency, he did his best to make his feelings about the agency and final reasons for his choice as clear as possible to its president, Humboldt Aesop. On the day that he chose to award the business to Aesop & Acton, he called the agency at 8:45 A.M. and asked to be connected with Mr. Aesop. He was held on the line for several minutes while the person who had answered Aesop's phone looked around for his secretary. Finally the secretary was located, having apparently been dragged from the ladies' room or a coffee conversation or something. Schneider introduced himself as "August Schneider, of Cacaphony Sound," and the secretary said, increduously, "Who?" Schneider repeated his opening statement but gave no additional information. The secretary suggested that he call back when the office was officially open at 9:00 A.M. and ask for Mr. Moran, the account supervisor on the Cacaphony Sound account. Schneider said that this was unsatisfactory and inquired whether Mr. Aesop was expected in the office on that day, because he was interested in speaking only to Mr. Aesop. By this time the hapless secretary began to realize that there was perhaps a bit more to all of this than met the eye and simply said that Mr. Aesop was expected around 10 A.M. and that she would give the message to him when he arrived.

Humboldt Aesop arrived in the office at his usual time, around 10 A.M. He was a man in his late fifties, a big, brisk, outgoing chap who had played football at Harvard, had disliked finance, and had got into advertising not because of desire or interest but because he perceived that at least some of his many college chums would eventually need an advertising agent, and this seemed as sure a way as any of cashing in on the fact that he had happened to meet and know many young men of enthusiasm and promise who would, in due course, become old men of commerce and affluence.

In the thirty years that had passed since he had reached this simple conclusion Aesop had moved through his apprentice and journeyman stages without distinction in other advertising agencies that had been founded on much the same assumption by Harvard or Princeton or Cornell or Yale men of a previous generation, and he had finally teamed with Winston Acton to open his own agency in 1950.

They had been successful. The Aesop premise had been correct and he had managed to bring in enough business over the years to develop a medium-sized agency of high profitability. Aesop was not now, nor had he ever been, much of an advertising man, but Win Acton was competent if unspectacular and he ran the agency down its solid if rather anonymous course as Aesop created a public figure of respectability, dependability, and intangible competence in the handling of the abstruse problems of communicating with the common man. He didn't know more about this than his Harvard school chums did, but because he was "in advertising" and because he alluded to mysterious communication processes, it never occurred to his old buddies to doubt his word as they gave him their business.

Somewhere along the line Aesop got to know G. N. Sternweiss, one of the founders of Cacaphony Sound, although Sternweiss had not done his undergraduate work at Harvard. None of the founding partners of Cacaphony Sound pretended to be knowledgeable about anything except designing and making better home entertainment products than anyone else in the business. There was a period in the early history of the company when they needed skills beyond those they professed and had not yet come to the point where they could afford to hire professional managers like Popeye Shortstreet and Uehlander and Anthony and Fiscigna. And in this early period, when the question of advertising came up, Sternweiss was the only one of the three founders that could remember ever having met an advertising man, and so Humboldt Aesop got the call and the Cacaphony Sound account.

Aesop, a man of the world, had been a great help to the founding partners. He knew the people in the world of finance and commerce whom they did not know and whom they needed to know, and as the years unfolded Sternweiss and his friends never forgot the debt they felt they owed to old Hum Aesop. But Aesop knew that this relationship was good only for so long. Sooner or later the actual control of the advertising agency assignment would drift away from the founders and even from their top managers. It was a day that Aesop did his best to anticipate and prepare for. He encouraged Win Acton to staff the Cacaphony Sound account (and the other accounts in the agency too) with sound professional people and with younger men who had trained in leading business schools. He also encouraged Acton to seek out the best creative talent that could be found.

But there was something rather old and stodgy about Aesop & Acton, and the young people in the advertising agency business sensed it and almost instinctively shied away. Humboldt Aesop recognized this and knew that his agency was gradually weakening as the circular process of aging and rejection by the young unfolded. Aesop himself tried to rectify this process, but he was not especially successful in his brisk, good-hearted ineptitude in hiring talent into his agency, and finally he turned his back on the matter while continuing to express the hope to Win Acton that Acton would do something about it.

So when Schneider's call came, the two principals were rather wary of each other. Schneider didn't like Aesop & Acton and would have chosen someone else if he had not thought it to be imprudent to do so. Aesop was unsure of himself with young professionals and had about given up trying to overcome his difficulties with them. When he received Schneider's message, Aesop had no idea who Schneider was, and he called his man Moran and asked. "He's product manager on the television set line at Cacaphony, Hum, but they'll never advertise that MAXIHUE product— it's in short supply and sells itself." "Why would Schneider want me?" continued Aesop. "I haven't the foggiest idea, Hum. He's kind of a queer bird—works long hours and is a real nut. You remember, he was the one who put in the sales potential business and some of those other computer things, and that's all he wants to talk about. A real weirdo, the boys think. Maybe he wants to explain his computer to you." This last was accompanied by a merry shout of laughter, and Aesop hung up the phone.

When he talked to Schneider, Aesop was stunned when he announced that he was considering awarding the MAXIHUE advertising assignment to Aesop & Acton and wanted to talk to him about it. Schneider asked if Aesop was available to discuss the matter that afternoon. Aesop was, and the two met for three hours, alone, in the Aesop & Acton offices that day.

Schneider came to the meeting with a voluminous set of handwritten notes. He made the following points:

1. He was willing to appoint Aesop & Acton, but only with considerable misgivings. He believed the agency to be rather slow footed in serving Cacaphony Sound, and he thought their creative work to be rather mediocre and dull.

2. He would make the appointment only after he had been assured

that a totally separate group of agency people would be formed to service MAXIHUE, totally independent of the other groups working on Cacaphony Sound business. He wanted a completely new set of faces.

3. He outlined the timetable that he had in mind for the development and placing of advertising for MAXIHUE. This timetable envisioned the public appearance of advertisements for MAXIHUE within ten weeks. He asked Aesop if this seemed reasonable, noting that it was a condition of appointment.

Aesop responded with a certain cool enthusiasm to Schneider's presentation. He didn't like many of the things that Schneider said about his firm and said so, but at the same time he acknowledged that Schneider might be at least somewhat right in his criticisms and he pointed out that it was much easier to provide adequate service to those who said what they did and did not want from an agency than to those who did not. By the time the meeting was two hours old, the two men knew each other well enough to know that their preconceptions of each other had been, to at least some extent, wrong and to suspect that they could work well enough with each other to make a success for MAXIHUE.

As the meeting came to a close, Aesop said that there was one area in which Schneider would have to give a great deal of help to the agency and that without his help the agency would be very significantly hindered both with respect to the quality of its creative work and with respect to its speed of response. This was in the briefing of the agency about the product characteristics of the MAXIHUE portable television receivers.

"You have to tell us what your products can do and what they can't do. We are an advertising agency. We are experts in communicating with the consumer. We do three things. We figure out what is the most compelling thing you can say about your product, given its peculiarities and characteristics. Then we figure out the best way to say what should be said, that is, execute the compelling characteristics in advertising form. Finally, we figure out the best media vehicles to put those messages in. Don't ask me how we do all these things in detail, because I don't know . . . that's what our employees are paid to do, and they are very good at it. But I do know that the crucial area is what your product can do and what it can't. The more clearly you explain the differences and advantages of your product, the better the ads we'll make. The more clearly you explain the disadvantages of your product and what it can't do, the surer we can be that your advertisements are not misleading or untruthful. That's getting to be more important every day—with the Federal Trade Commission, and Ralph Nader and the consumerists, and the junior Senator from South Dakota, and who knows who else.

"We're not technical people, don't you see, and we can only evaluate and put into consumer language the things that you tell us. So all I can say to you is that the more closely you work with us, the better your advertising is likely to be and the less chance you have of getting into hot water with the government."

Schneider was really quite surprised at this outburst. He had sized up Aesop as a rather facile and pompous extrovert, not profound and unlikely to become emotionally involved in anything, least of all his business affairs. But here he was, speaking with great enthusiasm and fervor about what the client had to do to help the agency. He was rather impressed by the old man's sincerity. "What do you mean, Mr. Aesop, when you say that if we tell you everything about the product, we only lessen the chance that we may get into trouble with the government? Truth is truth, isn't it?—if we're truthful, and our lawyers review every ad, isn't that all we have to do?" asked Schneider.

"Come on, boy," responded Aesop, with even more heat, "you must know better than that. Advertising is a part of everybody's life. A lot of people will tell you they don't like it. It's such an easy thing to be against. If you've got nothing else to talk about in Peoria, talk about advertising, about how dumb it is, and how condescending it is and how exploitive it is and how immoral it is and all the rest. Forget the economic case, or the communications needs of our great companies, or the importance of brands to our economy, and all that, and show your neighbor how smart you are, and be against advertising. When you can find one thing that lots of people agree on, and it's negative, and you're a politician—you've got a hold of something, Schneider, and you ride it and make a career out of it and damn it, I get so mad about this I sometimes get unglued over it. But that's what it's about, and even when you tell the truth, or think you do, someone is likely to object to it, and their objections are based on dislike and the possibility of political gain and, believe me, just telling the truth is all you can do and it may save you in the end, but it won't protect you from those people wanting to criticize your advertising and questioning it and forcing you to substantiate it and defend it in administrative and judicial processes.

"You'll win in court with the truth, Schneider, and thank God for our judicial system—without it we'd all be out of business—but that doesn't mean that they won't harass you to death with their press releases and proceedings and subpoenas and spend lots of your time and money until you can get the truth before a judge."

"Well, Mr. Aesop," responded Schneider, "I appreciate what you're saying to me. Believe me, we'll do anything in our power to give your people the facts and all the facts about our products, and we'll stand by you, and you can depend on it."

On that note the meeting between the two men came to an end. Schneider returned to his office secure in the belief that a good working relation with the agency had been established and that whatever else Humboldt Aesop was, he was sincere in his beliefs and could be counted on to do his best to make sure that his organization would service the MAXIHUE line of portable television sets as well as they could.

There followed several weeks of intensive briefing of the agency by MAXIHUE engineers, of guided plant tours, and of indoctrinations of one kind or another. Schneider did everything in his power to honor his pledge to Aesop of total information. And, in fairness to him and his people, everything was done that reasonably could be done to give the agency people the complete MAXIHUE story. If there was a problem in all of this it was in the disparate backgrounds and perceptions of the people involved: the MAXIHUE people were essentially technicians, trained to communicate to their peers in technical terms, and rather contemptuous of the apparently undisciplined and easy-going agency creative people to whom they were asked to impart their knowledge. The agency people, for their part, did their best to keep up with the labored and even premeditatedly complex presentation. But they were not technical people and had no pretensions of being technical people. They wanted to know enough to do their job, and do it well, but they had no interest in moving beyond this basic requirement for knowledge. The engineers felt that unless the agency people really knew everything, they could not communicate fairly and truthfully about the MAXIHUE product. The agency creative people wanted to know the essence but not, as one of them put it, "so much that we'll have to write seven-page ads to get all that junk across."

Schneider sensed this problem and discussed it forcefully with Wellington P. Crust, the management supervisor appointed by Aesop & Acton to work on the MAXIHUE account. Crust was concerned about the problem too. "Look, Augie," he said to Schneider, "I think we've got past the point where more seminars and forums are going to help very much. My guys simply don't want or need to become technicians. It would be wonderful if they knew as much as your engineers, but we both know that won't happen, and if it did they wouldn't be copy writers anymore but engineers. I guess they probably feel that they've been preached at enough. Maybe they've absorbed more than we know. It's hard to be sure and easy-going as these guys seem to be, don't let them fool you—they're quick students and they're smart as hell."

"Okay, Welly, if you say so," responded Schneider, "but it doesn't look to me as if they've been paying attention. I hope you're right about their knowing what's what. But let me suggest one more thing. We've got an engineer out there in the plant who is very facile with words— much better than most of the guys that your people have been exposed to. He's out in the plant doing a nothing job because, frankly, he's kind of a second-rate engineer, but he can describe systems simply and well, in writing, without getting all bogged down in the detail. His name is Julie Hendelman. I'll ask him to write a five- or six-hundred-word description of what MAXIHUE is for the use of your copy people: at least that will give them fundamental direction and a basis for coming back to us with specific questions about things they still don't understand.''

And so Julian A. Hendelman was asked to prepare a simplified statement describing the MAXIHUE portable television set, the design principle upon which it was based, and the ways in which it differed from and was better than competitive television receivers. The Hendelman statement is reproduced in Exhibit 15–1.

EXHIBIT 15–1
Statement by Julian A. Hendelman, Ph.D., Concerning the Technical and Performance Characteristics of MAXIHUE Portable Color Television Receivers

The MAXIHUE portable color television receiver utilizes a picture tube of totally new design that, in fact, produces demonstrably superior picture-color composition when the set receives normal over-air broadcast transmissions.

A number of factors inhibit colormetric fidelity in normal color TV signal reception. When the television receiver is designed it represents a series of compromises, as is so often the case with complex electronic equipment. Accordingly, the engineer must first make design decisions in the context of existing broadcasting practices, especially the lack of colormetric uniformity of signal as between transmitting stations as well as the materials that individual stations transmit. In addition, the engineer must juggle the inherent engineering limitations of fundamental system components, variations in color-tube phosphor capabilities, relations between capabilities and market pricing realities, and so on.

The traditional solution to this problem has been to depart in varying degrees from a literal or theoretically correct decoding of the signal received by the set in order to provide significantly more latitude in attaining acceptable flesh-tone reproduction, in response to both receiver adjustment and broadcast variations. The price paid in these flesh-tone compromises is a distortion in other colors, even to the extent of pink oceans and greenish egg yolks.

The fundamental design principle that has been followed historically is to accept the signal as transmitted, pass it through the receiving set, and then attempt to improve it as received by adjusting the receiving set itself, manually. Thus the final adjustment is given to the consumer to make, and he does it with greater or lesser facility, depending upon his own understanding of the gross parameters involved, his manual dexterity, and the condition and excellence of his receiving set. (There is at least, one might add parenthetically, a little bit of guile in making the consumer a crucial collaborator in the final picture quality that is achieved.)

MAXIHUE turns its back on this principle. We have developed a totally new concept in color picture reception. Briefly stated, it is that the received picture should be adjusted to standard mechanically *before* it is unleashed into the receiving set itself. The trick is to find a way to decompose or smash the picture signals, as received from the station transmitter, and then reintegrate them into a standardized picture for transmission into the receiving set itself. Once this decomposition and reintegration has been achieved, the pure picture elements are channeled into the set and it is neither necessary nor relevant to consider adjusting them in any further manual way.

Our first problem, then, was to develop the decomposition-reintegration mechanism and this was done. We call this the D–R box, and it is, of course, now fully covered by U.S. patents 1,628,247,311 and 1,628,247,312. The basic elements in this mechanism are a color-base unscrambler that is an engineering marvel. Received light is decomposed instantaneously into its five basic hues, analyzed with respect to computed hue intensities, and then recombined as the hue analyzer believes it should be. Very often the resulting picture is better than the one originally transmitted because the aesthetic monitoring program of the reintegration mechanism produces hue relationships that are inherently balanced and pleasing— disparate or threatening hue relationships are eliminated because, as the program dictates, they should not occur in nature and our circuitry is developed to reflect only the harmonies of nature, not the disharmonies or inconsistencies, real as they may occasionally be.

There are no manual picture-adjustment capabilities in MAXIHUE sets. None are needed. One simply turns on the set, adjusts the volume, and enjoys perfection. It is, of course, true that when the set malfunctions, it is beyond the capability of the consumer to adjust it. A malfunctioning set must be repaired by a professional. But the R–D box has been remarkably free of defects, and it is safe to say that it requires considerably lower levels of maintainance than the complex and now outmoded manual tuning subsystems that it has superannuated.

There is another advantage inherent in the MAXIHUE design. It is considerably less expensive to manufacture than the standard manual tuning designs that characterize its predecessors. This is so because the manual tuning systems involve complicated and extensive circuitry and systems, and all of these are eliminated by the MAXIHUE design. They are replaced, as I have explained, by the unique R–D box. The R–D box is an extremely sophisticated electronic system. Its design, however, emphasizes low-cost fabrication and trouble-free operation.

The product development group at Cacaphony Sound Company devotes its professional life to perfecting better entertainment systems for consumers. Because of this it is perhaps naïve to believe that others will accept as objective or unprejudiced our own evaluation of the performance of systems developed by us. Nevertheless, we are not in the business of misleading ourselves. Our own evaluation of the MAXIHUE system and the decomposition-reintegration principle upon which it is based is that it does produce a remarkably superior picture with inherent economies of manufacture and maintenance that make MAXIHUE sets unique among television receivers.

Meanwhile, Aesop & Acton representatives had been giving considerable attention to the development of a fundamental plan for MAXIHUE advertising. Crust and Schneider had agreed that a reasonable basis for establishing an advertising budget was a factory assessment of $1.15 per set. One dollar per set would be used for the actual purchase of media and $.15 per set would be used to cover administrative costs and the cost of actually producing television commercials and print advertisements. These per-set assessments, when applied against the projected number of

MAXIHUE sets that would be sold during the 1974-model year, yielded a media budget of $7,685,600, and a production/administration budget of $1,152,840 (see Exhibit 15–2).

EXHIBIT 15–2
Specimen Data: MAXIHUE Sales and Advertising Relationships, 1974 Model Year

Projected national television set sales	$6,160,100,000
Projected portable color television set sales	3,813,100,000
Projected MAXIHUE dollar share: 45%*	
Projected MAXIHUE dollar sales	1,715,895,000
Projected portable television set sales (units)	14,780,000
Projected MAXIHUE unit shares: 52%†	7,685,600
Projected MAXIHUE consumer advertising media expenditures @ $1.00 per unit	7,685,600
Projected MAXIHUE consumer advertising production and administrative expenses @ $0.15 per unit	1,152,840

* MAXIHUE share of dollar sales in prior years:
  1970   10%
  1971   32%
  1972   40%
† Details of the competitive pricing structure of the 1974-model year are not known; it is assumed that MAXIHUE prices will run about 16% lower than those of competitors, as in the past.

Schneider was somewhat distressed by what seemed to him to be a rather old-fashioned method of computing advertising budgets. This arbitrary allocation of dollars from projected sales did not, on the face of it, reflect in any way the causal relation between advertising and sales. Rather, advertising seemed to be conceived as a derivative from sales. He mentioned this to Crust when the decision had finally been made to set aside $1.15 per television receiver. "You make a good point, Augie," said Crust, "but you have to keep several things in mind about advertising expenditures. In the first place, unless there is good reason to make an abnormal investment of company profits in advertising, then advertisement expenditures must come from the sales of a brand, and they must represent a reasonable fraction of the sales of the brand. We have no experience whatsoever in the productivity of advertising expenditures in selling MAXIHUE television sets. We don't know how much a given expenditure in advertising will increase sales, if at all.

"If we don't know about this and yet can establish definite communication objectives for our advertising, then we ought to do two things. First, we should set aside an amount for advertising from sales that is reasonable in overall profit terms and that is adequate to accomplish the communication goals that we have set up. In other words, if you have valid communications objectives, you should advertise to accomplish them even though you can't predict extra sales exactly because you don't know just how responsive to advertising your product may be. But the second thing you should do is to try to find out, through market experience and testing, as much as you can about advertising productivity, so that the next time you have to make the decision about how much to spend for advertising, you'll have something to go by. Slowly but surely, you'll gather enough information so that one day you'll make that decision on purely cost-return grounds. But meantime, you've got to start somewhere.

"The one thing that I can tell you about the media level of seven million, seven hundred thousand dollars is that it is adequate to do the job that you have specified. You want the consumer to know that MAXIHUE is better and less expensive than its competitors. We can implant that understanding in the minds of two thirds to three quarters of your prime prospects in the next year with that level of expenditure and will be able to measure our success in doing it. Beyond that, we know that a level of seven million, seven hundred thousand dollars will equal, more or less, the total of the advertising expenditures from all of the competitors in the portable color television set market. We know this from our competitive expenditure analyses.

"So we may not know on a scientific basis just how much we should spend to make our advertising pay for itself in extra dollar sales, but we can say with certainty that we'll get the message we want to communicate into the minds of our prospects and that we will dominate our competitors in advertising expenditures. And those seem to me to be good enough business reasons to justify our advertising expenditure recommendations."

Schneider accepted this rationale in the absence of anything better. He admitted to himself both that it was a fairly weak rationale for an expenditure of such magnitude and yet that a lot of business expenditures of significant magnitude were made with even less sound reason, and he let it go at that.

About the first of April, Aesop & Acton asked for a date on which to make a formal presentation of advertising copy for the MAXIHUE line of television receivers. Schneider welcomed the copy presentation. It consisted of a series of hardboard charts in which, as presented by Wellington Crust, the basic rationale of the proposed advertising campaign was presented. Subsequently, the ads themselves were presented by members of the Aesop & Acton creative department. The Crust presentation made the following basic points about the advertising campaign for MAXIHUE portable color television sets:

1. MAXIHUE is a distinctly different and superior portable color television set. It is a better portable color system that costs less, and advertising about it must leave no doubt in consumers' minds that it is superior.
2. The advertising of television sets tends to be predictably "look alike." It is very hard to distinguish the advertising—in either print of TV—of one set

manufacturer from the other. All emphasize picture clarity, ease of tuning, and smiling, satisfied viewers.

3. If MAXIHUE is different, and better, its advertising should sound different and look different. We must make MAXIHUE advertising look and sound different. If it is conventional in appearance, the consumer may perceive that the television sets that it represents are, themselves, conventional.

4. Above all, MAXIHUE advertising must present aggressively the meaningful differences between MAXIHUE and its competitors. MAXIHUE is different and better in ways that are important to consumers and we must not flinch from a vivid and aggressive portrayal of these product superiorities.

In the copy presentation that followed, seven television commercials were shown in story-board form. In addition, three proposed print advertisements were also presented. The television commercials were all based on two fundamental elements: the use of a famous television cowboy actor as spokesman and an elaborate animated sequence to demonstrate how the MAXIHUE design differed from those of conventional television receivers. These two elements were also carried over into the proposed print advertisements.

In presenting this creative work, Lawrence L. Cappolla, creative director of Aesop & Acton, emphasized two points: (a) no other television manufacturer had ever used a television personality to speak for his product; and (b) animation could clearly present the real difference and superiority of the MAXIHUE design. Schneider took this all in and when the presentation came to an end sat silent for several minutes, obviously absorbed in thought. Finally he said, "Well, Welly and Larry, that's a provocative and professional presentation and I like the work, I really do. I'd just like to make a couple of points—really very small and insignificant points when you think about it. But you do want my response, and I really feel it important that I give it to you, isn't that right?"

Welly Crust replied instantly, "Right, yes sir, that's what we want, Augie, isn't that right, Larry?" Larry Cappolla didn't seem all that enthusiastic about hearing everything that August Schneider had to say, but he nodded assent with a little smile and looked at Schneider expectantly.

"Well," Schneider continued, "first of all, I think that that cowboy is a little over the hill—he must have been on the air for fourteen or fifteen years anyway . . . " At this point, Cappola interrupted, "He's been on for seven years, Augie, seven."

"Right, Larry, thank you. Well if it's seven, it's still a very long time and I think he's past his prime and I wonder if an actor is the right kind of person to talk about a serious product like MAXIHUE television sets— don't we need someone more authoritative?" No one from the agency volunteered an answer to the question. Wellington Crust chose to assume that the question was rhetorical. Larry Cappolla sensed that there was more to come and that he would like it even less than what he had just heard.

Schneider continued, "I wonder about the use of cartoons to demonstrate our design principles. I mean, don't you think they will make the whole thing seem a little too frivolous? After all, the MAXIHUE system is a scientific breakthrough. We're talking about complicated and sophisticated electronic equipment and a conception of genius—not a toy.

"But, Augie," countered Crust, "we do have to convey that marvelous design principle in some meaningful way. The consumer isn't an engineer, after all, and what is meaningful to you and the Cacaphony people may simply be incomprehensible to them. We really feel very strongly that the animation—and it will be animation, Augie, not a cartoon—will be plenty serious in feeling. Right, Larry? The animated treatment will permit us to dramatize the fundamental difference and superiority of the MAXIHUE system, Augie. Maybe the cowboy isn't the ticket, but the animation idea is absolutely essential. We can find spokesmen with more authority—that's easy, there are lots of authoritative people around for hire—but it's not easy to think of a clearer or more compelling way of presenting the complexities of that MAXIHUE design."

"Okay, Welly, I get the point, and maybe you're right," said Schneider. "But get me somebody that's better than that cowboy, more serious, someone we can really depend upon, and someone who can sell, too. And take it easy with that animation—make it serious, not frivolous. Uh, by the way, has Art Webster seen this stuff yet?" "Not yet, Augie. We thought we'd better get your reaction to all of this before we took it up with the lawyers."

"Okay, Welly, I got it. The language you've used in those ads looks okay to me—you'll want to change the beginning to fit the personality of the new man, but I'll leave that to you. Why don't you come back when you have the new man and then we'll go see Webster."

In the end Godfrey Arturo—the well-known television personality–salesman—was recruited as a spokesman for MAXIHUE television sets, and the television commercials and print advertisements were presented to Art Webster, vice president for legal affairs of Cacaphony Sound.

The key selling propositions of the advertising were two: first, that MAXIHUE receivers provided better television pictures to the viewer and, second, that the MAXIHUE television receivers cost less. The following standard phrases were used in all of the proposed television commercials and print advertisements to convey these key selling propositions:

The MAXIHUE receiver is different from all competitive makes. This receiver takes the incoming signal, smashes it, and rebuilds it into proper proportions before it enters the set itself. Result—no tuning is required. A perfect picture every time. MAXIHUE gives cable TV quality without the cable. No other television set can match MAXIHUE picture quality because compared to MAXIHUE all other sets are obsolete.

And the MAXIHUE set cost less than competitors—no one outperforms MAXIHUE and no one costs as little.

Webster reviewed the advertising for about a week before responding to Schneider's request that he approve it. His response was in writing and is reproduced here.

Cacaphony Sound Communication

TO: August N. Schneider

FROM: Arthur A. Webster

We have now received the Cacaphony Sound MAXIHUE portable color television receiver advertising that has been submitted by Aesop & Acton. We have the following comments:

1. How can we substantiate that MAXIHUE is different from all competitive makes? Have we examined all competitive makes? Do we have a complete list of competitive makes? How do we know that it is complete?

2. We do not believe that *smash* is an accurate description of what the MAXIHUE system does to the incoming picture signal. Mr. Hendelman has, in our judgment, used too much license in saying that the incoming picture is smashed: this is not a true synonym for *decompose*. (*See* Random House Dictionary of the English Language, the unabridged 1966 edition, p. 376.)

3. How do you define perfect picture quality? Even Hendelman admits that television set design is a compromise. Have we not compromised somewhere? How do we know that the standards we impose on the MAXIHUE set are perfect?

4. What is cable-TV quality? How do we achieve cable-TV quality? How can we substantiate that we deliver cable-TV quality?

5. How do we know that we cost less than our competitors? Do we know their prices at list? Do we know their prices at retail?

Legal Department approval of the proposed advertising is withheld pending satisfactory resolution of these problems.

(Perhaps I should also add my personal misgivings about the use of Godfrey Arturo in this advertising. I believe it to be morally wrong to use in persuasive communication for our product a persuader of his acknowledged skill. He is such an adroit presenter that he may force people to buy a MAXIHUE set against their own, rational, judgment.)

Schneider was not at all pleased with this rather cold and crusty communication from Webster. "Who does he think he is telling us it's morally wrong to use Godfrey Arturo in our advertising?" he remarked to Wellington Crust over a luncheon devoted to the task of developing responses to Webster's memorandum. "I mean, it's our job to develop advertising to get consumers to want what we have to sell. I don't care whether they want it on a rational basis or an irrational basis or what. Just as long as they want it—that's what advertising is all about. And after all, Welly, we're not selling small efficiencies: MAXIHUE is different, is better, is cheaper—you know it, I know it, and that stuffy meathead Webster knows it, and look at the trouble he's giving us. It's his bread and butter as well as ours, but you wouldn't know it from that memo."

"Cool off, Augie," countered Crust. "He's doing us a favor. He has to think about the FTC and the courts and Nader and all the rest of the gang that's out to get advertising and advertisers. You look at that memo of his. It doesn't say we can't say these thing: it simply says we have to be able to prove them. And I think when he asks for proof he's doing us both a favor. You're right about the morality crack, but don't forget, some of your best friends probably think that a lot of advertising is deceptive or immoral or whatever. If they ever thought about it they'd see soon enough that they were wrong, but it's an easy idea to half-bake."

With this exchange out of their systems, the two men proceeded to develop a point-by-point response to the issues raised by Webster:

1. They agreed that it was impossible to substantiate a claim that MAXIHUE was "different" from all competitors if it was necessary, as implied by Webster, to examine physically a sample of every television set available to consumers. But they wondered if the existence of the MAXIHUE patent on the receiving system was not sufficient to substantiate the exclusivity of the MAXIHUE receivers. "After all," said Crust, "if the patent doesn't mean that we have the thing to ourselves, what's the use of getting one? We don't license that patent to anyone do we?" "I don't think we do, Welly, but that's Webster's problem, isn't it? Let's ask him. Maybe he knows something we don't."

2. Crust had listed synonyms for *decompose* from the Random House Dictionary of the English Language in preparation for his meeting with Schneider. They were *distill, fractionate,* and *analyze.* "I don't like any of them very much and neither does Cappolla, but if we have to use a synonym we prefer *fractionate,* even thought it's not a very consumer-type word," stated Crust. "Okay, let's give him that one," said Schneider, "but why use the Random House? I mean, I prefer Webster's, don't you, Welly?" "Well, I do, but I notice all our copywriters have the Random House around, and if that's what Webster likes, with his name and all, maybe he has his reasons, and even if he doesn't, why argue with him about it?"

3. The men then agreed that *perfect* was a hard word to defend. Even though they both believed that the MAXIHUE picture was as near to perfect as any one could make it, they reluctantly agreed with each other that it would be hard to defend anything as "perfect,"

especially a mechanical system that inherently contained design compromises.

4. They had an equally hard time with "cable-TV quality." "The real point is that our system eliminated ghosts and snow, isn't it?" asked Crust. "Cable-TV quality is real consumer language. It really says that our picture is very good, and says it without puffery. We did a little research on that phrase and, believe me, the consumers know exactly what we're saying. I'd hate to lose that one." In the end Webster refused to approve "cable-TV quality" unless some substantiating research could be devised to justify the use of the term. Schneider and Crust agreed that a question about this might be included in a research project among television repairmen that they shortly intended to put into the field. But they decided to hold that up until the agency submitted the advertising to the networks' program practices departments to see what their regulatory view of "cable-TV quality" would be.

5. Schneider and Crust decided that a study should be made of the factory suggested retail list price of competitive portable color TV models with equivalent screen sizes. The study would be limited to those competitors who advertised their products in national media during the 1972 (preceding) model year. This would restrict the claim to "costs less than other leading nationally advertised brands," and this was judged acceptable, if cumbersome, by Crust.

Accordingly, these agreements were discussed with Webster and he accepted them as a basis for submission to the television networks with the proviso that he reserved the right to final review after the comments of the television networks were in hand.

Each of the television networks maintain a large and well-qualified staff whose sole function is to review the accuracy, tastefulness, and truthfulness of advertising submitted by advertisers for subsequent use on the networks. In their role as reviewers of proposed advertising, these advertising-practices staffs find themselves in a difficult and often precarious position. They must not be unnecessarily strict, lest the economic well-being of their network be threatened. Yet they cannot be too lenient, lest the outcry of the public threaten the tenure of their affiliated stations as government-licensed station operators. Neither can they be more lenient with one advertiser than another lest they find themselves besieged with cries of "foul" from the outraged competitors.

In this situation the network advertising-practices departments tend to pay very close attention to the literal truth of advertising claims and demand that they be fully substantiated, to the satisfaction of the network, before such claims can be made on the air. In addition, they tend to be very careful about claims that may be misleading to consumers, and a variety of special rules have grown up in individual product categories to protect the consumer against misleading or exploitative devices in advertising. The children's toy category and the proprietary drug category exemplify products that are closely regulated by the networks on these grounds. Finally, the networks watch carefully for statements judged to be derogatory to competitive products, and they watch carefully, too, for claims, statements, or innuendos that may be suggestive or in bad taste. As the years have passed, the trend has been for the television network advertising-practices departments to become increasingly narrow and restrictive in their review of the television commercials submitted to them by advertisers. Most of this narrowing restriction is due to the increased activity of the various governmental agencies and consumer groups. But some of it is undoubtedly due to increased pressure on the television networks by the various competitive advertisers within each product category. An advertiser who has been restricted in his own claims is all the more likely to become indignant if he sees a competitor running advertising on the air that strikes him as at least as unfounded or misleading as the material the same network has not permitted him to use.

So it was to the advertising practices departments of the three national television networks that Aesop & Acton now submitted the seven television commercials and the substantiation that had been developed for their product. The standard selling phrase from the television commercials now reads as follows (see pages 345–46 for the text originally submitted to Cacaphony's legal department by Aesop & Acton).

The MAXIHUE color television receiver is different from all competitive makes. The patented MAXIHUE circuitry takes the incoming station signal, fractionates it into basic color components, and then rebuilds it into a natural picture before it appears on the screen. Result: you no longer tune the MAXIHUE set—the picture reaches the tube in pretuned form. You get a better picture every time. In fact, MAXIHUE gives cable-TV quality—without the cable. No other television set can match MAXIHUE picture quality, because compared to MAXIHUE all other sets are obsolete.

And the MAXIHUE set costs less than other leading nationally advertised portable color television sets—no one of them outperforms MAXIHUE and no one of them costs so little.

The network replies were received by Aesop & Acton about two and a half weeks later. Although each of the networks responded separately and each used rather different language to express their concerns, there was substantial uniformity in the objections that they raised to the commercial:

1. All of them pointed out that *different* television receivers were not necessarily *better* television receivers. Each expressed the view that unless objective evidence existed that established the MAXIHUE picture as "better" in some substantial sense, the "better" claim would have to be dropped. One of the networks went on to say that

such evidence could be based either on technical tests carried out by competent laboratory technicians following recognized testing procedures or on controlled comparison tests of MAXIHUE and its competitors with consumers.

2. All of the networks questioned the meaning of "cable-TV quality" and asked for substantiation that the MAXIHUE picture was, in fact, of cable-TV quality. One of the networks made the additional point that cable-TV systems are used in smaller markets to receive and transmit television signals that originate in markets so remote from the cable-TV market that ordinary home sets could not bring them in. They wondered if the MAXIHUE picture was of "cable-TV quality" in this sense.

3. All of the networks agreed that the phrase "compared to MAXIHUE all other sets are obsolete" derogated the television sets of all other manufacturers and could not be used.

August Schneider and Wellington Crust met to discuss the network reactions to the MAXIHUE advertising. They agreed that further changes must be made if MAXIHUE was to receive network television advertising support. Specifically, they agreed:

1. That the line "you get a better picture every time" could not now be used in the MAXIHUE advertising. It was agreed that a study would be authorized in the Cacaphony Sound laboratories to develop substantiation for the "better" claim on technical performance measurements.

2. That a question would be added to the survey of repairmen to elicit their opinion about whether the MAXIHUE picture was of "cable-TV quality." "I think that guy is reaching for one when he talks about chassis strength and remote signals," said Crust. "But I'll tell you what, once we get the research on the repairmen, if they say we do have cable-TV-quality pictures, we'll create a context that can only mean good pictures but not from faraway markets." Schneider agreed and "cable-TV quality" was dropped from MAXIHUE advertising, at least for the present.

3. That the phrase "compared to MAXIHUE all other sets are obsolete" must be dropped.

All of these agreements were reviewed with Art Webster and the legal department. When he approved them the agency then revised the story boards and advertisements once again. The standard selling phrase from the television commercials now read:

The MAXIHUE color television receiver is different from all competitive makes. The patented MAXIHUE circuitry takes the incoming station signal, fractionates it into basic color components, and then rebuilds it into a natural picture before it appears on the screen. Result: you no longer tune the MAXIHUE set—the picture reaches the set in pretuned form. No other television set can match the quality of the MAXIHUE picture for color composition.

And the MAXIHUE set costs less than other leading nationally advertised portable color television sets—no one of them outperforms MAXIHUE and not one of them costs so little.

The seven television commercials, as revised, were subsequently approved by each of the networks and produced and, once finished, were approved by the appropriate Cacaphony officials, including the three founders. They were then released to the networks and finally, some two months after Schneider's original target date, national advertising for the MAXIHUE portable color television set line commenced.

About a month later, August Schneider received a copy of a letter through the good offices of Wellington Crust. The letter had been written to Humboldt Aesop by his old friend and Cacaphony founder, G. N. Sternweiss. Here is that letter.

CACAPHONY SOUND

THE ROOM OF
THE FOUNDERS   November 19, 1974

Mr. Humboldt Aesop, Chairman
Aesop & Acton Advertising Agency
549 Madison Avenue
New York, New York 10017
Dear Hum:

It was wonderful to be with you and Elaine at the Harvard-Princeton game last weekend. Margery and I loved every minute of it: it was good of you to have us, and we were delighted with you that Harvard finally pulled out the win.

One thing I meant to mention over the weekend was the new MAXIHUE advertising. I know you have your troubles with our legal people and the networks and all, but somehow the advertising that's on the air makes MAXIHUE sound too much like all the competitive models.

We both know how significant an advantage this MAXIHUE is: a real breakthrough in electronics. I had a great deal to do with its development personally, and it is a little upsetting to see this particular light under a bushel basket.

Maybe it would be productive to have a few of your creative folks meet with our technical gang so they can develop a real appreciation of what MAXIHUE is. What do you think?

Meantime, thanks again for the great weekend: I do hope your team does as well with its opponent this coming Saturday.

Fond regards,
/s/ Gregor
Gregor N. Sternweiss

Three days later Schneider received from Art Webster the text of a formal communication from the Federal Trade Commission.[1] It was a formal order from the commission to Cacaphony Sound Company to furnish to the commission, within sixty days, documentation to support three advertising claims for MAXIHUE portable color television sets. The three claims for which the FTC required documentation were these:

1. "The MAXIHUE set costs less than other leading nationally advertised portable color television sets."
2. "No other television set can match the quality of the MAXIHUE picture for color composition."
3. "The MAXIHUE color television receiver is different from all competitive makes. The patented MAXIHUE circuitry takes the incoming station signal, fractionates it into basic color components, and then rebuilds it into a natural picture before it appears on the screen."

Webster also sent with the formal FTC order a copy of a formal FTC resolution of July 1971 that described the rationale for implementing the advertising substantiation program, its intended design, and the public benefits projected by the commission for the program. The text of this resolution (actual, not specimen) is reproduced as Exhibit 15–3.

EXHIBIT 15–3
Text of Federal Trade Commission Resolution of July 1971, Initiating the FTC Advertising Substantiation Program

Production of Documentation

The claims made in advertising consumer products often lead the consuming public to believe that such claims are substantiated by adequate and well-controlled scientific tests, studies, and other fully documented proof.

If the public and the Commission knew whether substantiation actually exists and the adequacy of substantiation, they would be aided in evaluating competing claims for products, and in distinguishing between the seller who is advertising truthfully and one who is unfairly treating both consumers and competitors by representing, directly or by implication, that it has proof when in fact there is none or the proof is inadequate.

Considering the importance of these questions to consumers and businessmen, the Commission, in fulfilling its statutory responsibility under Section 5 of the Federal Trade Commission Act (15 U.S.C. 45) with respect to false and deceptive advertising, and unfair methods of competition, *resolves* that advertisers shall be

---

[1] The following events are based on an actual advertising substantiation program undertaken by the Federal Trade Commission and reported in a publication entitled "Staff Report to the Federal Trade Commission on the Ad Substantiation Program Together with Supplementary Analysis of the Submissions and Advertisers' Comments," Committee on Commerce, U.S. Senate, Washington, D.C., July 31, 1972. Quotations in the text are taken from this source.

required, on demand by the Commission, to submit with respect to any advertisement such tests, studies or other data (including testimonials or endorsements) as they had in their possession prior to the time claims were made and which purport to substantiate any claims, statements or representations made in the advertisement regarding the safety, performance, efficacy, quality or comparative price of the product advertised.

The claims, statement or representations subject to the above requirement will be identified in Orders to File Special Reports which will be issued to such advertisers as may be selected from time to time by the Commission. If the advertiser had no data to substantiate these claims before they were made, he shall notify the Commission of this fact before the return date of the Order to File Special Reports.

The Commission will compel the production of said tests, studies or other data (including testimonials of endorsements) in the exercise of the powers vested in it by Sections 6, 9 and 10 of the Federal Trade Commission Act (15 U.S.C. 46, 49 and 50), and with the aid of any and all powers conferred upon it by law and any and all compulsory processes available to it.

Publication of Documentation Submitted

Except for trade secrets, customer lists or other financial information which may be privileged or confidential, pursuant to Section 6 (f) of the Federal Trade Commission Act, the material obtained by the Commission pursuant to this solution will be made available to the public under such terms and conditions as the Commission may from time to time determine. In addition, the Commission may release summaries, reports, indices, or such other publications which will inform the public about material delivered or not delivered to it hereunder.

In deciding to make this material available to the public, and to publish summary reports, the Commission is persuaded by the following policy considerations:

1. Public disclosure can assist consumers in making a rational choice among competing claims which purport to be based on objective evidence and in evaluating the weight to be accorded to such claims.
2. The public's need for this information is not being met voluntarily by advertisers.
3. Public disclosure can enhance competition by encouraging competitors to challenge advertising claims which had no basis in fact.
4. The knowledge that documentation or the lack thereof will be made public will encourage advertisers to have on hand adequate substantiation before claims are made.
5. The Commission has limited resources for detecting claims which are not substantiated by adequate proof. By making documentation submitted in response to this resolution available to the public, the Commission can be alerted by consumers, businessmen and public interest groups to possible violations of Section 5 of the Federal Trade Commission Act.[2]

Webster and Schneider discussed the FTC order between themselves, with the general counsel of Cacaphony Sound, and with the outside counsel retained by Cacaphony Sound for advice in such matters.

[2] Ibid, pp. 3 and 4.

Schneider was mad as a bee. "They seem to be accusing us of dishonest claims, Art," he said to Webster. "We told the truth, and we leaned over backwards to tell the truth, and then we satisfied you and your gang and then we satisfied the networks and I know those ads are true. But they're accusing us without a trial or a hearing, or anything. I feel like a criminal of some sort and I really have no recourse. What are we going to do?"

"Well, I don't want to give you any direction until I've cleared it with all the senior lawyers," said Art, reflectively and seriously sucking on his pipe, "but I believe that we will finally consider it prudent to respond to the order. We have, I believe, Augie, no choice."

There was considerably more pipe sucking, and veiled reference to the views of this and that commission, and allusions to proceedings in lower courts in prior years and similar cases, and several meetings and legal memoranda and all, and then the combined legal talent proceeded to consider it prudent to respond to the order.

Three documents were then submitted to the commission in response to its order.

The first was a summary analysis of factory-suggested retail list prices of nationally advertised competitive portable color television models of equivalent screen size (see Exhibit 15–4).

The second was the "Statement by Julian A. Hendelman, Ph.D., Concerning the Technical and Performance Characteristics of MAXIHUE Portable Color Television Receivers," reproduced above (p. 340) as Exhibit 15–1.

EXHIBIT 15–4
Specimen Data: Analysis of Factory Suggested Retail List Prices of 1974 Portable Color Television Sets—Nineteen-Inch Screen Size
Nationally Advertised Brands Only

MAXIHUE	MH 74–131	$279.99
	MH 74–132	269.99
	MH 74–135	249.99
SDB	384 Q 66	299.99
	384 R 66	324.99
Apex	18 C 74A	299.99
	18 C 74B	329.99
	18 C 74C	359.99
Nagami	884221	299.99
	193284	284.99
Marco	187433	284.99

The third was a series of twenty-eight pages abstracted from the original MAXIHUE patent application. This seemed the simplest and most direct way in which to demonstrate the fact that MAXIHUE sets were different and that the essential difference was patentable.

Some months passed before the FTC announced that the material submitted in response to the orders to file special reports had been collated and indexed by the commission staff. Claims of confidentiality were then reviewed by the commission, and any of the material submitted by manufacturers, claimed to be confidential, and judged by the commission to be, in fact, of a confidential nature was withdrawn. All of the remaining material (the bulk of it) was placed on public display, without editing. The documents were available for public perusal in commission offices in Washington, Atlanta, Boston, Chicago, Cleveland, Kansas City, Los Angeles, New Orleans, New York, San Francisco, and Seattle. Copies were also offered for sale to the public by the National Technical Information Service.

Subsequently, the staff of the commission prepared its "Staff Report to the Federal Trade Commission on the Ad Substantiation Program Together with a Supplementary Analysis of the Submissions and Advertisers' Comments." These documents were then released to the public by the chairman of the Consumer Subcommittee of the Committee of Commerce of the U.S. Senate.

In this staff report to the Federal Trade Commission on the ad substantiation program, the following statements were made about the general quality of the submissions by the advertisers in the television set and other consumer-durable categories:

The Commission staff's preliminary analysis yields a number of general conclusions. With respect to those claims that were made, at least 30% of the substantiating material was so technical in nature that it apparently required special expertise, far beyond the capacity of the average consumer, to evaluate. The quality of substantiation varied greatly from company to company, and claim to claim. Many claims were documented in a most impressive manner; on the other hand, serious questions as to the adequacy of data to support the claims they purported to document arose in about 30% of the responses.

Preliminary experience with the responses and the public's use of these responses leads to some tentative conclusions about the advertising substantiation program. Although the returns are not all in, it appears that few individual consumers are likely to request the substantiating material, and those who do receive it probably will not find the material very useful. Given the complexity of the documentation submitted, it seems apparent that the educational function of any such program will be minimal, unless interested consumer groups undertake to analyze the materials and translate them into language the consumer can understand. It is understood that various academic and public interest groups are presently engaged in such analytical work, but none has been published to date. Similarly, it is simply too early to judge the deterrent value of placing on the public record an entire industry's substantiation of advertising claims, since most of the ads questioned were prepared before the program was announced. . . .

The analysis of the substantiating material, limited as it is to applying the principles of logic and common experience, cannot replace the comprehensive investigation normally required to support a formal legal proceeding. A fully definitive evaluation of the substantiating material would require an extensive investigation, with expert technical assistance, of statistical data, engineering specifications and testing procedures. It is therefore conceivable that some documentation, presently viewed as adequate, may upon more investigation prove insufficient to support an advertising claim. Conversely, it is possible that additional material, not submitted by the respondent companies, may exist to support the claims.[3]

In the case of the substantiating material submitted by television set manufacturers who had received orders to file special reports, the staff concluded that the majority of the material submitted was either too technical to be evaluated without assistance or raised questions as to whether, in fact, it supported the advertising claim made. Of seventy-eight specific responses on particular claims examined by the staff, twenty-six were believed by the staff not to be adequate, thirty to be overly technical and could not be evaluated by the non-technically-trained members of the staff, and twenty-two might be adequate to support the advertised claims.

In its evaluation of specific claims (presented in the "Supplementary Analysis of the Submissions"), the following statements were made with respect to material submitted by Cacaphony Sound in order to substantiate its advertising.

---

1. *Under the general category of "Adequate Responses."* A Cacaphony Sound analysis of retail list prices of nineteen-inch portable color television sets in support of its claim that "the MAXIHUE set costs less than other leading nationally advertised portable color television sets." This documentation satisfactorily covered the claim. But the value to the consumer of this documentation may be questionable because the actual difference revealed by the analysis was less than two per cent in two instances.

2. *Under the category of "Instances Where the Material, Despite Its Relevance, Was of Doubtful Adequacy to Support the Claim."* In support of its claim that "no other television set can match the quality of the MAXIHUE picture for color composition," Cacaphony Sound presented a statement reflecting the judgments of a member of its technical staff, but this claim was not further substantiated by specific tests or other data.

3. *Under the category of "Technically Complex Responses."* Cacaphony Sound excerpted twenty-eight pages from its patent application for the MAXIHUE tube to substantiate its claim that "the MAXIHUE color television receiver is different from all competitive makes. The patented MAXIHUE circuitry

[3] Ibid, p. 2.

takes the incoming station signal, fractionates it into basic color components, and then rebuilds it into a natural picture before it appears on the screen." The information extracted from the patent application appears to be relevant to the claim, but it is probably incomprehensible to anyone without a background in electronics.

When August Schneider received this report he felt exasperated and helpless. He called Art Webster on the telephone: "Art, I've just read the FTC staff report. What in heaven's name do we do next?"

"Sit tight, Augie," said Webster. "One thing I should tell you is that we have had a chance to respond to this already. The chairman of the Consumer Subcommittee of the Committee on Commerce of the Senate sent us a copy of the FTC staff 'supplementary analysis' and invited us to comment on it with the promise that our response would be published with the supplementary analysis. We chose not to do that for a lot of reasons—but we *were* given the opportunity. As far as the commission is concerned, they may use this as a basis for a formal complaint that our advertising is false and misleading. And they may not. Who knows? And then too, we may get complaints from the Code Authority of the National Association of Broadcasters and from the National Advertising Review Board of the Better Business Bureau. Or some Senator may make a speech. Or Nader, or you name it. One thing's for sure, Augie, it isn't over. It's just begun."

Questions for Case 15

1. What advertising strategy underlies the advertising for MAXIHUE portable color television sets? Can consumer research help to resolve strategic alternatives?
2. What does a senior account executive in an advertising agency do? Using as a model Messrs. Moran and Crust of the Aesop & Acton agency, describe the primary functions of the senior account executive.
3. What function does an advertising agency fulfill? Why do most companies prefer to use outside advertising agencies? Why should Cacaphony Sound depend upon an advertising agency in preference to developing their own in-house advertising capability?
4. The purpose of advertising is to convey information to consumers. How does the Federal Trade Commission define the informational needs of consumers? How does this differ from the definition favored by Schneider? Is it likely that these two points of view can be totally reconciled by the administrative processes of the government regulative agency?
5. Why should advertising be regulated? How many regulatory levels are depicted in this case? From the standpoint of business operations, do you believe this to be too many or too few regulatory levels? From the consumer's standpoint? From the public policy standpoint?

6. How much does an advertising agency creative person have to know about a product to write successful advertising about it? Would a good engineer make a good writer of consumer advertising? Why or why not?

7. Appraise the "advertising substantiation" program of the FTC. Do you believe it should be continued? Should it be changed in any way? How?

Case 16

Corporate Social Responsibilities

Wonder Foods Develops Programs for Corporate Communications

T
HE WONDER FOODS COMPANY, INC. is the third largest food manufacturing company and the forty-ninth largest company in the United States (see Case 2). It is an immense organization: it has over thirty thousand employees throughout the world, and of these some twenty-eight thousand are employed in the United States. About six thousand of these work in the corporate headquarters in a small New Jersey town about an hour and a half away from New York City. The balance are spread throughout the country in forty-odd sales and warehousing locations and thirty-five separate manufacturing facilities.

A portion of the Wonder Foods organization chart is shown in Exhibit 16–1. It shows the major officers of the company and several of the major marketing functions that report to the executive vice-president in charge of marketing, Elton H. Markell. Markell has held this post for seven years. During this period, he has made a great many organizational and personnel changes as he attempted to shape a marketing structure that could produce growing sales and profits for Wonder Foods in the market conditions of the 1970's. As he reflects upon the job he has done over the years he wonders whether he has done rather more reorganizing than perhaps was necessary. He had, for example, abolished the old advertising department almost as soon as he had taken over. He then split the communications function into two parts: (a) a paid advertising component (with responsibility assigned to specific product managers under the director of marketing, Theodore W. MacMahoner); and (b) a public relations component. With the organizational change he had promoted the former director of advertising, V. J. Curry (deposed on the demise of the corporate advertising department), to vice-president for public relations and had hoped that all of this would work out for the best. But it had not, because Curry simply didn't know what public relations was and made little or no attempt to find out.

Instead, Curry devoted a great deal of his time trying to tell the brand product managers how to assess advertising copy and make advertising

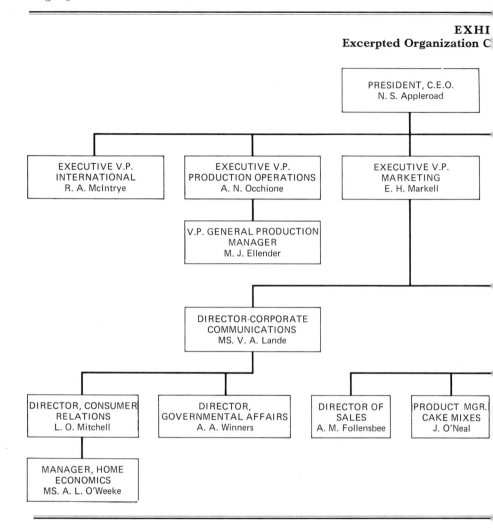

media decisions. His advice was not especially welcomed by the young product managers, not only because they resented his intrusion but also because they thought of Curry as an older man with rather outmoded points of view about advertising. Markell observed this state of affairs for a year and a half and then, after the complaints of the product managers reached an unbearable level, finally asked Curry to accept early retirement. Curry didn't like the suggestion and at first said he wouldn't do it, but he finally was told that he was in fact being fired and had no choice but to accept it quietly and with as much grace as he could.

There was then the question of who would replace Curry. This wasn't an easy decision for Markell either. The fact that he had chosen Curry in the first place demonstrated conclusively that there was no outstanding

1
Wonder Foods Company, 1974

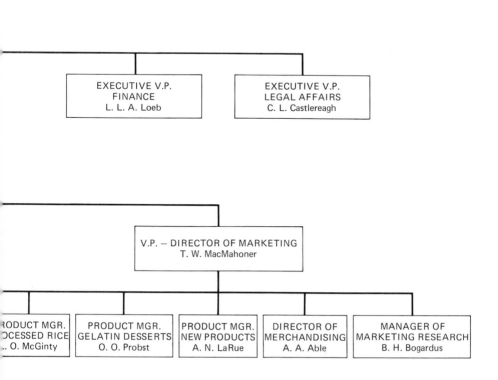

| EXECUTIVE V.P. FINANCE L. L. A. Loeb | EXECUTIVE V.P. LEGAL AFFAIRS C. L. Castlereagh |

V.P. – DIRECTOR OF MARKETING
T. W. MacMahoner

| RODUCT MGR. OCESSED RICE . O. McGinty | PRODUCT MGR. GELATIN DESSERTS O. O. Probst | PRODUCT MGR. NEW PRODUCTS A. N. LaRue | DIRECTOR OF MERCHANDISING A. A. Able | MANAGER OF MARKETING RESEARCH B. H. Bogardus |

candidate available within the company to take on the public relations job. What little public relations had been done during the year and a half that Curry had been responsible for the function had emanated from the public relations firm of Anderson, Anderson & Young, under the direction of the Anderson, Anderson & Young account executive, Virginia Lande.

Anderson, Anderson & Young had been retained as public relations counsel to Wonder Foods since 1948. Over the years as the Wonder Foods organization had grown and changed, the public relations firm had found itself reporting first to one executive and then another, its role undefined and its activities barely directed. A. B. "Sandy" Anderson did his best to maintain good relations with the various executives who were responsible for the P.R. activity, but he realized that the major reason that Anderson,

Anderson & Young seemed shunted from pillar to post had nothing to do with his firm but with Wonder Foods itself. "They don't know what public relations is, that's what," said Sandy Anderson to his partner, "Dusty" Young. "Some day we'll figure out a way to make it important to them, or something will happen to get what we do into proper perspective, or one of our competitors will get a break and take the business away from us. Someday, they're going to be one big PR account for somebody, and I sure hope it's us."

When Curry retired, Anderson was surprised to get a phone call from Markell. "I want to talk to you, Sandy, about what we should do to replace old Vance Curry. You know he decided on early retirement, and now we're up a tree, Sandy, because I really don't think there's anyone in the Wonder Company that can do the job, and I really believe there ought to be a professional handling it." Anderson might have been nonplussed by this, but he had been at the game too long not to know that a critical point in the relationship had arrived and that he had to make the right moves, right then, to survive. "Maybe you'll have to think about hiring from the outside, Elton. I know that isn't the Wonder way, but sometimes it may just be the only way to do it right."

"That's why I called you, Sandy. You've got a lady over there—a Miss or Mrs. Lande, or is it Ms.? Anyway, the people over there think she's done a good job in pretty difficult circumstances in the last couple of years and I thought she might be interested in coming over, but before I talked with her, I thought I better let you in on what I was thinking and see if you had any objection."

Without a split second of hesitation, Anderson responded, "It's OK with us, Elton. Virginia—it's Ms. quite emphatically, by the way—is terrific. And she really likes Wonder, enjoys working on it. You really should talk to her. I don't know what her reaction will be. You know as well as I do that people who work on the outside in ad agencies and PR firms and all have kind of different personality needs. I've never discussed it with Virginia. Some of our people don't want to work for big companies—they'd rather work on the same problems in a smaller house of professionals, get more interplay with other people in the same business that way and that seems to be important to them. So I don't know what she'll say—I honestly don't. But you really should talk to her, because whatever her personal view, she'll know your problem probably better than anyone and she'll know who you should talk to, if it isn't her."

And while he was saying all of this with total sincerity, he was also thinking that this was the break he'd been waiting for. Finally Wonder Foods would have a professional in charge of public relations, and if Virginia Lande took the job, or recommended a candidate, the professional would be someone who understood Anderson, Anderson & Young and respected the kind of work that it could do.

And so it came to pass that Virginia Lande was hired on September 1,

1973, as director of public relations of the Wonder Foods Company. When he hired her, Markell took a certain satisfaction in the fact that he was the first of the executive vice-presidents of the company to place a woman at the level of director of a corporate activity (the most senior Wonder Foods personnel grade below vice-president). And he hoped she did the job well: the better she performed the less trouble he'd have, and he'd had fully enough of sub-par public relations work in the days just passed.

* *
*

The late 1960's and early 1970's were turbulent years for major manufacturers of consumer goods. Their relations with the public were tested in many ways. Their hiring policies with respect to minority groups and women were subjected to public scrutiny. The truthfulness of their advertising and the integrity of their products were publicly questioned. Whether they were an environmental polluter or not was discussed openly. And in scores of other areas, ranging from significant to unimportant, a dialogue developed with the public and its governmental representatives about the ways in which the leading companies were responding to the needs of that public for better products at fairer prices, produced under policies that were democratic with respect to both the human resources needs of the community and the natural resource utilization of the community.

An era had finally come to an end. The corporation and its management were no longer responsible only to the shareholders for profitability. Now the management and its policies were required to reflect a broader responsibility to everyone the corporation touched in its dealings. The corporation management was required, in this broader responsibility, to be aware of the interest of all these publics and to preserve the integrity of these interests as well as to make a reasonable profit for its stockholders.

For many corporations these were years of self-regulation and shock. When a company changes its basic conception of how and to what end it will conduct its affairs, very fundamental processes are involved and very profound changes may be set in motion. In the opening rounds the company tends to respond in a perfunctory legalistic way. The legal officers try to define and limit the exact areas in which reform will come and the extent of the reform that is required. Lawyers talk to lawyers at the interface with government regulatory agencies. But while this is going on the company gradually discovers that its representatives are required at other interfaces too—interfaces that are not legalistic in nature or tone—with de facto consumer groups, with individual consumers, with representatives of suppliers of raw materials, with executives of advertising media, with representatives of distribution channel trade associations, and on and on.

Gradually the corporation perceives that there is more to the problem than lawyers can solve and that it must reform itself at least to some extent: the issue is one of change from within rather than simply negotiation with those outside. The realization comes slowly enough and its full dimension depends both on the degree to which the corporation really has been derelict in its social responsibilities and on the degree of really constructive pressure that the leaders of reform bring to bear. More often than not the corporation has done a much better job, almost inadvertently, than its critics suggest. And often enough, too, the constructive pressure of the critic evaporates with the passage of time because some other short-term political goal has been achieved by the reformer that diverts his attention from the corporate target.

But regardless of the situation in the particular company, it is soon enough obvious that some person or persons must be designated to become concerned with social responsibility. This person must assess the position of the company on the major social issues of the day and identify ways and means of coping with them that will satisfy the company's critics while doing as little harm as possible to the company's earnings.

For Wonder Foods, the first really serious problem arose when a young food scientist questioned the nutritional value of two of the company's leading brands: Fluffy Quick preprocessed rice and Sparkle Mucho Gelatin Desserts. The young man—Oswald Reincke, by name—was an associate professor of food chemistry at a smallish Northern Plains agricultural school. No one at Wonder Foods, or in most other business organizations for that matter, had ever heard of Reincke before he appeared before a Senate subcommittee to testify about the nutritional levels achieved by the typical American family and how they might be improved. To dramatize the point that the consumer was being nutritionally shortchanged, Reincke had listed fifty leading processed foods and presented an evaluation of their food value. Both Fluffy Quick preprocessed rice and Sparkle Mucho Gelatin Desserts were named, as were products of other leading food manufacturers. And both brands appeared, on the basis of data presented by Reincke, to have only negligible nutritional value.

All of this was headline news around the country and it was clear that the reputation of Wonder Foods and two of its leading brands had been significantly hurt. Because the statement had been made before a congressional committee and because he hadn't the foggiest idea what else to do, N. Stuart Appleroad, president and chief executive officer of Wonder Foods, directed his chief legal officer, C. L. "Clutch" Castlereaghe, to make a noncommittal public statement and subsequently to launch an investigation of Reincke's charges. The Wonder Foods statement, which was the only public response made by the company, follows (page 365).

Appleroad himself refused to be interviewed about the statement and he suggested that when Castlereaghe met with the press that he should make no comment beyond that contained in the statement.

The whole matter was then investigated by Wonder Foods in some

WONDER FOODS COMPANY PRESS RELEASE

FOR IMMEDIATE RELEASE

The Wonder Foods Company has become aware of certain statements made by Dr. Oswald Reincke on October 16, 1973 before a Senate subcommittee about two Wonder Foods products: Fluffy Quick preprocessed rice and Sparkle Mucho Gelatin Desserts.

Wonder Foods has not examined the studies upon which Dr. Reincke based his testimony and cannot, therefore, comment specifically upon his allegations at this time. We state unequivocally that Wonder Foods products and, specifically, Fluffy Quick Rice and Sparkle Mucho Gelatin Desserts are superior products with excellent nutritional characteristics.

We would welcome an opportunity to study and appraise the Reincke data and report more fully to the American public.

(October 18, 1973)

---

detail. Reincke's material was published weeks later in the formal proceedings of the committee hearings. It was then determined that his methods of data collection were outmoded and his methods of analysis had serious flaws. It was finally decided that no respected nutritionist would take his views and conclusions seriously and that most of the products included in his analyses (including the Wonder Foods brands) were in no way deficient nutritionally nor less nutritious than the raw ingredients used in their manufacture.

Three months had then passed since Reincke's original testimony, and Wonder Foods was hard pressed to find a way to redress the wrong that they were now sure had been visited upon them by Reincke.

The senior staff members in the office of the Senator under whose aegis the hearings had been held advised Wonder Foods that the hearings and their record were closed, that the Senator had no intention of reopening the hearings, and that there was no further interest in the topic.

Dr. Reincke had, meanwhile, retreated to his university post. Although he answered promptly all letters addressed to him, his answers were perfunctory and reflected no interest on his part in further debate about or clarification of his earlier data and research.

By this time, Virginia Lande (and Anderson, Anderson & Young) had been brought into the picture by Appleroad and Markell. The best advice that Ms. Lande could give was to prepare a dispassionate report, repudiating the Reincke testimony, scientific in nature and tone, but simple and straightforward enough to interest the scientific and nutritional editors of the mass media, and then to distribute this report and other related materials in a press kit to these editors, perhaps at a press luncheon called for the occasion. "We're too late, Elton," remarked Virginia Lande as she discussed the problem with Elton Markell. "We've got a lot of work to do to get into a position where we can instantly respond to statements and testimony like Reincke's. But more than this, we've got to find a way to be there while the band is still playing and make darn sure our side of the case is presented in the same hearings and on the same platform. There are ways to do that, and we'll do 'em, but we're too late to accomplish much this time. Anyway, it's a start and we can at least be slow but self-righteous and that's better than just being dumb. But let's give a lunch. If we don't and these science and nutritional people get wind of what's up, they'll stay away in droves. We've got to give to get and the free lunch is about as cheap as you can give."

Twenty-eight nutritional or science editors appeared at the Wonder Foods press luncheon held at the Fifth Avenue Hotel in New York City, and fourteen appeared at a similar function held at the Noble Western Hotel in Chicago a week later. The response of the editors was one of appreciative boredom, and almost nothing subsequently appeared in their respective media to suggest that they had absorbed the Wonder Foods message. "Well, it's a start," Virginia Lande thought to herself. "Maybe they'll call me before they write their stories next time, and maybe I'll be able to tone it down a little before it gets out to the public."

For the next eighteen months a whole series of similar incidents occurred as one group after another expressed public concern over the ways in which Wonder Foods Company conducted its affairs.

Early in 1971, the American Activists for Women issued a press release from its Washington headquarters about Wonder Food advertising in behalf of Pretty Picture DeLuxe Cake Mixes. The complaint alleged that a particular Pretty Picture DeLuxe Cake Mix commercial showed the heroine in the commercial in a demeaning and degrading way relative to the product portrayed in the commercial. (The commercial was a rather whimsical treatment of the dilemma faced by an attractive young married woman who wanted both to bake a cake for her new husband and to look pretty for him on his arrival home from the office. The tag line of the commercial was "If you want to be Pretty as a Picture, use Pretty Picture DeLuxe Cake Mixes in your kitchen.") The American Activists for Women was, the press release announced, boycotting Pretty Picture DeLuxe Cake Mixes until "a totally new perspective and tonality is achieved in Pretty Picture DeLuxe Cake Mix consumer advertising. The life of woman is not tied to home and kitchen: it is the destiny of woman to transcend her historic submission to the male." In addition, A.A.W. picket lines were thrown up around Wonder Foods corporate headquarters and the headquarters of several major food chains, as customers of Wonder Foods.

"OK, Virginia," said Markell, "What do we do about this one? I've had my doubts about that commercial, all right, but my worry was that it might not sell any cake mixes because it really isn't very hard sell and it doesn't come down on the reasons why PPD is a better product. But does it really degrade women, Virginia?"

"You've got me, Elton," said Virginia. "I think it's a nice, innocuous little commercial, which I don't like very much, but I don't know anything about advertising and from what I've seen of it, I don't want to know anything. What are the plans for that commercial? Do you plan to keep it on the air for a long time? Are you going to make more like it?"

There had been enough discontent within the organization about this particular advertising so that plans were already well along to scrap it and put a totally new campaign into production. The new campaign was a straightforward statement of the virtues of Pretty Picture DeLuxe Cake Mixes delivered by a male announcer, with various table top demonstrations, visualizing the various product superiorities that characterized the Pretty Picture DeLuxe brand.

It seemed to all concerned that the American Activists for Women could find little enough to object to in this proposed advertising. The question was what to do about the picketing and the boycott. Castlereaghe was reluctant to make a legal issue out of it. "Look," he said to Markell, "they probably haven't got any real right to picket us and I'm not even sure what their boycott means. And I'm not sure about their right to picket our customers. Maybe we should try to get an injunction, but this is a very murky area in the law. At the best it can take a long time in the courts and generate lots of publicity, most of which would be favorable to them and not to us. Even if we win they'll appeal it and it will go on and on. And if we happened to lose, heaven only knows what kinds of precedents might be set."

"But, Clutch, I don't want to knuckle under to these ladies," said Markell. "We give them this one, and who knows what they'll want next. The next time it might be something that we really do care about, you know, and then what will we do? You know, there are precedents in practice as well as in the law." "Let it ride, Elton, let it ride," replied Castlereaghe. "Don't do anything except replace that commercial and let the whole thing fall of its own weight. You do anything else and you're playing into their hands."

Next, a conservation club in Biloxi, Mississippi exposed the fact that the local Wonder Foods rice-processing plant was dumping hundreds of gallons of dilute sulfuric acid (a by-product produced in the rice conversion process) into a local stream, killing certain varieties of fish under certain circumstances and potentially endangering the eyesight of downstream bathers. (On investigation, Wonder found the allegations to be true and rebuilt the plant so that acid wastes would be treated and rendered harmless before being discharged into continuous aqueous aerator waste-disposal units, rather than into the river.)

In another plant city, Schenectady, New York, another rather more serious pollution issue arose. A crusading television reporter discovered that the Mucho Sparkle Gelatin Dessert processing plant in Schenectady was emitting a colorless, odorless gas into the atmosphere that, if sufficiently concentrated, could cause irritation of the entire upper respiratory tract as well as significant eye tearing. This gas, known as PHPLAP, had been identified and named only after forty workers in a gelatin processing plant in Lille, France all became mysteriously afflicted with severe manifestations of these symptoms when an air circulator failed to function for a period of about a week. Finally, two of the Lille employees died, and the ensuing investigation led to the identification of PHPLAP as well as to the establishment of new ventilation standards (including back-up air circulators) in the French gelatin-processing industry.

The Schenectady newsman happened upon this story while visiting relatives in New York City whose next door neighbor had lost an uncle in the Lille incident. At first, the newsman was only vaguely interested in what had happened to the neighbor's uncle. But then, suddenly, it dawned on him that there was a Wonder Foods gelatin-processing plant in Schenectady, and he began to listen more closely and think a little harder about what he heard. When he returned to Schenectady he visited the Wonder Foods plant, was courteously received, and was given a guided tour of the plant by the senior engineering officer who was charged with overall responsibility for employee safety. This officer explained that the existence of a noxious gas as a by-product in the gelatin processing had long been known about, although it was only recently that this gas had been given the name PHPLAP by the French, following the disaster of Lille.

Moreover, when the Schenectady gelatin plant had been built in 1938, the potential danger had been anticipated. A very powerful exhaust-fan system had been designed for the Schenectady plant. It replaced the air within the plant four times every minute and accomplished this so efficiently that the PHPLAP was gone before it could come to rest in the eyes or within the respiratory tract of the workers. "Where does all that PHPLAP go?" asked the television reporter. "Why outside, of course," responded the engineer. "You mean, into the Schenectady atmosphere?" asked the reporter.

And thus, with this innocent exchange, began the great SNAP episode. The reporter announced, on his station's evening news program on the very day that he had had his plant tour, that an environmental hazard of significant proportions existed in Schenectady, recounted the tragic events of Lille, and implied that the discharge of PHPLAP into the Schenectady atmosphere threatened all of the residents of Schenectady with upper respiratory infection, tearing, and even death. The existence of PHPLAP in the atmosphere was, of course, bad enough, said the reporter, but what about when the conditions of atmospheric inversion existed (that is, a windless atmospheric condition in which the atmospheric temperature in a particular geographic area inverts and tends to hold pollutants down against their origin rather than exhausting them outward)? Atmospheric inversions and attendant severe air pollution had been known in Schenectady in times gone by, and they had inevitably caused discomfort among those affected with respiratory disease; there were even occasional deaths attributable to the conditions that the inversion produced. The television reporter ended his exposé with the question, "How many inversion deaths have been due to the continuing presence of Sparkle Mucho PHPLAP in our atmosphere?"

Within a week, an ad hoc group called SNAP (Schenectady Neighbors Against PHPLAP) had been formed. This group included representatives of a very large number of concerned Schenectady organizations, including conservation and anti-pollution groups, of course, but ranging through Boy Scouts, church groups, service groups (like the Elks and Lions), and even several PTA's. Perhaps it had been a slow winter in Schenectady and maybe the city was ripe for a pollution crisis, but whatever the reason, the SNAP activity took hold throughout the city in a way that was unprecedented. Within a week after the formation of SNAP, a formal plan of action had been drawn up. This included (1) a demand to Wonder Foods that all gelatin formulation be halted in Schenectady until some device had been found to dispose of PHPLAP totally and with no atmospheric discharge; (2) the institution of a class-action suit against Wonder Foods in behalf of all the citizens of Schenectady whose present and future health and well-being had been endangered by the discharge of PHPLAP into the Schenectady atmosphere: and (3) twenty-four-hours-a-day, seven-days-a-week picketing of the Schenectady Wonder Foods plant. In the first several days the picketing was so effective, although totally nonviolent, that almost no Wonder Foods employees reported for work and almost no deliveries to the plant could be made. Within a week the plant was effectively shut down, even though no such decision, or any decision at all, for that matter, had been made by Wonder Foods management in the remote New Jersey headquarters.

In New Jersey, there was a good deal of confusion about just what to do. The senior corporate officer immediately affected by the Schenectady crisis was A. N. Occhione, executive vice-president for production operations. Al Occhione was a superb production man. He knew as much as any man about the ways in which abstract chemical and physical processes could be harnessed to the mass production of food products under absolutely sterile conditions at low cost. And what he didn't know, he knew how to find out. But Occhione was completely nonplussed by the thought of pickets around his plant because of a health danger his plants might be causing to a community. "It's just not so, Stuart," Occhione exclaimed in his first meeting on the topic with N. S. Appleroad. "We know all about PHPLAP, and it might hurt some people if they breathed about 50 per cent PHPLAP for an hour or two—but what we discharge up there would need an atmospheric inversion six weeks long to get up to a concentration of 50 per cent. The longest known inversion in Schenectady lasted eight days in 1924. After eight days the PHPLAP concentration in the atmosphere is at maximum one fortieth of one per cent. Our plant safety regulations say a PHPLAP concentration of one per cent is not harmful, and I know those safety regulations are right because I had three separate authorities work on them. Anyway, all we have to do is shut off the plant during an atmospheric inversion and there's no harm anyway. What are these people trying to do to us, anyway? You've got to go up there, Stuart, and see the mayor or the SNAP people and get them on our side."

Appleroad called a meeting of Occhione, Elton Markell, Clutch Castlereaghe, and Virginia Lande to decide what to do in Schenectady. After considerable discussion it was decided that Virginia Lande and Al Occhione would go to Schenectady the next day, talk to as many of the local public, media, and SNAP officials as they could, and make recommendations to Appleroad as to what course should be followed.

Ms. Lande and Al Occhione found a good deal of sympathy among the public officials of Schenectady for the plight of Wonder Foods. After they heard Al Occhione out, they stated strongly their belief that if all the facts were made public, it would be a relatively easy matter to bring the SNAP leaders to their senses and stop the demands, class-action suits, and picketing. "Will you support us with SNAP, Mr. Mayor?" asked Virginia Lande during a meeting with the mayor of Schenectady, several of his aides, and Occhione. "Of course I will, Ms. Lande, if you really get your story across to the people so they understand how little real danger there is, just as Mr. Orchonne explained it to me."

"It's *Occhione*, Mr. Mayor," responded Virginia Lande. "But what I mean is, will you, yourself, help convince them that there is no danger?"

"Well, I'm not an engineer or anything like that, Ms. Lande. You don't know my background, of course, but all I know is what little law you pick up studying nights along with the common sense the good Lord gave us all. So I really couldn't be expected to act like an expert with that SNAP group, now could I?"

"Mr. Mayor," said Ms. Lande, "I assume that you do want to help, because it couldn't be very good for Schenectady if Wonder Foods had to pull out, and the word got around that you weren't very hospitable to companies that want to put factories in here to help the tax rate and give jobs and all."

"Well of course we want to be helpful, Ms. Lande. You know that just as well as I do. And you know we do everything in our power to accommodate folks who want to bring new industry in here. I suppose if you folks announced that you had agreed to give me the right to shut your plant any time in my judgment there was a danger to public health or safety, that might be enough to convince these SNAP folks that their interests had been taken care of right down here in the office of the mayor."

"But, Mr. Mayor," said Ms. Lande, "don't you have that right already, and even if you don't, don't you believe that Wonder Foods is public-spirited enough and has a sufficient sense of its social responsibility to shut its own plant down if the public health was endangered?"

"Well, Ms. Lande," replied the mayor, "maybe I do have that power already, but I've certainly never exercised it, have I? And maybe you've got a terrific sense of social responsibility, but I don't remember you folks ever shutting that plant down during an atmosphere inversion, do you?"

"No, Mr. Mayor, we never did do that, because, as I've explained, there is simply no need," responded Occhione, who had not quite understood the reason Virginia Lande had put up with all this long-winded conversation with this dotty old pol.

"Well, I think the mayor makes a pretty good point, Al," said Virginia Lande. "In a way that's what this is all about, Al. The point is that nobody has ever done anything before, and now a lot of people here in Schenectady think that something should have been done, and so now the mayor feels that he has to be able to reassure his people that he'll shut our plant if there's any danger. I think we'll be able to do that without any trouble at all, Mr. Mayor. I suspect our president, Mr. Appleroad, will want to come up here and talk to the press and to you and your officials and perhaps go on TV, and I don't see any reason why he wouldn't want to give you that power, just as long, of course, as it was limited to bona fide atmospheric inversions, authenticated by the National Weather Service."

N. Stuart Appleroad did travel to Schenectady, did preside at a press conference, did appear on each of the three television stations on time paid for by Wonder Foods, and did lunch with the mayor. In each of these appearances he gave the basic story of the safety of the Wonder Foods ventilating system, the very low and innocuous concentrations of PHPLAP normally found in the Schenectady atmosphere, and the joint agreement between the mayor of Schenectady and Wonder Foods, Inc. that in the future, during atmospheric inversions over Schenectady, the mayor would have the right to close the Wonder Foods plant if he believed there to be any danger to the public health and safety. The SNAP leaders accepted this resolution, and although they did not promise to disband, it was clear that the Wonder Foods story and the Mayor's intercession had taken the wind out of SNAP's sails and the PHPLAP issue was dead.

On the drive back to New Jersey, after this long day in Schenectady, Stuart Appleroad, Al Occhione, and Virginia Lande had a long conversation about the events of the day and all the things that had caused SNAP. "That old mayor is a cagey fellow, all right," mused Appleroad. "He worked us over pretty good when you analyse it. He made all the political hay there was to be made out of the situation and then some, and, in a way, in the end it looks like he is running our plant rather than us. Not a bad day's work for him, when you think about it. But we got out of it OK. Let's hope there isn't one of those atmospheric inversions for a while, and let's make sure we know enough about them technically to protect ourselves in court, Al, in case he wants to get fancy. OK?"

"OK, Stuart," responded Occhione glumly. He didn't like anything about the entire sequence of events in Schenectady. The facts, after all, seemed to speak for themselves, and he neither liked nor understood public relations people, and mayors, and television appearances by his boss on subjects that he considered to be his own domain, and days in Schenectady in general.

"Virginia, I think we have a major problem," said Stuart Appleroad. "All year long it's been one thing after another. First it was that nut nutritionist from South Dakota, and then it was the ladies who didn't like our television commercials for some reason or other, and then it was the acid discharge in Mississippi, and now this, and who knows how many other things. I'll take it as given that we have to be more aware of the public interest than perhaps we have been in the past, and I'm willing to accept that this is going to cost us profit dollars, and I'm willing to do whatever we have to do to handle the situation. The thing that bothers me is that we've been on the defensive from the start, and we really haven't been doing very well. Nobody knows that that nutritionist was dead wrong and the ladies weren't answered or fought—they were just bypassed. And we rebuilt the plant in Mississippi, and up here we let an upstate apple knocker take credit for something that he seems to have fixed for us, that we all know didn't need fixing in the first place. These people are taking advantage of us, Virginia, and we've got to do something about it. I never did understand what public relations was all about. but I do know what not being taken advantage of is all about and that's what public relations means at Wonder Foods from now on, OK?"

Neither Ms. Lande nor Al Occhione had any response to this. Virginia had no idea whether what Appleroad had just said was something he simply felt deeply and wanted to get off his chest or whether he was making a sharp and determined criticism of her own work, and she said nothing as she tried to figure out what was really on Appleroad's mind. Occhione, on the other hand, had had enough of public relations, whatever that was, for one day and didn't want anything more to do with it.

"Virginia," Appleroad continued, "I want you to do something for me. I want to know what we should do—what kind of a program, that is—to go on the offensive. Give me a plan and tell me how much it will cost to get us out of this position we seem to be in. We can't drift along from one crisis and embarrassment to another any longer."

"Right, Stuart," said Virginia Lande, and then she was silent as she wondered what kind of a plan she should put together for the boss.

She thought about it for several days and then drafted and redrafted a formal memorandum to Appleroad that summarized the immediate and long-term steps that she felt the company should take to discharge its social responsibilities more fully. Here is the memorandum she wrote.

WONDER FOODS MEMORANDUM

TO: N. Stuart Appleroad
FROM: Virginia Lande
SUBJECT: Wonder Foods Social Responsibilities

You asked me to recommend a program to deal with the recurring social responsibilities problems and crises that Wonder Foods has been faced with over the last year or two.

The several incidents with which we have been faced have all had a single characteristic: they have been totally unexpected. And because we have not, as a company, consistently discharged our social responsibilities over the years, we have not been sure, in each instance, whether the company was in the right or in the wrong. If anyone were to challenge our plant sanitation, we would know immediately that he was wrong because it has been our consistent policy over the years to maintain the highest sanitation standards in our plants. But we have not had similar policies with respect to pollution, or toward the women's lib implications of our television commercials, or even with respect to the degree of nutritional carry-through in our processed foods. Thus we are vulnerable to an attack in any of these areas.

The public is in a mood to expect that corporations aren't very good citizens these days, and so there is a more receptive audience to attacks of these kinds than there has been in times past. I doubt very much that the public receptivity is going to decline, and so we can continue to expect incidents of the type we've had in which someone points a finger at us and cries "foul."

It is probably true that we cannot totally protect ourselves against this sort of thing in the future. It is one thing to clean up a plant that really is polluting a river, and it's a totally different thing to anticipate the PHPLAP problem and do something about it before it begins. The first kind of situation can be handled before it happens, but there really is nothing we could have done in Schenectady to forestall the SNAP crisis.

With this background, it seems to me that we can establish some realistic and practicable goals for a social responsibility program for Wonder Foods and outline some policies that we can implement immediately to achieve those goals.

Here are three goals we should set for ourselves immediately:

1. We should discharge our social responsibilities wherever it is practical for us to do so.
2. We should build a public reputation for social responsibility.
3. We should reduce our vulnerability to irresponsible attacks on the part of those who wish to take advantage of us for their own selfish gains.

To achieve these goals, we should take the following steps:

1. We should inventory our progress in matters of social responsibility. That is,

we should identify areas in which we are socially responsible—pollution control, minority group recognition and training, product-standard maintenance, plant sanitation standards, nutritional development programs, and so on—and inventory those things that we have done and those areas in which we are, in fact, vulnerable. Such an inventory would have identified the Biloxi pollution problem, for example. And such an inventory would give us materials immediately at hand with which to answer accusations such as those made by Oswald Reincke in congressional testimony.

2. We should develop comprehensive information concerning what other competitor and comparable firms have done and are doing to discharge their social responsibilities.

It is one thing to know what Wonder Foods has and has not done, but it's important to have some kind of idea about the standards of social responsibility that prevail in the rest of the industry.

Fixing the Biloxi plant seemed like the only thing that could be done in the circumstances. But it cost us four million-odd dollars to fix it, and I think it might have been helpful to know what other firms had done in similar circumstances—exactly how they handled themselves, with what results, and at what expense. This will be important to know when our own inventory indicates places where we have been derelict in our social responsibility and we have to decide what to do and when to do it.

3. We should consider a program of corporate communication based both on public relations activities and advertising to convey to the public our recognition of social responsibilities and on the steps that we are taking to discharge our obligations in this area. We want to create an aura of good practice around Wonder Foods. The public should think well of us before the fact. If they do, it will make it that much more difficult for the irresponsible to attack us and just that much easier for us to respond.

The fodder for such a program of corporate communication will come from our social responsibility inventory. And I assume that we will find plenty of good works in the closet—because there must be a solid basis for such a communication program. The days of being virtuous through proclamation are long behind us. You have to deliver the goods before you can brag about it.

4. Finally, one corporate officer should be continuously on call to respond to every social responsibility situation that develops. This officer will be responsible for building and maintaining a posture of strength in this area. So far, every time something of this kind has come up we have run away and hidden for two or three days and then either issued a mealymouthed press release or let the local politicians make monkeys out of us. Someone should be ready to tell the Wonder Foods story in the strongest way at a moment's notice. The more that person knows about what we've done in the past (the social responsibility inventory) and the more the public believes that Wonder Foods does care and is doing socially responsible things, the better the job he'll be able to do.

But, there must be a Wonder Foods spokesman and a Wonder Foods point of view, not just a slow-to-respond committee that talks out of several sides of its mouth. Incidentally, this is a job I'd like for myself.

* *
*

Meanwhile, T. W. MacMahoner had been working on a totally different area of corporate communications. He had become increasingly concerned about the decline in sales of the nonadvertised products produced by Wonder Foods Company. These nonadvertised brands had contributed $65,106,224 in sales and $16,927,568 in profits in 1971. But they had declined sharply in 1972 and 1973. The 1973 sales were $58,521,821 and the 1973 profits were $9,498,992. There were some seventy-odd Wonder Foods products not actively promoted by the Wonder Foods Company. These included the Friendly Girl line of dessert toppings, Eureka brand dry cooking ingredients (Eureka Brand powdered sugar, granulated sugar, brown sugar, cornstarch, baking powder, cream of tartar, cake flour, all-purpose flour, long-grain rice, cocoa, and so on); Tangy Land brand dry spices (salt, ground white pepper, ground black pepper, whole black pepper, thyme, marjoram, rosemary, basil, coriander, dill, tarragon, parsley, mint, all-spice, cardamom, MSG, turmeric, and so on); Sparkling Drop brand line of wet cooking ingredients (molasses, cider vinegar, wine vinegar, plain vinegar, soy sauce, cane sugar syrups, pancake syrups, and so on); and the Bertram Bunny line of children's jams and jellies.

Taken as a group, these nonpromoted brands produced a sizeable dollar volume and profit for the Wonder Foods Company, although specific individual items were typically of little consequence. Over the years these nonpromoted lines had shown slow but steady sales growth following the upward trend in the general population. Within the nonpromoted group, some items had declined as attractive substitutes were developed in the marketplace. For example, Eureka Brand long-grain rice was, at one time, a relatively big seller. In 1953 the sales on this brand surpassed $16 million. But the growing popularity of preprocessed rice had a sharp impact on Eureka long-grain sales in the late 1950's. Thus in 1965 Eureka long-grain rice sales had fallen to about $10 million. But meanwhile Wonder Foods Fluffy Quick preprocessed rice sales had burgeoned as Eureka long-grain languished. At the same time some other items within the line prospered. For instance, in the late 1950's the Tangy Land line had begun to show sharp sales increases as a growing preoccupation with sophisticated cookery developed among American housewives. Finally, the sales of some items had declined as underlying consumer preferences inexplicably declined. This has been the recent fate of the Sparkling Drop line.

The overall effect of the gains and declines within the line was a gradual sales increase from year to year. This trend is seen in Exhibit 16–2 in the years 1956 thru 1971. Suddenly and unexpectedly, in 1972, the nonpromoted items showed a sales decline. This was followed by an even sharper drop in 1973.

As this change in the fortunes of the nonpromoted products unfolded, MacMahoner turned the problem over to Hunty Johnson, who had recently been given the assignment of Product Manager–Advertised

EXHIBIT 16–2
Specimen Data: Sales and Gross Profit of the
Nonpromoted Wonder Foods Brands 1956–73

	TOTAL SALES	GROSS PROFIT CONTRIBUTION
1956	$48,142,672	$10,772,384
1966	58,428,789	14,022,723
1967	59,133,406	14,783,254
1968	61,245,662	15,311,258
1969	62,578,999	15,018,722
1970	64,052,767	15,372,488
1971	65,106,224	16,927,568
1972	63,021,448	13,234,419
1973	58,521,821	9,498,992

Lines (see Case 2). "Here's another headache for you, Hunty," said MacMahoner. "Heaven only knows what's happened to all those products, but we've got to find out fast and do something about it."

Hunty Johnson's first response to the sales decline was to initiate a series of trade deals to stimulate dealer stocking and pushing of the various nonpromoted items. Under these trade deals, substantial discounts were offered to those merchants buying a specified (and substantial) quantity and variety of Wonder Foods nonpromoted brands. Much to Johnson's consternation, these trade deals failed to generate any substantial new volume. The large chains gave three basic reasons for disinterest in these Wonder Foods promotions.

1. First, inventories on the Wonder Foods line were generally very, very high. The chains continued to buy isolated items for open stock to maintain adequate inventory levels on these particular items. But the chains were not interested in making substantial additional purchases of the nonpromoted items, regardless of how attractive the deal prices were. For example, one of the offered deals involved the Eureka brand. Wonder Foods offered major chains one case of any Eureka brand merchandise free with the purchase of one case each of seven different items of Eureka brand merchandise. This offer was very generous, representing an extra discount of about 12.5 per cent when the deal terms were met (the case prices of the various Eureka brand items were approximately the same). It had been estimated that 100,000 of these Eureka "deals" would be sold to the major chains. Actually, 16,236 of these deals were sold, although during the deal period almost every major chain did order small quantities of individual items to fill out depleted inventories on particular Eureka products.

2. Several of the chains also pointed out that even if their inventory position on the nonpromoted items had not been very high, they would have had little interest in the trade deals without specific extra advertising or consumer promotion support to accelerate consumer demand for the products in the deal. In other words, the chains had little interest in making substantial deal purchases unless they received help from the manufacturer in moving the merchandise out of their stores. They were not interested in buying extra quantities of nonpromoted generic items, regardless of how attractive the price might be.

3. Finally, several chains revealed that they had been expanding their own private labels into many of the areas that had been the exclusive preserve of the major food producers like Wonder. Thus, for example, many chains were in the process of introducing private-label items directly competitive with the leading nonpromoted Wonder Foods brands. This seemed to be a major reason underlying the sales decline of the Wonder Foods nonpromoted brands. But it was also an important reason why Wonder Foods could do relatively little to force the trade to buy and push this nonpromoted merchandise. It was virtually impossible for Wonder Foods to price these products, through periodic deals or price reductions, so that they would be more profitable to the food chains than their own private labels. And, of course, Wonder Foods could not, over the long haul, offer price concessions on their nonpromoted brands without seriously reducing their profitability to Wonder Foods.

Johnson studied this situation closely and with growing alarm throughout the latter months of 1974. The obvious solution was to create consumer demand for the various nonpromoted brands through advertising or continuous consumer promotion. But any adequate advertising and/or promotion program across these previously non-promoted lines would be likely to be so expensive that Wonder Foods profits would be cut far below acceptable levels. And, of course, any price increase to support new advertising or promotional activities would play directly into the hands of the chain stores by giving their own private-label brands an even greater price advantage at the consumer level. Johnson was keenly aware that almost all of the Wonder nonpromoted items were essentially generic: in almost every instance there was no differentiation from the private-label brands that could serve as a basis for effective advertising. After a thorough analysis it seemed clear to MacMahoner that the promotion and advertising of individual Wonder Foods lines could not be made economic.

At this point, Johnson proposed an alternative course of action. First, he suggested that *all* of the Wonder Foods packages—for both advertised and nonadvertised brands—be redesigned to include a common corporate identifying mark. This common mark would, under Johnson's plan, appear on all of the advertised Wonder Foods brands as well as on the nonpromotional brands. Second, he recommended that a corporate or umbrella advertising campaign be developed in support of the previously nonadvertised brands that would emphasize the fact that they carried the common corporate mark and would indicate specifically the kinship existing between the advertised and previously nonadvertised brands.

Johnson suggested that 20 per cent of the gross profits of the non-advertised brands in 1973 (see Exhibit 16–2) be established as the budget for this umbrella advertising campaign. He also suggested that marketing research be used to help develop and evaluate alternative common corporate identifying marks and to develop and evaluate the umbrella advertising campaign.

A lengthy series of meetings between MacMahoner, Johnson, and various other representatives of Wonder Foods sales, marketing, and advertising departments were held to examine Johnson's suggestions. Sitting in these meetings as a representative of the marketing research department was Jacob D. Jack, the associate manager of the Wonder Foods marketing research department.

Jack suggested that before any package development or advertising development work was undertaken some attempt be made to establish that an overt association between Wonder Foods and the previously non-promoted brands would enhance the appeal of these brands in the consumer's eyes. To this end, Jack recommended that a simple brand-rating study be undertaken.

This study, as he envisioned it, would consist of two separate parts. In one part, respondents would be asked to express their attitudes toward a list of brand names. These brand names would not be identified as products of a particular corporation. Some of these brands would be heavily advertised brands from the Wonder Foods stable; some would be nonadvertised brands from Wonder Foods; and some would be non-advertised brands from leading food chains. In the second part of the study, a matched group of respondents would express their attitudes toward the same list of brand names, except the brands would now be identified as the products of either Wonder Foods or the food chain sponsor. The two parts of the study would be identical except for this difference in the brand name list. The measurement device in each case consisted of a five-item scale ranging from "a fine brand, one of the best" to "a brand of second quality, but worth the price."

Jake Jack recommended that this study be administered to two stratified random-probability samples of one thousand five hundred persons, each projectable to the northeast geographic area as defined by the U.S. Census. Jack recommended the northeast census region because his analysis showed that 65 per cent of the sales of Wonder Foods nonpromoted items were made in that area and because the major private-label food chain competition was concentrated in that area.

EXHIBIT 16–3
Specimen Data: Consumer Attitudes Toward Selected Groups of Wonder Food Brands and Chain Private-Label Brands Measured With and Without Corporate Auspice*

	NORTHEAST GEOGRAPHICAL REGION	
	AVERAGE ATTITUDE RATING WITHOUT CORPORATE AUSPICE	AVERAGE ATTITUDE RATING WITH CORPORATE AUSPICE
Wonder Foods, Advertised brands	1.89	1.94
Wonder Foods, Nonadvertised brands	3.26	2.11
Chain private-label brands	4.52	4.09

* The lower the rating, the more favorable the attitude.

The recommended study was quickly undertaken and its major findings are summarized in Exhibit 16–3.

In the final report on this research, the following three conclusions were drawn:

1. The advertised Wonder Foods brands were very favorably regarded by the consumers. Their identities were sufficiently distinct and positively perceived so that a more intimate association with Wonder Foods did nothing to enhance the appeal of these brands to consumers.

2. This was not the case with the nonadvertised brands. Although these nonadvertised brands were not in total disrepute, they did not enjoy, on average, a favorable consumer evaluation. And when these brands were associated in the simplest possible way with the Wonder Foods Company, their reputation was immediately enhanced.

3. The chain private labels did not enjoy a favorable reputation with consumers, at least when they were rated in a contest limited to chain brands and Wonder Foods advertised and nonadvertised brands. Although the recognition of the chain auspice did improve their consumer reputation, it was still not very strong.

The Wonder Foods marketing research department strongly recommended, on the basis of these results, that the recommended programs of corporate package identification and umbrella corporate advertising be developed at once as a basis for the sales rejuvenation of the nonadvertised Wonder Foods brands.

Hunty Johnson endorsed this recommendation, as did Theodore Mac-Mahoner. "But, Hunty," said MacMahoner, "we better let Elton Markell in on all of this before we think about advertising budgets and new advertising agencies and all." And so, in due course, the research presentation was made to Elton Markell. He followed the material closely and at the end gave his approval to the development of a new corporate logo and the development of a corporate advertising program: "Go ahead, boys. Work out your program. But I'm not approving any budgets today. Once you get a corporate mark and corporate advertising that we all like, I suppose you'll want to recommend some sort of test program so that we can find out if it really works as you say it will. And when you appoint an advertising agency to do the work, I'd suggest you put the whole assignment on a fee basis, so we don't have any mortgages on our future."

And with that, the meeting with Markell was over. Johnson and MacMahoner had his approval to proceed, but whether or not the whole program would be undertaken would depend upon the quality of work done by Johnson and MacMahoner and whatever advertising agency they chose.

The corporate advertising assignment was given to the major Wonder Foods advertising agency, the P. Williams Houston Agency. The Houston Agency was the largest advertising agency in the world. It was the first advertising agency ever appointed by the Wonder Foods Company; this original appointment occurred in 1908. Houston was responsible for nine of the seventeen advertised Wonder Foods brands and their advertising billings for 1965 amounted to $17,428,000. This total was about 56 per cent of the Wonder Foods domestic advertising expenditure in 1965.

After extensive study, the Houston Agency agreed that a corporate umbrella advertising campaign should be undertaken for the non-advertised brands with the following specific objectives:

1. To introduce the new corporate mark and the redesigned packages.
2. To relate specific nonpromoted products to those Wonder Foods advertised brands with which they are logically related.
3. To create an awareness of the non-promoted product lines and to create a consumer belief that any Wonder Food product stands for quality, dependability, and modern technology.

The agency then presented their own recommendation for the new corporate mark, the package designs, and a two-phase magazine advertising campaign. In the first phase of this campaign the objective would be simply to develop consumer familiarity with the new corporate mark and establish its relation with the various advertised and nonadvertised brand names. The recommended campaign theme was "The mark with seventy names." In the second phase of the campaign, the quality, dependability, and modernity of the various Wonder Foods nonpromoted brands would be developed under the campaign theme "Confidence when you start from scratch."

The agency also recommended that the proposed institutional campaign be tested in three market test areas. They suggested that store audit measurements be made of sales movement of the nonpromoted product lines in each of the test markets. In addition, the agency recommended that the communication accomplishment of the new advertising be measured to determine its effect in creating new consumer knowledge and attitudes toward the nonpromoted Wonder Foods brands as well as to relate varying levels of communications success with actual consumer purchase of the nonpromoted brands.

The test market auditing of sales results was cut and dried and would be handled in a routine manner by the Wonder Foods research department. The measurement of the communications effect of Wonder Foods advertising was, however, another matter and one in which Wonder Foods had no prior experience. Therefore, Johnson directed that the Houston Agency and the Wonder Foods marketing research department work together to develop appropriate plans to measure the effects of a limited test of the proposed new advertising campaign.

The first step in the development of this program of marketing research was to develop some concrete idea of how the proposed corporate advertising campaign was expected to affect consumers, at least in theory. This was the first issue to which Jacob D. Jack and James B. Bridgeall (director of research for the Houston Agency) addressed themselves as they set about designing the research program. They concluded that the proposed advertising program could have at least five specific objectives:

1. To create consumer awareness of the new Wonder Foods identifying mark.
2. To increase consumer knowledge of the composition of the Wonder Foods line.
3. To increase consumer awareness of the connection between the nonpromoted brand names and the Wonder Foods Company.
4. To improve consumer attitudes toward Wonder Foods products and especially to improve the quality, dependability, and modernity image of Wonder Foods products.
5. To create sales of Wonder Foods brands, especially among persons who had received the messages directed at them by the advertising campaign.

It was not considered a foregone conclusion by Jack and Bridgeall that the proposed advertising campaign would do any of these things, or some of them, or all of them. But they agreed that these were the five things that the advertising would accomplish if it were totally successful. And if these objectives were not accomplished, it could be fairly stated that the advertising had not been a success. Jack and Bridgeall agreed that these putative effects of the advertising should occur gradually over a period of time. Thus they reasoned that it would be necessary to make a series of measurements over time to test the effect of the advertising and to be sure that any observed effect had in fact been caused by the advertising, rather than developing without any direct connection to the advertising.

The two men designed a research program to accomplish these objectives and presented it along with recommendations for test markets to Johnson and MacMahoner.

And, in turn, the whole package of proposed new corporate mark, proposed label design, proposed corporate advertising, and proposed research plans was taken to Elton Markell. As it happened, the presentation was made two days after Virginia Lande's memorandum to Stuart Appleroad outlining a program for corporate social responsibilities had been received by Markell.

As he listened to MacMahoner, Johnson, and the Houston Agency people talk, he wondered what relation there could be between these programs and the one Ms. Lande had recommended and whether they could be coordinated in any way to accomplish what might be related purposes at a somewhat lower expense.

Questions for Case 16

1. To what extent is the problem of corporate social responsibility a marketing problem? Can the corporate marketing organization make a contribution to the way in which corporate social responsibilities are identified? Can the corporate marketing organization make a contribution to the way in which corporate social responsibilities are discharged? What are the marketing consequences of an indifference to corporate social responsibility likely to be?

2. Is the public relations function properly positioned within the corporate marketing organization? Should Ms. Lande be given the responsibility that she requests in her memorandum? To whom should she report?

3. What does Ms. Lande mean when she says, "The days of being virtuous by proclamation are long behind us"?

4. What is the long-term prognosis of the nonadvertised Wonder Brands? Is there any good reason to believe, save for the research results shown in Exhibit 15–3, that advertising can improve their profitability? Is Markell right or wrong to ask that MacMahoner's proposal be tested?

5. Contrast the objectives of the corporate communications programs recommended by Ms. Lande and Mr. MacMahoner. In what ways are the objectives similar? In what ways are the objectives dissimilar?

6. Can the same advertising campaign accomplish the purposes set out by Ms. Lande and Mr. MacMahoner? Are sales results ever translatable into social responsibility results? What are the implications of such translatability, if any, for advertising campaigns that are designed to enhance the consumer acceptance of all corporate products?

7. When Ms. Lande says, "We should consider a program of corporate communication based . . . on public relations activities," to what kinds of activities does she refer?

8. When Ms. Lande says "We should discharge our social responsibilities wherever it is practical to do so" what exactly does she imply? Where does the corporation draw the line between that which is practical and that for which it is socially responsible? What criteria does the corporation use in drawing such a line? Short of specific legislation, who makes the final determination of corporate social responsibility?

INDEX